The Rise of Confucian Ritualism in Late Imperial China

Ethics, Classics, and Lineage Discourse

The Rise of Confucian Ritualism in Late Imperial China

Ethics, Classics, and Lineage Discourse

Kai-wing Chow

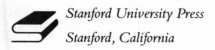

Stanford University Press
Stanford, California

Stanford University Press
Stanford, California
© 1994 by the Board of Trustees
of the Leland Stanford Junior University
Printed in the United States of America

CIP data appear at the end of the book

Publication of this book was partially
underwritten by a grant from the
Chiang Ching-kuo Foundation for
International Scholarly Exchange (USA).

Stanford University Press publications
are distributed exclusively by
Stanford University Press within
the United States, Canada, Mexico, and
Central America; they are distributed
exclusively by Cambridge University
Press throughout the rest of the world.

Acknowledgments

Acknowledging one's debts to those who contributed in various ways to the completion of a work is perhaps the most enjoyable ritual scholars perform. Many friends and colleagues read earlier versions of this work, either in part or in its entirety. I thank Cynthia Brokaw, R. Kent Guy, John Henderson, Tze-ki Hon, Whalen Lai, Evelyn Rawski, Richard Smith, Lynn Struve, Bin Wong, and Alexander Woodside for their invaluable comments and criticisms. Several colleagues at the Department of History of the University of Illinois, Thomas Haven, Harry Liebersohn, Don Queller, and Winton Solberg, have either commented on some part of the manuscript or kindly made available their expertise.

I also acknowledge the invaluable advice of Benjamin Elman, whose critical reading of an earlier draft helped me rethink some of the important issues. His careful reading spared me many mistakes. I am as well deeply indebted to the anonymous reader for the Stanford University Press, whose suggestions and criticisms corrected some of my personal biases. If the present work is more balanced in its treatment of Chinese thought in the high Ch'ing period, I owe it to this reader and to Benjamin Elman.

Although I was unable to incorporate all their suggestions and respond to all their criticisms, they guided my revision significantly. Whatever mistakes that this book may have, I am personally responsible.

Two friends deserve special thanks. Without the encouragement and enthusiasm of William T. Rowe, the publication of the present work would have taken a few more years. From him I have learned the importance of collegial support. I am also immensely indebted to my colleague Patricia Ebrey. She is always supportive, and her contributions to the present work have gone beyond criticism and suggestions for improvements. She constantly reminds me of my own biases. Her own works have convinced me that intellectual historians have much to learn from social and cultural historians.

Among my many mentors, my teachers Kwang-ching Liu and Don C. Price occupy a special place. Both were extremely helpful throughout my graduate work. My debt to K.C. is enormous. I could not have completed my studies without his consistent support and unfailing confidence. The influence of his view of Chinese culture and society is evident everywhere in this work. From the inception of this work as a dissertation to the completion of the final manuscript of this book, he kindly gave of his time. Both K.C. and Don read the final manuscript and corrected many mistakes.

Chi-kong Lai's friendship and help deserve special thanks. His devotion to scholarship always reminds me how much more I can do to improve myself. I am fortunate to have John Ziemer as my editor. His meticulous editorial work and his critical reading have spared me many mistakes. My wife, Teresa, has been supportive and tolerant of reduction of family time. My daughters, Roxanne and Lorraine, also have suffered from the consequence of having a father whose academic profession often deprives them of attention and care. I thank my wife for her devotion to the caring of our children.

Finally, I would like to thank the Research Board of the University of Illinois for granting me a Humanities Released Time Award, which has provided me with the needed time for the final revision.

K.-W.C.

Contents

Reign Periods of the Ming and Ch'ing Dynasties   ix

Introduction   I

1   The Crisis of the Confucian Order and
     Didactic Responses   15

2   Ritualist Ethics and Textual Purism in the
     K'ang-hsi Reign   44

3   Lineage Discourse: Gentry, Local Society, and the State   71

4   Ancestral Rites and Lineage in Early Ch'ing Scholarship   98

5   Ritual and the Classics in the Early Ch'ing   129

6   Linguistic Purism and the Hermeneutics of the
     Han Learning Movement   161

7   Ritualist Ethics and the Han Learning Movement   187

8   Ritualism and Gentry Culture: Women and Lineage   204

     Conclusion   223

REFERENCE MATTER

     Notes   233
     Bibliography   281
     Character List   315
     Index   327

Reign Periods of the Ming and Ch'ing Dynasties

	Reign Title	Temple Name
	Ming (1368–1644)	
1368–99	Hung-wu	T'ai-tsu
1399–1402	Chien-wen	Hui-ti
1403–24	Yung-lo	Ch'eng-tsu
1425	Hung-hsi	Jen-tsung
1426–36	Hsüan-te	Hsüan-tsung
1436–50	Cheng-t'ung	Ying-tsung
1450–57	Ching-t'ai	Tai-tsung
1457–65	T'ien-shun	Ying-tsung
1465–88	Ch'eng-hua	Hsien-tsung
1488–1506	Hung-chih	Hsiao-tsung
1506–22	Cheng-te	Wu-tsung
1522–67	Chia-ching	Shih-tsung
1567–73	Lung-ch'ing	Mu-tsung
1573–1620	Wan-li	Shen-tsung
1620	T'ai-ch'ang	Kuang-tsung
1621–27	T'ien-ch'i	Hsi-tsung
1628–44	Ch'ung-chen	Ssu-tsung
1644–45	Hung-kuang	An-tsung
1646	Lung-wu	Shao-tsung
1646–62	Yung-li	
	Ch'ing (1644–1911)	
1644–61	Shun-chih	Shih-tsu
1662–1722	K'ang-hsi	Sheng-tsu
1723–35	Yung-cheng	Shih-tsung

1736–95	Ch'ien-lung	Kao-tsung
1796–1820	Chia-ch'ing	Jen-tsung
1821–50	Tao-kuang	Hsüan-tsung
1851–61	Hsien-feng	Wen-tsung
1862–74	Tung-chih	Mu-tsung
1875–1907	Kuang-hsü	Te-tsung
1908–11	Hsüan-t'ung	

The Rise of Confucian Ritualism
in Late Imperial China

Ethics, Classics, and Lineage Discourse

Introduction

Objective and Scope of Study

This study is an interpretive essay in Chinese intellectual history from the seventeenth century through the early nineteenth century. This period witnessed the emergence of Confucian ritualism in the last decades of the Ming dynasty (1368–1644) and its eventual ascendancy in the K'ang-hsi (1662–1722) and Ch'ien-lung (1736–95) reigns. This intellectual movement primarily involved, but was not confined to, the scholar-gentry of the Lower Yangtze area. Ch'ing (1644–1911) Confucian scholars underscored the central role of ritual in their approach to ethics, Classical learning, and social order. Ritual became the confluence of various intellectual currents—purism and classicism—that sought to re-interpret Confucian tradition in order to cope with a wide array of problems besetting Chinese society since the late Ming. Its ascendancy in the early Ch'ing was inextricably linked with the gentry's attempt to reform their culture, which had been transformed dramatically in the sixteenth century by commercialization and urbanization. Beginning in the early Ch'ing there was a moral clampdown on various forms of urban culture. The upsurge of social conservatism and the growth of the cult of women's purity betrayed the gentry's growing fear of the subversive effects of literacy on the social hierarchy and their concern about the social and geographical mobility of women. The rise of Classicism, ritualism, and purism attested to the gentry's attempts to reform educational and training programs. Ch'ing literati were urged to immerse themselves in the difficult language of the Classics and to conduct research on ancient rituals and institutions, with the ultimate goal of rediscovering the authentic rituals of the sages. The ritualist approach to moral cultivation and to social solidarity through strengthening kinship ties helped re-establish the gentry as the intellectual, moral, and social leaders of local society.

All these developments were different but related aspects of an extensive endeavor by the gentry to redefine their Confucian heritage in relation to other beliefs, their relationship with the common people, and their relation to the imperial state. All aspects of this cultural reformism revolved around the axis of ritual.

This study is an attempt to trace and explain this ritualist re-orientation of Confucianism. To argue for the rise of Confucian ritualism is to reconsider the intellectual history of the Ch'ing period from a new perspective.

Our understanding of the intellectual history of the Ch'ing period has been shaped by the strong interest in explaining the origins and growth of a particular form of Confucian Classicism—the "evidential" (*k'ao-cheng*) movement of the mid-Ch'ing period. This "evidential Classicism" has been examined and documented from many perspectives.[1] The empiricism of evidential scholarship continues, however, to be the dominant theme of recent studies. Ying-shih Yü regards Ch'ing empiricism as the rise of "Confucian intellectualism." Benjamin A. Elman argues that the intellectual changes in the seventeenth and eighteenth centuries amount to no less than an epistemological revolution, which, through the accumulated effect of "evidential research," "advanced the front of objectivity and the cause of unbelief."[2] This "empiricist" thesis tends to treat the moral and social commitments of Ch'ing Confucians as a given or as something being eroded by the critical edge of evidential scholarship.

By focusing on the Ch'ing scholars' interests in Classical studies, philology, and an empirical methodology, current studies have by default obscured the profound commitment of the Confucian literati to a *specific* vision of Confucian society—a vision of a new social order based on pure Confucian rituals and doctrines. The ritualist approach to social order contributed significantly to the rise of ritualism in many aspects of Confucian thought of the early and mid-Ch'ing period.

This study is concerned with only three aspects: ethics, Classical learning, and lineage discourse. This study seeks to understand how these aspects of Confucianism changed as the sociopolitical matrix of Ming-Ch'ing China shifted.

Reform of Gentry Culture

Confucian ritualism is treated in this study as the discursive expression of a cultural reform movement that began in the early Ch'ing, a movement envisioned and in varying degrees undertaken by Confucian scholars in their capacity as gentry. Studying the rise of Confucian ritualism in the context of the gentry's cultural reform is important for understanding a larger question: Why did the Manchus succeed in consolidating their control over China? The Manchu success depended to a great extent on the collaboration of the Chinese gentry.[3] Beyond the defeat of the Ming forces, however, the accomplishment of this "great enterprise," as Frederic Wakeman calls it, was contingent upon the ability of the Chinese gentry to regain their dominance or hegemony in local society. The Manchu regime provided the Chinese gentry with the stability and authority needed to carry out their agenda for political reform, which included tax registration and collection, elimination of abuses of gentry privileges and the eunuchs' encroachment on the bureaucracy, and bureaucratic control of education and recruitment of officials. These political reforms, however, were not conceived solely as a means of restoring the Ming imperial system. As responses to the dire problems besetting Chinese society in the late Ming, they were essential to the creation of a social order that depended less on the imperial government for the maintenance of order at the local level. The Ch'ing dynasty was not a reincarnation of the Ming regime. It found stability in a new social order with a broader basis of support, which the gentry helped to create and control. In this social vision, the gentry reasserted their duty to local communities as a necessary basis for their dominance. This attempt at reclaiming moral leadership and hegemony in local society involved reform of the culture of both the gentry and the common people. The articulated vision and the practice of cultural reform were inextricably intertwined. The focus of this study is primarily restricted to the discourse on ethics, Classical learning, and lineage, which constitute a major part of the reform movement. In order to show how wide the scope of the cultural reform was, however, it is useful to provide a brief discussion of how the attitudes and sensibilities of the Ch'ing gentry regarding other cultural aspects differed from their Ming predecessors.

The Ch'ing gentry displayed great rigor in upholding the core values of Confucian orthodoxy—filial devotion, loyalty to the monarch, and wifely fidelity.[4] The Ch'ing period saw the unprecedented growth of the Confucian cult of women's purity. A woman was expected to be faithful and subservient as a wife and to remain chaste as a widow.[5] By the eighteenth century, widow chastity had become a "religion,"[6] and the obsession with sex segregation and female chastity had reached the point of absurdity.[7] There were even attempts to remove from circulation sex manuals distinguished by a healthy acceptance of female sexuality.[8]

Students of Ch'ing society have noted the attempts among the conservative literati to impose rigid moral norms on many facets of social life. This social conservatism found expression in the denunciation of the major forms of urban culture. In the sixteenth century and throughout most of the seventeenth, women from gentry and merchant families in the Kiangnan area had been both consumers and producers of literary culture.[9] After the early Ch'ing, however, women were exhorted not to read vernacular novels, not to watch dramas, and not to walk in the street or mix with men in public.[10]

Theatrical performances that during the Ming dynasty had often been staged in the imperial palace, in the private homes of officials and merchants, or on public platforms in front of temples and ancestral halls underwent significant changes in the Ch'ing period. The creation of drama in the Ming had been a serious literati enterprise.[11] Among the more than 400 playwrights in the Ming were princes, grand secretaries, and board presidents. At least thirty of them were holders of the *chin-shih* degree.[12] Since the mid-sixteenth century, the major form of elite drama had been K'un-ch'ü.[13] But it began to wane from the mid-K'ang-hsi period on.[14] Performances became increasingly stereotyped as fewer literati devoted themselves to creating new librettos.[15] K'un-ch'ü also declined because the gentry of the Lower Yangtze area ceased to train their maids and servants in the art of musical and theatrical performance, a common practice in the late sixteenth century.[16] As K'un-ch'ü declined progressively with the Ch'ing regime,[17] local dramas remained popular.[18] Their inferior literary quality clearly indicates the lower social status of the audience and the writers.[19]

The conservative segment of the Ch'ing literati strove to bring the content of dramas in line with their norms, which they were redefining in an increasingly rigid manner. There were even attempts to outlaw theatrical performances altogether, even though the content of most librettos was hardly inimical to social morality.[20] Whereas many Ming playwrights regarded drama as a means to cultivate and promote Confucian values, influential Ch'ing scholars opposed the drama for its baleful effects on social morality. Some even went so far as to claim that certain widows who saw some plays depicting romantic love broke their vows of chastity and remarried.[21]

Vernacular fiction was subject to no less criticism and censure.[22] Novels had been so popular at all levels of Ming society that the literati regarded this genre as "a serious exercise in writing, one requiring careful planning and deliberateness in execution, a vehicle worthy of the most profound

political, social and psychological insight."[23] Unlike their Ming predecessors, however, the Ch'ing literati displayed a growing opposition to
novels on the grounds of their virulent effects on customs and social
morality.

Throughout the Ch'ing, frequent imperial rescripts and official injunctions banned vernacular novels and plays, and there were government
orders to close theaters.[24] There were cases in which Manchu and Chinese officials were punished for either watching a play in public or hiring
theatrical troupes for private entertainments at home.[25] For a time during the Ch'ien-lung reign, theaters and plays were completely banned in
Peking.[26] The Ch'ing Code made organizers of public theatrical performances and local officials who failed to enforce the proscription liable for
punishment. Officials conniving in the publication, collection, and circulation of licentious novels were also to be punished.[27] Similar strictures
against immoral novels and theatrical performances were included in two
widely read instruction books for officials, *Complete Reference for Com-
missioners of Education* (*Hsüeh-cheng ch'üan-shu*) and *Essentials for Magistrates*
(*Mu-ling chi-yao*).[28]

To be sure, the tightened control on popular literary forms in part
resulted from the Manchu court's attempt to stamp out seditious sentiments in novels and to reaffirm the state ideology.[29] One segment of the
literati, however, called for censorship of popular literary forms on other
grounds. During the K'ang-hsi reign, high officials and eminent scholars
such as T'ang Pin (1627–87), Lu Lung-ch'i (1630–92), Li Kuang-ti (1642–
1718), T'ien Wen-ching (1662–1732), Chu Shih (1665–1736), and Li Fu
(1675–1750) recommended and carried out proscriptions of those popular
entertainments.[30] Most of them were followers of the Ch'eng-Chu school.
T'ang Pin, however, was inclined more toward Wang Yang-ming's teachings, and Li Fu was one of the most important critics of Chu Hsi in the
early Ch'ing.

Ming scholars such as Yang Shen (1488–1559), Hu Ying-lin (1551–
1602), and Wang Shih-chen (1526–90) have been lauded for their pioneering efforts in Classical and philological studies. They included novels,
dramas, and even Buddhist scriptures in their philological agenda.[31] By
contrast, with the possible exception of Chi Yün (1724–1805), few *k'ao-
cheng* scholars of the mid-Ch'ing showed much interest in writing or commenting on novels. Even Chi's main purpose was to promote the basic
Confucian orthodox values—filial piety, loyalty, chastity, and observance
of other Confucian norms.[32] Perhaps the *k'ao-cheng* scholars' preoccupa-

tion with Classical studies left them no time for novel writing. But this was more than a matter of priorities. Some evidential scholars were repelled by the novel. The polymath Ch'ien Ta-hsin (1728–1804) went so far as to consider vernacular novels a new heterodoxy.[33] The undogmatic Classicist Chiao Hsün (1763–1820) recommended burning and proscribing all novels not written with a didactic purpose.[34] There is no question that novels and plays continued to appeal to the wider public and, to a lesser degree, to the literati.[35] But the energies of the best minds in the Ch'ing were expended in literary exercises of a "higher order"—Classical studies.

The power of social conservatism is further revealed by research on lineages, especially analyses of lineage rules in genealogies. Studies have shown that the literate elite and lineage elders sought to impose hard-and-fast rules of behavior on their kin.[36]

The Ch'ing period also witnessed a general trend of growing severity in interpreting the statutes and in meting out punishments by the Board of Punishment for violators of moral norms. People professing to abide by Confucian norms received maximum legal protection, and violators of these norms were dealt with harshly.[37]

Social Conservatism and Classical Scholarship

The preceding sketch of changes in the Ch'ing literati's attitudes toward various literary forms and social practices clearly evidences the prevalence of a social conservatism. How can this cultural reorientation be explained in terms of the rise of evidential Classicism in the mid-Ch'ing? Did k'ao-cheng scholarship or the revival of Han commentarial traditions (Han-hsüeh) operate on a plane different from that of the society at large? It is clear that evidential scholarship did not affect the larger circle of the elite directly, to say nothing of the common people. It might be argued that the increasing social conservatism resulted from the Manchu government's willingness to endorse Ch'eng-Chu learning as the state orthodoxy and that evidential scholarship had no role in perpetuating such a conservative vision. But if Ch'ing empiricism operated within the perimeters of Confucian order, how was it related to the growing rigidity in interpreting social norms? It would otherwise be baffling if this intellectual movement, divorced from the broader developments of social conservatism, had such an appeal among the literate elite.[38] If, however, Ch'ing empiricism did serve some social purposes in connection with the Confucian literati's commitment to upholding Confucian norms of social behavior, how did it accomplish this? Despite the greater depth and complexity of Ch'ing thought that recent scholarship has revealed, these questions have not been addressed adequately. Of particular interest to me is the question of how Ch'ing intellectualism and Classical learning came to bear on ethical practices and such social developments as lineages, which proliferated during the Ch'ing period.

Other questions pertaining to intellectual change in this period need to be addressed as well. Wing-tsit Chan and recently William Theodore de Bary have documented the powerful revival of Ch'eng-Chu "orthodoxy" among scholars both inside and outside the Manchu government during the K'ang-hsi period.[39] Why, then, was this revival followed by the complete rejection of the Ch'eng-Chu school in the latter half of the eighteenth century by k'ao-cheng scholars, who believed in the superiority of the Classical scholarship of the Han period (206 B.C.–A.D. 220)? One needs to know the forces that reinvigorated Ch'eng-Chu learning in the K'ang-hsi period and to examine the manner in which this revived tradition departed from earlier forms. One also needs to consider what forces worked to bring about its rejection by the Han Learning scholars in the latter half of the eighteenth century.

The present study is an attempt to answer these questions. The book is divided into eight chapters. Chapter 1 treats the emergence of a ritualist ethics as one of many social and intellectual responses to a sense of imminent social crisis in the late Ming. Chapter 2 explains how the Manchu conquest in the mid-seventeenth century added fuel to the ritualist movement as rituals took on not only a dynastic but also a cultural symbolism. The concern for cultural purity and its ritual expression resulted in the rediscovery of the ritual and Classical scholarship of the Ch'eng-Chu tradition and in the rejection of the teachings of Wang Yang-ming and his more radical followers as heterodox. But a more radical strain of purism, represented by Yen Yüan and Li Kung, was taking shape; it criticized the Ch'eng-Chu tradition as no less heterodox in its exposition of Confucian doctrine. Chapters 3 and 4 examine how early Ch'ing scholars came to grips with the exegetical legacy of Ch'eng I and Chu Hsi regarding ancestral worship, and how ritual studies and Classical learning were important to the gentry's attempt to build lineages. Chapter 5 explains how the debates over two major Classical rituals were crucial to the discourse and practice of Ch'ing kinship organization. By examining private and official projects on ritual studies in the early Ch'ing, Chapter 5 also shows the beginnings of various intellectual positions that were to character-ize the Han Learning movement. Chapter 6 examines the hermeneutical principles of the Han Learning movement, underscoring the connection between Classical research and its ritualist agenda, as well as the relation-ship between linguistic purism and its profound anti-heterodox stance. Chapter 7 focuses on the ritualist ethics in the thought of Tai Chen, Ling T'ing-k'an, and Juan Yüan. Chapter 8 shows how ritual studies both chal-lenged and reinforced Confucian values and ethics regarding the cult of widow chastity and ancestor worship.

Ritualism, Purism, and the Gentry

Confucian thought in this period was propelled by three powerful cur-rents: *ritualism, purism,* and *Classicism. Purism* here designates an intellectual impulse that demands the recovery of the "original" or "pure" Confucian norms and language.[40] The urge was prompted by the belief that Sung-Ming neo-Confucianism had been sullied by heterodox teachings, espe-cially Buddhism and Taoism.[41] Until the 1820's, leading scholars in the Ch'ing rejected any form of syncretism.[42] The purism of the Ch'ing schol-ars was not a clearly defined set of Confucian doctrines; rather, it was an aspiration, or an attitude, that fueled the persistent effort to purge heterodox elements from the Confucian Classics and rituals.

In their attempt to recover the original meanings of Confucian doc-trine, Ch'ing scholars did not plunge into the Classics without pre-exist-ing concerns and presuppositions. They were seeking knowledge of an-cient rituals. Ritual had always been important, and all Confucians were expected to know and practice it. In contrast to the general importance of ritual in Confucian discourse, however, "ritualism" stresses ritual prac-tice as the most effective method for cultivating Confucian virtues and a reliable way to exclude heterodox practices. In conjunction with purism, ritualism not only played a significant role in shaping Classical scholar-ship but also emerged as the Ch'ing literati's primary approach to ethics and social order through the end of the eighteenth century.

Ideas and values need bearers. The major agents of Confucianism in Ming-Ch'ing China were the gentry.[43] *Gentry* here refers to two major privileged groups: the *shen* (official-gentry) and the *shih* (scholar-gentry). The *shen-shih* or *shen-chin* held titles, examination degrees, or offices in the government. Many scholars with great learning, however, refused to take the civil service examinations or failed to earn a degree. Although they possessed neither degrees nor office, they shared the same educational experience and social identity, and often the same life-style, as the gentry. The majority of the Ch'ing literati belonged to the gentry stratum.

Confucianism, Ritual, and Station

As background for this account of the rise of Confucian ritualism in the Ch'ing, a brief discussion of the meanings of the term *li* (ritual) in Confucian thought, the nature of ritual phenomena, and the relationship of ritual to culture and social structure will be useful. The importance of ritual in Chinese culture can hardly be exaggerated. As James Watson aptly remarks, "If anything is central to the creation and maintenance of a unified Chinese culture, it is the standardization of ritual."[44] Although ritual was important to religious Taoism and Buddhism and Confucianism was not the only intellectual force that had shaped the discourse and practice of ritual in imperial China,[45] ritual is often associated with Confucianism. "Rites and music" (*li-yüeh*) in fact stands for the Confucian approach to moral cultivation and social order.

The English word *ritual* inadequately renders the broad range of meanings of *li*. *Li* began as a term for sacrifices to ancestors and to deities. Its meanings later expanded to mean the institutionalized and stylized behavior of the nobility, ranging from political institutions such as the "feudal system" (*feng-chien*) to ceremonies and life-cycle rites to standards of decorum and social manners. *Li* has come to mean all patterns of behavior—both stylized and non-stylized—and their symbolism.[46] By extension it also means the dispositions, inclinations, and emotions essential to the appreciation and performance of ritual.[47] The comprehensive connotation of *li* arises because the scope of order it concerns is all-encompassing. As Benjamin Schwartz has aptly remarked, "The order that the *li* ought to bind together is not simply a ceremonial order—it is a sociopolitical order in the full sense of the term, involving hierarchies, authority and power. The *li* must themselves support this authority and power."[48]

In Confucian thought, *li* is often treated as the behavioral expression of the inner moral quality *jen* (humanity or perfect virtue). *Jen* and *li* represent the two poles of the moral philosophy of Confucius. *Jen* is the all-encompassing virtue, an umbrella term for all the values that define the ideal humanity.[49] Often Confucius had to clarify the meaning of *jen* in terms of the observance of *li*. He said: "To subdue oneself and return to propriety is perfect virtue."[50] It is *li* that sets the perimeters for the elusive virtues.[51] To conduct oneself in the "correct" or "moral" manner prescribed by ritual constitutes a large part of the effort to cultivate *jen*. The inner moral quality of *jen* likewise manifests itself in conforming to the correct patterns of behavior, both formalized and non-stylized.

In Confucius' thinking, one major function of *li* was the "rectification of names" (*cheng-ming*). To observe *li* was to conduct oneself in accordance with the "name" of one's social station. Ritual not only conveys "religious, moral, and aesthetic meanings" to the participants but also encodes a hierarchy of social relations.[52] A major concern of Confucians is how to represent political ranks and status distinctions in ritual. As will become apparent in the discussion of ancestor worship in Chapters 4 and 5, many controversies stemmed from conflicts between status and political rank.

Of the two major interpreters of the teachings of Confucius—Mencius and Hsün-tzu—Hsün-tzu has been known for an emphasis on the regulative function of *li* in his approach to the sociopolitical order. Whereas Mencius confessed he knew little about ancient rituals, Hsün-tzu was well learned in the theoretical and technical aspects of ancient rites.[53] It is believed that his writings were the major source of the ritual knowledge and Classical learning of Han dynasty scholars.[54]

According to Hsün-tzu, *li* is important to all aspects of human society.[55] It regulates one's daily life and interaction with others, channels emotions properly, distinguishes civilized patterns of behavior, and maintains the political order.[56] A fundamental function of *li* is to distinguish the *fen* (station) of the members of society. Humanity is defined in terms of humans' ability and interest in organizing themselves into differentiated social stations.[57] The "name" (*ming*) in Confucius' phrase *cheng-ming* is what Hsün-tzu called *fen* (station). *Ming* is simply the name of the station. Therefore, in common usage, the term *ming-fen* is often used to denote social station. Teachings about social stations, the crux of Confucian social ethics, are called either *ming-chiao* (doctrine of names) or *li-chiao* (doctrine of propriety-and-ritual).[58] Whereas *ming-chiao* refers to the sum total of social ethics, *li-chiao* can be used both in the sense of *ming-chiao*, the content of the teachings, and in the sense of a method of cultivating virtues, *i li wei chiao*, (employing ritual as the method of teaching values).

The core values of Confucian social ethics since the Han dynasty have been the Three Bonds (*san-kang*): the obligations of official to monarch, son to father, and wife to husband. Despite their strong interest in metaphysics, Sung and Ming neo-Confucians continued to espouse the Three Bonds, often included within the variant term Five Relations (*wu-lun*), and continued to practice rituals that expressed these values.[59] Insofar as core values are concerned, Ch'ing scholars were as Confucian as their Sung and Ming predecessors. What distinguished them was an unprecedented rigor in demanding the expression of these values through ritual practice grounded in pure Confucian doctrine.[60]

The Symbolic and Performative Domains of Ritual

The reasons Ch'ing scholars came to stress ritual as the major approach to ethics and social order will become clear in the following chapters. But the historical context cannot explain fully why they preferred ritual over other methods for inculcating values. The following general discussion of the nature of ritual as a social phenomena will supplement the historical explanation for the rise of Confucian ritualism.

As a node in the web of meanings of social interactions and in the sprawling tangle of their patterns, ritual can be studied from many perspectives. From the perspective of social integration, ritual is an important mode of communication essential to the spread of values. As such, ritual has several characteristics. First, ritual exhibits dual properties. This fundamental characteristic is best illustrated by the existence of two major approaches to the study of ritual—the "intellectualist" and the "functionalist." As Maurice Bloch has pointed out, both approaches are unsatisfactory. The intellectualist treats ritual as embodying the cosmology of a society, whereas the functionalist stresses the power of ritual performance.[61] The general difference between these two approaches is that "the intellectualist approach considers the ritual as a statement, the functionalist one as an action." These two approaches fail to recognize the fundamental characteristic of rituals as "events that combine the properties of statements and actions."[62]

Second, ritual symbols are multivalent. All rituals have an object or a group of objects in whose name the rituals are created and performed. The objects can be persons, ancestors, deities, the spirits in exorcist rites, the body in a funeral and burial ceremony. Except in rituals involving living persons, the objects often are represented by symbols: the tablets used in ancestor worship; the trees, rocks, or mountains of animist cults; or the animals in the Buddhist rite of releasing life. Major rituals often have an open-ended "repertoire of meanings" inscribed and "superscribed" onto them by various groups over time.[63] The various meanings of a ritual symbol may not always be structured, but for the participants there is always a set of "primary meanings" in whose terms they understand their participation in the ritual. They may know, accept, or reject other meanings in the repertoire of the ritual, but these meanings are only secondary.

The primary meanings are those that bind the local group most strongly. The secondary meanings for that local group may in turn be the primary meanings of another group. The sharing of the same ritual symbol allows for some degree of integration. But different understanding of the meanings of the symbol may also draw the different groups into a battle of interpretation. Because of the multivalence of ritual and its social nature, ritual is a major arena in which social groups compete for control of the public meaning of symbols. By using the same ritual symbols, different social groups contribute to the expansion of the symbolic integrative power of the rituals. The more open the symbolic domain, the greater the potential for the ritual to incorporate new meanings and, paradoxically, the greater the danger that the primary meaning of the ritual for a given group will be transformed.

The third characteristic of ritual is its integrative effect on participants' behavior. Scholars of ritual often point out that rituals are repetitive, constant, and conservative. Ritual performance calls for conformance to clearly prescribed acts. The habitual behavior of a novice participant is transformed and brought into line with the ritual structure. Those who grow up performing a ritual, through the constant repetition of the same sequence of formalized acts, form habits that conform to the ritual structure and, in most cases, internalize the value the ritual practice embodies. Ritual therefore produces effects of social integration both at the normative and behavioral levels.

In this study I refer to the two aspects—patterns of meanings and social interaction—as the "symbolic" and "performative" domains of ritual.[64] These aspects are differentiated in the Confucian discourse on ritual by such terms as *li-i* (ritual propriety), which denotes the symbolic meaning of a ritual, and *li-chieh* (ritualized acts), which refers specifically to the formalized action.[65]

Communication of Values: Ritualism and Didacticism

Cultural values can be transmitted visually by symbols, orally and textually by language, and experientially by participation in ritual. In cultural practice, all three are often involved in transmitting values. But in terms of the conscious propagating and spreading of a particular set of values such as a religion, a political ideology, or a social vision, we can distinguish "didactic" and "ritualist" approaches. The peculiar manner in which ritual transmits values differs from other methods of communication that utilize ordinary language.

The symbolic meanings of ritual differ from those of ordinary language in that they do not constitute an argument. As Maurice Bloch aptly remarks, "Ritual language and material symbols can never express propositions similar to the propositions expressed in other language uses. Ritual cannot form a true argument, because they imply no alternative."[66] Ritual does not present logical arguments about values to its participants even though it exhibits some properties of statements. Ritual conveys values embodied in the formalized acts. It does not explain why certain actions are valued; rather, it prescribes how actions are performed. The values ritual transmits are not meant to be discussed by the participants during the performance. Since the ritual process itself does not articulate a logical statement, the participants need not know all the meanings of ritual symbols in relation to one another.

Ritual does not appeal to the intellect in achieving its goal of inculcating values. It manipulates material symbols and the ritual setting to create awe and to arouse the emotions of the participants. The participants may not know or understand the meaning of a specific ritual, but by taking part in it, they submit to the authority and values encoded in the ritual structure. Because of the requirement of participation and the strong appeal to emotions and conduct, ritual frequently succeeds in conveying otherworldly values for which human reason either provides no logical and systematic explanation or, when it does, presents conflicting cosmological claims.

In contrast, a didactic approach appeals more to the exercise of human intellect to comprehend values. Its methods range from instruction to persuasion to discussion. In a didactic mode of communication, an authority figure—the teacher or instructor—always plays the key role in imparting knowledge and values, and the students "receive" the teachings. Any discussion among the students or even between the students and the teacher is meant not to provoke new thinking in the teacher but to help students understand the issues. The exchange of ideas takes place horizontally rather than vertically, even though in effect the teacher may benefit from the discussion.

As a method of communicating values, rituals require different degrees of participation, depending on the nature of the ritual. The role of the participant in a ritual ranges from mere presence as audience or witness to full participation as performer. In a wedding ceremony, for example, the bride, the groom, and the priest are the main performers, and the guests are witnesses. Despite this difference in degree of participation, the participants in a ritual do not play the *roles* of teacher and student. They have only to perform the proper ritual sequence. They already know the meaning of the ritual, which is not discussed, deliberated, or contested during the ritual. To be sure, prior to taking part in a ritual, the novice participants have to learn from the ritual specialists or officiants, who may be Buddhist or Taoist priests or Confucian scholars. Therefore, in *preparing* for performance, there is still a teacher-student relationship between the ritual specialists and the participants. But *during* the ritual performance, the role of the officiants in instructing the participants is that of a conductor rather than a teacher. His role is to orchestrate, rather than to impart new knowledge. Since the instructions given during the ritual process are the same for every performance, they are not comparable to the instructions of a schoolteacher responsible for imparting new knowledge to students *during* each lesson. To be sure, in many religious rituals that involve the participants more as audience than as performers there is still need for the services of ritual specialists whose knowledge of such subjects as geomancy, exorcism, and sutra incantation is important but not meant to be transmitted to clients.

In sum, the didactic method transmits values by engaging the participants in a dialogue, a conversation, or a discussion in either a personal or a textual encounter. In contrast, participants in a ritual learn values experientially through witnessing or performing ritual acts. By following the formal procedures of a ritual, one either accepts its symbolic meaning or willingly suspends any doubts regarding its professed meaning.

These two approaches to conveying moral knowledge are not mutually exclusive in practice. In fact, both contain some elements of the other. The didactic mode and the ritualist mode of transmitting values do, however, differ in terms of their means of communication. As is argued in the next chapter, most of the major intellectual movements of the late Ming adopted the didactic method as the major means of transmitting values. The rise of ritualism in the Ch'ing represents a shift away from the didactic mode. To understand why ritualism became a defining characteristic of Confucian thought, we first need to understand why the didactic mode appealed to the late Ming religious and intellectual leaders.

1

The Crisis of the Confucian Order and Didactic Responses

Chinese society in the sixteenth century was full of contradictions and paradoxes. Concerned gentry were profoundly disturbed by the near dissolution of the Confucian order, the very core of the political, social, and moral world. Powerful forces were undermining the foundation of the Confucian system. The expansion of the domestic economy, especially in the commodity sector, brought dramatic economic and social changes characteristic of an increasingly fluid social structure: urbanization, the flourishing of urban culture, an increase in educational opportunities and literacy, absentee landlordism, a decline in paternalism and kinship ties. These socioeconomic changes took place as the Ming government showed every sign of decline: the indifference and incompetence of the Chia-ching (1522–67) and Wan-li (1573–1620) emperors, the extravagance of imperial relatives, the decline in tax revenues, factional struggles, expansion of eunuch power, and external threat from the Manchus in the north.[1] These may seem symptoms of yet another cycle of dynastic decline, but there was no recurrence of a pattern in which social, economic, and political forces declined concurrently. Indeed, the late Ming was a period of dynastic decline, but many of the ways it declined were peculiar to Chinese society in the sixteenth and early seventeenth centuries.

Economic Expansion and the Transformation of the Literati

Commercial growth and the monetization of silver were two of the most important forces behind the social and economic changes of the sixteenth century. Early in this century silver became the major medium of exchange in the areas linked to the rapidly expanding interregional and national markets.[2] The increasing use of silver bullion after the early fifteenth century is evidenced by a series of reforms in tax collection that sought to impose silver as the means of tax payment.[3] The Chia-ching reign saw the emergence of silver as the major medium of exchange throughout China.[4] Along with the indigenous growth of the economy, the rapid expansion of overseas trade in the late sixteenth and early seventeenth centuries quickened the pace of social and economic changes. A flourishing foreign trade brought huge amounts of silver bullion into China from Japan and Spanish America. This new supply of silver made possible further domestic economic expansion and accumulation of monetary wealth on a grand scale.[5] The prosperity of various trades resulted in greater economic integration and regional specialization.[6] Expansion of the commercial sectors of existing towns and cities contributed to the rapid growth in urban population. Towns and cities with greater economic specialization multiplied along the veins of trade and commercial networks.[7]

The benefits of economic prosperity, however, were not evenly distributed. Those who had power and entertained no scruples about enriching themselves were the biggest beneficiaries. Officialdom was the first group to reap the extra wealth. Before the Cheng-te reign (1506–21), the number of officials engaged in commercial enterprises was relatively small.[8] Toward the end of the sixteenth century, it became a fashion among both acting and retired officials, especially in Kiangsu, to engage in business.[9] The majority of gentry families in Kiangsu established family textile workshops.[10] Officials not only invested in and operated commercial enterprises but also sought to control major production, transaction, and transportation facilities. According to Ku Yen-wu (1613–82), after the Wan-li reign irrigation works, watermills, ferries, and markets came to be owned by powerful gentry (hao-shen).[11] Grand Secretary Hsü Chieh (1503–83), an important promoter of Wang Yang-ming's teachings at court and a fervent patron of "public lecturing" (chiang-hsüeh), kept a number of women in his house to produce textile products for sale in the market. Like many other officials, he owned scores of pawnshops.[12]

Commercialization and the Gentry's Abuse of Privileges

The greater supply of silver in the economy and increasing commercialization rendered the quest for more wealth desirable now that wealth could be accumulated on a greater scale. More important, the supply of luxury products and the variety of entertainments available in the urban centers in the Lower Yangtze area were growing. To a lesser extent, these social changes were also evident in cities in north China.[13] The gentry not only took advantage of the booming economy but also sought to increase their wealth by dint of their privileges. They themselves led the way in subverting the central principle of the Confucian political system—government by example. The most common ways to increase wealth were to invest in commerce, evade tax payments, and serve as protectors of the powerless in return for services and payments.

The gentry legally enjoyed certain economic privileges. They were exempted from labor service, and a portion of their land was not subject to taxation. After 1436 active and retired officials and degree-holders were exempted from the ad hoc "miscellaneous labor services" (tsa-yao) either in full or in half.[14] The sixteenth-century increases in land tax and corvée exemptions granted to officials and degree-holders shifted the tax burden onto small landlords and peasants. Between 1521 and 1610 the land tax exemption for first-rank officials increased twenty-five-fold and for eighth-rank officials twenty-seven-fold. Ku Yen-wu estimated that in one county 50–90 percent of the land was owned by the gentry and hence exempt and that the tax was paid by only 10–50 percent of the landowners, who had only small holdings.[15] Moreover, since the gentry were exempted from the labor service of collecting taxes, the small landowners in the li-chia system were obliged to undertake the duty of extracting taxes, which often brought ruin to families of moderate means.[16] By the sixteenth century, most powerful gentry, especially those in central and south China, sought to evade even the regular corvée.[17]

As tax responsibilities fell more and more on independent cultivator-owners, those who could not resist extortion by clerks and runners sought protection from powerful gentry. As T'ang Shun-chih (1507–60) observed, the privileges the gentry enjoyed allowed them to provide shelter to land commended to them by friends and relatives, or even unrelated persons—a fraudulent practice known as t'ou-hsien. It was particularly extensive in Kiangsu. The seriousness of commendation and false registration was borne out in the land survey of 1610, which showed that unregistered land exceeded registered land by 42.3 percent to 345 percent.[18] The gentry had no scruples against expropriating commended land as their own.

Peasants were forced to desert their land under the combined pressures of tax and rent payments, numerous exorbitant surcharges (tsa-pan),[19] and relentless oppression from landlords and gentry as well as clerks and runners. Many became vagrants; others entered towns and cities as hired laborers. They became a major source of bondservants (*nu-p'u*) who worked as hired hands and agricultural laborers for powerful families with extensive landholdings and various commercial operations.[20] Many became bondservants through adoption (*i-nan*) because Ming law forbade commoners and officials below the third rank to possess bondservants.[21] By stretching the meaning of the term *family* to accommodate the new social and economic relations, the late Ming elite subverted the basing of the family on kinship, a principle fundamental to the Confucian notion of social order.

The gentry, the presumed exemplars of Confucian virtues, deviated in every possible way from Confucian social ethics. By dint of their special status and access to political power, they preyed upon the common people with impunity. As Lü K'un (1536–1618) and Li Chih (1527–1602) observed in the late sixteenth century, the gentry were acting like rapacious merchants bargaining in the market.[22] They had betrayed their duties toward society and become a detestable source of oppression in the local community.[23] By illegal as well as immoral means—fraud, deceit, and threats—the gentry sought to acquire buildings, farmland, and other forms of property.[24] The rapacity of the gentry had become so common that morality books had a special category of demerits for such malfeasance.[25] The notorious case of the burning of T'ung Ch'i-ch'ang's (1555–1636) residence in 1616 was but one example of the long-standing hatred the local people harbored toward the exploitative gentry.[26]

No doubt there had been corrupt officials since the founding of the Ming dynasty. But corruption was regarded as conduct unworthy of an official. After the Chia-ching reign, however, not only was corruption not condemned, but it became the criterion of "success" for officials. Local officials were concerned only about whether a new appointment was to a "profitable" county. Anyone who failed to line his pockets was ridiculed for incompetence.[27] From the Chia-ching reign on, only a few officials won mention in the "good officials" (*hsün-li*) section of the *Ming History*.[28]

In the eyes of the common people, the gentry no longer appeared to be Confucians fulfilling their primary duties of providing the common people with an orderly society and conducting themselves in accordance with the basic Confucian virtues. They were a corrupt and rapacious class that gave no substance to Confucian precepts. In Li Chih's pungent depiction, the officials were no more than "great robbers clad in official robes and caps." The eminent monk Tzu-po Ta-kuan (1544–1604) explained that officials were even worse than real thieves: "Thieves are easy to catch because they live in mountainous regions and forests and use weapons, but those who live under the protection of official robes and caps and who take advantages of their names and ranks are difficult to catch." [29] It was imperial authority that provided the gentry the license to rack the people.

The growing tendency of the gentry to move to the cities and the extensive abuse of their privileges point to the transformation of the gentry's role in local communities. They had abandoned their role as community leaders in the countryside. They no longer served as the brokers between the imperial state and the commoners in their rural communities. Their absence allowed the clerks and runners of the magistrate's office to extort more taxes and surcharges from the rural populace. Their dependence on bondservants for rent collection not only weakened their tie with the tenants but also contributed to the growth of exploitation in the countryside. Their managerial bondservants often become village bullies.[30] As Jerry Dennerline aptly puts it, by the late sixteenth and early seventeenth centuries, "the last vestiges of a multiplex of social network binding tillers by personal obligations to a classically educated civil service elite had given way to the pervasive influence of specific contractual ties." [31]

Society had come to recognize only power and money. In fact, they had become inextricably intertwined.[32] With money, the nouveaux riches bought degrees and positions in the government.[33] With these imperial insignia, one obtained not only the privilege of exemption and gentry status but also the license to exploit the people for more profit. Doubt arose as to the purpose of practicing conventional virtues such as industry, honesty, harmony, and doing one's duty while unscrupulous exploiters rose high on the social scale.

Erosion of Confucian Social Ethics

The common people exhibited no stronger desire to hold to traditional values. With rapid commercialization, urbanization, and population growth came a society characterized by new patterns of social relations, fierce competition, the constant lure of wealth, and a growing sense of uncertainty regarding proper conduct. The paternalism that landlords exhibited toward tenants in the early Ming gave way to impersonal and businesslike relations.[34] Bondservants and tenant-tillers received less and less personal support from their masters.[35]

The new patterns of social relations demanded a greater ability to survive in an increasingly competitive environment. The attitude of striving to get ahead at the expense of others was widespread.[36] But accompanying the greater opportunities for economic and social advancement was an acute sense of uncertainty about one's fate. However successful, no man could feel certain of his achievements or possessions.[37]

The great social mobility was not created and structured by a new sociopolitical order, but resulted in part from the breakdown of the existing system. Advancement on the social ladder was often achieved by breaking the rules rather than by abiding by them. Survival and success depended on one's willingness and ability to victimize others. A gloomy portrait of human relations in this period can be found in the *San-chiao k'ai-mi kuei-cheng yen-i* (The romance of the three teachings clearing up the deluded and returning them to the true way), a novel published in the 1610's.[38] As this novel shows, the common people's major concerns were money and influence. The traditional virtues central to the Confucian social order had been abandoned. Families were plagued by quarrels—marital, fraternal, generational.[39] The perceived breakdown of the Confucian order also found powerful expression in such "literati novels" as the *Water Margin, Journey to the West, Romance of the Three Kingdoms*, and *Golden Lotus*. According to Andrew Plaks, these four sixteenth-century novels are full of narratives of "subversion of conventional ideals." "The common denominator in all four works is an emphasis on the breakdown of order or failure of the will."[40]

Under relentless exploitation, the common people became increasingly restless and disrespectful toward the government and the gentry. Concerned officials such as Lü K'un were alarmed at the growing discontent of the people and felt sympathy for their sufferings. Lü was deeply worried about popular riots and uprisings, and not without reason.[41] The White Lotus sect expanded rapidly in the mid-sixteenth century.[42] To prevent popular grievances from turning into mass uprisings, Lü came to stress that inculcating Confucian precepts among the people through the "community compact" (*hsiang-yüeh*) and mutual surveillance (*pao-chia*) systems was fundamental to preventing mass actions.[43]

Confucian teachings were no longer confirmed by social relations. Social experience had ceased to be the most reliable source to test the substance of Confucian teachings. In fact, people's conduct was governed by greed, conflict, and corruption. The contrast between Confucian precepts and "knowledge gained from the external world" (*wen-chien chih chih*) raised doubts about Confucianism and the conduct of the gentry. Those gentry, Confucian or otherwise, who recognized the critical state of the Confucian order sensed that the belief of the literati as well as of the common people in the truth of sages' teachings needed to be re-confirmed through didactic moral instruction. Only through didacticism based on faith or subjective authentication could Confucianism be sal-vaged in a world of money and power. It was in the minds of the people rather than in social experience that the truth of Confucianism could be substantiated.

Didacticism, Syncretism, and Populism

Although sharing the same conviction on the need to reaffirm and re-store the failing social order, gentry and religious leaders diverged on the means for achieving the goal. Their differences stemmed from their dis-parate diagnoses and, more important, from the different networks and institutions to which they had access. Of the various responses to this crisis, three major trends can be identified. First, a movement of popular Confucianism with a strong syncretic outlook was manifest among Con-fucians, Buddhists, and Taoists. Second, a small number of local officials tried to resolve social tension at the local level by promoting community solidarity through such methods as the "community compact" and vol-untary associations for mutual help. Third, there were attempts to reform the bureaucracy and to re-educate the literati as the basic steps necessary to rejuvenate the Confucian order. These three trends were not mutually exclusive. Individual literati and officials might be involved in all of them, or they might support one or two of these activities at the same time or at different phases of their involvement.

The intellectual and social milieus in which each of these three trends evolved were too complex to be explained solely in terms of a concern for upholding social order. Nonetheless, it was an important concern under-lying these trends. Common to these three trends, whether the audience was the common people or the literati, was the didactic approach. As discussed in the Introduction, didacticism appealed more to the intellect as a method of inculcating values. One obvious reason that didacticism emerged as a more practical method was the greater fluidity of social ranks. The uncertainty of status attending the erosion of conventional authority made it impossible to impose precepts on an audience who as-sembled freely for lectures or instructions. The populist and syncretic movements approached the restoration of social order didactically because they, unlike the local officials and the reformist gentry, could not depend on political authority to mobilize the people.

Expansion of the Literati Class and the Syncretic Movement

Since the introduction of Buddhism into China in the second century A.D., Confucians had confronted a Buddho-Confucian syncretism of some sort.[44] Chu Yüan-chang, the first emperor of the Ming dynasty (r. 1368–99), officially proclaimed his commitment to harmony among Confucianism, Taoism, and Buddhism.[45] Syncreticism, however, was much more than a state ideology. Its extraordinary appeal in the late Ming cannot be explained in terms of state patronage.[46] Throughout the Ming dynasty, syncretism was a living tradition among the gentry. Toward the close of the dynasty, it gained exceptional strength. But the late Ming syncretic movement did not owe its popularity to gentry lecturers' attempts to spread their syncretic outlook among the common people; popular practice had always undogmatically mixed Confucian worship of ancestors with worship of various Buddhist and Taoist deities. Buddhist monks and Taoist priests were often hired for funerals, burials, and other ritual occasions.[47] Indeed the common people had no need for the religious leaders and gentry to convince them of the compatibility, if not union, of the Three Teachings.

By the latter half of the sixteenth century, syncretism had undergone drastic changes and moved beyond the perimeters of the imperially endorsed position. Unlike its Sung predecessors, Ming syncretism assumed greater organizational coherence and group identity. It drew followers from all walks of life, including the gentry themselves. It had become a religious movement, involving the gentry and Buddhist and Taoist leaders.

The late Ming Confucian elite's tolerance for heterodoxy and its active search for a path unifying the Three Teachings can be explained in terms of both social and intellectual changes. The increasingly sympathetic reception and open espousal of Buddhism among the Confucian elite were in part a corollary of the injection of diverse social elements into the Confucian elite through the civil service examinations. Economic growth and the advance in printing technology had made education more affordable. From 1500 on, private printing became common. Individual literati, printing shops, and academies turned out a great variety of books, in addition to extensive commentaries on the *Four Books* and the *Five Classics*.[48] The widespread availability of encyclopedias intended for civil service candidates testified to the expansion of the literati class and the growing importance of wealth based on commerce.[49] Sons of merchants and in some cases bondservants of wealthy families could afford an education and managed to succeed in the civil service examinations.[50]

The failure of the bureaucracy to expand to accommodate the growth of the literati class, however, resulted in a lower success rate in the examinations and a greatly extended period of preparation for the majority of the aspirants. To support themselves, many took up tutoring or one of the great variety of professions created by the flourishing printing industry. Many candidates wrote novels, plays, or examination aids or edited and collated books for commercial consumption. In most cases preparation for the examinations became a secondary pursuit.

Among other impacts, this professionalization of the literati diluted gentry culture. The classical education the literati acquired was put to uses not directly related to the examination system or government service. As David Johnson warns, it is a mistake to assume "the classically educated in Ming-Ch'ing times" were a "homogeneous group."[51] The connection between education and government service was no longer absolute; nor was it always desirable. Willard Peterson has pointed out that some of the classically educated were actually "men of culture," who were "only minimally involved in government" or "eschewed ambitions of wealth and standing as officials in order to devote themselves to literature and art."[52] As professional writers, they had to cater to the diverse needs and interests of the reading public. To be sure, the Confucian values they had internalized appear in their writings. But unlike examination papers they were not in these writings obliged to stress these values. Nor were they required by professional demands to conform to the moral code of the gentry and the commitment to government service. Consequently, the literati were much more inclusive than the gentry. From the gentry's standpoint, the literati class was not fully "gentrified." The growing distance between the literati and the political arena also lessened constraints on the pursuit and expression of personal interests in religious and cultural matters.

Populism and Syncretism: Wang Yang-ming's Legacy

The syncretic movement, which often overlapped the populist movement, would not have gained such momentum among the Confucian elite in the second half of the sixteenth century had it not been for the soaring popularity of the innovative teachings of Wang Yang-ming. In some degree this success owed much to the political importance many of his disciples achieved in the 1550's and 1560's.[53] The appeal of Wang's teachings lies in two basic ideas of his moral philosophy—the "innate knowledge of the good" (liang-chih) and "lecturing" (chiang-hsüeh). By identifying the presence of "innate knowledge" in the human mind and reducing morality to a matter of commitment to the basic Confucian precepts regarding "human relationships" (*jen-lun*), he was able to transform Confucian social ethics into a subjective moral quality that of itself was deemed sufficient to qualify one as a sage. Wang Yang-ming said, "There is no learning independent of human relationships" and "knowledge of these does not require thinking because it is innate knowledge."[54]

The combined effects of Wang Yang-ming's belief in a common moral nature and his commitment to the moral self-transformation of people gave rise to an urge to popularize Confucianism. Commenting on the failure of a student's attempt at proselytism, Wang explained that the best way to get one's ideas accepted by the common people was for oneself to become a common person (*yü-fu yü-fu*).[55] The adoption of such a populist approach to Confucianism reflected both the influence of Wang Yang-ming's philosophy of the mind and the need to spread the belief in the moral orthodoxy of Confucianism among the common people, who either did not share the same beliefs or had doubts about Confucian claims. This concern to preach Confucianism to a large degree explains the stress Wang Yang-ming and his followers put on "public lecturing." It was a radical teaching method because the audience of the lectures was not confined to candidates preparing for the civil service examinations. It was a more direct way of teaching the public the basic values of filial piety, loyalty, and social harmony. Wang Chi (1498–1583) explained why it was a pressing need to give lectures: "When the master's teachings are established, the number of good people will multiply."[56] Wang Ken (1483–1541) defended "lecturing" as a means of "ordering the world" (*ching-shih*) on the grounds that lecturing produced "useful people."[57]

Although Wang Yang-ming himself did not actively seek a synthesis of the Three Teachings, he was accommodative toward unorthodox (*i-tuan*) teachings.[58] In an answer to the question regarding the meaning of heresy, he said: "What can be understood and practiced by men and women of simple intelligence is called universal virtue. What cannot be understood and practiced by men and women of simple intelligence is called a heresy."[59] It is worth noting that Wang Yang-ming's definition of heresy had a strong populist appeal. Orthodox teachings were those simple and easy enough for illiterate people to understand and practice. Doctrinal quibbles had no place in Wang's mind. The populist strain in Wang's thought drew him closer to the mental world of the common people, who were eclectic in their religious and normative outlook. Wang's toleration of unorthodox ideas paved the way for the vigorous attempt among many of his students to synthesize the Three Teachings. Wang Chi went so far as to say, "Confucians of today do not know that the teaching of Buddhism was originally the great way of Confucianism."[60]

The Variety of Syncretism in the Late Ming

The rise of syncretism in sixteenth-century China, however, was more than an intellectual movement among the Confucian elite.[61] It was part of a religious and intellectual movement manifested in Taoism and Buddhism as well.[62] It is not surprising that these new intellectual and religious movements gained popularity in the late sixteenth and the early seventeenth centuries, a time of deepening social and political crisis. Nor was it any accident that attempts to defend and reaffirm the Confucian patterns of social and political mores reached an unprecedented magnitude at that time. These movements included Buddhist syncretists such as Yün-Ch'i Chu-hung (1535–1615) and Han-shan Te-ch'ing (1546–1623), the Taoist-inclined official Yüan Huang (1533–1606), and the Confucian lecturers of the T'ai-chou school.[63] The efflorescence of all varieties of religious activism indicated both the growing sense of insecurity and disappointment with the worldly situation and the more active role religious leaders played in addressing social and economic needs.

Lay Buddhism and Moral Ledgers

Lay Buddhism at this time was itself strongly pervaded by syncretism. The major leaders of this religious movement shared a commitment to reaffirming Confucian social ethics. Otherworldly as its ultimate concerns might be, the lay Buddhist movement was "more activist than contemplative, more moralistic than theological, more world-affirming than world-rejecting."[64] The eminent monks Chu-hung and Te-ch'ing are the best examples of Buddhist participation in sustaining the crumbling moral order of Confucianism. According to Chun-fang Yü, what is remarkable about Chu-hung's proselytism among lay Buddhists was "his emphasis on moral action and his relative neglect of theological speculation."[65] Te-ch'ing believed that the doctrine of the mind was inherent in both Buddhism and Confucianism.[66] What provided a common ground for the Three Teachings was their stress on the evils of desires and the destruction of egoism. He taught that Confucian precepts such as filial piety were integral to Buddhist discipline.[67]

Lay Buddhism was not alone in benefiting from its active involvement in buttressing the social ethics of Confucianism; the same factor can account for the popularity of morality books such as the ledgers of merits and demerits (*kung-kuo ko*). Despite their debut in the fourth century, moral ledgers were not popular among the literati until the sixteenth century. Tadao Sakai has noted that "the emphasis [of the morality books] shifted in the Ming from religious salvation in another world to a man's conduct in this world."[68] The sixteenth-century moral ledgers chose elements freely from the Three Teachings. These books were written in simple language and aimed at a wide public. They were generous with admonitions to perform the duties of one's station, to reduce familial and social conflicts by restraining oneself from oppressing others, and to render help to kin, tenants, servants, and indigents.[69]

The moral ledger, with its method of keeping an account of one's good deeds and wrongdoings, was widely used by literati, Buddhists, and Taoists with a syncretic bent.[70] Notable examples are Lü K'un, Chu-hung, and Yüan Huang.[71] The system of merits and demerits they developed represented "a 'Confucianized' version of a system originally associated principally with Buddhism and Taoism."[72] The idea of quantifying morality no doubt reflects the calculational mentality of the urban populace. More important, it can be argued, it points to a pressing need for assuring the public of the practical utility of conventional morality. Morality, like money and power, was useful and accumulable.[73] The wide circulation of these morality books bears witness to the need felt among the literati to provide moral instructions to the reading public.

As a type of didactic text, the moral ledgers reveal the general shortcomings of didacticism as a method for cultivating values—the limitation of moral persuasion. They had to enlist the concept of retribution to encourage good conduct and warn against wrongdoings.[74] Although the ledgers presumably would give their user a sense of control over his or her fate through the accumulation of merits, the principle of retribution on which the system rested remained the ultimate source for delivering the worldly reward. To be effective, didacticism could not depend entirely on persuasion; retribution served as the ultimate explanation for the actual punishment or reward.

Popular Confucianism and the Syncretic Religion of Lin Chao-en

Perhaps the most unique phenomenon in the sixteenth century was the rise of "popular Confucianism," represented best by the syncretic religion of Lin Chao-en (1517–98) and the T'ai-chou school founded by Wang Ken. These two forms of popular Confucianism actively propagated the social ethics of Confucianism. In addition to a personal quest for sage-hood, they shared a moralistic approach to the social crises that deeply troubled their leaders.

Lin Chao-en, the founder of the Three-in-One religion (*san-i chiao*) began to "preach" Confucianism in 1551. The main objective of his school was to cultivate students in accordance with Confucian canons.[75] In 1563 he devoted himself to the diffusion of the doctrine of the Three Teachings by traveling about southeast China. According to Judith Berling, Lin's "Confucian syncretism" of this period "was even more conservative than that of many of his Ming contemporaries."[76] In 1571 when he wrote new regulations for his expanded school in P'u-t'ien, Fukien, he required every student to continue doing duties befitting his "apportioned lot." The message was much more than passive acceptance of one's own station. It sought to reaffirm in action the hierarchy of the Confucian social order.[77]

There is no question that in Lin's later years he no longer accorded Confucianism a reigning position over Buddhism and Taoism. But insofar as social and familial ethics are concerned, Confucianism retained its supremacy.[78] To stress the "conservative" aspects of Lin's syncretism is in no way to underrate the religious and spiritual quest of Lin and his followers. As Berling admirably puts it, "Lin's style was to affirm within Confucianism the levels of spirituality which rendered it hospitable to Taoist and Buddhist forms of spiritual cultivation, while at the same time affirming, and bringing Taoist and Buddhists to affirm, the basic social and ethical values of Confucianism."[79] If Lin's method was radical and syncretic and his ethics traditional, so were those of the T'ai-chou school.

The T'ai-chou School: Populism, Heroism, and Syncretism

In the sixteenth century, the public lecture became a pedagogical method used by both gentry and non-gentry activists not just to educate the literati but to promote Confucian precepts in large public assemblies of examination candidates and common people. Sometimes the size of the audience exceeded a thousand.[80] The populist potential of Wang Yang-ming's idea of the innate knowledge of the good was fully realized in the teachings of Wang Ken, the popular lecturer and founder of the T'ai-chou school. He promoted the idea that the realization of one's moral will lay in the spontaneous fulfillment of the natural (*tzu-jan*) self.[81] The epitome of this doctrine was the phrase *tzu-jan liang-chih* (spontaneous realization of the moral will). The extension of the moral will required neither a rigorous regimen of behavior nor intense spiritual cultivation. With his populist approach to public lecturing, Wang Ken was able to build an extensive movement; his large number of followers of diverse extraction and huge audience of lowly station included agricultural laborers, servants, artisans, and clerks.[82]

Wang Ken found conveying messages through songs a powerful technique. His famous "Learn to Be Happy Song" ("Hsüeh-le ko") taught that happiness comes from the elimination of selfish desires as the "innate knowledge" detects their appearance. What "innate knowledge" recognizes are the basic Confucian human relationships.[83] Even his barely educated student Yen Chün, who was known for his heroic activism, wrote a song to promote filial piety among the common people.[84] Yen's student Lo Ju-fang (1515–88) focused in his lectures on the basic values of filial piety and familial harmony, with frequent reference to the "Six Injunctions of Ming T'ai-tsu."[85] He also compiled lyrics to admonish the peasants to make tax and rent payments on time.[86] Another of Yen's students, Ho Hsin-yin (1517–79), was concerned to urge his kin to pay their taxes promptly.[87] The T'ai-chou school's zeal in popularizing basic Confucian morals among villagers was nothing less than religious.[88] If their zeal was religious and their approach populist or perhaps radical, the moral message of their lectures remained traditional.

Far from being a monolithic lineage of teachings, the T'ai-chou school underwent significant changes. Although the followers and students of Wang Ken shared the same populist didacticism and intuitive approach to ethical behavior, social activism and syncretism characterized the thought of some members of this school at different stages. To be sure, the particular combination of these elements varied with the individual.

Some followers of Wang Ken such as Yen Chün and Ho Hsin-yin began to promote social reforms. The career of Yen Chün has been described as that of a "knight-errant" (*yu-hsia*). He and Ho Hsin-yin acquired a reputation for their heroic commitment to helping friends and to changing society. Ho Hsin-yin became involved in a clandestine plot to destroy the power of the grand secretary Yen Sung (1480–1565).[89] More disturbing to the authorities, however, was his proselytizing among the common people. Ho was renowned for his ability to instigate people to action. His heroic style of social activism caused alarm among more conservative officials.[90] Ho Hsin-yin's criticism of current politics and his involvement in political intrigue clearly suggest that some members of the T'ai-chou school were moving from didacticism to heroic activism to bring about changes in society. Ho's intellectual development bears witness to the complexity of the T'ai-chou school and its gradual fracturing. Ho's thought differed from that of other members of the T'ai-chou school, especially those who entered the bureaucracy. Syncretic didacticism, rather than heroic reformism, distinguished followers of the T'ai-chou school in the bureaucracy such as Lo Ju-fang, Yang Ch'i-yüan (1547–99), and Chou Ju-teng (1547–1629?).[91]

Although Ho Hsin-yin was critical of Buddhism and Taoism,[92] other followers of the T'ai-chou school exhibited a tendency toward syncretism. Lo Ju-fang and his students—Chiao Hung (1541–1620), Yang Ch'i-yüan, Chou Ju-teng—openly advocated a synthesis of Confucianism and Buddhism.[93] In 1592 in Nanking, Chou Ju-teng proclaimed his teaching on the amorality of the original mind.[94] Chou championed Wang Yang-ming's idea that the substance (*pen-t'i*) of the mind was neither good nor evil. What was more alarming to such conservative Confucians as Hsü Fu-yüan (1535–1604) was Chou's total disregard for the cultivation of good conduct. To refute Chou's teaching, Hsü wrote a series of critical essays called *Chiu-t'i* (The nine absolute truths). Chou in reply wrote *Chiu-chieh* (Nine explanations).[95] Ironically Chou was attacked by the Buddhists as well, despite his sympathetic promotion of Buddhism. Chu-hung, the Buddhist leader, criticized Chou Ju-teng for his total neglect of attempts to eliminate evil.[96]

Li Chih and the Iconoclastic Turn of Syncretism

To conservatives, the dangers of syncretism reached alarming proportions in the teachings of Li Chih (1527–1602). The populism of followers of the T'ai-chou school and the social activism of Yen Chün and Ho Hsin-yin combined with a strong inclination toward syncretism resulted in an iconoclast. Li Chih, the "heretic," published his first collection of essays under the title *Fen-shu* (A book to be burned) in 1590. It was a critique of traditional Confucian morality and the Ch'eng-Chu school of neo-Confucianism.[97] Among other heretical stances, he praised the first emperor of the Ch'in dynasty and ridiculed the idea of unswerving loyalty so dear to neo-Confucianism by lauding Feng Tao (882–954), an official traditionally condemned for serving four different ruling houses.[98]

His views on personal relations were even more distasteful to traditional Confucianists. Li argued against distinguishing rulers and commoners. In commenting on the *Lao-tzu*, he said, "Commoners are not inferior; dukes and kings are not superior."[99] He also shared the radical view of Ho Hsin-yin, who considered relations with friends as the most important obligation for an individual. As de Bary has noted, Li Chih took "less practical interest in familial relations than in the broader social ones."[100] Li went so far as to deny as inconsequential all Confucian obligations toward family and society in his quest for the common quiddity of Confucianism, Buddhism, and Taoism.[101] Both Ho and Li exalted friendship and genuine affection at the expense of normative roles and hierarchical relationships, and both relegated core Confucian ethical duties to the periphery of their concerns.

Li Chih made no effort to hide his disregard for the authority of Confucius, the Classics, and Chu Hsi's teachings.[102] He praised vernacular novels as better than the Classics or history for learning the truth.[103] He complained that criteria for judging right and wrong were lacking because everyone had taken Confucius' teachings as absolute.[104] Given his condemnation of blindly accepting beliefs, the later official charge against him of repudiating Confucius' teachings was no slander.[105]

For Li Chih, no one needs to learn norms and rules of proper behavior. The moral will—or in Li's favorite term, the "child mind" (*t'ung-hsin*)— with which a person is born is capable of knowing and realizing moral values. The child mind in Li's thought transcends empirical distinctions of good and evil. Stemming from this conviction was a moral teaching that denied the need to conform to external constraints in moral cultivation. For Li Chih, "doctrines, restrictions and regulations are of no avail."[106] Authentic morality could be at odds with conventional standards of behavior. Conformity could be hypocrisy in disguise. In a vehement attack on literati hypocrisy, Li Chih indiscriminately and belligerently reviled the followers of the Ch'eng-Chu school: "Those who speak of the teachings of Chou [Tun-i], Ch'eng [I and Ch'eng Hao], Chang [Tsai], and Chu [Hsi] with their mind set on high office and great wealth deserve capital punishment."[107]

In the eyes of the conservative gentry, the most forthright attack on Confucianism was Li's refusal to recognize Confucius as the ultimate authority on morality. Li advocated the importance of "selfishness."[108] He saw no difference between fulfilling basic appetites and practicing the Way of the sages: "To wear clothing and eat food—these are the principles of human relations. Without them there are no human relations."[109] By equating daily life with the ideal ethical principles of Confucianism,

Li Chih came to stress the natural expression of human desires rather than their restraint. At least, that was the impression other scholars obtained from his teachings. Even a syncretist like Kuan Chih-tao (1536–1608) found his teachings about abandoning human relations offensive.[110] But Li Chih's teachings were widely popular among the literati.[111] Ironically, what Li Chih detested most—hypocrisy—was a major factor in the popularity of his writings; his approach to sagehood became a handy masquerade for indulgence and avarice among officials.

Contrary to the early phase of religious and popular syncretism, some late developments not only led to an iconoclastic attack on Confucian ethics but also aroused greater suspicion among conservative gentry about a possible connection in some cases with peasant rebellions. The eminent writer Wang Shih-chen (1526–90) was deeply disturbed by the populist efforts of the lecturers. He accused them of instigating the common people and predicted that the lecturers' activities would "cause a disaster like the Yellow Turban and Five Pecks of Grain [rebellions]." [112] The official and writer Hsieh Chao-che (1567–1624) was equally suspicious of the disciples of Lin Chao-en for the way they employed talismans and for the resemblances between the ritual documents they used in exorcisms and the practices of the White Lotus sect.[113] As far as the teachings of Wang Ken and Lin Chao-en are concerned, the charges of instigating popular uprisings and of colluding with millenarian sects may seem farfetched. In view of the growing restlessness in the countryside, however, the acute fears of those hostile to the populist lecturers and religious activists are understandable.

Ritualism and the Reorientation of Neo-Confucian Ethics in the Late Ming

Not all gentry activists, however, agreed on the form of pedagogy. As argued above, although most lecturers from the T'ai-chou school and religious leaders were greatly concerned about the disintegration of the Confucian order, they were not particularly appreciated by conservative gentry. Although some like Lo Ju-fang and many followers of Wang Ken valued public lecturing for its power to mobilize the populace, others, such as leaders of the Tung-lin Academy, preferred to restrict their audience to the literati. They condemned the populist and syncretic tendencies for diluting the distinction between gentry culture and popular culture.

The populism and syncretism characteristic of most didactic endeavors were denounced by some officials and gentry whose didactic attempts followed more conventional lines. A small group of officials—notably Ku Hsien-ch'eng (1550–1612), Kao P'an-lung (1562–1626), Chao Nan-hsing (1550–1628), and Shih Meng-lin (*chin-shih* 1583)—continued to strive to reform society through the government and through educational reform and mobilization of the literati. Their attempts focused on the periodic evaluations of officials by the Board of Personnel.[114] By recommending rewards and punishments for officials, they hoped to fill the government with good officials who would rejuvenate the dynasty, but they were frustrated by the power of the Grand Secretariat and the eunuchs. Since the Chia-ching reign, the Grand Secretariat had encroached on the authority of the Six Boards.[115] From 1593 to 1605 it continually thwarted reformist attempts by officials. Among the officials recommended for demotion by the Board of Personnel were relatives and protégés of the grand secretaries. As a result of their effrontery, many officials working in the board were punished and cashiered.[116] In the 1590's, removal from the political arena led some ex-officials to concentrate on addressing intellectual problems and reforming the education of the literati.

The Tung-lin's Critique of Syncretism and Buddhism

The completion of the rebuilding and expansion of the Tung-lin Academy in 1604 marks the symbolic beginning of a new phase in late Ming intellectual history. The academy served as a center for frustrated ex-officials to exchange and crystallize their views regarding the major problems besetting the empire. It also provided a rallying point for conservative scholars and officials to join forces in combating what they believed to be the sources of the rampant social and political evils of their times.

Ku Hsien-ch'eng, who was cashiered in 1594 and had been staying in his home in Wu-hsi in Kiangsu since his dismissal, rebuilt and expanded the Tung-lin Academy with the support from a group of ex-officials and officials living in the area.[117] Most of the initial patrons of the academy were ex-officials dismissed or degraded in 1592–94.[118] Although these officials believed in working through the bureaucracy to save the dynasty, they were left with no choice but to resort to didacticism as a means to promote moral conduct among the gentry.

The Tung-lin Academy differed from the T'ai-chou school in its strongly elitist approach to revival of the Confucian order. Its leaders, such as Ku Hsien-ch'eng, directed their criticisms primarily against the gentry's negligence of ethical obligations toward fathers, the monarch, and the people.[119] The programs conceived by Ku Hsien-ch'eng and Kao P'an-lung did not include educating the common people.[120] The Tung-lin assemblies were oriented toward reforming the literati themselves. The high proportion of *chin-shih* among the membership of the Tung-lin Academy and those involved in its political movement suggests its upper-gentry social background. More than 90 percent of the members had earned the highest degree.[121] The elitist composition of the Tung-lin becomes apparent when it is contrasted with the T'ai-chou school, the majority of whose followers were neither officials nor holders of the *chin-shih* degree.[122]

Like the populist lecturers of the T'ai-chou school and the religious leaders, the founders of the Tung-lin Academy were deeply troubled by the imminent collapse of the Confucian order. But unlike the T'ai-chou activists and the syncretists, they traced the roots of moral anarchy among officials in part to the extensive influence of heterodox teachings and the prevalent syncretic and populist movements.[123]

From Syncreticism to Purism

The Tung-lin leaders focused on three issues in their attempt to rectify the literati's education and the exposition of the Confucian doctrine: Wang Chi's teaching of the absence of moral standards in the substance of the mind; syncretism and Buddhism; and the idea of spontaneous knowledge of the good championed by the T'ai-chou activists. In their view, these "wayward" ideas were at the heart of the moral anarchy of their times. The appalling iconoclasm they saw in Li Chih's social critique was viewed as inextricably linked to the radicalization of ethical thought since Wang Chi and Wang Ken. They held these radical trends responsible for dissolving the boundaries of Confucian morality and leading to a pervasive moral decline among both the gentry and the common people.

Wang Chi was a fervent advocate of the Union of the Three Teachings movement (*san-chiao ho-i*).[124] His syncretic view was based on what he believed to be the ultimate teaching of Wang Yang-ming at the Bridge of Heavenly Spring. Wang Yang-ming reportedly said that the original substance of the mind was neither good nor evil. This account had come to be known as the "verification of the Way at the Bridge of Heavenly Spring" (*T'ien-ch'üan cheng-tao*).[125] This teaching undermined not only mainstream Confucian moral orthodoxy but also the distinctiveness of Confucianism. In fact, Wang Chi regarded this doctrine as the metaphysical ground on which he could reconcile Confucianism, Taoism, and Buddhism.[126]

Notable followers of the T'ai-chou school, such as Lo Ju-fang,[127] his student Chou Ju-teng, Chiao Hung, Kuan Chih-tao, and Yüan Tsung-tao (1560–1600), all of whom harbored a strong interest in syncretism, embraced this teaching in varying degrees.[128]

To rectify what they considered the perversion by Wang Yang-ming's followers of his teachings, Ku Hsien-ch'eng and his younger brother Ku Yün-ch'eng (1554–1607), Kao P'an-lung, Feng Ts'ung-wu (1556–1627?), and Liu Tsung-chou (1578–1645) made a personal commitment to repudiating the doctrine of the moral will being beyond good and evil.[129] Ku Hsien-ch'eng believed that Wang Chi had fabricated the "Verification of the Way at the Bridge of Heavenly Spring."[130] Ku Yün-ch'eng ruefully remarked:

All Mencius strove to accomplish was the refutation of the idea that there is no distinction between good and evil. To the contrary, lecturers of present time [try to] prove the teaching of the identity between good and evil. . . . Since the Three Dynasties, [they contend,] all have been "sanctimonious conformists" [hsiang-yüan] given to seeking profit and fame, receiving favors without compunction. Although these lecturers have yet to kill their fathers and rulers, so self-centered are they that they have sown the seeds of patricide and regicide.[131]

The Tung-lin leaders' attacks on the Union of the Three Teachings movement and Ch'an Buddhism were particularly strident. Ku Yün-ch'eng called Wang Chi's idea of the amoral mind as identical with the basic doctrine of Buddhism.[132] According to Kao P'an-lung, the threat had never been greater because the advocates of syncreticism came not from heterodox camps but from "followers of the [Confucian] sages"—it was disaffection from within the ranks.[133]

The Tung-lin leaders had reason to blame syncretism and Buddhism for contemporary problems. In the sixteenth century, lay Buddhism, which was strongly syncretic in orientation, attracted a large body of followers among the gentry in the Lower Yangtze region and other parts of China.[134] Even Confucians did not consider themselves the sole guardians of the truth. Confucianism was at best on a par with the other two teachings.

To the Tung-lin leaders, the T'ai-chou activists had further eroded Confucian ethical norms. The T'ai-chou defiance of conventional social morality was anathema to the scholars of the Tung-lin Academy.[135] They regarded Wang Ken's radical teaching of the spontaneous extension of innate knowledge of the good as one of the root causes of moral degeneration among contemporary scholars, especially high officials at court.[136]

Ku Hsien-ch'eng was appalled that some scholars justified their unscrupulous pursuit of private interest by saying they were following naturally the dictates of their moral will.[137]

Shih Meng-lin, a Tung-lin member, pointed out the danger of the T'ai-chou school's intuitive approach to the moral will:

When asked about their method, they say: "Eat when you are hungry and sleep when you are tired. All comes naturally without any exertion. . . ." Moreover, they themselves were given to natural instincts, following their emotions and desire. . . . If humans eat when hungry and sleep when tired, how are they to be distinguished from beasts![138]

To Ku Hsien-ch'eng the T'ai-chou school's emphasis on the spontaneity of the moral will and its subjective moralism had undermined the Confucian scholar's commitment to familial and social obligations. To the Tung-lin scholars Li Chih's criticism of traditional Confucian morality was the logical outcome of the perverted teaching of the innate knowledge of the good.[139]

Ku Hsien-ch'eng was troubled by the radical implications of Wang Yang-ming's teachings, from which the radicalism of the T'ai-chou activists derived. Nowhere were his misgivings more explicitly disclosed than in a comment on the inherent shortcomings of the Ch'eng-Chu school and the Wang Yang-ming school. Whereas the Ch'eng-Chu teachings tended to promote "conformity" (chü), the Wang Yang-ming school was prone to "recklessness" (tang). If forced to choose, he would rather live with "conformity."[140]

Compared with the T'ai-chou activists, the ethical thought of the Tung-lin leaders was conservative. Heinrich Busch has characterized the Tung-lin school as "a center of conservative Confucianism,"[141] and Charles O. Hucker has noted that Tung-lin partisans can be identified by their "common respect for the old moral standards."[142] But what were these "old moral standards"? In Ku Hsien-ch'eng's words, they were nothing but "the [Three] Bonds and the [Five] Constant Virtues."[143]

To the conservative Confucians, all problems could be solved by reestablishing the hierarchically structured order in which everyone knew his or her station and acted accordingly. The Confucian elite at the top would exercise a paternalistic authority over the people. To combat "subjective" moralism and iconoclasm, the Tung-lin scholars came to stress ritual practice in moral cultivation. They saw ritual practice in general as serving to cultivate and reinforce Confucian values regarding the five fundamental human relationships, which had been undermined by the market economy, urbanization, and the breakdown of central government.

From Ontological Discussion to Moral Practice

To the Tung-lin scholars, the syncretic view of the Three Teachings accentuated the diminution of the Confucian socio-moral order, since not all Buddhists honored mundane socio-moral obligations as defined in Confucian terms. More important, Buddhist rituals and methods were employed to achieve such Confucian values as filial piety and loyalty. At first glance, the syncretic thinking of late Ming Buddhists seems to lead to the impression that Buddhism had accommodated Confucian ethical values quite successfully. But as pointed out earlier, the symbolic realm of ritual was multivalent and could be expanded without much change in the performative structure.

Good examples of how the symbolic realm of ritual can accommodate different values are such Buddhist good deeds as "nonkilling" and "release of life," advocated by Chu-hung and other Buddhist leaders. The call for releasing animals captured for food and for other purposes was based on the belief that "all the beings in the six paths of existence are my parents. If I should kill and eat them, it is the same as killing my own parents."[144] The rite of releasing a captive animal is presented as fulfilling the central Confucian obligation of filial piety. A closer examination, however, reveals that Confucian values have been transformed to serve Buddhist precepts.

In Chu-hung's view, one's parents were simply two persons among many in the endless cycle of reincarnation. This notion indubitably undermined the absolute aura Confucianism had built around filial piety, for, according to Chu's understanding, one had more than one's earthly parents to attend to. Others also held a claim on one's filial duties. This concept of filial piety was based on the Buddhist ideas of karma, retribution, and the equality of all living beings, ideas at variance with Confucianism. Compared with the Confucian association of the father with Heaven, the idea that one's father could be any animal was even more damaging than Mo-tzu's idea of treating all humans equally. From the perspective of Confucian purists, this insinuation of Buddhist ideas into Confucian ethics did the greatest damage to the Confucian claim to absolute moral authority.

The Buddhist ritual act of releasing animals was thus invested with Confucian symbolism. Confucian filial piety was understood as the motivation of pious patrons of Buddhism who donated money for the purchase and release of animals. The Buddhist meaning of the ritual provided the cosmological explanation for the creation of the ritual. The participants' perception of their act as fulfilling a Confucian obligation and their acceptance of the act's Buddhist meaning transformed filial piety into a value attained by ritual of non-Confucian origin.

Kao P'an-lung took the "subversive" effect of Buddhist rites especially seriously. For him, the illusion that the Three Teachings essentially taught the same thing had not only blurred the line between Confucianism and heterodox teachings on the ideological level but fostered the fallacy that the observance of Buddhist rituals and the practice of Buddhist good deeds helped uphold and promote Confucian values. In Kao's view, to depend on Buddhist rites to fulfill Confucian obligations led to an impasse because the means as well as the goals were validated in Buddhist rather than Confucian terms. In explaining the nature of human existence, Kao P'an-lung insisted: "When man practices continuously the way of [Confucian] sages, he will be a [Confucian] sage; when he practices Buddhism continuously, he becomes a Buddhist; when he practices Taoism steadfastly, he will be a Taoist. . . . Therefore, a gentleman must be careful in forming his habits." [145]

Kao's remarks make it perfectly clear that Confucian obligations such as filial piety and loyalty could not be fulfilled by performing Buddhist and Taoist prescriptions for proper conduct such as the accumulation of merits as defined by Buddhism. Kao's purist approach to ritual clearly distinguishes the Tung-lin scholars from the syncretists, who were inclusive in their methods of moral instructions. For Kao, one could never become a Confucian except by committing oneself to a Confucian way of life. Kao's idea was shared by Feng Ts'ung-wu, who argued that "we Confucians have our own effort [kung-fu], and the Buddhists have their own effort. Since the doctrines are different, so are the efforts." [146]

Tung-lin leaders such as Kao P'an-lung recognized that dwelling on ontology would only further erode the distinctiveness of Confucianism. The need to re-draw the line between Confucianism and heterodox teachings was the most pressing task. As early as 1605, Ku Hsien-ch'eng had written a small pamphlet entitled I-tuan pien (On differentiating heterodoxy [from orthodoxy]) to defend Confucianism and refute Buddhism. [147] The hard-line emphasis on the distinction between Confucianism and heterodox teachings was a major element of the Tung-lin ideology [148] and would emerge as a powerful trend in the early Ch'ing period.

One major area the Tung-lin scholars found fundamental and useful for identifying the Confucian stance was the strict observance of ethical relationships, that is, the Three Bonds, and cultivation of the Five Constant Virtues, such as *jen* (humaneness), *i* (duty), *li* (ritual propriety), *chih* (wisdom), and *hsin* (honesty). Such concern for ethical obligations and moral performance was prominent in many Tung-lin scholars' emphasis on *kung-fu* (moral effort) over speculative discussion of *pen-t'i*, the ontological dimension of mind and human nature. As noted above, in the realm of ontology and subjective morality, many similarities could indeed be found between neo-Confucianism and Buddhism.[149] But what mattered to the Tung-lin leaders was the differences between the two teachings and the need to apply Confucian moral standards to one's conduct. Shih Meng-lin pointed to the abuses in the T'ai-chou teaching of the spontaneity of the moral will: "They don't realize that the mind's original substance and moral effort are inseparable. There will be moral effort when one has the original substance [in his mind]; no original substance will ever exist without moral effort."[150]

It is clear from Shih's remarks that the growing concern about moral effort among the Tung-lin scholars resulted from their apprehension about ideas that encouraged indulgence in emotions and desire. They held the doctrine of the spontaneous realization of the moral will responsible for the rampant social dissolution. This position was succinctly articulated by Kao P'an-lung: "[One] need not be anxious about inadequate understanding of ontology [*pen-t'i*] but one must be concerned about laxity in moral effort [*kung-fu*]."[151] This emphasis on moral exertion was meant to rectify the disquieting teachings of the T'ai-chou school that a person's moral nature could realize itself spontaneously and naturally. According to the Tung-lin scholars, humanity is the product of culture that has resulted from efforts to make humans increasingly different from beasts. Humanity is characterized not by what humans do spontaneously but by what they do in accordance with Confucian norms.

The Tung-lin's stress on moral effort was the first step away from the more optimistic, spontaneous, and populist approach to moral cultivation. For the Tung-lin scholars, moral effort entailed discipline, control, and conformity to rules; the implicit premise for this approach is a *ch'i* ontology. Moral behavior is no longer the result of the spontaneous extension of the innate knowledge of the good but the control and molding of one's physico-psychological self in accordance with external rules. In light of this line of reasoning, small wonder that both Kao P'an-lung and Feng Ts'ung-wu found Chang Tsai's teachings on moral cultivation pertinent.

Ch'i Ontology and the Rediscovery of Chang Tsai

It has been noted that Kao P'an-lung strongly endorsed Chang Tsai's *ch'i* ontology.[152] Chang Tsai's method of moral cultivation began from the proposition that the "physical nature" of humans was bound to be either deficient or excessive (*p'ien*); this of necessity produced "improper desire," which evolved into bad habits.[153] Therefore, for Chang, moral cultivation primarily involved weaning oneself from bad habits by observing correct rites. His idea is best epitomized in his favorite phrase, "transforming physical nature" (*pien-hua ch'i-chih*). Since the experiential moral nature of humans was "created" by observing proper ritual, Chang also referred to his method as *chih li ch'eng hsing* (learning ritual to establish one's moral nature). Extensive learning had an important place in Chang's method, for proper ritual could only be acquired—thus his dictum *po-wen i chi-i* (to learn extensively in order to accumulate [knowledge of] propriety).[154] Moral nature was not close at hand and did not come instantaneously as a consequence of "enlightenment." It had to be cultivated incessantly. Hence, moral cultivation called for discipline and knowledge of proper ritual rather than abstract deliberations on human nature.

Kao P'an-lung's appreciation of Chang Tsai's ethical teachings was shared by many late Ming scholars. Like Kao, Liu Tsung-chou grounded his view of moral cultivation in a *ch'i* ontology.[155] In his *Manual of Man* (*Jen-p'u*), he compared his own demand for a moral regimen to Chang Tsai's method of moral cultivation.[156] Elsewhere, he echoed Chang's view on the need to be vigilant about one's habits. Moral nature in its experiential embodiment results from the habitual practice of ritual.[157]

The renewed interest in Chang Tsai's method of moral cultivation is part of the broader re-orientation of Ming neo-Confucianism that "rediscovered" the importance of ritual practice and the thinking of neo-Confucians of the Northern Sung. It represents an attempt to reopen the question of the core of the Ch'eng-Chu orthodoxy and marked the initial shift of focus in Confucian ethical discourse from the innate moral aspect of the mind to its intellectual faculty, and from autonomy to authority.

Ritual Practice and Moral Cultivation

This shift from subjective to objective moralism was, among other changes, an intellectual development common to almost all persuasions of neo-Confucianism in the Ming-Ch'ing transition. The intense interest in *li-chiao* (doctrine of ritual) was in fact evidenced by the revival, associated with the Tung-lin Academy, of the Ch'eng-Chu school of neo-Confucianism. Ritual became the common ground for those who strove to reconcile the teachings of Wang Yang-ming and Chu Hsi regarding the interiority and exteriority of morality.[158] These attempts at reconciliation were a prelude to the full rejuvenation of the Ch'eng-Chu wing of neo-Confucianism in the K'ang-hsi period. And one of the most important areas in which these two traditions intersected was the emphasis on the centrality of ritual in moral cultivation.[159]

Ch'ien I-pen (1539–1610), an important Tung-lin figure, believed that the moral mind should be preserved (*ts'un-hsin*) by practicing humanity (*jen*) and ritual (*li*). Only through humanity and ritual could the moral mind be preserved.[160] In Ch'ien's teaching, ritual and the external norms of conduct replaced innate knowledge of the good as the reference of morality. Ritual was essential for its function in defining proper ethical relationship and moral attitudes. Keng Chü (fl. 1610), in a slightly different way, echoed Ch'ien's idea. He rejected the quest for moral nature (*te-hsing*) through abstract and speculative discussion. For him moral nature is nothing but adherence to ritual.[161]

Liu Tsung-chou, an avowed follower of Wang Yang-ming, considered moral cultivation as existential testimony to one's unity with the universal essence of human nature. His teacher, Hsü Fu-yüan, who had criticized the syncretism of Chou Ju-teng, had taught him the significance of ethical duties and rituals.[162] Liu explained the importance of ritual in connection with human nature: "Ritual and nature are identical. Ritual is the manifestations of nature. If one is determined to develop one's nature, ritual cannot be ignored for one moment. An instance of departure from ritual is a moment without nature."[163]

Liu was repelled by Buddhist influence on popular morality. To replace a popular morality book by Yüan Huang, in 1634 he wrote his pamphlet of moral instructions, the *Manual of Man*. The first part of this pamphlet dwells on the ontological and cosmological dimensions of human beings. The second part spells out the essentials of practical ways of cultivation. The section on cultivation essentially deals with details of proper conduct. The *Manual* also affirms the five human relationships as internal to man's nature. His interest in the metaphysics of the mind and human nature notwithstanding, Liu insisted that cultivation of the mind must be manifested in ritual behavior. In the last years of his life, he dedicated himself to the study of the *Book of Etiquette and Decorum* (*I-li*), a major Classic on ancient rites.[164]

Classical Studies and the Quest for Canonical Rituals

The Chinese Classics are by no means a homogenous entity. Despite a general recognition of the basic Confucian ethical values, the Classics are a rich repository of ancient events and ideas, capable of supporting different emphases and amenable to multiple interpretations. The *Rites of Chou* (*Chou-li*) was to Wang An-shih's political reformism as the "Great Learning" and the "Doctrine of the Mean" in the *Book of Rites* were to Sung neo-Confucian metaphysics, and as the *Kung-yang Commentary* on the *Spring and Autumn Annals* was to the radical political thinking of the late nineteenth century. The same can be said of late Ming Classicism.

Ying-shih Yü has demonstrated that the revived interest in the study of Confucian Classics, which began in the mid-Ming, was a logical extension of the continuous debate between the Ch'eng-Chu school and the Wang Yang-ming school over the meaning of the Way.[165] The Classics became the testing ground for any exposition of the sages' teachings.[166] From as early as the refounding of the Tung-lin Academy in 1604, the Classics were not just the battlefield for the neo-Confucians themselves but also a major means to distinguish "pure" Confucianism from Buddhism and to cleanse Confucianism of such "perverted" teachings as the syncreticism of many of Wang Yang-ming's followers. Besides their concern for reaffirming the established ethical relationships central to Confucianism, the Tung-lin leaders were strong exponents of Classical studies. The third regulation in the Tung-lin Academy rules of membership required the study of the Five Classics. Confucian Classicism took as its purpose the defense of Confucian ethics and political activism. Ku Yün-ch'eng explained his perspective on Classical studies as follows:

The moral will [*tao-hsin*] requires no constraints, but man's mind cannot be relied upon entirely. To understand the moral will is difficult, and man's mind is subject to delusions. Only recently have I found the moral meanings [*i-li*] in the Six Classics appropriate and agreeable. Every sentence enlightens my moral mind, and every remark awakens my human mind [*jen-hsin*]. No learning is authentic if it is not predicated upon the Classics; no statecraft is genuine if it does not originate from them.[167]

The Tung-lin leaders' emphasis on the Classics as the only source for the authentication of ethics and statecraft became the raison d'être of the Restoration Society (Fu she). Their concern for reaffirming traditional socio-moral standards and their solutions to political and social ills were perpetuated in the ideas of leaders of the Restoration Society, which sought to incorporate the political and moral platforms of the Tung-lin scholars. The leaders of the Restoration Society, Chang P'u (1602–41) and his brother, Chang Ts'ai (1596–1648), made it a rule in their public lectures to exhort the audience to abide by the law and to observe strict moral standards.[168]

The stress the Restoration Society put on Classical studies further attests to its elitist orientation. The reasons for "reviving ancient learning" (*fu-hsing ku-hsüeh*) were explicitly laid down by Chang P'u:

From the time education [began to] decline, scholars have not understood the wisdom embodied in the Classics. . . . There are fewer and fewer talented men and the government gets worse every day. . . . I [only] hope to join with many scholars from all over the empire to revive the ancient teachings so that future generations will be able to provide useful service [to the country]. For this reason, [our group's] name is the Restoration Society.[169]

Like Ku Yün-ch'eng and Kao P'an-lung, Chang P'u concluded that the deterioration of education, resulting from the neglect of the Classics, had led to the political and moral crises of their times. Of great interest is the way in which the Restoration Society associated Classical studies with service to the state. In the rules of the Tung-lin Academy, the regulation requiring Classical studies came after regulations enjoining "knowing the basics" (*chih-pen*, i.e., human nature as essentially good) and "establishing one's will" (*li-chih*). For the members of the Restoration Society, however, drilling in the Classics was the most important objective of learning.

Like Ku Hsien-ch'eng and Kao P'an-lung, the Chang brothers and their friends confined the membership of their society to the literati. Unlike the populist lecturers and the T'ai-chou activists, they did not seek to mobilize the common people in their attempt to rejuvenate the dynastic order. By making Classical studies the core of the curriculum of the members and by restricting membership to the literati, the leaders of the Restoration Society, like the Tung-lin academicians, clearly distinguished themselves from the populist lecturers.

The increasing emphases on Classicism and ritualism in the late Ming were intimately related developments. The correlation of Classical studies and the concern for ritual practice is epitomized in the catchphrase from the *Analects*, "learning extensively and disciplining oneself in accordance with ritual" (*po-hsüeh yü wen, yüeh chih i li*). The regard for erudition was growing among scholars.[170] Ku Hsien-ch'eng's good friend Feng Ts'ung-wu considered that the term *po-yüeh* (erudition and discipline) referred to effort (*kung-fu*) rather than to the original mind (*pen-t'i*). "Learning extensively" (*po-wen*) was the "investigation of things and the extension of knowledge" (*ko-chih*). By *yüeh*, he meant *yüeh-li* (self-discipline through ritual).[171] Incidentally, Feng had great admiration for Chang Tsai's teachings.[172] Like Chang, he made ritual the objective criterion of proper conduct.[173]

The term *po-yüeh* began to gain currency in the early Ch'ing. The major realm of "extensive learning" was seen as Classical studies; *yüeh* referred mostly to "discipline through rituals." In the perspective of growing ritualism, the rise of Classicism can be related to the concern for ancient rituals. In the late Ming, however, the relationship between Classicism and ritual studies was not as conspicuous as it would be in the wake of the Manchu conquest.

2

Ritualist Ethics and Textual Purism in the K'ang-hsi Reign

Ritualism, Culturalism, and the Manchu Conquest

The instant collapse of the Ming regime had an enormous impact on the thinking of the gentry. In the wake of the Manchu conquest, a powerful current of culturalism further fueled the growth of ritualism and purism. These intellectual currents were indicative of the gentry's three major concerns—cultural identity, Confucian ethics, and social hierarchy. These three concerns converged on ritual as a general approach to a great variety of problems. This chapter deals with the first two concerns; the problems of social hierarchy are taken up in the next chapter.

Insofar as ethical thought was concerned, the Manchu conquest furthered the shift of interest from ontological questions to moral effort and the proper expression of ethical values through Confucian ritual. The large number of literati who either surrendered to the peasant rebels and the "barbarian" conquerors or sought refuge in Buddhist monasteries convinced the committed Confucian literati that lay Buddhism had eroded the Confucian commitment to social duties. Serving the emperor was, after all, not a Buddhist imperative. Studying sutras and releasing animals did not produce loyal officials. Early Ch'ing Confucians demanded moral action and ritual expression of ethical beliefs.[1]

Ritual became more than a practical means to resist Buddhism. It became a powerful symbol of Chinese identity. To practice it was to show defiance of Manchu authority. The need to express Chinese identity through ritual practice in part explains the growing importance of ritualism in early Ch'ing ethical thought. The sense of cultural identity became acute as the Manchus required all Han Chinese officials and commoners to adopt the queue and shave the forehead during the 1640's and 1650's. Even the common people were easily provoked into mob violence against such humiliating imposition of a "barbarian" hairstyle on the Chinese.[2]

Ritual practice was a powerful way to express cultural identity during the first two decades of Manchu rule when the Chinese were fighting a losing battle against the Manchus' political and cultural oppression. Perhaps no scholar exemplified this state of mind better than Ku Yen-wu. In a 1663 letter to Wang Wan (1624–90), Ku confided that he had not recognized the primacy of ritual propriety until recently.[3] In a preface written several years earlier to Chang Erh-ch'i's (1612–78) I-li Cheng-chu chü-tu, Ku wrote that nothing was more important than ritual propriety; the Duke of Chou had ruled the realm with ritual, and Confucius based his teachings on it.[4] Rituals became the quintessence of Chinese culture and a powerful system of enabling symbols for Confucians like Ku Yen-wu. An oft-quoted passage makes explicit his notion of the relation of ritual to the duty of the Confucian elite:

There is a distinction between the destruction of a dynasty [kuo] and the destruction of the realm [t'ien-hsia]. Where [does one] draw the line? The change of imperial house [i-hsing] is what is called the destruction of a dynasty; the realm is said to have been destroyed when humanity and duties [jen-i] are abandoned to the extent that human beings eat one another.[5]

At a time when canonical teachings (chiao) were completely forgotten, these statements were indictments against scholars who violated Confucian teachings about moral obligations such as loyalty and filial piety. For Ku, serving the Manchus was the best evidence of the "destruction of the realm." Many others, such as Chang Erh-ch'i and Wang Fu-chih (1619–92), shared the tendency to see political apostasy as a crime against culture.[6] Committing oneself to rituals was for many an act of symbolic resistance to the Manchu conquest, however politically unproductive such an act might be. The psychological comfort that it brought was not insignificant.

Ironically, culturalism and its ritual expression could serve the opposite goal. By identifying with culture rather than with the Ming regime, Chinese literati could justify their participation in the Manchu government. Belief in the universality of Chinese culture and one's commitment to preserving it under an alien regime could help mitigate the sense of guilt of those who served the Manchus.[7]

In the light of the powerful surge of culturalism, the general interest among scholars in the history and the institutions of the Three Dynasties, that is, in the Classics, can be viewed as an expression of both an implicit rejection of the Manchu regime and a justification of rendering service to it. For many, Classical studies were hardly anachronistic exercises. The upsurge of interest in Classical studies and ritual learning was a political statement in disguise. The ambivalence of the political implications of culturalism contributed significantly to a strong sense of Chinese identity. The literati became more concerned with "our tradition" and "our culture."[8] The preservation of the cultural tradition called for action, whether political or ethical.

Ritualism and Moral Cultivation

The Ming disaster proved to many the futility of a didactic method that depended on "empty talk" about human nature and moral principles in abstraction. Discussion of human nature became meaningless when a literatus had to decide whether to die a martyr, to withdraw from government service in order to preserve his integrity, or to accept the identity-racking hairstyle imposed by the Manchus. These choices made action the testing ground of morality.

Emphasis on moral effort in terms of proper behavior became more pronounced among the students of Liu Tsung-chou, such as Huang Tsung-hsi. In the preface to his influential *Records of Ming Scholars* (*Ming-ju hsüeh-an*), Huang said: "The mind has no essence; the mind's essence is the totality of moral effort."[9] For the most part, Huang owed this idea to Liu Tsung-chou's teaching that moral effort and the substance of mind are identical (*chi kung-fu chi pen-t'i*).[10] From the perspective of the Wang Yang-ming school, Liu's innovation lies not so much in his emphasis on moral practice as in his doctrine of "vigilance in solitude" (*shen tu*), a regimen of introspection that allowed one to experience the essential mind.

In stressing moral effort as the essence of the mind, Huang Tsung-hsi departed from his teacher's position in a subtle way. When speaking of moral effort, Liu emphasized the mind's vigilance over conduct. By contrast, for Huang, moral effort involved cultivation more of virtue (*hsiu-te*) than of the mind.[11] In terms of self-cultivation, he underscored the molding of conduct (*hsiu-shen*) rather than control of the mind. Huang did not so much deny the controlling function of the mind as stress the ritual expression of morality. In the Confucian context, proper cultivation of the person in the main involved the observance of social morality and ritual propriety (*li*). Liu Tsung-chou's study of the *Book of Etiquette and Decorum* also provided a basic procedural form for Huang Tsung-hsi's colloquiums on the Classics in the 1660's.[12]

Huang Tsung-hsi's interest in the Confucian doctrine of ritual (*li-chiao*) was noted by Ch'üan Tsu-wang (1705–55). In his epitaph of Huang, Ch'üan pointed out that one major component of Huang's learning was "Chang Tsai's doctrine of ritual."[13] For Huang, ritual provides the objective standards for behavior. Commenting on Liu Tsung-chou's discussion of the relationships among human nature, destiny, and mind, he subtly altered his master's formula by emphasizing "destiny" (*ming*). Moreover, Huang equated "destiny" with the "universal principles of all things" (*kung-kung chih li*). By "universal principles," he meant "the principles of the Three Bonds and Five Constant Virtues [*kang-ch'ang*] and of human relationships and things. They are considered by man as the universal principles of all things and are used to regulate the ethico-moral order. This is the reason why these principles constitute destiny [or command; *ming*]."[14] In Liu's thought, mind controls nature (*hsing*) and destiny (*ming*). Huang's comment, however, in effect externalizes the mind into "universal principles"—observable human relationships and the corresponding virtues. Huang might have inadvertently misread his teacher, but his "misunderstanding" should not come as a surprise in view of his concern for objective rules of behavior as well as for moral exertion.

Huang's emphasis on moral practice was shared by his fellow student Ch'en Ch'üeh's (1604–77). Ch'en strongly criticized Ch'an Buddhism and Sung neo-Confucianism for their doctrine of the self-sufficiency of the moral will. Anticipating the methodology of the eighteenth-century evidential school, Ch'en pointed out that the term *pen-t'i* (original substance), a phrase currently used to denote the essential rather than the experiential aspect of human nature, was not in the Classics. Rather, it originated in Buddhism.[15] Human nature was, of course, good, but its goodness, Ch'en insisted, could be discerned only after its "full extension" (*k'uo-ch'ung*). By "extension" he meant moral exertion (*kung-fu*). Vacuous speculation on the abstract nature prior to physical existence could easily lead people into believing Ch'an Buddhism.[16] Ch'en regarded moral endeavor as empirical testament to human nature.

Huang Tsung-hsi's ethical thought echoed Ch'en's views. In the preface to *The Records of Ming Scholars*, he wrote: "The substance of mind is where moral effort is extended."[17] Phrased differently, human nature, in this case empirical nature, depends exclusively on the sum of one's moral exertions. Both Huang and Ch'en had come to understand morality in terms of human endeavor to realize the good. The good nature of human beings could not exist in abstraction, any more than moral acts could

spring naturally from a sheer "discovery" of the moral will. Moral will is
not sufficient to ensure moral conduct.

Although important as a forerunner of later developments, Liu Tsung-
chou belonged more to the generation of Ku Hsien-ch'eng and Kao P'an-
lung, which still took a strong interest in metaphysics and spiritual cultivation. By contrast, Ch'en Ch'üeh's concerns lay largely in the realm of
developing habits in accordance with moral standards and rituals, a tendency already nascent in Liu's ethics. Nowhere is Ch'en's regard for ritual
more forcefully expressed than in his instruction to his son: "What distinguishes human beings from beast is their capacity to devote themselves to
ritual practice. Humans also set themselves apart from beasts by practicing ritual in earnest." [18] Ch'en's ideas exemplify a striking departure in the
development of ethical thinking in the early Ch'ing; more will be said in
subsequent chapters about his views on a wide range of rites.

Chang Tsai and Ritualist Ethics

Developments in ethical thinking parallel to those in Kiangnan are discernible among eminent exponents of Wang Yang-ming's teachings in
north China. Sun Ch'i-feng (1584–1675) and Li Yung (1627–1705) incorporated the ritualism of the Ch'eng-Chu tradition into their own thinking. In ways reminiscent of the Tung-lin scholars, Sun reaffirmed Confucian ethical relationships and the role of ritual in regulating behavior. [19]
The basics of self-cultivation lay in the fulfillment of one's ethical duties
and the observance of ritual. [20] Sun pointed out that one difference between
Chang Tsai and Ch'eng Hao lay in Chang's emphasis on ritual practice in
his approach to moral education (i-li wei chiao). [21]

Li Yung believed that Chang Tsai's stress on ritual was a remedy for
the moral crisis of his time. [22] Rectifying misconduct occupies an important place in Li's ethical teachings. Concern about wrongdoing and attempts at rectification through confession were evident in the thinking of
several late Ming thinkers. [23] Li Yung's major precept in this regard was
expressed in the dictum "Repent and renew yourself" (hui-kuo tzu-hsin). [24]
The stress on correcting one's wrongdoings and evil ideas resembles the
moral instructions afforded in Liu Tsung-chou's Manual of Man. Centered
on awareness of one's mistakes in thought and action, Li's teachings represent a more realistic view of the human proclivity to err. He recognized
the strong human tendency to depart from moral standards. For Li, it
is in the empirical realm of human action that we can work to improve

ourselves morally. Compared with the doctrines of the T'ai-chou school, Li's ethical teachings smack of pessimism. His profound recognition of human moral inadequacy, however, comes close to Chang Tsai's view that the "imbalanced" physical nature of humans gives rise to bad habits. Both men stressed the need to cultivate moral conduct.

Cultivating behavior through ritual practice was no less emphasized by the leading scholars of the Ch'eng-Chu tradition in the south. Lu Shih-i (1611–72) of Kiangsu, who attended Liu Tsung-chou's lectures at the Chi-shan Academy,[25] noted, as had Liu, that Chu Hsi devoted his last years to study of the *Book of Etiquette and Decorum*. Lu believed that Chu's formula "the investigation of things and the extension of knowledge" referred mostly to the discussion of ritual.[26] Lu took issue with the view that the emperor had the sole authority to decide matters concerning ritual. That he stressed this point bespoke the difficulties he confronted as a scholar who refused to serve the Manchu regime. For him, ritual was much larger than political authority. By putting rituals above the vicissitudes of dynastic regimes, he sanctified Chinese rituals as a universal system of rules of behavior, an unmistakable symbol of cultural identity for the Confucian elite under alien rule in Lu's time. To drive this point home, he availed himself of Chu Hsi's view of ritual as the "manifested rules of Heavenly principle" (*t'ien-li chih chieh-wen*). With Chu Hsi as authority, he argued that it was a Confucian scholar's (*ju*) duty to discuss ritual.[27]

Chang Lü-hsiang (1611–74) of Chekiang, after switching allegiance from the Wang Yang-ming school to the Ch'eng-Chu school, stressed the cardinal importance of learning ritual in the development of man's nature (*chih li ch'eng hsing*).[28] In all likelihood, Chang's view owed much to Chang Tsai, who stressed the importance of learning and practicing ritual in transforming one's nature.[29] The growth of interest in Chang Tsai's method of moral cultivation further attests to the increasing dissatisfaction with the intuitive approach to morality. It explained to some degree the reversal in the relative appeal of Wang Yang-ming's teachings and the Ch'eng-Chu school.[30]

Those Ch'eng-Chu scholars concerned about ritual were attracted to Chang Tsai's views on teaching moral conduct through ritual practice. A good example was Ku Yen-wu. During his sojourn in north China after 1656, Ku made the acquaintance of scholars such as Chang Erh-ch'i, Li Yin-tu (1631–92), and Wang Hung-chuan, who were devoted followers of Ch'eng-Chu neo-Confucianism.[31] Ku was impressed as much by Chang Erh-ch'i's study of the *Book of Etiquette and Decorum* as by the advocacy by Li Yin-tu and Wang Hung-chuan of Chang Tsai's method of moral cultivation.[32] Through interaction with these scholars, Ku came to underscore the importance of ritual in maintaining the Confucian ethico–moral order.[33] Chang Tsai's teaching provided an example for him to follow once he found the Ming restorationist cause beyond hope.[34] Ku's interest in ritual grew as he aged. He found it rather deplorable that not until he was over 50 did he realize one could not establish oneself without learning ritual.[35]

The stress on cultivating one's nature by ritual practice was prominent in Wang Fu-chih's moral thought as well. According to him, whereas Mencius speaks of human nature, Confucius speaks of practice (hsi).[36] On one occasion he even reduced learning to the knowledge and practice of ritual: "To know is to know ritual. Ritual is to practice what one knows."[37] He argued that the Buddhists "suppressed the ego" (k'o-chi) without "returning to ritual" (fu-li) because they believed in ontological nothingness. In the process of "suppressing the ego," the Confucians brought themselves in line with ritual, which embodied the core values of Confucianism.[38] Among the Sung neo-Confucians, Wang was particularly interested in Chang Tsai's philosophy and wrote a commentary on Chang's philosophical work Cheng-meng (Rectifying the ignorant).[39]

Ritualism and New Interpretations of the Ch'eng-Chu Orthodoxy

As is true of any system of thought, the Ch'eng-Chu school of neo-Confucianism lends itself to multiple emphases. Within late Ming and early Ch'ing versions of Ch'eng-Chu neo-Confucianism, new interpretations of the Four Books pointed to the centrality of ritual.

Chu Hsi regarded the gist of the Doctrine of the Mean to be "thoroughly talking about the effort of vigilance in solitude" (shen-tu kung-fu).[40] It is the most important text on which he derived his explanation of the distinction between two states of the mind: the state before the rise of emotions and the state when they arise. The mind without emotions is the heavenly endowed nature (t'ien-ming chih hsing). The effort of cultivation before emotions arise is "reverence" (ching).[41] Reverence means "keeping a sense of caution and vigilance, and not daring to become permissive."[42]

Chang Erh-ch'i, whose devotion to ritual studies is indicated above, argued that the message of the Doctrine of the Mean had been obscured by a mistaken explication of the term *chung-yung* (the mean). According to Chang, *chung-yung* means the modality of proper behavior as regulated by ritual: "Only when one abides by ritual can one behave properly. Only with proper behavior can one attain the way of the mean. . . . The *Doctrine of the Mean* is nothing but a general and epitomized discourse on ritual."[43] Chang was convinced that the crux of the *Doctrine of the Mean* is the primacy of ritual rather than, as emphasized by Chu Hsi, the cultivation of the mind. Chang stressed the regulation of conduct by ritual by saying that "ritual is the manifestation of the Way."[44] Chang's statement rephrases Chu Hsi's remark "Ritual is the particular manifestation of Heavenly principle" (*li che t'ien-li chih chieh-wen*). Chang merely substituted "Heavenly principle" for "the Way."[45]

The growing concern for ritual is indicated no less prominently in contemporary interpretations of the intellectual development of Chu Hsi. Lu Shih-i lamented that Chu Hsi did not live long enough to finish his *General Exposition of the Book of Etiquette and Decorum and Its Commentaries* (*I-li ching-chuan t'ung-chieh*). Lu was dissatisfied with the extant work, which was completed by Chu Hsi's disciples.[46]

Lu Shih-i was by no means the only scholar who devoted himself to painstaking study of ritual. After 1677, Hsü Ch'ien-hsüeh (1631–94), Ku Yen-wu's nephew, worked on a voluminous compendium of ritual entitled *Tu-li t'ung-k'ao* (A comprehensive study of rituals; 120 *chüan*). During the period 1677–90, he enlisted the help of many noted scholars, including Huang Tsung-hsi's student Wan Ssu-t'ung (1638–1702).[47] Chiang Yung (1681–1762), a faithful follower of the Ch'eng-Chu school, also believed that the *Etiquette and Decorum* was the basis of the work on ritual to which Chu Hsi devoted himself in his last years.[48] Like Lu Shih-i, he found the work of Chu Hsi's students unsatisfactory. He decided to finish Chu Hsi's incomplete project himself. The resulting *Li-ching kang-mu* (An outline of the Classics on rituals) was a voluminous work in 80 *chüan*, organized under the conventional five categories of rituals.[49] Ch'in Hui-tien's (1702–64) well-known *Wu-li t'ung-k'ao* (Comprehensive study of the five categories of ritual; 260 *chüan*) was probably an expanded and revised version of Wan's colossal work.[50] Like Chiang Yung, Ch'in's work was intended to finish what Chu Hsi had begun.[51] Chapter 5 has more to say about the legacy of Chu Hsi's scholarship in the ritual studies of the K'ang-hsi period.

Classics and Ritual

Although like their late Ming predecessors early Ch'ing scholars were drawn to ritual studies, they came to place greater stress on the relevance of research on the Classics. In his preface to a critical study of rituals by Wan Ssu-ta (1633–83), Huang Tsung-hsi went so far as to say that the Classics were records of ancient rituals: "The Six Classics are records of the Way, and rituals are the main structures."[52] Huang regarded the Classics as the basis of learning and promoted their study among his students. What is more revealing is his understanding of the Way as ritual. Huang's unusual command of ritual is evidenced by his letters to Wan Ssu-t'ung.[53] Huang required all his students to learn the Classics well.[54] Like his older brother, Wan Ssu-t'ung devoted himself to research on Classical institutions and rites.[55] They perpetuated and advanced Liu Tsung-chou's and Huang Tsung-hsi's ideas on the role of proper ritual in the maintenance of the moral order.[56] As discussed below in Chapters 3 and 4, Wan Ssu-ta and his contemporaries also became engrossed in ritual studies because of the need to clarify kinship rituals crucial to the building of lineages.

These dual tendencies—ritualism and Classicism—were equally manifested among scholars of the Ch'eng-Chu school. Ku Yen-wu exhibited a deep interest in the study of the Classics, especially after the fall of the Ming dynasty.[57] Despite his criticisms of neo-Confucian speculations on mind and human nature, Ku Yen-wu had great respect for the breadth of Chu Hsi's learning.[58] Ku's goal was to apply Classical knowledge as clarified by textual investigation. One area of application was ritual, as revealed by his maxim "Broaden oneself with learning, and behave with a sense of shame" ("po-hsüeh yü wen, hsing chih yü ch'ih"). Shame resulted from violation of proper ritual and moral standards. Knowledge of rituals could be acquired through broad learning, in which Classical learning was critical.[59] Nowhere is Ku's Classicism more clearly disclosed than in the oft-quoted statement "The study of the Classics is the study of principle" (ching-hsüeh chi li-hsüeh).[60]

Lu Lung-ch'i (1630–92), a partisan Ch'eng-Chu scholar, studied the three ritual Classics during his mourning for his father.[61] He reviewed the commentaries on the Book of Etiquette and Decorum and criticized them according to what he took to be Chu Hsi's ideas.[62] His notes on rituals were completed in 1679 and given the title Tu-li chih-i (Doubts raised in studying rituals).[63] According to Chang Po-hsing (1651–1725), Lu's study of the three ritual Classics was inspired by Chu Hsi's inquiries into the commentaries and the original text of the *Book of Etiquette and Decorum*.[64] In his preface to Lu's work, Chang said:

Rituals are the manifest rules of Heavenly Principles, the regulations for human activities. . . . When even one minor act is not in accordance with ritual, the Heavenly Principle is lost. Therefore, when [Confucius' disciple] Yen Yüan was studying with the sage, he learned extensively and disciplined himself with ritual [*po-wen yüeh-li*]. In the [Northern] Sung Chang Tsai also devoted himself to the teaching of "developing [human] nature by learning ritual" [*chih-li ch'eng-hsing*]. Study without learning ritual amounts to steering a boat without oars. Formerly Chu Hsi did a general exposition on the *Book of Etiquette and Decorum* that is superior to those written by scholars of the Han dynasty.[65]

Chang Po-hsing's remarks make it clear that these early Ch'ing scholars considered ritual essential for developing proper conduct and that Lu Lung-ch'i's study of the ritual Classics grew out of his concern for practical application of these ancient norms of behavior.

Textual Purism, and the Critique of Neo-Confucian Classicism

The vigorous revival of the Classical tradition of the Ch'eng-Chu school in the second half of the seventeenth century continued to shape ritual studies and research on the Classics in the early eighteenth century. This revival developed in conjunction with the purist movement of the K'ang-hsi and early Ch'ien-lung reigns. In this second phase of the movement, the purist goal was well served by Sung scholarship, which provided a window on Classical doctrines and rituals and the "intellectualism" needed to refute the intuitionism of Wang Yang-ming's teachings.[66] But this rapport between Sung scholarship and the purist quest for the pristine Confucian doctrine gradually broke down as some Confucians came to dismiss Sung neo-Confucian scholarship on the Classics and ritual as unreliable because of the pervasive influence of heterodox notions that had crept into the thinking of the Sung neo-Confucians.

From the 1650's on, ominous signs were visible that presaged the loss of interest in Sung neo-Confucian scholarship among *k'ao-cheng* Classicists a century later. We need to know, therefore, why the reinvigorated Ch'eng-Chu school, especially the exegetical tradition forged by Chu Hsi, came to be condemned as an inaccurate presentation of the Classics. To put it differently, we need to understand why scholars gradually gave up Sung-Yüan Classicism and ritual scholarship for a new system of Classical and ritual learning—the Han Learning movement that was to dominate the intellectual scene from the mid-eighteenth century on.

The emergence in the mid-eighteenth century of distrust of the Sung-Yüan exegetical traditions can be traced to a flurry of purist attempts to eliminate non-Confucian textual elements from the Classics in the K'ang-hsi period. These textual critiques not only considerably undermined the cosmological and ontological systems of the Sung neo-Confucians but also gradually fostered a deep suspicion about the soundness of Sung and Yüan scholarship.

Ch'en Ch'üeh
and P'an Ping-ko

Although Ch'eng-Chu neo-Confucianism re-emerged as the dominant school in the second half of the seventeenth century and continued the battle against Wang Yang-ming's teachings and all forms of syncretism and heterodoxies, a more "radical" strain of purism was taking shape in the 1650's that worked to undermine the theoretical and textual basis of neo-Confucianism. This purifying effort came to focus on identifying heterodox elements in the commentaries on the Classics. Confucian texts would be correctly understood only after non-Confucian phrases and expressions had been identified and excised.

The foremost scholar to use linguistic purism to shatter the textual foundations of neo-Confucianism was Liu Tsung-chou's student Ch'en Ch'üeh. Ch'en differed significantly from Huang Tsung-hsi in his attitude toward neo-Confucianism. Ch'en's writings show little interest in metaphysics and cosmology. He attacked neo-Confucianism of all varieties for being skewed by Buddhism, an act that alienated most of his contemporaries, and he held the Sung neo-Confucians accountable for this, an accusation to be reiterated by Yen Yüan (1635–1704) and the Han Learning scholars.[67]

Ch'en disparaged attempts to discuss the metaphysical foundation of ethics and strove to show that many terms prominent in Confucian discussions of human nature originated in heterodox teachings. He noted, for example, that the term *pen-t'i* (essential nature), a notion central to neo-Confucian ontology, was used neither in the Classics nor in the earliest commentaries. It was originally a Buddhist term.[68] Ch'en was not alone in striving to identify terms of unorthodox origins employed by Sung neo-

Confucians. His contemporaries Li Yung and Ku Yen-wu also shared his interest.[69]

The most disturbing writing of Ch'en Ch'üeh is the treatise "Distinguishing the *Great Learning*" (*Ta-hsüeh pien*), a critique that he began to work on as early as 1654.[70] Ch'en argued that the *Great Learning*, a basic text of neo-Confucianism, was not the work of Confucius' disciples but the crass writing of some Han scholar.[71] Its teachings departed fundamentally from those of the sages for it stresses "knowing" (*chih*) to the neglect of "practice" (*hsing*). Ch'en had no doubt that the *Great Learning* exemplified the teachings of Ch'an Buddhism. One reason for his judgment was the phrase *chih-chih* (knowing where to stop): "How could a scholar's quest for knowledge stop?" "Knowing where to stop" was to entertain the Ch'an idea that no further knowledge was necessary once one attained perfect knowledge.[72] In dismissing the *Great Learning*, Ch'en rendered the controversies over the textual arrangement and the meaning of *ko-wu* irrelevant to the proper understanding of Confucianism. Ch'en clearly was unconcerned about the damage his views might cause neo-Confucianism. Despite his admiration for Wang Yang-ming, who venerated the *Great Learning*, Ch'en never apologized for his vehement attack on this central text of neo-Confucianism.[73]

Ch'en Ch'üeh's textual criticism presents an excellent example of a general problem often encountered in philology—the fusion of canonical texts and commentaries on them due to errors in copying, printing, and oral transmission. Like his Sung predecessors, Ch'en, by extending his criticism beyond the existing commentarial tradition, called into question texts conventionally accepted as authentic. Critical scholarship, if allowed to move beyond the text, can be as dangerous as heterodox teachings.

Ch'en's iconoclastic treatise immediately elicited protests, even from such friends as Chang Lü-hsiang.[74] As Ch'ien Mu has noted, Huang Tsung-hsi initially took exception to Ch'en's view but, in a revised epitaph on Ch'en, eventually admitted that the origin of the *Great Learning* was indeed problematic.[75] Ch'en was moving ahead of his contemporaries in abandoning Sung traditions. He called for a return to the authentic Confucian teachings of the Classics. Ch'en was among the first in the early Ch'ing to call for a demarcation between Sung neo-Confucianism and Classical Confucianism. He criticized the teachings of Chou Tun-i, Ch'eng I, and Chu Hsi for their strong element of Ch'an Buddhism.[76]

Ch'en's critique of Sung neo-Confucianism paralleled that of P'an P'ing-ko (1610–77), who dismissed neo-Confucianism in its varied forms as either Taoist or Buddhist. After Huang Tsung-hsi restored the Cheng-jen Academy in Chekiang in 1667, scholarly meetings resumed in that area. P'an P'ing-ko attended the meetings and impressed Huang Tsung-hsi's students such as Wan Ssu-t'ung and Cheng Liang (1637–1713) with his disquieting remark that both Chu Hsi and Lu Chiu-yüan preached heterodoxy, the former Taoism and the latter Buddhism. P'an went so far as to dismiss all the scholars from the Sung on as a crowd of Buddhists and Taoists.[77]

As Ch'ien Mu long ago noted, the distinction that Ch'en and P'an strove to make anticipated the scholarship of the late seventeenth and early eighteenth centuries.[78] Without question both Ch'en and P'an exemplified a radical purism congruent with that of Yen Yüan and Li Kung (1659–1733). Small wonder that Li Kung felt sympathetic toward P'an's views.[79] However, the shocking categorical condemnation of neo-Confucianism by Ch'en Ch'üeh and P'an P'ing-ko failed to attract a large audience, for, as we have seen, most contemporary scholars were drawn to the Ch'eng-Chu school for inspiration and solutions to various problems that were created, they believed, by the radicalization of the teachings of Wang Yang-ming.[80]

Although the "radical" and thorough indictment of neo-Confucianism proposed by Ch'en Ch'üeh and P'an P'ing-ko created only ripples in the intellectual circles, some purist efforts to excise textual appendages from the Classics gained extensive support from the 1660's on. Although these efforts ultimately presented a substantial challenge to neo-Confucianism, these attacks did not target the Ch'eng-Chu school intentionally. Textual criticism was, for the most part, undertaken by adherents of the Ch'eng-Chu school. But by unraveling the extraneous origins of texts attached to the Classics, scholars, in effect, contributed collectively to dismantling the authority of neo-Confucianism, whose cosmology was based on texts infused into the Classics.

A Purge of Textual Impurities

As discussed in the preceding chapter, the interests of Tung-lin scholars gradually shifted from metaethics to the cultivation of proper behavior in accordance with Confucian rituals. Their polemical efforts to mark off heterodox teachings aimed to discredit syncreticism and the amoral view of human nature. Although there was already a strong commitment to Classical studies, few members of the Tung-lin Academy foresaw that their battle against heterodoxies would result in damaging the integrity of the Classics. From the 1660's until the end of K'ang-hsi reign, however, the purist effort to demarcate Confucianism from unorthodox teachings was carried out as a purge of non-canonical texts and rituals.

In 1661 Huang Tsung-hsi fired the first shot at the basic text of neo-Confucian cosmology. In *I-hsüeh hsiang-shu lun* (A discussion of the images and numbers associated with the study of the *Book of Changes*), he concentrated on exposing the heterodox origin of texts incorporated into the *Book of Changes*. Huang Tsung-hsi took exception to Chu Hsi's acceptance of the numerological interpretations advanced by the Sung neo-Confucian Shao Yung.[81] Later, in a similar vein, Mao Ch'i-ling (1623–1716) chastised Sung neo-Confucians for corrupting the Confucian Classics by infusing into them heterodox cosmologies based on Taoist scripture.[82]

On the bases of the pioneering works by Huang Tsung-hsi and Mao Ch'i-ling, in 1700 Hu Wei (1633–1714) completed a more comprehensive and definitive study. Hu Wei's celebrated work, the *I-t'u ming-pien* (A clarifying critique of the diagrams associated with the *Book of Changes*) revealed the heterodox origin of Chou Tun-i's "Diagram of the Great Ultimate" (*T'ai-chi t'u*).[83] Others agreed. In tracing the origins of the "Diagram of the Great Ultimate" and of the *Ho-t'u Lo-shu* (Yellow River chart and Lo River diagram), Li Kung, a friend of Hu Wei, reached a similar conclusion in 1708. Both men rejected the various diagrams as additions to the *Book of Changes*. Their views were shared by another friend, Wang Fu-li (fl. 1695), a descendant of Wang Yang-ming. All concurred that the diagrams were Taoist in origin.[84]

Equally devastating was Yen Jo-chü's (1636–1704) systematic exposure of the fabrication of the *Old Text Book of History* (*Ku-wen Shang-shu*). Yen completed the first draft in 1683, but the work had no impact until a decade later.[85] The fabricated Classic contained a passage that, it was believed, provided Chu Hsi with a textual basis for his ontological dualism. The passage drew parallels between the terms *jen-hsin* (human mind) and *tao-hsin* (moral mind) and the dichotomy between human desire (*jen-yü*) and "heavenly principles" (*t'ien-li*). The credibility of this Classic had been questioned by Wu Yü (fl. 1124), Chu Hsi, and Wu Ch'eng (1247–1331). But as Benjamin Elman aptly points out, few Sung and Yüan Confucians allowed their philological skepticism to override their philosophical belief in the *jen-hsin tao-hsin* passage.[86] Through meticulous comparison with ancient texts, Yen was able to demonstrate that the *Old Text Book of History* was a forgery. The verdict undermined the textual basis of the Ch'eng-Chu idea of moral cultivation and its dualism of the moral mind and human desire.

K'ang-hsi period critical scholarship cannot, however, be taken as a general strike against Ch'eng-Chu learning. The criticism and skepticism exemplified by the enterprises of Yen Jo-chü and Hu Wei should not be viewed as an indiscriminate onslaught consciously directed against Sung and Ming neo-Confucianism. As Elman has demonstrated, Yen's critique grew out of a tradition of scholarship dating back to Sung neo-Confucian suspicions of the *Old Text Book of History*.[87] Yen's skepticism was in line with the strong critical and skeptical stance of Sung and Yüan neo-Confucians.[88] In a similar spirit, Hu Wei traced the creation of the diagrams by the Sung Taoist Ch'en T'uan (d. 989) to a misreading of Han apocryphal writings.[89]

The notion that neo-Confucianism, as it evolved under the Sung or under the Ming, had to be forsaken before authentic Confucianism could be restored had yet to gain stature. The textual skepticism characteristic of the scholarship of the K'ang-hsi reign, therefore, has to be treated as part of the attempt to purify Confucian textual traditions. Those who engaged in such purgative exercises did not conceive of themselves as promoting a form of Confucianism diametrically opposed to the ethical teachings of the Sung neo-Confucians. They did not intend to degrade the authority of the Ch'eng-Chu school. In fact, many sought to prove the spurious origins of the texts attributed to Chu Hsi in order to exonerate him from the charge of slanting Confucianism. Hu Wei was a good example of such an attempt.[90] Another scholar who set himself the same task was Wang Mou-hung (1668–1741). In order to defend Chu Hsi against accusations of attaching heterodox writings to the *Book of Changes*, Wang argued that a comparison of the personal writings of Chu Hsi and the "Nine Diagrams" placed at the beginning of the *Book of Changes* clearly showed that the diagrams had been falsely attributed to Chu Hsi.[91]

The Ambivalence of Textual Purism

Textual purism knew no boundaries, and like critical scholarship without doctrinal constraints, it could cut both ways. The line between authentic and spurious texts was not always clearly drawn. To those purists more sensitive to the precarious nature of critical scholarship, following the logical path of criticism could wreak havoc on the textual integrity of

Confucianism. Indeed this was already evident in Yen Jo-chü's rejection of the *Old Text Book of History* as a forgery. Criticism of this sort alarmed some scholars, including those hostile to the Ch'eng-Chu school. If unharnessed, textual criticism could destroy their attempts to restore the authentic teachings of the Confucian Classics. Many scholars promptly took up the defense of the discredited text. The most celebrated scholars were Wan Ssu-t'ung, Mao Ch'i-ling, and Li Kung.[92]

Li Kung, like his teacher Yen Yüan, committed himself to expurgating heterodox ideas from the exegetical traditions of the Classics. He made a distinction, however, between, on the one hand, non-canonical texts and exegeses that skewed Confucian doctrines and, on the other hand, the Classics themselves. Despite his purist and anti-neo-Confucian positions, Li did not regard Yen Jo-chü's critique of the *Old Text Book of History* as a major blow against Ch'eng-Chu neo-Confucianism. Nor did Yen himself.[93] Li Kung agreed with Wan Ssu-t'ung that the text was authentic in terms of the moral teachings it embodied, regardless of some problems of style.[94] However critical he might be of the neo-Confucians' expositions on the *Great Learning*, he did not go as far as Ch'en Ch'üeh and dismiss it as a Ch'an Buddhist text.[95] Casting doubt on the Classics was a self-defeating perversion of the attempt to expunge heterodox elements.

The lack of scholars in the K'ang-hsi period who sought to apply critical methods systematically and thoroughly to the study of all the Classics can be seen in the reception accorded the critical scholarship of Yao Chi-heng (1647–1715?), a student of Mao Ch'i-ling who committed himself to revealing false texts. Yao raised doubts about many Classics, including the *Rites of Chou*, the *Rites of the Senior Tai* (*Ta-Tai li*), and the *Old Text Book of History*. Even the *Classic of Filial Piety* did not escape his skeptical eye. Yao declared that all four were blatant forgeries.[96] Of interest is the relative lack of popularity of his works among scholars of the K'ang-hsi and Ch'ien-lung periods in comparison to Yen Jo-chü's expose of the *Old Text Book of History*. The contrast in reception is best explained by the unwitting subservience of critical methods to the purist impulse that sought to restore the textual integrity of the Confucian Classics. The employment of textual and linguistic methods was guided by the attempts to expose and eliminate heterodox elements and to protect the Classics from excessive skepticism.

Skepticism did not serve the purists well. As Liang Ch'i-ch'ao has noted, attempts to expose false texts were a major trend in early Ch'ing scholarship, but they declined with the rise of evidential scholarship in the mid-eighteenth and early nineteenth centuries.[97] In fact, the major achievements of evidential scholarship of the eighteenth century lie less in uncovering spurious portions of the Classics and more in eliminating heterodox ideas and texts attached to the Classics by Sung neo-Confucians. A brief discussion of Yen Yüan's and Li Kung's critique of neo-Confucianism will show how purism was related to the "evidential scholarship" both as a methodological movement and as a system of ethics. Yen's and Li's ethical thinking foreshadowed that of Tai Chen (1724–77) and Ling T'ing-k'an (1757–1809), the foremost ethical thinkers of the Han Learning movement.

Purist Critique of Neo-Confucian Ritual and Ethics: Yen Yüan and Li Kung

No sooner had ritualism gained ascendancy in the ethical thought of the early Ch'ing than competing exegetical traditions emerged to engage scholars in heated debates. Whereas Ku Hsien-ch'eng and others demanded observance of rituals largely shaped by the Ch'eng-Chu tradition, some scholars in the second half of the seventeenth century began to realize that the rites promoted by the Sung neo-Confucians deviated from Classical norms. Among them were such eminent scholars as Ch'en Ch'üeh, Yen Yüan, and Li Kung. The growing Classicism and purism undoubtedly played an important role in precipitating the battle between "neo-Confucian ritualism" and "Classical ritualism." The link between neo-Confucian rituals and Classical studies began to dissolve as scholars realized the differences between neo-Confucian and Classical rituals.

Nothing exemplifies the conflict between these two approaches to ritual better than the intellectual development of Yen Yüan and his disciple Li Kung. The ethical theory of the Yen-Li school, as it came to be known, cannot be understood as strife *within* neo-Confucianism. The two men represent the beginning of the final stage of purist ritualism—a rejection of both the Ch'eng-Chu school and the Wang Yang-ming school, or, to use Liang Ch'i-ch'ao's term, a broad "reaction" against neo-Confucianism.[98] They did not, however, confine their attack to neo-Confucian "empty talk" about metaphysics. Much of their critique, especially that of Li Kung, was aimed at Ch'eng I's and Chu Hsi's writings on rituals and the Classics.

Yen Yüan: Purism and Ritual Practice

Yen Yüan, who first turned away from Wang Yang-ming's teachings and then from the Ch'eng-Chu school, represents an extreme in the Ch'ing scholarly search for correct ritual.[99] He considered the practice of ritual the fundamental doctrine of the Duke of Chou and Confucius and rejected the neo-Confucian approach to moral education of "understanding principles" (ming-li). What Confucius taught, he argued, was "practice" (hsi). His choice of sobriquet, Studio of Practice (hsi-chai), is indicative of the central position ritual practice held in his thought.

When he was committed to the Ch'eng-Chu school, his life-style was already highly ritualized.[100] Around 1664, he began keeping a diary solely to record his faults.[101] He modeled his behavior on the *Family Rituals by Master Chu* (Chu-tzu chia-li), a work attributed to Chu Hsi.[102] Four years later, when his foster grandmother died, he strictly observed the mourning rites prescribed by the *Family Rituals* and almost died from the intense austerity they required. This physical crisis led him to doubt what he believed to be Chu Hsi's system of rituals and eventually to reject neo-Confucianism of any persuasion as Buddhism in disguise. After 1668, he committed himself to exposing the Buddhist origins of the central teachings of Sung neo-Confucianism.

As mentioned earlier, the rise of culturalism in the wake of the Manchu conquest further fueled anti-Buddhist sentiments. Opposition to heterodoxy and syncretism continued to pervade intellectual circles in Yen's time. Among the anti-Buddhist literati were high officials and influential scholars of diverse persuasions—from the staunch Ch'eng-Chu admirer Lü Liu-liang to Chu Shih, an exponent of Chang Tsai's teachings, to Li Fu, an eminent scholar in the Lu Chiu-yüan tradition.[103] Li even denied that Buddhist renunciation of the world could explain the martyrdom of some scholars during the fall of the Ming dynasty because Buddhism excluded "human relationships," including loyalty to the emperor.[104]

As argued above, the demise of the Ming dynasty discredited the teachings of Wang Yang-ming.[105] Many of Yen Yüan's contemporaries denounced Wang Yang-ming's teachings as Buddhist. Chang Lieh (1622–85) penned the widely known *Wang-hsüeh chih-i* (Critique of Wang [Yang-ming]'s teachings). This relentless attack on Wang Yang-ming's teachings from the position of Ch'eng-Chu neo-Confucianism so impressed Lu Lung-ch'i that he underwrote its printing in 1686.[106] Lu himself was one of the foremost exponents of the Ch'eng-Chu school who criticized the Buddhist undertone of Wang Yang-ming's teachings. His *Hsüeh-shu pien* (Distinguishing [proper] learning) exemplifies the partisan charge by Ch'eng-Chu scholars of Ch'an influence in Wang Yang-ming's teachings.[107]

Yen Yüan, however, reminded adherents of the Ch'eng-Chu school that Wang was only continuing a practice begun in Sung neo-Confucianism.[108] Yen argued that Sung neo-Confucianism was nothing but an amalgam of Buddhism and Taoism.[109] Chu Hsi, he noted, had referred to the pervasive influence of Buddhism among Ch'eng I's students, many of whom were drawn to Ch'an Buddhism after Ch'eng I died. Yen Yüan pointed out that these students had been immersed in Ch'an Buddhism even before Ch'eng I's death, for what they learned from Ch'eng I bore a great resemblance to Ch'an Buddhism.[110] The same could be said of Chu Hsi's teachings.[111] Yen was accusing both Ch'eng I and Chu Hsi of practicing a form of syncretism not far removed from that of Wang Yang-ming. In his view, those who embraced Ch'eng-Chu neo-Confucianism deserved no less condemnation for their distortion of Confucianism than those in the Wang Yang-ming tradition. Yen went further than most of his contemporaries in rejecting all forms of neo-Confucianism, including the rejuvenated Ch'eng-Chu school.

Yen was therefore opposed to any attempt to reconcile the teachings of Wang Yang-ming and Chu Hsi, such as that of Sun Ch'i-feng. To Yen, neither faithfully represented Confucianism.[112] The attempt by Ch'eng-Chu neo-Confucians to purge heterodox teachings left much to be desired; they would never accomplish this task, for they themselves were irremediably influenced by Buddhism. The purification of Confucianism called for a full-scale critique of the entire neo-Confucian system and its perverted doctrines.

By tracing the heterodox ingredients in the teachings of Wang Yang-ming to Sung neo-Confucians, Yen broke with the trend of purism that began with the Tung-lin Academy.[113] The Tung-lin critique of syncretism did not call for a total rejection of neo-Confucianism, and Ku Hsien-ch'eng and Kao P'an-lung focused their attack only on the radical syncretism of Li Chih and Chou Ju-teng. In contrast, Yen directed his attack against both Sung and Ming neo-Confucianism. When Lü Liu-liang and Lu Lung-ch'i were vociferously attacking the teachings of Wang Yang-ming for being imbued with Ch'an Buddhism and other heterodoxies and hence responsible for the Ming demise,[114] Yen was battering the ideological foundation for these Ch'eng-Chu scholars' polemics. The task Yen saw for himself was clear: "The more [the teachings of] Ch'eng-Chu are removed, the more [the teachings of] Confucius and Mencius will be revealed." [115]

To Yen, crucial to Ch'eng-Chu neo-Confucianism was a dualistic view of human nature that posited an essential nature and a physical nature. The essential nature was "good"; the physical nature was the source of evil. This negative attitude toward physical nature fed suspicion of feelings and appetites. Because of this dualistic ontology, the Sung neo-Confucians formulated a program of moral cultivation that called for the suppression of feelings and desires.

Yen Yüan himself became a victim of such asceticism when he took seriously the strict mourning rules prescribed in the *Family Rituals by Master Chu*. That ordeal raised doubts in his mind as to the canonical origin of those neo-Confucian rites and their ethical foundation. As he saw it, these rites ignored the limits of human endurance because of the neo-Confucian view of human nature. Yen came to reject this bifurcation of human nature and regarded nature (*hsing*), feelings (*ch'ing*), and talents (*ts'ai*) alike as "good" (*shan*). Physical being was human nature. He argued that by regarding physical nature as the source of evil, Ch'eng I and Chu Hsi were in effect applying the Buddhist notion of *liu-tsei* (six destructive elements). For Yen, neither Confucius nor Mencius spoke of physical endowment as evil. Only Buddhist doctrine led Sung neo-Confucians to identify physical nature as such.[116]

Like Lu Shih-i, Yen endorsed a monistic view of human nature and claimed that "without physical nature, there is no [human] nature; without physical nature, [human] nature cannot be seen." [117] The natural endowment of human beings was not inherently evil. The formation of bad habits accounted for human evils.[118] Crucial to Yen's ethical theory was therefore a stress on the development of good habits. The neo-Confucian practice of quiet-sitting was of no avail in cultivating moral conduct.[119] Good habits were formed by practicing rituals that inculcated specific modes of behavior. Yen took exception to the neo-Confucian approach to moral cultivation for its emphasis on understanding and teaching ethical principles (*i-li*) as the proper path to moral development.[120] He insisted that only by making proper behavior habitual could morality be ensured. But once acquired, bad habits were difficult to eradicate. Yen Yüan therefore proposed a program of moral cultivation stressing the elimination of "acquired misconceptions and bad habits" (*yin pi hsi jan*).[121] This view of moral cultivation is reminiscent of those of Chang Tsai and Kao P'an-lung.[122]

This ritualist approach to moral conduct discourages questioning of the reasons behind rituals and tends to promote behavioral conformism. Unlike Wang Yang-ming's ethics, it distrusts human willpower regarding moral cultivation. As will be demonstrated below, Yen's ideas foreshadowed Tai Chen's and Ling T'ing-k'an's views of human nature and moral cultivation.

Yen may have rejected the ritual prescriptions in the *Family Rituals* as uncanonical but not a ritualist approach to moral cultivation. Rather, his ritualism underlay the drive to ensure that *correct* rituals were being practiced. In the *Rites of Chou*, Yen found what he believed to be the authentic teachings of ancient sages. The ancients were taught "six arts, six virtues, and six standards for proper conduct" (*liu i, liu te, liu hsing*).[123] The Classics also provided correct prescriptions for political institutions, including the "well-field" system and the feudal system. Yen insisted that the "great peace" of the Three Dynasties could be restored if these rituals and institutions were revived, though with some modifications.[124]

The purist impulse called for purging the rites of their neo-Confucian elements and for reviving canonical rituals. This of necessity entailed a thorough investigation of the Classics.[125] Yen's strong pragmatism, however, prevented him from total devotion to the Classical research then beginning to come into vogue.[126] He took issue with Chu Hsi's teaching regarding extensive learning[127] and opposed indiscriminate pursuit of knowledge. His belief that the study of rituals, music, archery, writing, and mathematics were essential to an authentic curriculum of Confucian education only suggests his pragmatic approach to learning. It is inaccurate to represent his thinking as an extreme case of anti-intellectualism. His ideas on statecraft called for the mastery of the technical as well as the theoretical disciplines essential to government. He may be guilty of entertaining a narrow definition of knowledge, but he was without question a Confucian purist who sought knowledge in order to attain the goals of order and peace.[128]

Li Kung: From Ritual Practice to Classical Studies

Li Kung and Wang K'un-sheng were the most notable disciples of Yen Yüan; both were faithful to their master's teachings on ritual practice. Li believed ritual was the quiddity of the "Way."[129] Wang modeled his life-style after that of Yen Yüan and was attentive to every minor act lest it violate ritual.[130] Both shared Yen Yüan's view that the Six Arts were nothing other than rituals.[131] Wang, like Yen, kept a diary recording his progress and his failings in moral cultivation.[132] In fact, Li Kung and all Yen's students kept diaries as records of moral practice; they showed these to each other regularly to gain the benefits of mutual watchfulness and exhortation.[133]

Yen Yüan was concerned primarily with practicing ancient ritual; he gave little thought to textual verification of their authenticity. He dismissed exegetical work as nugatory and considered statecraft a more urgent matter than textual problems in the Classics.[134] His idiosyncratic commitment to pragmatic learning and his secluded life-style shielded him from the disturbing currents of critical scholarship in the Lower Yangtze area.

Li Kung, however, could not avoid textual issues. Yen's thought contains an inherent tension between resurrecting ancient rituals and practicing them. Li Kung began to find textual study of the Classics increasingly indispensable to his effort to revive the ancient ritual of the sages.[135] His interest in ritual studies arose from the practical need to clarify what rituals the ancients had practiced. During his mourning for his parents' death, he did some research on the *Book of Rites* (*Li-chi*) and wrote treatises on several important ancient rituals.[136] The relevance of ritual studies to practice was clearly revealed when Li corrected Yen. In 1702 Yen followed Ch'eng I's account of ancient ritual and worshiped his grandparents in the spring and his parents in the fall. Li told him that in antiquity both grandparents and parents had been worshiped on the same day. Yen referred to the Classics and was convinced that Ch'eng was wrong. He abandoned Ch'eng I's program for the Classical one.[137]

Li Kung's interest in Classical studies grew after he made the acquaintance of Wan Ssu-t'ung and Mao Ch'i-ling, who were among the best Classical scholars in the Lower Yangtze area.[138] Despite Yen's profound interest in ancient rituals, he had always warned against excessive book learning to the neglect of practical purpose. Yen was disturbed by Li's growing interest in textual investigations of the Classics and the commentaries.[139] In response to his teacher's disapproval, Li explained:

I also study books for the purpose of learning. My practice is only slightly different from Master Yen's view. That we engage in the Six Arts [*liu-i*] requires us to study antiquity in order to correct present practice [*k'ao-ku i chun-chin*]. . . . Besides, without practice, one will not be familiar with the rituals of passage to maturity [*kuan*], marriage, mourning, and worship; without study, [ancient] etiquette cannot be known. . . . Rituals regarding ancestral temples [ts'ung-miao], worship of heaven and sacrifices to Heaven and Earth [chiao-she], grand worship and collective worship [ti-hsia] can be studied for future implementation by the monarch and prime minister. It is not appropriate to decide [on the proper form] of practice as an individual. . . . Even Confucius had to study [ancient rituals and institutions]. Presently, all follow the *Family Rituals* by Chu Hsi, but most of the rituals are arbitrary and imaginary creations and are not practical. How urgent is the study and discussion of rituals! Within the four seas, no one knows more than Mao Ch'i-ling in matters of rituals and music; Wan Ssu-t'ung has no peer in his broad knowledge of rituals.[140]

Although Li might have been influenced by the concern for textual research that was making its impact felt in the academic community in the south, his justification for textual studies and his departure from Yen Yüan cannot be dismissed as mere pedantry.[141] Li's strong interest in ancient ritual as a guide to practice may be seen in a response to a student's question: "To study extensively to acquire knowledge of ritual is learning ritual [*i li po-wen, hsüeh li yeh*]; to discipline [oneself] with ritual is to practice ritual [*yüeh-li, hsing-li yeh*]."[142]

In terms of ethical thought, Li Kung owed much to Yen Yüan. But that heritage was jeopardized by a rising tide of skepticism and critical scholarship that threatened to destroy the canonical basis of Yen's view of Confucianism. Li Kung's acquaintance with the Classical research circle in the Lower Yangtze area presented him with tasks requiring immediate attention if he was to uphold Yen Yüan's teachings.

The need to consult the Classics to verify rituals had led Li Kung to Classical research despite his mentor's warnings. More important was that Li realized the considerable stake Yen's teachings had in Classical research. Ying-shih Yü has aptly pointed out that the doctrines Yen Yüan singled out as the "original" teachings of Confucianism—"hsiang san-wu" and "liu-fu san-shih"—derive from the *Old Text Book of History* and the *Rites of Chou*.[143] The *Old Text Book of History* had come under the fierce attack from Yen Jo-chü, and a significant portion of the *Rites of Chou* was rejected by Wan Ssu-ta and Fang Pao (1668–1749) as spurious.[144] Fang Pao, a good friend of Li's, questioned the wisdom of basing his teachings on the *Rites of Chou* when its canonical status was in doubt.[145]

Li Kung was caught between the need to purge heterodox elements from exegetical traditions predominantly shaped by neo-Confucianism and the recognition of the ominous import of critical scholarship, which had been brought to a higher level of perfection by Yen Jo-chü and others.

Critical scholarship could cut both ways. Li clearly saw the peril in Yen Jo-chü's use of critical methods. He felt compelled, as his good friend Wan Ssu-t'ung did, to defend the *Old Text Book of History*.[146] Li failed to see the spuriousness of the text, but his apology for the text is indicative of his purist concern for the integrity of the Classics.

The authority of the Classics indeed was at stake during the K'ang-hsi period as Confucian purists strove to purge them of heterodox and uncanonical elements. Critical scholarship knew no boundaries, and there was the danger that it would backfire. For instance, Mao Ch'i-ling proclaimed that ancient rituals had been lost by the Spring and Autumn period, and the three ritual Classics were works of the Warring States period.[147] From his studies of the *Spring and Autumn Annals*, Ku Tung-kao (1679–1759) also came to the conclusion that the *Rites of Chou* had been fabricated by scholars of the Han dynasty and was no more trustworthy than the *Book of Etiquette and Decorum*.[148]

In order to combat the current of skepticism, Li felt obliged to take issue with Mao Ch'i-ling on the spuriousness of the three ritual Classics. He marshaled evidence from many sources showing that ancient ritual had survived Confucius' times and that the three ritual Classics constituted the most valuable surviving records of the rites of the Three Dynasties.[149] He contended that the *Rites of Chou* was an authentic Classic.[150] Li Kung's attempt to curb skepticism became important in the hermeneutics of the second half of the eighteenth century, a point to which we shall return.

Apart from combating skepticism, Li attacked the latitude with which the Sung neo-Confucians changed the characters in the Classics and re-ordered their texts. In a treatise on the *Great Learning*, the *Ta-hsüeh pien-yeh* (Exercises in defending the *Great Learning*), Li argued for restoring the work's original textual arrangement in the *Book of Rites* after it had been shuffled by neo-Confucians at will. To be sure, he had an ideological ax to grind. For example, he glossed the controversial phrase *ko-wu* as "practicing the *hsiang san-wu*," thus enlisting the neo-Confucians' most important canon in support of Yen Yüan's view of the content of ancient teachings.[151]

Not only did Li criticize Sung scholars for making arbitrary changes in the Classical texts, but he also accused them of taking liberties in interpretation.[152] In this respect, Yen Yüan and Li Kung pioneered in the critique of some fundamental passages of neo-Confucianism. Yen had been critical of the excessive attention neo-Confucians devoted to the discussion of "principles" (*li*) of human nature and destiny (*hsing-ming*).[153] Long before Tai Chen did, he pointed out that the lexical meaning of *li* referred to the grain of wood.[154] Li Kung further argued that the word *li* figured insignificantly in the Classics and pointed out that it occurred infrequently. Its usage in the *Doctrine of the Mean* was identical with that of *t'iao-li* (sense of order) in the *Mencius*.[155]

The importance of the passage *k'o-chi fu-li* in the Analects did not escape the attention of Yen Yüan, who disliked neo-Confucian austerity in matters of ritual practice. Since many neo-Confucians despised human physical nature, their program for moral cultivation inevitably stressed asceticism with no regard for human feelings. But Yen found no evidence for Chu Hsi's reading of the phrase *k'o-chi* to mean suppressing selfish desires. In ancient usage, Yen pointed out, *k'o* meant "can" and "overcome," but never "eliminate." Nor did the ancients equate *chi* with selfish desires. The Sung neo-Confucians' understanding of the phrase owed much to their dualistic view of human nature, which they heedlessly adopted from Buddhism.[156]

Here Yen's point is relevant to one of the methodological principles of the Han Learning scholars of the eighteenth century. In his view, Sung neo-Confucians did not consciously distort the meaning; rather, their understanding of the passage was mediated by the dualistic view of Buddhism, which had entered their thinking as they immersed themselves in Buddhist scriptures. Yen therefore opposed studying the writings of such neo-Confucians as Ch'eng I, Chu Hsi, Lu Chiu-yüan, and Wang Yang-ming except with great care.[157] Li Kung strongly endorsed the view that heterodox teachings had insinuated themselves into Confucian doctrines through Han, T'ang, Sung, and Ming commentaries.[158] These cautions against reading exegeses perverted by heterodox ideas predated the Han Learning scholars' insistence on bypassing Sung exegetical writings and going directly to the Han commentaries.

This distrust and avoidance of Sung exegetical traditions presented, however, a great problem. If not the Sung glosses, what could one resort to when confronted by the often obscure texts of the Classics? This partly explains the growing dependence on Han scholarship, especially for information on ancient objects, knowledge of which was essential to understanding the ancient rituals. This was precisely the task to which Li Kung devoted himself, despite his mentor's warnings against pure academic exercises. Yen Yüan needed only to speak of his faith in Confucianism to his students and followers; Li Kung had to convince an audience with textual support from the Classics. Unlike his mentor, he wrote commentaries on the *Book of Changes*, the *Book of Odes*, the *Spring and Autumn Annals*, the

Analects, the *Great Learning*, and the *Doctrine of the Mean*. Li Kung's intellectual undertakings clearly indicated the path purism would take later in the eighteenth century—a deeper commitment to exegetical commentaries on the Classics.

Most textual critiques of the K'ang-hsi period were not designed to dismantle Sung neo-Confucianism in toto. Its textual foundation suffered immensely, however, as a result of the purist drive to weed out non-Confucian elements. Sung neo-Confucians were thus discredited considerably by the attempts of textual criticism to expose hidden heterodox elements. Although adherents of the Ch'eng-Chu school strove to clear the Sung neo-Confucians from charges of conscious promotion of heterodox teachings, the Sung thinkers were nonetheless found responsible for introducing alien elements into the Classics and the exegetical literature. They at least had to bear the blame for failing to distinguish unorthodox teachings from genuine Confucianism.

The reputation of Sung Classical scholarship was further undermined by attempts to trace the metaethical teachings of Sung neo-Confucianism to Buddhism. The seminal critiques of the ethical thought of Sung neo-Confucians by scholars such as Li Kung and Yen Yüan were to provide Han Learning scholars with a philosophical platform for their own ethical thought. An emphasis on Han exegeses carefully protected the ethics of the evidential scholars from the perverted views of the Sung neo-Confucians. The need to subordinate textual criticism to the goal of Confucian purism and the growing recognition of the importance of philology and historical research helped to shape the methodology of purist hermeneutics—a system of interpretive principles for reconstructing original Confucianism designed to ensure an unperverted understanding of the Classics. How the Han Learning scholars came to regard philology and historical research not only as *the* methods to understand the Classics but also as safeguards against future subversion of Confucianism by heterodox teachings is the main concern of Chapter 6.

The growth of culturalism and the concern for moral conduct in the early decades of the Manchu conquest rendered the study and practice of rituals highly relevant to the gentry. The heightened sense of cultural identity further goaded the purist quest for Confucian doctrines and rituals. As ritualism became the dominant trend in Confucian thought, competing exegetical traditions began to emerge. The shift from metaethics to moral practice encouraged a rediscovery of the ritual scholarship of

Chu Hsi. A more radical strain of purist ritualism, represented by Yen Yüan and Li Kung, however, looked beyond Sung neo-Confucianism for original doctrines and rituals. Its categorical rejection of all forms of neo-Confucianism remained an undercurrent during the K'ang-hsi and early Ch'ien-lung periods.

How this radical strain of purist ritualism emerged in the mid-eighteenth century as the Han Learning movement will also be the subject of Chapter 6. The following chapter focuses on the other major factor in the growth of ritualism in the K'ang-hsi period: the gentry's concern to rebuild the sociopolitical order on a more solid foundation.

3

Lineage Discourse: Gentry, Local Society, and the State

The ritualist ethics of the late Ming purists developed in conjunction with a social and political vision that gave more weight to the non-bureaucratic functions of the gentry in maintaining order at the local level. The lineage emerged as the fundamental organization through which the gentry could exercise leadership in supporting and promoting social ethics. It also provided the needed institutional basis for transmitting values to the common people. Such a social vision, however, did not spring from utopian thinking or from Classical idealism. It grew out of both social practice and the need to deal with practical problems of local government as a result of the paralysis of the central government and the breakdown of local administration in the late Ming.

Local Order: Liturgical Governance and Gentry Dominance

G. William Skinner has noted that the fivefold increase in population from the T'ang through the Ch'ing was not accompanied by a corresponding expansion of the county-level bureaucracy. For the number of local administrative units and related personnel to increase in proportion to the population growth, the state would have had to be capable of imposing and collecting taxes at the local level and of controlling the bureaucracy below the county level. This capability was, however, beyond an agrarian state. Only by keeping the number of regular officials small could the state hope to control the bureaucracy. This was accomplished at the expense of direct control over local administration.[1]

The maintenance of local order in the Ming-Ch'ing period depended on both a formal governmental structure (the magistrate's office) and non-bureaucratic "liturgies" (mostly under the control of the gentry and other local elites, such as big landlords and wealthy merchants). In the Chinese context, Max Weber's term *liturgies* refers to a wide range of associations such as kin organizations, local defense systems, and merchant guilds. Members of these associations were not bureaucrats drawing a salary from the state coffer. They rendered services to the state and the public at their own expense.[2] In Ming China the extremely small bureaucracy governed an enormous population over a vast continent; this necessitated a dependence on liturgical agencies. By performing liturgies, the gentry gained authority and enhanced their status in local society.

To legitimate their leadership of local society, the gentry could not depend exclusively on state-conferred authority. They had to establish and maintain their leadership by performing communal services for the local populace, such as organizing religious and kinship associations, serving as creditors and arbiters, or contributing to public works and charitable funds. These were the networks and organizations that constituted what Prasenjit Duara has called the "cultural nexus," through which the gentry strove to maintain and compete for legitimate leadership and control in their communities.[3]

But in the late sixteenth century, urban gentry in the Lower Yangtze area did not have deep roots in their communities. Their power depended more on personal networks and possession of examination degrees and official status. The elite mobilization by Tung-lin leaders and later by the Restoration Society clearly indicated the relative weakness of the gentry's ties to their local communities.[4] The late Ming collapse of local administration and decline in the civil authority of the gentry compelled some gentry and other local elites to take a greater initiative in providing services to the local populace. Some gentry were aware of the need to strengthen their local ties. The upsurge of gentry activism in supporting charities, in organizing lineages, and in patronizing didactic lectures and community compacts is evidence of a social change that called for a localist approach to social order which the gentry then used to justify greater autonomy and power in maintaining local order.

To be sure, there were variations in the activities that the gentry undertook and in the resources available to them. Recent studies have demonstrated the complexity and vast number of patterns of domination by local elites in late imperial China. Although the gentry constituted a major component of the local elite in most areas, the two did not overlap completely. Since the gentry was first and foremost part of the local elite, its activities were to a significant degree shaped by the social and ecological conditions in the local community. From the perspective of local society, it is therefore a gross simplification to speak of a homogenous gentry possessing a status granted by the imperial state.[5]

This caveat against treating the gentry as a homogenous class is warranted. But even though the gentry played a major role in local society, their common ties with the state and the Confucian culture should not be ignored. Through the civil service examination system and the bureaucracy and its networks, the gentry continued to partake in a national culture and, more important, benefited (or suffered) from the cultural resources that circulated in these elements of gentry culture.

Gentry Activism and Local Order in the Late Ming

The corruption of local officials and the rapacity of clerks and runners had reached alarming proportions by the late sixteenth century. As discussed in Chapter 1, under the combined pressures of high rents, extortion, and inflation, the common people became restless. Popular violence was rampant. Some gentry came to realize that their survival and prosperity depended on their ability to ease social tension in their local communities. They had to shoulder more responsibilities in order either to protect and promote their own interests or to keep the increasingly restless populace from turning into rioting mobs or from engaging in large-scale uprisings. This need, however, was not uniformly felt among the gentry. It came to weigh heavily only on those who continued to feel obligated to perform their duties. The majority of local elites abandoned their paternalistic role toward the local population.

In their attempts to sustain order and dominate their communities, late Ming gentry experimented with and learned from one another methods for dealing with the vast range of problems vexing local communities. One way was to promote morality books and sponsor public lectures;[6] a more efficacious way to maintain local order was direct improvement of local environment and the welfare of its residents. To achieve this goal, local elites built and repaired dikes in order to improve irrigation and farming, supported public relief in times of natural disasters, contributed regularly to help social dependents and the impoverished, sponsored charitable foundations to help kinsmen and the needy in the community, set up relief granaries, and contributed to the building and repairing of public facilities.[7]

One social activist, Yang Tung-ming (1548–1624) wrote an illuminating defense of the added duties of retired officials. He insisted that in times of crisis resulting either from natural disasters or from military uprisings, former officials residing in the country were obliged to take appropriate action of their own accord. Yang was one of the few ex-officials who devoted himself to alleviating tension within his community. When famine victims in his hometown reached an alarming number in the mid-1590's, Yang helped sponsor soup kitchens. He also contributed to funds to repair dikes and to establish a granary to help regulate the price of rice. Clearly, Yang was doing far more than was expected of a retired official. As Joanna Handlin Smith has noted, he knew very well that unless he and others with means did something to assuage the suffering and discontent of the victims of natural and social disasters, these restless elements could precipitate social upheavals.[8]

Yang was also known as the first to found a "benevolent society," the Society for Sharing Goodness. The members of this archetypal society used monthly dues and fines to finance the repair of bridges and roads and to fund wedding and funeral ceremonies.[9] His effort was emulated by such leaders of the Tung-lin Academy as Ch'ien I-pen and Kao P'an-lung, who established in their native places benevolent societies devoted to raising funds for the indigent, the sick, and the undernourished.[10] Ch'en Lung-cheng (1585–1645), a disciple of Kao P'an-lung and an active Confucian philanthropist, founded the Society of Joint Benefit to promote "good deeds" through dispensing alms to the poor.[11] This special criterion distinguished benevolent soceieties patronized by Tung-lin academicians from those run by the Buddhists.

Insofar as these founders were concerned, these societies were meant to promote Confucian morality. Unlike the Buddhist principle of charity, moral qualities rather than practical needs determined who received support.[12] The moralistic intention is clearly spelled out in Ch'en Lung-cheng's and Kao P'an-lung's explicit statements that the basic goal of their societies was encouragement of moral conduct by means of discrimination in dispensing aid. They saw in charitable activities an instrument for inculcating Confucian moral standards, such as filial piety and widow chastity.[13]

In fact, they were meant to be institutions competing with those operated by Buddhists. As Smith has noted, the societies sponsored by Ch'en Lung-cheng and later Lu Shih-i were created as "alternatives to available Buddhist institutions."[14] Ch'en explained clearly why donations to these benevolent societies meant more than those to the Buddhist societies for releasing (animal) life. It was because these benevolent societies "save human lives and support good people." [15] This is clearly a statement of what gentry social activism should be. Those members of the Tung-lin Academy who devoted themselves to these welfare organizations appear to have been motivated by purist concerns.

Apart from ad hoc activities such as famine relief and public work construction and repair, gentry activism was displayed in two major forms of organizations that were used to promote communal sentiment and mutual support—the "community compact" or the "village compact" (*hsiang-yüeh*) and the lineage. The first can be covered briefly. Since Wang Yang-ming, the community compact had been used increasingly in conjunction with the *pao-chia* system to maintain local order. [16] In Hui-chou in Anhwei, for example, a community compact was used to defend against Japanese pirates in 1555. [17] This organizational skill was promoted by such gentry activists as Lü K'un, Hsü Fu-yüan, and Lo Ju-fang. [18]

Lineage and the Gentry

Lineage was another form of social organization crucial to the emerging localist approach to social order. [19] During the Ming-Ch'ing transition, the lineage gradually emerged as one of the most important institutional remedies that the gentry used to cope with problems. This form of social organization appealed to Confucian purists because it was a form of organization sanctioned by the Classics through which Confucian social ethics could be transmitted to kin through ritual practice. This localist approach to social order furthered the growth of ritualism in early Ch'ing thought.

Some general comments on the situation of lineages in the late Ming will help put gentry efforts to strengthen kinship ties in perspective. As recent studies have shown, the large lineage with corporate estates that Maurice Freedman found in Kwangtung and Fukien came into existence as a result not of fission but of fusion. [20] These findings caution against any assumption that the lineages characteristic of Ch'ing China were common earlier in Chinese history. Recent studies have pointed to the need to consider variation both in regional development and over time. [21]

I discuss the history of Ming-Ch'ing lineage development in more detail in the next chapter. Suffice it to say here that since the Northern Sung there had been a "cultural repertoire" of institutions—ancestral hall, the *tsung* (descent-line) system, offerings at the graves of stirps, charitable estates, family instructions, and genealogies—whereby the sense of descent and kinship ties could be strengthened.[22] None of these was an entirely new development. For various reasons—custom, practical need, or reverence for the Sung neo-Confucians—some of these institutions had been adopted as a means to achieve greater kinship cohesion since Sung times,[23] but they were not considered "standard" features that a lineage must have, and there was no clear concept of what constituted a lineage.

By the late sixteenth century, there were at least three major types of lineages: the "north China" type studied by Myron Cohen, the "Lower Yangtze" type described by Patricia Ebrey and Keith Hazelton, and the "south China" type of large lineage with corporate estates that Maurice Freedman found in Kwangtung and Fukien in the twentieth century.[24] In north China, few lineages had a freestanding ancestral hall. Most had little or no corporate estate.[25] Ancestral halls and corporate estates were of more importance in the Lower Yangtze area. But compared with the south China type, which had the largest corporate estates and membership, lineages in the Lower Yangtze had only modest estates. Despite these general distinctions, one can find large lineages with the substantial corporate estates characteristic of south China in the Lower Yangtze area, and lineages of the north China type in the Lower Yangtze area and south China as well.

Among those descent groups that supported some of these institutions, there was no deeply felt need to study the Classics for knowledge of ancient models. As the discussion below of the cases of Chang Lü-hsiang and Ch'en Ch'üeh will show, in the mid-seventeenth century there was no consensus either in theory or in practice on the proper way to organize a kin group, especially as regards the questions of the scope of the lineage and of the fundamental ancestral rite for the entire lineage. But there was a growing tendency among the Confucian elite to consider that a lineage capable of binding kin effectively could not do without a free-standing ancestral hall for the entire lineage, a genealogy, often some corporate estate, and occasionally a lineage school.

Kinship Organizing Activities in the Late Ming

Building and maintaining lineages were never easy tasks. Resources were the main problem. Few could emulate Fan Chung-yen's example of setting up a charitable estate to help his descendants.[26] Corporate estates often disappeared as a result of family division,[27] especially in the Yangtze Delta, where the effects of commercialization and urbanization worked against kinship solidarity. The common practice of dividing properties among sons was a major factor working against the perpetuation and accumulation of landed estates. "Living in different households" (*fen-chü*) was particularly common in urban areas in Kiangnan.[28] Whereas genuine kinship ties were diluted, false kin relationships were created. The common practice of allowing bondservants to become "adopted sons" (*i-nan*) of the master further rendered kinship a less desirable criterion for promoting bonds among kin.[29]

In addition, the efforts of powerful branches to control property and other interests continued to make it difficult for tightly organized lineages such as those in T'ung-ch'eng to develop.[30] Maintaining an authentic record of descent had become difficult for many kin groups because genealogies were sold and falsified descent became common in the late Ming.[31] Existing lineages showed signs of decline in their ability to resolve tension arising from growing economic and social differences. This was evident even in areas such as Hui-chou in Anhwei where lineages had been strong.[32] There is ample reason to believe that in the late Ming kinship ties were much weaker within existing lineages than they had been in earlier times.[33] Nonetheless, kinship organization continued to provide a viable and respectable model for gentry and non-gentry local elites in maintaining their leadership.

There was a growing concern about kinship solidarity on the part of Confucian elites of widely divergent political and philosophical affiliations. Kinship remained one of the few bases for mobilizing local people for protection against all contingencies. Lineage solidarity was used, for example, in direct negotiations with tax collectors in order to minimize extortion.[34]

Some leaders of the T'ai-chou school (see Chapter 1) actively promoted kinship cohesion as a means of resolving social tension and as an experiment in building a utopian "commune." In 1552 Wang Ken's son, Wang Pi (1511–87), inaugurated a regular gathering of his kinsmen in the hall dedicated to the memory of his father. He also planned to establish an ancestral hall with its own land endowments or "sacrificial fields"; he compiled a genealogy and opened a charitable school for his lineage.[35] His students Lo Ju-fang and Han Chen (1516–85) underscored the same idea that kinship harmony was essential to the maintenance of social order.[36]

Ho Hsin-yin was not satisfied with his kinsmen's "parochialism and selfishness" and introduced measures to centralize lineage activities based on "a collective and egalitarian basis."[37] Ho intended to transcend religious, economic, and vocational distinctions in the larger entity of the lineage. One example of the accommodating nature of Ho's lineage was the inclusion of kin who were Buddhists and Taoists.[38] The simple, colloquial language in which he set down the lineage rules points to Ho's populist approach to kinship organization, which was in keeping with the T'ai-chou scholars' general willingness to cross class lines to reach less fortunate kinsmen.[39] Ho's utopian commune was clearly aimed at attenuating the growing tension among kinsmen. His reform measures suggest that the existing institutions of his kin group had failed to forge an integrated lineage. What is significant here is that Ho did not deem it necessary to consult the Classics for the changes he carried out. As is demonstrated in the next chapter, the concern to build lineages in accordance with Classical norms became acute among the scholar-officials in the wake of the Manchu conquest.

The concern for kinship solidarity was felt no less among leaders of the Tung-lin Academy. In 1607 Kao P'an-lung's belief in molding behavior by ritual practice prompted him to compose family instructions (*chia-hsün*) in simple language, in which he encouraged the study of Chu Hsi's *Hsiao-hsüeh* (Elementary learning).[40] He also compiled a genealogy for his lineage.[41] Ku Hsien-ch'eng, after completing the reconstruction of the Tung-lin Academy, established an ancestral hall for his lineage in 1611. With aid from his father and brother, he founded a charitable estate, which was to benefit their kindred in critical times.[42]

Although there were attempts to create institutions to improve communications and mutual help, many found the existing lineage in need of reform. In 1626 Liu Tsung-chou began to cleanse his lineage's ancestral rites of usages he found improper. He undertook to set down a series of new ceremonies in the *Tsung-tz'u ssu-tien* (Worship ceremonies for the lineage hall) for practice in the ancestral hall, which he finished revising in the spring of 1631.[43] At the close of that year, he succeeded in adding more acreage to his lineage's sacrificial land.[44] In 1639, he added to the land endowments for each ancestor.[45] To resolve conflicts stemming from differences in social position, he began to organize his kin by a set of "lineage compacts" (*tsung-yüeh*). He designated lineage elders as *tsung-chang* (lineage elders) and *tsung-chiao* (lineage instructors) and made them responsible for overseeing the conduct of all kindred.[46] Liu's effort to build a well-organized lineage included the writing of a genealogy for his descent group in 1638.[47] His interest in the practice of ritual led him to ritual studies, and in his last years he devoted himself to the study of the

Book of Etiquette and Decorum, a primary source of Classical rituals.[48] The connection between ritual studies and lineage building is evident in Liu Tsung-chou's intellectual development.

If the Confucians agreed that kinship could be used to resolve social and economic conflicts, they were by no means unanimous in regard to the principles of lineage organization. As noted above, the kinship organization promoted by Ho Hsin-yin was to a certain degree egalitarian, and as a result hierarchical relationships were de-emphasized. The main purpose of Ho's lineage reform was to promote kinship solidarity on an egalitarian basis by downgrading occupational and financial distinctions.

From the perspective of statecraft, the T'ai-chou school represented a more radical approach to social reform through kinship reorganization. Members of this school rarely modeled their kinship organizations on the descent-line principle (see below), which was at the heart of Chu Hsi's *Family Rituals*, the standard ritual manual for the gentry in the sixteenth century.[49] Tung-lin leaders regarded this work as the standard reference for proper rituals,[50] and they seemed to have generally emulated its model of kinship organization. But as we shall see in the next chapter, the lineage model prescribed in *Family Rituals* imposed serious limitations on any attempt to build a large lineage including agnates beyond the third collateral line. Nonetheless, despite the discord over how to build a lineage, the interest in strengthening kinship bonds intensified and culminated in nothing less than a national movement of lineage building in the late seventeenth century.

Lineage and the State in Early Ch'ing Discourse

Perhaps no factor outweighs the collapse of the Ming dynasty in explaining why the Confucian elite came to emphasize even more the localist approach to political order in the mid-seventeenth century. Kinship organization came to provide the institutional foundation for this approach. Indeed, with the demise of the Ming, scholars began to focus increasingly on the political and social functions of kinship organization as the major locus of local power. Many were astonished by the sudden overthrow of the Ming house by peasant rebellion and Manchu invasion. When Ming restorationist hopes evaporated in the 1660's, some scholars began to search for an explanation for the Ming collapse in terms other than Manchu military prowess. In their agonized reflection on its causes, many singled out overcentralization of political power in the imperial hierarchy.

The Ming house could have withstood domestic uprisings and external incursions far longer but for the total impotence of the local resistance, which in turn was owing to the absence of powerful local lineages.

The consensus on local political impotency was borne out clearly in the writings of such eminent thinkers as Huang Tsung-hsi, Ku Yen-wu, Wang Fu-chih, and Lü Liu-liang by their call for political decentralization under an imperial system. They proposed different solutions to the same problem—the great peril in reposing all power in the imperial structure and the need to develop centers of local power founded on a broader institutional basis than that of the formal government.[51]

Ku Yen-wu's Localist Approach to Social Order

The most prominent exponent of limited political decentralization in the early Ch'ing was Ku Yen-wu. More than anyone else, he probed the structural defects of the Ming political system and suggested remedies. For him the growing concentration of power in the central government had undermined local powers; the absence of strong lineages (ch'iang-tsung) at the local level accounted in great measure for the disruption of domestic order by peasant rebellion.[52] The Ming principalities might have effectively resisted domestic and external threats during the last years of the dynasty but for the success of officials in the central government in undermining their power ever since their installation in the early Ming. The ability of these "feudal" elements to protect the imperial house existed in name only.[53] Despite his enthusiasm for reviving a truncated form of feudalism, Ku was not oblivious to the notorious exploitation of the inhabitants of these principalities.[54] Feudal princes could not be considered a reliable resource for maintaining local order. For Ku, the gravest flaw of the Ming system was not so much the absence of "feudalism" as the lack of locally powerful social groups.

To the late Ming Confucian elite, the inordinate concentration of power in an irresponsible government resulted either in the eclipse of officialdom by extralegal agents such as eunuchs or in the inevitable delegation of administrative power to clerks and runners. Ordinary officials were the victims in either case. In his widely read *Jih-chih lu* (Records of daily learning), Ku Yen-wu explained the dilemma of local officials:

In later ages there appeared inept rulers who gathered all authority into their own hands, but the countless exigencies of government are so broad that it is quite impossible for one man to handle them all, so the authority then shifted to the laws.

With this a great many laws were promulgated to prevent crimes and violations, so that even the greatest criminals could not get around them nor the cleverest officials succeed in evading them. People thereupon expended all their efforts in merely following the laws and trying to stay out of difficulty. Thus the authority of the son of heaven came to reside not in the officials appointed by the government but in the clerks and assistants. Now what the world needs most urgently are local officials who personally look after the people, and yet today the men who possess least authority are precisely those local officials. If local officials possess no authority and the grievances of the people are not made known to the higher authorities, how can we hope to achieve peace and prosperity and prolong the life of the country?[55]

Ku's call to restore to the local official political power sufficient to run his office effectively represents one major prescription for the political evils he saw in the centripetal development of the imperial system.[56]

In a treatise on local administration, *Chün-hsien lun* (On prefectures and counties), Ku argued for a modified feudal system. A magistrate who proved his worth in office after a probationary period of twelve years should be made the permanent ruler of the county. On retirement, he could bequeath his office either to a son or brother or to a man of virtue he recommended. The advantage of this system was that the strong ties forged between the magistrate (and his heirs) and the county would serve as a powerful incentive to keep the county prosperous and peaceful.[57]

Philip Kuhn aptly points out that Ku Yen-wu and his followers advocated not a "return to political decentralization, but rather an infusion into the centralized state of certain 'feudal' principles."[58] Kent Guy, among others, notes the strong localist orientation in Ku Yen-wu's political thought and characterizes it as "feudal localism."[59]

For two reasons, I find Guy's term useful in understanding the major orientation of Ku's political thinking. First, his idea of an inheritable magistracy was a motley institution that combined feudal and non-feudal elements. It warrants the characterization "feudal" only because the magistrate's position was inheritable. Second, the "feudal magistrates" did not enjoy as much power as the ancients, and their feudal status was far from complete. Ku's magistrate, unlike the ancient archetype, would operate within a centralized state. Moreover, after the twelve-year probationary period, the power that determined whether a magistrate's office would become hereditary was the central government. Even after the hereditary status was vouchsafed, his chief assistant was still to be chosen by the Board of Personnel.[60] Thus Ku, like Huang Tsung-hsi, never conceived of a completely decentralized political system. Nonetheless, his proposal for a quasi-feudal system of inheritable magistracies exemplifies the serious theoretical consideration given in the late seventeenth century to political decentralization at a time of increasing centralization of the imperial system under an alien regime.

This semifeudal form of local government, however, constituted only the political dimension of Ku Yen-wu's broader vision of feudalism. For Ku Yen-wu, formal government in itself was not the key to a stable social order. In his view, dependence on county magistrates as the lowest institutional bulwark of social order was necessary but insufficient. Local government, as part of the state system, was vulnerable to the unpredictable variations in the caliber of the emperor and to the vicissitudes of court politics. Despite his commitment to the reform of government institutions, Ku Yen-wu apparently did not have complete faith in the emperor and the bureaucracy as the sole guardians of the people's welfare. His disenchantment grew out of his experience and knowledge of the numerous defects of the late Ming political system—the ineptitude and license of emperors, the demoralization of bureaucrats, the eunuchs' avarice and infringement on the authority of the officials.

Yet another factor helped shape Ku Yen-wu's localist approach to political order. His anti-Manchu stance rendered it extremely desirable to have centers of local power—however limited in resources—that would provide sanctuary to political dissenters. A centralized and despotic state was capable of wreaking even greater havoc when combined with the hostility and high-handedness of alien conquerors. The policies of the Manchu regime did not assuage Ku Yen-wu's anxiety about an undisciplined state controlling most of the power. The discovery of large-scale tax defaults in 1661, which implicated more than 13,500 officials and gentry of the Lower Yangtze region,[61] further attested to the helplessness of the gentry in any confrontation with the state. One of those implicated was Ku's nephew Hsü Yüan-wen (1634–91). He was found guilty and removed from his position of compiler in the Hanlin Academy.[62] This vivid picture of gentry and officials at the mercy of a powerful alien state deepened Ku's conviction of the need for a much broader institutional basis than an inheritable magistracy.

A variety of institutions could serve the purpose of building a social basis for local political autonomy, including different kinds of voluntary associations, whether brotherhoods of outlaws or literary associations (she). Ku lamented that the ancient usage of the term she to signify an administrative unit had been lost and the word had come to denote voluntary organizations of dubious objectives. Ku criticized the late Ming literati for choosing such a term for their clubs. One senses a deep hostility on Ku's part toward these voluntary associations. He saw an unpleasant resemblance between *she* and the seditious organizations of peasants and urban ruffians in the late Ming.[63] No doubt the horrifying consequences of the peasant rebellions, rent resistant uprisings, and urban riots of the 1640's still haunted Ku. In rejecting the *she*, Ku limited the means available for developing institutions to promote local autonomy. He looked to the lineage as a solution to this problem. Ku's censure of *she* therefore does not constitute a renunciation of a true base of local power, much less a localist approach to social order that cherished nothing but "a vaguer pride of place and an appreciation for locality as such."[64]

In organized lineages Ku Yen-wu saw the potential to develop a much broader social institution, the mainstay of social order, on which a stable political regime could rest. Both *she* and lineages had a claim, however tenuous, to antecedents in the Chou dynasty, whose institutions were pristinely feudal (*feng-chien*). But the hoary institutions of Chou feudatories also exemplified political decentralization, with power vested in local fiefdoms and the heads of clans. Viewed against the background of the strong tradition of political centralization, Ku Yen-wu's stress on local institutions represented a "localist" approach to social order.

The lineage did not emerge in full in Ku Yen-wu's localist approach to social order until his sojourns in north China. In 1657 he went to Shantung, where he made the acquaintance of Chang Erh-ch'i. Ku was impressed with Chang's extensive knowledge of Classical rites. Very likely it was this encounter that opened Ku's eyes to a more fundamental solution to political centralization. Ritual did not become central to his thinking until 1663, however.[65] The change in Ku's thinking can be traced in several events.

When a friend built an ancestral hall in 1652, Ku Yen-wu noted the event with respect and celebrated the filial undertaking in encomiastic rhetoric without reference to its implications for the problem of local power.[66] The treatment of lineage as an important institution of local power first became conspicuous in Ku's writings in 1663, six years after he met Chang Erh-ch'i. In that year, when Ku visited P'ei-ts'un, a locality in Wen-hsi county in Shansi,[67] he was impressed by the kinship solidarity of a relatively large number of agnates descended from the P'ei clan of the T'ang dynasty. In his admiration, he traced the P'eis' resilience under adverse circumstances through history and alluded to their resistance to coercion under the T'ang.

In Ku's analysis, powerful organized lineages (*tsung-tsu*) had served essential political and social functions in the past. Before the Five Dynasties, the big lineages had stood both as buffers of the state against subversive forces and as sanctuaries for the common people in turbulent times. Lineages were so indispensable to the imperial house that changes in their strength signified the rise and fall of a dynasty. When lineages diminished in power and their ability to extend protection to local communities declined, so did the emperor's control over the realm. "As the way of government declines further, the state has no powerful lineages. . . . Therefore, internal disintegration and external rebellion result in eventual collapse. The practice of the descent-line system is to uphold human relationships and to expand the state power."[68]

Ku was unequivocally arguing that it was in the interest of the imperial house to allow powerful lineages to exist. Elsewhere he wrote even more explicitly from the monarch's point of view on the need for organizing lineages. China was too vast for the emperor to oversee the proper management of every quarter. Governance of lineages by their descent-line (tsung) heirs would relieve the state of much of its administrative burden. The volume of litigation would be reduced substantially if descent-line heirs assumed the duty of resolving conflicts among their kin and meted out punishment.[69]

Tsung-fa, Ancestral Worship, and Lineage

Tsung and tsung-fa are crucial terms in Ming-Ch'ing discourse on lineage.[70] Following Patricia Ebrey's usage, tsung is rendered "descent-line" and tsung-fa "descent-line system."[71] A descent-line is a group of agnates sharing the same ancestry. A "descent-line system" refers to the method of designating an heir (tsung-tzu), originally the firstborn of the main wife in the main line of the descent group. The ritual authority to make sacrifices to the ancestors in the main line is vested in the heir alone. Except for the primogenitor, the ancestors of a descent-line are by the same token themselves firstborns in the main line. The heir's kinsmen, whether uncles, cousins, or nephews, would participate in the sacrifice conducted by the heir.[72]

There are two types of descent-line systems. The "great descent-line" (ta-tsung) is a descent group with an unlimited generational depth and hence an infinite number of ancestors. In contrast, the "lesser descent-line" (hsiao-tsung) is a descent-line with a fixed depth of five generations. The heir of a lesser descent-line worshiped his ancestors only up to the great-

great-grandfather. When the heir died and was succeeded by his first son, his great-great-grandfather ceased to be worshiped to keep the number of generations at five. The lesser descent-line system required the constant splitting of the descent group whenever the heir died. The practical implications of the differences between the two types of descent-line are discussed later in this chapter and the next one. For now, let us return to Ku Yen-wu's view of the role of the descent-line in lineage building.

As Ku envisioned it, the descent-line heir would draw on the income from the lineage estates to dispense aid to less fortunate kin—the widowed, the crippled, and the sick. Charitable estates would ease the hardships resulting from the extremes of wealth and harmful social and natural circumstances, thus mitigating the sufferings that could drive poor relatives to riot. Nothing is more revealing about Ku's view of lineages than his remark that the hapless members of a descent group would receive material support "without depending on governmental benevolence" (*pu tai wang-cheng chih shih*).[73]

Ku's enthusiasm for the political role of powerful lineages should not, however, be interpreted as a call for setting lineage against the state. In Ming and Ch'ing discourse, the lineage and the state were conceived as complementary to each other rather than competitive. Far from conceiving its function in antagonistic terms, Ku regarded the lineage as a social institution fundamental to a stable society and the monarchical order and may have entertained the notion that powerful lineages could serve as rallying points for resistance against foreign invasion. It is clear, however, that he merely sought some adjustment within a centralized imperial structure.

There is no denying that Ku distrusted the imperial monarchy and criticized past emperors. But who would be the key players in local leadership? Ku demanded that the Confucian elite play a greater role, especially in their local communities. Since the Three Dynasties the state had been derelict in its duty to provide for and to teach its subjects. For Ku, all dynasts since the golden age were nothing but rapacious despoilers. They racked their subjects with all kinds of taxes without giving a thought to their welfare. The people were left to attend to their own needs. The duty to educate them fell on the shoulders of non-office-holding Confucians (*ju-che*). Since the Han dynasty, Confucians knowledgeable about ritual had helped maintain the moral order of society. The need for the Confucian elite to assume greater responsibility toward their kindred and local communities in matters of moral instruction was growing. Ku called on them to fulfill these duties not as officials but as private individuals, as members of the Confucian elite and leaders of their kin groups.[74] Organized kin groups were essential for fulfilling duties the state no longer undertook.

In antiquity lineages had constituted an integral part of the feudal political system. In Ku's political vision, lineages, unlike their ancient counterparts, would not owe their existence to the state. They would be institutionally dissociated from the state, and they were therefore not feudal in the conventional sense of the Chinese term. However minimal Ku thought the tension between them might be, these two institutions nonetheless represented two potentially antipodal tendencies. By stressing the primacy of lineages in maintaining the local socio-moral order, Ku further dissociated his localist orientation from state-oriented approaches. As argued above, however, Ku's position does not imply a sanction for local autonomy outside the monarchical structure under normal circumstances.[75]

The Lineage as an Institution for Promoting Confucian Values

Ku Yen-wu came to stress kinship organization from a different and yet related perspective. Ku never thought of political stability independently of the Confucian moral order; for him, the political order is an extension of the moral order. In such a perspective, an inheritable magistracy served only to retain sufficient power at the local level for effective governance. The institution of itself would not ensure morality or social harmony within the county, both of which depended on the observance of proper ethical relationships. "Only after human ethical relationships are established can there be custom; only when there is custom will there be government affairs; with government affairs comes the state." [76] Without these Confucian principles, an effective local government could turn a magistrate into a satrap.

For Ku, cultivation of proper "custom and beliefs" (feng-su jen-hsin) was the basis of order and peace.[77] Social cohesion was contingent on proper beliefs and the proper conduct of members of society. For morality to become an effective means for reducing conflicts and harmonizing human relationships at the community level, it was necessary to have an institution capable of transcending distinctions in wealth, vocation, and status. The lineage was an ideal organization for these purposes.

The emergence of the lineage as the fundamental institution in the social vision of Ku Yen-wu and many early Ch'ing scholars testifies to the rejection of the didactic method employed by public lecturers in the late Ming.[78] The implicit optimism about the innate sense of morality that informed most of the populist and syncretic movements had dissipated. The didactic approach to the transmission of values to the common people had been discredited by peasant rebellions in north China and widespread urban riots, especially in the Lower Yangtze areas, Fukien, and Kwang-tung.[79]

The perils of treating the common people as equals of the literati in terms of moral capacity were revealed in the massive uprisings of bond-servants against their masters, most of whom were literati. The institution of bondservants, common in the Lower Yangtze area, proved to be dis-astrous. Maintenance of the social hierarchy could not depend on helping the common people understand the principle (*li*) behind social distinc-tions through didactic lectures and texts. Li Kung criticized the public lecturing common in the late Ming on the grounds that the more the common people were helped to reason or to understand principle, the more stubborn they became.[80] Li's view can be regarded as representative of the general change in the attitude of the gentry toward the common people. Neither moral ledgers nor the appeal to the "innate knowledge of the good" helped make the common people content with their lot. Rather than lecturing (*chiang*) to the common people and engaging them in conversation or even debate, Confucian scholars in the early Ch'ing emphasized the need to "practice" (*hsi*) ritual under the guidance of the Confucian elite, a method of transmitting values that did not engage the common people in a dialogue.

Ku's disillusionment with the inconstancy of imperial performance and the didactic method of public lecturing led him to look for an alterna-tive institution to propagate and instill orthodox ethical values. He came to see the lineage and its rituals as the best institutional solution to the problems of local government in relation both to the imperial state and to the common people. Unlike public lecturers, the leaders of the lineage appealed more to rituals and the ancestors as the sources of authority. Kin were taught to practice the proper rituals centered on the cult of the ancestors.

In 1677, when he wrote an essay to commemorate the founding of an ancestral hall by his good friend Wang Hung-chuan, Ku commended scholars who abided by the descent-line rules and erected shrines to celebrate ascendants and to enhance kinship ties.[81] Ku observed that in the past even at times when "chaos overran the government, the sages' teachings [*chiao*] continued to be properly provided to society." Families that had adopted the descent-line principle and erected ancestral halls were often able to hold to the proper teachings and preserve them.[82] It was to the credit of the scholars from these families that Confucian teachings were perpetuated in times of political upheaval. To Ku the ancient descent-line system was the key to kinship organization. In the Chou dynasty, the descent-line system had kept subjects together and prevented families from division. But to his regret, the practice of the descent-line system had become a great rarity ever since the Ch'in dynasty had required families to divide their property when the male children came of age.[83]

Lu Shih-i and Descent-Line Rites

Ku Yen-wu was not unique in stressing a localist approach to social order that regarded the lineage as a broad social basis for stable government. Nor was he alone in displaying a strong interest in lineages and in the descent-line system. Like Ku, Lu Shih-i had been a member of the Restoration Society and vigorously endorsed the introduction of a truncated model of feudalism. Lu believed that the possibility of realizing peace and perfect order hinged upon the revival of Classical institutions—the feudal aristocracy, the well-field system of land tenure, and scholarly academies.[84] The main reason for reinstating some feudal elements was to redress the virulent centralizing tendency of the "prefectural and county system." Of the various consequences of this inherent problem, Lu referred in particular to the powerlessness and impoverishment of local society, which could result in the toppling of the state by rebellions.[85] One cannot but suspect that as much as Ku Yen-wu, Lu was haunted by vivid memories of the extensive devastation wrought by peasant rebellions toward the end of the Ming.

Inspired as he was by Classical precedents, Lu was keenly aware of the structural weaknesses of feudal institutions and did not advocate a full-scale restoration. After deliberating the relative strength and drawbacks of the feudal system and the prefectural and county system, he reached a solution that attempted to capitalize on the best aspects of both systems. Within the framework of the prefectural and county system (that is, within a centralized government), the offices of provincial governor, prefect, and county magistrates were to be made hereditary with plenipotentiary power over such matters as administration and recruitment of local functionaries. Lu's suggestions for preventing these local rulers from developing into satraps parallel those of Ku Yen-wu, who called for the installation of supervisory officials above the hereditary magistrates and sub-prefects. In Ku's design, censors with one-year tenure were to be directly appointed by the central government to oversee the magistrates.[86] In Lu's version, however, even the office of governor was to be hereditary. Only the chief deputies (*ch'ing*) to the governor and to the magistrate were to be appointed by the emperor.[87]

Like Ku Yen-wu, Lu Shih-i regarded the descent-line principle as an important institution of Classical antiquity and thought it should be resurrected. His notion of the relation of the descent-line system to political order is, however, not identical to Ku Yen-wu's. Ku saw organized lineages as effective institutions that would aid the government in maintaining order, both moral and political and become autonomous enclaves under such exceptional circumstances as the disintegration and fall of dynasties. Lu, however, conceived of the lineage mainly as an extension of the family. Small wonder that his reflections on lineage and descent-line systems appeared under the rubric "Self-cultivation and Managing the Family" (*hsiu-ch'i*) rather than under "Order and Peace" (*chih-p'ing*).[88] Lu apparently did not approve of the political function that Ku Yen-wu envisioned for the organized lineage. Whereas Ku was delighted to see large descent groups providing some institutional basis for local organization, Lu denounced the practice of having multitudes of kin living in clustered villages as was the case in southern Anhwei and Kiangsi. The largest descent groups in such areas could boast of over ten thousand members.[89]

For Lu, the scope of a lineage should not extend infinitely. Lu condemned not so much the practice of forming large kin groups as the abandonment of the descent-line principle in their organization.[90] Lu took exception to Ch'eng I's proposal that everyone should worship ancestors up to the great-great-grandfather. This theory of ancestor worship would render the descent-line system nugatory, for there would be no need for agnates to congregate to make offerings en masse under the direction of the descent-line heir. Ch'eng I's prescription did not take into account "differentiation" by status, which for Lu meant essentially seniority. In Lu's view, only descent-line heirs (*tsung-tzu*) were eligible to worship lineal ancestors; agnates properly participated on the side.[91]

The descent-line system was for Lu by no means mere ritual. To him the descent-line heir performed duties comparable to those of a monarch:

"The *tsung* is to a family as the monarch is to a state. . . . Therefore, *tsung* means to regulate. If there is a *tsung*, there is order; without it, chaos will prevail."[92] Lu clearly regarded the descent-line system as much more than a system of rules pertaining to ancestral worship. He saw its revival as essential to social and familial order as prescribed by the Classical canons.

Lu Shih-i believed that it was possible to revive the descent-line system and that even scholars without government office must incorporate it in the system of ancestor worship. Lu proposed to vest in the descent-line heir the exclusive right to preside over all oblations held in the ancestral hall. In any one descent-line system, there were four lesser descent-line heirs and one great descent-line heir. All other agnates were obliged to participate and assist the descent-line heirs in performing the liturgies in the hall and in defraying expenses.[93]

Lu held the *Family Rituals by Master Chu* in high esteem but cautioned against dogmatic adherence to its minor ceremonials.[94] To him, the ancestral rites laid down in the *Family Rituals* were originally designed for descent-line heirs who possessed office and considerable wealth. Proper execution of its ceremonies required large expenses beyond the means of poor scholars. Lu therefore proposed a reduction in the number of meetings, thus curtailing expenses. Instead of making individual offerings to all four immediate ancestors—father, grandfather, great-grandfather, and great-great-grandfather—and to the first ancestor during every worship gathering, each ancestor and the descendants he sired were to be honored collectively.

In the first month of every year all descendants of the "first ancestor" would assemble to make an oblation in his memory under the direction of the great descent-line heir. In the second month of spring, each set of agnates sharing the same great-great-grandfather would convene to pay tribute to the four immediate ancestors with the great-great-grandfather receiving the main oblation. This ceremony was to be led by the eldest descent-line heir in the lesser descent-line sired by the great-great-grandfather. In the second month of summer, the great-grandfather, the main benefactor of this worship, would receive similar offerings from his descendants, who subordinated themselves under the ritual authority of the lesser descent-line heir, in this case the eldest great-grandson. The grandfather, the main benefactor, and the father were worshiped in the second month of autumn by their scions with the eldest grandson presiding. The father became the main object of worship in the second month of winter. His sons would follow their eldest brother in rendering service.[95]

Lu's proposal of a simplified liturgy for his kin group was clearly intended to save money. It was meant to be a compromise between the *Family Rituals* model and practical considerations of expenditure. In brief, it was an attempt to enhance the kinship bond and to build a viable lineage institution flexible enough to accommodate the ideal of kinship solidarity without overstraining resources.

Lu's system of ancestral rites was predicated on the principles of the descent-line system. His conception of descent-line heir accorded with the conventional view—the position was to be filled by the firstborn in the descent-line. But other scholars who felt a similar need to revive the descent-line system did not conceive of the meaning of descent-line in the same sense. Officials such as Hsü San-li (1625–91) and Li Kuang-ti (1642–1718) were disposed to determine the descent-line heir by government rank and office. The complicated issues involved in reviving the descent-line system are discussed in the next chapter. Let us now turn to attempts to build more organized lineages in the second half of the seventeenth century.

Lineage Building in the Early Ch'ing

In the wake of the Ch'ing conquest, scholars—for reasons other than considerations of political balance—expressed equally strong interest in the organization of lineages in accordance with proper rites. As mentioned in the preceding chapter, with the Manchu conquest rituals took on a special significance. For those scholars who avowed loyalty to the ill-fated dynasty and refused to seek refuge in self-exile, the study of Classical rituals and the attempt to practice them offered a third alternative to eremitism and service to the alien conquerors. These undertakings provided them with a purpose in life, as well as a means of making a token condemnation of the "barbarian" regime. By devoting themselves to the study and practice of proper rituals, Chinese scholars were consciously setting themselves apart from the alien conquerors. They had lost control to the Manchus in the political arena, but they were still able to live as Chinese and to show contempt toward the culturally inferior "barbarians." Military failure was compensated by a sense of cultural superiority. From the 1660's on, restorationist efforts were channeled into preserving and glorifying Chinese rituals and Chinese culture in general.

This deep devotion to rituals among scholars who displayed no interest in a career under the new regime is not surprising. This intellectual disposition was conspicuous among some of Liu Tsung-chou's students. Many devoted themselves to the study and practice of rituals. Like their predecessors in the late Ming period, most of them consulted the *Family Rituals* for specific instructions on mourning, funeral, and ancestral rites.

Chang Lü-hsiang, who began as a student of Liu, later became a staunch exponent of Ch'eng-Chu neo-Confucianism. After the collapse of the Ming dynasty, Chang and his inner circle of friends strove to rectify ritual abuses. They came to realize that the descent-line principles formed the basis of the *Family Rituals*, as the famed Ming statesman Ch'iu Chün (1420–95) had noted.[96] Chang's best friend, Ch'en Ch'üeh, on learning the descent-line principle that "secondary sons do not make sacrifice" (*chih-tzu pu chi*), renounced his right to worship his father since he was not the eldest son.[97]

For Chang Lü-hsiang, the descent-line system and the building of an ancestral hall were crucial to the lofty ideal of "honoring the descent-line so as to unify kin" (*ching-tsung shou-tsu*). He lamented that few official families had established family shrines (*chia-miao*). Far fewer still were ancestral temples built to the specifications of the *Family Rituals*. In his native T'ung-hsiang county in Chekiang, he found that this type of building, the *chia-miao*, was so rare that there was not one in a thousand families.[98]

Ch'ai Shao-ping (1616–70), a native of Jen-ho in Chekiang, had a similar impression of the scarcity of *chia-miao*: "In recent times few officials establish family shrine [*chia-miao*]. There are a small number of 'big clans' [*shih-tsu*] that have founded ancestral halls. But their structures accord neither with ancient institutions nor with the provisions in the *Hui-tien*."[99]

Ch'ai was a Ming government student who declined to serve the Manchu dynasty. By *Hui-tien*, he meant the *Collected Statutes of the Ming Empire* (*Ta-Ming hui-tien*). The building of an ancestral hall in the official style of the Ming dynasty was unequivocally a symbolic expression of loyalty to the fallen dynasty. The officially approved type of ancestral hall that few officials in the Ming dynasty had taken the trouble to build suddenly became a powerful symbol of loyalty.

Hardly had he consolidated his power over China in 1373 when Ming T'ai-tsu granted officials the right to establish "family shrines" after the model outlined in the *Family Rituals*.[100] But for reasons discussed in the next chapter, the imperial prescriptions were not taken seriously. In 1377 Fang Hsiao-ju (1357–1402), in an essay celebrating the building of an ancestral hall by a Ch'en lineage in Chekiang, alluded to its deviation from the official model, which permitted the installation of ancestor tablets up to the great-great-grandfather and did not provide for the inclusion of the first ancestor (*shih-tsu*) in the hall.[101] A memorial submitted by Hsia Yen (1482–1548) in 1536 revealed the scarcity of the official type of ancestral hall.[102] Even in Hui-chou, Anhwei, where the gentry boasted of their faithful observance of Chu Hsi's teachings, the *Family Rituals* model was outnumbered by the popular model of lineage hall (*tsung-tz'u*), which enshrined a far greater number of ancestors than the official limit of four.[103] It is apparent that the current practice of ancestral worship in *tz'u-t'ang* departed from the *Family Rituals*.

Scholars in Fukien were no more faithful to the instructions of the *Family Rituals* despite their claim of being Chu Hsi's ardent followers. When writing an essay to commemorate the founding of an ancestral hall in Foochow, Ch'iu Chün related with regret that the "four-generations" type of ancestral hall was the least built.[104] No significant changes seemed to occur in the next two hundred years. Li Kuang-ti, a native of An-hsi, Fukien, played a crucial role in bringing the K'ang-hsi emperor under the influence of neo-Confucianism. When his father erected a family shrine in 1665, Li observed that families of many officials had temples founded in memory of their first ancestors, but hardly any had built a "lesser descent-line temple" (*hsiao-tsung tz'u*) to honor their "four ancestors."[105] Li was referring to the model in the *Family Rituals*.

To be sure, domestic ancestor worship was as common as ever. But in most family altars Chang Lü-hsiang saw in Chekiang, Buddhist, Taoist, and many other deities were tended side by side with the ancestors. Those who had some knowledge of proper rituals would establish a family ancestral hall (*chia-t'ang*), placing in the center a tablet inscribed with words such as "Heaven, earth, emperor, parent, and teacher" (*t'ien ti chün ch'in shih*). But the ancestors' tablets were arranged on both sides in defiance of "generational order" (*chao-mu*). No clear distinction was made between "displaced ancestors" (*t'iao-chu*) and "appended ancestors" (*fu-chu*). More seriously in error was their schedule, which was based on Buddhist and Taoist custom.[106]

To rectify these wayward practices, Chang stressed the need to build ancestral halls, which would provide a location for strengthening kinship ties through participation in ancestral rites. The *Family Rituals* was the best guide to the structure and meaning of the ancestral hall. Chang, however, was willing to compromise regarding its size, because of the wide discrepancies in wealth. It is apparent that Chang was not speaking to the scholar-officials per se. No less than Lu Shih-i, he hoped to see worship in an ancestral hall become a common practice for most people, regardless of wealth and station.[107] He regarded the founding of an ancestral hall and the compiling of a genealogy as the easiest means for private individuals to promote order within the domain of kinship.

Chang's good friend Ch'en Ch'üeh, whose ritualist approach to ethics is discussed in Chapter 2, saw in the ancestral hall an important institution to bring otherwise loosely linked kin together. Ch'en was a native of Haining county in Chekiang. The two most distant ancestors of the Ch'en lineage were buried in different locations. The kin group had erected ancestral halls near each grave. But the one at the "northern" grave was built by the main-line descendants and used exclusively for worshiping this line of ancestors. The hall, however, was no more than a simple structure, lacking a roof and in need of major repairs. The hall at the "southern" grave was in a similar condition. Ch'en proposed to his kin that both halls be reconstructed.[108]

These halls were not the "four-generation" temples prescribed by the *Family Rituals* but *ta tsung-tz'u* (temple of the great descent-line) or *shih-tsu miao* (temple of the first ancestor). In all, eighteen ancestors were enshrined. Although these halls were built to honor ancestors, those outside the main line of the "northern" ancestors were not worshiped in the "northern" temple. Ch'en proposed that it become a lineage hall dedicated to the entire ancestry. In other words, Ch'en attempted to unite the hitherto disassociated branches by honoring a common "first ancestor" (*shih-tsu*). Combining separate schedules of ancestor worship, Ch'en wanted to make existing facilities available to a wider group of kinsmen. This was to be achieved by cutting expenses. Some ancestors had set up estates to defray the costs of sacrifices made in their memory, and separate offerings had been made to each of these endowing ancestors. Ch'en suggested that they be tended as a group, which would help curtail expenses. As part of a collective ancestry, those ancestors buried in the same area who had not left behind estates for the purpose of worship would be able to receive oblations. The savings from such a reform would fund a charitable lineage trust to subsidize expenses of weddings, funerals, and education of kinsmen.[109]

A number of observations may be made on Ch'en Ch'üeh's proposed reforms. Despite the existence of ancestral halls, they were not meant to be inclusive, and little attempt was made to unify agnates within the two branches until Ch'en made his proposal. The tendency toward internal differentiation was stronger than the need to attain greater ritual unity. The situation in Ch'en Ch'üeh's lineage is reminiscent of the similar absence of a strong bond in the Ho lineage that Ho Hsin-yin strove to reform. The pre-existing practice of sacrifices both at the grave site and at the ancestral hall should be taken as parallel and yet separate developments of a fully integrated worship system. There was some periodic interaction among a group of loosely linked agnates. Yet Ch'en's proposal to channel the savings into a charitable trust was indicative of the low degree of kinship organization in his kin group.

The ancestral halls of the Ch'en kin group in Chekiang were not the *Family Rituals* type of "four-generation" temple. Ch'en Ch'üeh did not share Chang Lü-hsiang's view on restricting worship to the "four generations" and took exception to Ch'eng I's idea that everyone could worship the "four ancestors" because of mourning obligations. To Ch'en, Ch'eng I's view represented no more than the "personal opinion of a private scholar."[110] Ch'en did not believe that rules of mourning were analogous to the method of ancestral rite. Inasmuch as a *shih* (officer) in Classical antiquity was entitled to only one temple, he was accordingly authorized to worship only his father. It was a breach of propriety for an officer of the lowest rank to make sacrifice to four generations of ancestors.

In 1650 Ch'en withdrew his father's tablet from his household altar and chose to participate in the ancestral rite led by his eldest brother. He rescinded his right to worship ancestors independently of the descent-line heir and pledged to observe the canonical rule—"secondary sons [chih-tzu] do not perform sacrifice," a principle of the descent-line system. However, Ch'en's attempt to incorporate the descent-line principle into the ancestral rite did not go unchallenged. His fellow students pointed out that Manchu regulations had no such restriction. Ch'en argued that a concession could be made to accept the descent-line heir's worship of four generations, but it was intolerable to see "secondary sons" offering oblations personally.[111]

It is apparent that Ch'en regarded the Classical ritual not as a set of arbitrary rules but as sacred principles that transcended variations in dynastic institutions.[112] Whether the Manchus granted one the right to worship four ancestors, it remained everyone's obligation to abide by the Classical regulations. The Classical rituals were meant to be followed strictly, and Ch'en equated them with "heavenly principle." Any action going beyond the heavenly principle was nothing but human desire (*jen-yü*).[113] The strong cultural symbolism that Classical ritual came to represent was striking in Ch'en's remark.

Ch'en Ch'üeh and Chang Lü-hsiang were at the center of a group of scholars and officials who shared a kindred interest in ritual reform and the revival of "ancient rites." Their attempts revolved around the building of lineage ancestral halls and rectifying ancestral sacrifices and mourning ceremonies.

In 1654 their friend Wu Ch'ien-mu (1631–59) came into a large estate of over 230 *mou*. He decided to turn it into a lineage corporate estate to support the periodic worship of ancestors.[114] When Ch'ien-mu and his elder brother, Chung-mu, built an apical lineage hall (*ta-tsung-t'zu*), Chung-mu sent both Ch'en Ch'üeh and Chang Lü-hsiang a tentative agenda for comment on the structure and liturgy of the hall.[115] The 230 *mou* was to be divided into three parts, with 100 *mou* for supporting ancestor worship by "lesser descent-line" heirs. Another 100 *mou* was dedicated to maintaining the apical lineage hall. The remaining 30 *mou* became a charitable estate for the lineage school.[116]

In 1666 Chang Lü-hsiang received a letter from his student Chang Chia-ling, seeking advice on burial ceremonies and ancestral rites.[117] Chia-ling intended to rehabilitate the descent-line principle in ancestral rites and had encountered the most common obstacle—its implementation entailed either an imposition of ritual unity or a voluntary adjuration of worship rights by other agnates to the descent-line heir. Being the first son, Chia-ling was the heir of the descent-line sired by his father. But neither his father nor his grandfather had been the first son, and Chia-ling had no claim to ritual submission from his collateral kin. Furthermore, like most people, his agnates limited their worship to three generations. Since Chia-ling's younger brother had been adopted by his uncle, who was the first son, the adoptee's son became the "lesser descent-line heir" for three generations. Chia-ling's great-grandfather, who was the great-great-grandfather of his cousin, the descent-line heir, would have to be displaced. However, if the rites were based on Chia-ling, his great-grandfather should still receive oblation. Chia-ling was at his wit's end and wrote to Chang Lü-hsiang for advice on how to overcome the practical difficulties stemming from attempts to revive the descent-line institution.[118]

Chang Chia-ling's case clearly shows that although there was ancestor worship practiced in halls called *tz'u-t'ang*, the number of ancestors worshiped was not always the four stipulated by the *Family Rituals*. The existing practices in ancestral halls were at variance with the prescriptions of the manual. The renewed interest in the rituals prescribed in the *Family Rituals* and in reforming ancestor worship accordingly gave rise to conflicting opinions that could be settled only by Classical studies. Research on the Classics thus became one of the most urgent tasks facing scholars in the second half of the seventeenth century.

4

Ancestral Rites and Lineage
in Early Ch'ing Scholarship

The desire to strengthen kinship ties grew to claim priority on both the social and the scholarly agendas of the Confucian elite. As noted in the preceding chapter, the zeal for building lineages and kinship solidarity seized a large spectrum of scholars and officials either out of deference to the teachings of Ch'eng I and Chu Hsi or out of the desire to develop an extra-bureaucratic basis of local power. To be sure, some of these activities were attempts by wealthy non-gentry to emulate the life-style of the gentry. Although united in their goals, however, they remained divided over the rituals of the lineage—institutions of ancestor worship, temple structure, descent-line principle, and criteria of membership, to name but the important ones.

As noted in the previous chapter, rituals, especially those approved under the Ming dynasty, came to acquire a special significance in the early Ch'ing. The triumph of the alien regime not only helped keep the Confucian purist movement alive but also gave it a new impetus. The convergence of anti-Manchu sentiment with the resurgent Ch'eng-Chu school added fuel to the quest for authentic Confucian rituals. Never was the study of the Classics a more pressing task.

Although many followers of the Ch'eng-Chu school accepted unquestionably the rituals set forth by Ch'eng I and Chu Hsi as standard, opposition to equating Sung rituals with Classical ones was growing. Conflicts between diverging views perforce had to be settled by appeal to the Classics. As the interest in building lineages grew, disputes over ancestral rites drew Confucians deeper into investigation of the Classics. The controversies over the theoretical basis of kinship organization in the late seventeenth and early eighteenth centuries in significant ways not only stimulated but also shaped the development of Classical scholarship.

From the wide range of views on lineage organization current in the second half of the seventeenth century, two general approaches emerged—one favoring a fixed generational depth; the other partial to an unlimited kin group size. Each was based on a different set of principles of ancestral rites. An analysis of the issues involved in the polemics will help explain not only the practical reasons behind scholarly interest in the study of ancient ritual but also lineage development in the early Ch'ing.

A host of issues were directly and indirectly related to lineage building. Driven by the purist quest to recover Classical ritual forms, much of the controversy over the ancient rites involved the practice of ancestor worship. The following discussion is limited to the four most important issues in order to demonstrate the relationship between Classical research and the lineage-building movement. (1) What was the system of ancestral rites in the Chou dynasty? (2) Was the number of ancestors entitled to memorial services identical to the number of temples people of different ranks could have? (3) What was the *tsung-fa* (descent-line) system, and could it be resurrected? (4) How were these issues related to lineage organization?

It is not my purpose to examine these issues purely as academic quibbles or to provide "correct" answers to these questions. We are as much victims of contradictions in the Classics as scholars in the past were. Whether Ch'ing scholars and their predecessors understood the ancient world "objectively" is only a peripheral concern. What matters is how they understood these issues and where they differed. More important still are the implications of these differing views for lineage organization. It is therefore to the conceptual disparities among scholars, rather than to the verities of these Classical institutions, that this chapter is addressed.

Ch'eng I and Two Approaches to Kinship Organization

The efforts of early Ch'ing scholars to probe Classical antiquity owe much to preceding scholarship. They encountered the ancient world through the mediation of exegetical traditions currently accepted as paradigms. Classical scholarship as much as Confucian teachings had changed significantly in the hands of neo-Confucians since Sung times. These changes included attempts to ground ritual innovations in the Classics. Through the efforts of Ssu-ma Kuang (1019–86), Ch'eng I, and Chu Hsi, a somewhat different system of ancestral rites related to kinship had evolved. Their attempts to find solutions to problems concerning these issues in the Classics had served as the point of departure for Yüan and Ming scholars. For this reason, before we can attempt an analysis of early Ch'ing discourses on ancestral rites and lineage organization, an overview of the great changes in these areas since the Sung is in order, despite the risk of oversimplification. A second reason is that current scholarship on Sung scholars' "innovations" in ancestral rites is inadequate, despite excellent exploratory efforts.[1]

As Patricia Ebrey has noted, a few prominent Northern Sung neo-Confucians strove to revive the *tsung-fa* system in their attempt to reform kinship practices. Both Chang Tsai and Ch'eng I advocated the establishment of a *tsung-tzu* (descent-line heir) for a descent group with a depth of five generations; this was the *hsiao-tsung* (lesser descent-line) system.[2] Ch'eng I, however, ventured changes that deeply influenced theories regarding kinship organization and ancestral rites in Late Imperial China.

According to exegetical traditions evolved since the T'ang dynasty, in high antiquity ancestor worship was practiced in temples and on a graduated basis. Under the Chou regime only the king and the feudal lords could worship ancestors as distant as the great-great-grandfather in addition to a permanently honored "first ancestor" (*t'ai-tsu*). A memorial temple (*miao*) was erected to each of them.[3] "Great officials" (*ch'ing ta-fu*) were granted the right to worship up to the great-grandfather; "officers" (*shih*) only to the father. Accordingly, the former could have three temples, and the latter only one.

This view negated the Sung neo-Confucians' attempt to unify kinsmen descended from the same great-great-grandfather; according to this interpretation, even the highest Chou officials had been denied the right to worship their great-great-grandfather in the temples.[4] The implication for any attempt to use ancestral rites to enhance kinship solidarity was obvious. Were the great-great-grandfather not honored in memorial services, there would be no reason to convene agnates beyond the second collateral line; nor could there be a complete lesser descent-line system.

Worship of the Four Immediate Ancestors

In order to give kin groups sufficient generational depth, Ch'eng I had to justify everyone's right to worship the "four immediate ancestors" (*ssu-ch'in*): father, grandfather, great-grandfather, and great-great-grandfather. To this end he reinterpreted ancestral rites in the light of "five mourning grades" (*wu-fu*). In the Classics the systems of the five mourning grades and of ancestral rites were separate. Ch'eng I reasoned that inasmuch as agnates related through the great-great-grandfather fell within the five degrees of the mourning circle, it was perfectly legitimate for the descent-line heir and his siblings and cousins to worship that common ancestor. Since everyone from emperor to commoner observed the mourning rite, there was no reason not to use the same principle in ancestral rites.[5]

Ch'eng I also questioned the view that drew a parallel between the temple system and ancestor worship. He argued that the number of temples had nothing to do with the number of ancestors that could be worshiped. Great officials, low-ranking officials, and even commoners had the right to worship their ancestors up to the great-great-grandfather. Whether they housed the ancestors' tablets in one, two, or three temples did not matter.[6] By equating the generational scopes of mourning grades and ancestral rites, Ch'eng I in effect created a new principle of ancestor worship. As Chu Hsi acutely pointed out, the resulting ancestral rite had no Classical precedent. Ch'eng I was the first to identify ancestral rites with mourning grades.[7]

The significance of Ch'eng I's exposition was profound. In dissolving the theoretical link between the ancient temple system and the number of ancestors and aligning the latter with mourning grades, Ch'eng took the first step in making ancestral rites the institutional basis of kinship organization in Late Imperial China. With this new interpretation of an-cestral rites and temple system, Ch'eng I was able to proceed with the implementation of the lesser descent-line system.

The right to worship ancestors as distant as the great-great-grandfather did not in itself constitute kinship organization. Everyone could serve his four immediate ancestors at home or in a family shrine. Only when this rite was practiced in conjunction with the lesser descent-line principle was there a common ground for kinship organization.

Ch'eng I conceived the lesser descent-line system as an institution for a descent group delimited by shared mourning obligations and a common pedigree—the immediate four ancestors.[8] The lesser descent-line principle required all agnates descended from the same great-great-grandfather to subordinate themselves to the authority of the descent-line heir in matters of ancestral rites. By applying the lesser descent-line system to ancestral rites, Ch'eng I centralized ritual authority in the descent-line heir, who alone had the right to sacrifice to the lineal ancestors of his descent-line system. Under the descent-line system, secondary sons in the descent line and agnates in the collateral lines were required to relinquish the right to worship their common ancestor. In order to repay their debts to the ancestors, such kinsmen were obliged to participate in a collective ceremony led by the descent-line heir.

Insofar as kinship organization is concerned, this form of worship has obvious advantages over other rituals such as sacrifices at graves and mortuary rites. One great strength of conjoining the descent-line system and ancestor worship was that it demanded more frequent formal meetings of kindred. Offerings at graves did not require organized congregational ceremonies, nor necessitate constant meetings of agnates. Mortuary rites provided occasions for the assembling of kin members only at the demise of a relative. With the descent-line system, however, all rituals otherwise independently and domestically supervised by the head of each household were performed in the ancestral hall and involved all agnates. The descent-line heir presided not only over memorial services to ancestors, but also over marriage, mortuary, and mourning rituals. These ceremonies and periodic assemblies held in the name of ancestors, both monthly and seasonally, renewed interpersonal ties among kindred on a regular basis.

The scope of *tsu* (kin group) for Chang Tsai, Ch'eng I, and, in fact, most Sung Confucians interested in ritual reforms and kinship organization did not reach beyond the limits defined by the five grades of mourning dress. Their ideal kinship group coincided with the lesser descent-line system and the mourning circle. Agnates related through a forebear in the sixth generation in the ascending order had no obligation toward each other, since they belonged to different sets of "mourning grades." Ch'eng I unequivocally explained that the duty of a descent-line heir to keep kin together ended where the mourning circle terminated and where the obligation to perform ancestor worship ceased to be binding on the descent group.[9] None of the Sung neo-Confucians attempted to revive the "great descent-line" system (*ta tsung-fa*).[10] They believed that system was an inalienable right of the ancient hereditary aristocracy.[11]

Worship of the First Ancestor: The Ritual Foundation of the Modern Lineage

Ch'eng I made yet another important innovation in ancestral rites: the annual worship of the "first ancestor" (*shih-tsu*). In a modified form, this would provide an institutional basis for the development of a type of kinship organization capable of embracing a much larger descent group than the five-generation or lesser descent-line model. Among Northern Sung writers on ancestor worship, only Ch'eng I recommended the worship of the first ancestor.[12] In addition to the regular service for the four immediate ancestors, Ch'eng I provided for the worship of the first ancestor in an annual service held at the winter solstice. By *shih-tsu* he meant "the first progenitor of humankind" (*chüeh ch'u sheng-min chih tsu*).[13] The ceremony conducted to honor this shadowy forebear was essentially symbolic. This putative ancestor was not represented by a tablet installed in the ancestral hall, nor did he receive as many offerings as the enshrined did.[14] Without a tablet to lodge his spirit, this fictive figure was addressed in an invocation and tended only once a year at the winter solstice. As Ch'eng I explained, this was the date when the "productive energy" (*yang-ch'i*) of nature began to wax and the cosmos entered a state analogous to the human procreator giving birth to scions.[15]

Clearly Ch'eng I did not intend the worship of the first ancestor to be a means of achieving greater kinship cohesion beyond the mourning circle. Nor did Chu Hsi entertain such an idea. In the beginning Chu Hsi was faithful to Ch'eng I's advice to make an offering to the first ancestor, but he later abandoned the ritual because of its resemblance to the ceremony of *ti* (grand worship). In his view, this was the prerogative of the emperor.[16] Another reason was that only the great descent-line heir had the right to make such sacrifice to the first ancestor and only the "differentiated sons" (*pieh-tzu*) of the feudal lords could be designated such heirs. Ordinary officials therefore were not permitted to worship the first ancestor.[17] Chu Hsi's argument is predicated on the conventional view that the great descent-line system was part of the ancient hereditary political structure and, failing the revival of that system, could not be practiced.

Ch'eng I's ambiguous definition of *shih-tsu* confounded his followers in the Southern Sung. Even Chu Hsi was unable to reach a judgment on what Ch'eng I had in mind. In response to a student's question, Chu Hsi gave two alternative definitions of *shih-tsu*: the ancestor who received a surname and hence a fief from the Chou king (*shou-hsing chih tsu*), and the original progenitor of the human species. Another student asked if it was proper to worship the ancestor who "first laid the foundation" (*shih-chi*) for his descendants. Chu Hsi told him to honor this first ancestor at his grave.[18]

Hsü Heng and the "First Migrant Ancestor"

The meaning of *shih-tsu* hitherto had no connection in ancestral rites with the derivative connotation of first forebear who migrated to a locale, which was to become the most common usage in Ming and Ch'ing genealogies and ancestral rites.[19] In all likelihood, the practice of worshiping the first migrant ancestor grew out of offerings at graves by agnates descended from a common local ancestor.[20] More important, perhaps, was the emergence of a "lineage orientation" among scholar-officials during the Southern Sung. According to Robert Hymes, this was an integral part of a broader shift in the survival strategy of the elite, who attempted to strengthen their local position through the "promotion, celebration, and in some cases, creation" of localized descent groups.[21] This change in strategy is hypothesized from a change in the contents of prefaces to genealogies in the Southern Sung. Genealogies of this period began to embrace agnates related through ancestors beyond the great-great-grandfather and to treat collateral kin in equal detail.[22]

When ancestry expanded to accommodate the growth of the descent group from five generations to scores of generations, the *Family Ritual*'s provisions for kinship organization became inadequate. Less than seventy years after Chu Hsi died, an attempt was made to legitimize the worship of the "first migrant ancestor" by tincturing Ch'eng I's notion of first ancestor with Classicism.

Despite Chu Hsi's personal injunction against it, he had included Ch'eng I's advice for the worship of the first ancestor in the *Chin-ssu lu* (Record of reflections at hand) and the *Hsiao-hsüeh* (Elementary learning).[23] Some literati took Ch'eng I's recommendation seriously. Hsü Heng (1209–81), a renowned follower of the Ch'eng-Chu school under the Yüan, required his students to study the *Hsiao-hsüeh*.[24] In 1269, Hsü sought to ground the worship of first migrant ancestor in the Classics when he wrote an essay to commemorate the founding of an ancestral hall dedicated to the first migrant ancestor of his lineage.[25] Taking a cue from Chu Hsi's linkage of the worship of first ancestor and the differentiated son (*pieh-tzu*), Hsü found in commentaries on the *Book of Rites* two definitions of *pieh-tzu*: a person who established himself in a new locality and fathered a group of descent; the first ancestor to gain government office.

There is little doubt that these two meanings derived from remarks by the Han commentator Cheng Hsüan (127–200) and the T'ang exegete K'ung Ying-ta (574–648). In three different chapters, they noted as many categories of *pieh-tzu*: secondary sons of feudal lords; ducal sons settling in a domain other than their father's; officials from clans other than the imperial one (*i-hsing*).[26] In their comments, however, *pieh-tzu* did not mean commoners who attained office or settled in a new locality. Rather, both referred to descendants of *i-hsing*—that is, different aristocratic clans—

and specifically to ducal sons (*kung-tzu*) from a different domain. But Hsü Heng quoted the comments out of context and made both migration and first attainment of office the defining criteria of *pieh-tzu*.[27] In so doing, he forged a new meaning for *shih-tsu*, replacing Ch'eng I's obscure usage with a definition derived from Han and T'ang glosses.[28]

Ch'eng I's idea of worshiping the first ancestor provided the necessary link between practice and the Classics.[29] Hsü's view of first ancestor, however, departed from those of both Ch'eng I and Chu Hsi. To Hsü, the first ancestor was neither a mythical figure nor a descendant of an aristocrat, but either a first migrant ancestor or the first official in one's ancestry. In either sense of the word, the apical ancestor of Hsü's lineage qualified for a memorial hall.

Hsü Heng's pursuit of a Classical explanation for the building of an apical lineage hall is revealing. First, it is quite clear that the *Family Ritual* model was inadequate for a lineage that included agnates beyond the third collateral line.[30] Hsü's justification was desirable because Chu Hsi opposed Ch'eng I's idea and the ancestral hall Hsü's kinsmen built was based on the idea of Ch'eng I rather than Chu Hsi. There can be no doubt that the hall Hsü's lineage built was a prototype of what came to be called "hall of the great descent-line" (*ta-tsung tz'u*), or apical lineage hall.[31]

Second, from the Yüan dynasty on, Ch'eng I's recommendation to worship the first ancestor was often invoked to legitimize the worship of first migrant ancestor, a grafting of Ch'eng I's idea onto the evolving practice of kinship organization.[32] First ancestor in the sense of either the first migrant or the first winner of government office became the most common term for apical ancestor in Ming and Ch'ing genealogies and ancestral rites.[33] The two senses Hsü Heng extracted from the commentaries had become the most commonly cited reasons for building an apical lineage hall, a type of ancestral hall distinguishable from that envisioned by either Ch'eng I or Chu Hsi.

Official Model and Private Practice

Clearly, the rituals proposed by Ch'eng I lacked Classical sanction as far as Chu Hsi was concerned. The right to perform the rituals of the quaternary ancestral system was not granted officials during the Chou dynasty, and the consecration of all four ancestors in one hall was at variance with the ancient practice of single-generation temples.[34] The Classics contain no reference to annual sacrifices to the original human progenitor, who should not be confused with the "first ancestor" (*t'ai-tsu*) of feudal rulers in the Classics. Despite Chu Hsi's objection to Ch'eng I's proposal to make offerings to a first ancestor and the idea's questionable claim to a Classical origin, it came to have an enormous appeal for the Confucian elite in the Ming and Ch'ing times.

These ideas—the worship of the first ancestor and the use of mourning grades as the basis for organizing ancestral rites—became widely known from their discussion in such basic neo-Confucian texts as the *Chin-ssu lu* and the *Hsiao-hsüeh*.[35] Another important source for Ch'eng I's ideas was the *Family Rituals*, one of the most comprehensive reference works on Sung ritual.[36] During the Ming, Ch'eng I's views on ancestor worship were made known to the literati through imperial publications. Acting on the decree of the Ming emperor Ch'eng-tsu (r. 1403–24), in 1415 Hu Kuang (1370–1418) completed the *Hsing-li ta-ch'üan*,[37] which was essentially an expanded version of the *Chin-ssu lu*.[38] The text of the *Family Rituals* included in this text spanned three *chüan*.[39] Nothing proved more effective for disseminating Ch'eng I's ideas than making the *Hsing-li ta-ch'üan* a required text for the civil service examination.[40]

More than merely knowledge to be acquired for the civil service examinations, the *Family Rituals*' ancestral rite became the code of ceremonies for officials in the Ming dynasty. The costliness of its ceremonies made it suitable for this purpose, since only families of officials could afford to stage grand ritual performances.[41] Observance of the ceremonies prescribed in the *Family Rituals* was therefore limited to a small number of families of either high official position or considerable means. The *Ta Ming chi-li* (Collected Ceremonies of the Great Ming), completed in 1370 under chief editor Hsü I-k'uei (1318–ca. 1400),[42] modeled its description of the "family shrine" (*chia-miao*) of officials on the *Family Rituals*.[43] Three years later, Ming T'ai-tsu ordered royal and official families alike to establish a family shrine to the east of their residence. Four generations of ascendants were to be enshrined in it.[44] But officials' response to the imperial fiat was far from enthusiastic. Around 1377, a scholar remarked with disapproval on the nonchalance of officials and gentry with respect to setting up the official version of the ancestral hall.[45] Ch'iu Chün (1420–95), a famous official and scholar, made a similar observation in 1449.[46] Those who did build one did not always follow the imperial specifications.

Numerous examples point to the wide spectrum of variation in ancestral halls built by Ming officials. Wei Chi (1374–1471), a native of Hsiao-shan in Chekiang and a onetime vice-president of the Board of Personnel, founded an ancestral hall enshrining his four immediate lineal ascendants. In addition, he set up a separate niche for the tablet of the first migrant ancestor.[47] This appears to have been a common arrangement in the Ming— a combination of the quaternary system and Hsü Heng's idea of honoring the first migrant ancestor. In the mid-fifteenth century, when Ch'iu Chün added supplementary notes to the *Family Rituals*, he made reference to the practice of some families, including the widely acclaimed Cheng family of Chin-hua in Chekiang, of installing the tablet for the first ancestor permanently in their ancestral hall. Ch'iu Chün, however, deemed the practice presumptuous for officials.[48]

Unlike the ancestral hall founded by Wei Chi, these halls honored a descent group with no specific limit on the number of consecrated forebears. A good example is the hall built in 1377 by a Ch'en lineage for which Fang Hsiao-ju wrote a commemorative panegyric.[49] There are a number of references to this type of apical ancestral hall in the Ming dynasty.[50]

Official Recognition of Offering to the First Ancestor

Despite its imperial recognition, the *Family Rituals* model of ancestral hall for officials was far less appealing than the apical hall. In the sixteenth century, in the wake of the Great Rites controversy (*Ta-li i*) that inaugurated the reign of the Chia-ching emperor (r. 1522–1566), ritual emerged as a great concern of officials.[51] In the eleventh month of 1536, Grand Secretary Hsia Yen, a native of Kiangsi, submitted a memorial to the Chia-ching emperor urging him to allow officials and commoners to worship the first ancestor as well as the four immediate lineal ancestors.[52] Thus far imperial regulations about the gradations of ancestral rites to be observed by the various ranks of officials had not been specific. Neither the *Ta-Ming chi-li* nor the 1373 edict set up a graduated system of family shrines for officials.

Hsia Yen recommended that all officials establish family shrines with a structure and rites befitting their rank. Those of the third rank and above were enjoined to erect a temple with five niches. The center niche would house the tablet of the first ancestor with the four immediate lineal ancestors arrayed to either side. If no one in the genealogy was worthy of such an honor, the official himself would become the first ancestor on his death. Officials of the fourth rank and below were entitled to worship only their four immediate lineal ascendants in the shrine. The first ancestors of lower officials and commoners, represented by a card, would be commemorated in accordance with Ch'eng I's schedule. The card would be burned at the conclusion of the service.[53]

Two facts in Hsia Yen's memorial are noteworthy. First, despite the edict of 1373, few officials had constructed family shrines in accordance with the imperial rules. Second, some elite families preferred the practice of erecting first ancestor or apical lineage halls. In the mid-sixteenth century, even in Hui-chou, Anhwei, a stronghold of Ch'eng-Chu neo-Confucianism, Wang Tao-k'un (1525–93) observed that gentry families preferred to worship in apical ancestral halls.[54] As noted above, even before 1536, there were a number of apical lineage halls in which the first ancestor was worshiped, in violation of government regulation. Hsia Yen's memorial could therefore be viewed as a plea for official recognition of existing practices. But Hsia Yen proposed to limit the permanent enshrinement of the first ancestor in the ancestral hall to a few high-ranking officials. Furthermore, for those high officials the ancestral halls were family shrines, not public lineage halls, and the officials themselves conducted the ceremony. The offering to a first ancestor with a tablet installed in a hall was recognized only as a family rite, not as a lineage ceremony.

Two Types of Ancestral Hall

Why the greater appeal of the apical hall? The most critical factors working against the official model for the ancestral hall—the family shrine—were the bureaucracy and the civil service examination. The right to build an official family shrine was a privilege of officials, awarded to distinguish them from commoners. It was a personal honor that could not be inherited. If an official had no descendants who succeeded in attaining office, the family shrine had to be demolished. As the editor of the Ta-Ming chi-li noted, since Sung times attempts to revive some form of family shrine for officials had been futile. More often than not, the male descendants of officials failed to maintain their forebears' rank and status, and the court was unable to grant hereditary status to all.[55]

Moreover, the family shrine was a privilege granted to an individual. A family producing more than one official could claim as many family shrines as it had family members in office. For some this was perhaps an excellent way to display status, but for others building more than one ancestral hall was undesirably ostentatious. A Ming scholar noted, undoubtedly with exaggeration, that official shrines would outnumber commoners' abodes, for some families had produced more than one official for three generations.[56]

The ancestral hall dedicated to a primogenitor, on the other hand, was free from these limitations. Its raison d'être was not directly linked to government office, and it was built chiefly to honor an apical ancestor of a descent group, rather than to recognize a scion for his personal accomplishment as an official. Whereas the family shrine of an official might have to be demolished or deserted because of a loss of official status, the worth of the first ancestor was unaffected by the unforeseeable political and bureaucratic fortunes of family members. Once founded, an apical hall could continue to serve as a center for ancestor worship. An official family shrine honored the living; the apical hall commemorated the dead.

Inasmuch as the family shrine was awarded to the official himself, it was essentially the shrine of the official's family. It had nothing to do with his agnates. The official was the principal worshiper regardless of his status within his descent group. Its genealogical depth of five generations also prevented the official from involving agnates sharing ancestors more distant than the great-great-grandfather. Officials of the third rank and above could invite remote kinsmen to worship their first ancestor, but whether to tender such an invitation was entirely the official's personal decision.

Although the official family shrine was modeled on the *Family Rituals by Master Chu*, there was a major departure. As Ch'iu Chün noted, descent-line principles lay at the heart of the *Family Rituals*.[57] A "descent-line heir," who was the firstborn of the immediate lineal ancestry, officiated at all the ceremonies in the hall. His natal status qualified him as the principal worshiper. In contrast, in the official's family shrine, the official enjoyed ritual leadership regardless of his natal status. The abandonment of the descent-line principle in the official ancestral rite was inevitable, for it was at odds with the meritocratic basis of the bureaucracy. The conflict between these two principles came to a head in the early Ch'ing literati fervor to build ancestral halls. This occasioned a great debate on the rites and the structure of ancestral hall described in the *Family Rituals*, a development to which we now turn.

The Early Ch'ing Controversy over Ancestral Rites

Several factors contributed to the renewed interest in the *Family Rituals* model. As pointed out earlier, with the Manchu conquest, ritual took on a distinctly cultural meaning for the Chinese elite, especially for those who resolved to shun a political career in a government presided over by "barbarians." At the risk of psychological speculation, we might suppose that their enthusiasm for rituals betrayed a need to seek consolation in practices that reaffirmed their Chinese identity. It is in this connection that *Family Rituals* carried particular significance. For some, its ritual prescriptions obviously came to represent not just Chinese culture but also the institutions of the Ming dynasty. Even Huang Tsung-hsi, normally considered a follower of Wang Yang-ming, recommended in 1662 that the *Family Rituals* be made the standard manual of rituals for all subjects.[58] To be sure, this explanation holds only for the period before 1690, when the Manchu regime adopted the Ming structure for the family shrine of its officials in the *Collected Statutes of the Ch'ing Empire (Ta-Ch'ing hui-tien).*[59]

As discussed previously, this heightened concern owed much to the social vision of such influential scholars as Ku Yen-wu and Lu Shih-i, who saw in lineages the prospect of providing a broader institutional basis for gentry power. Their emphasis on reviving the descent-line system lent support to the importance of the *Family Rituals'* approach to lineage organization. The confluence of these currents of thought gave added impetus to attempts to organize lineages in accordance with the *Family Rituals'* model. Differing views on ancestor worship and lineage organization in turn provoked scholarly controversies.

Challenges to the *Family Rituals*

Many upheld the *Family Rituals* as the great reference for ritual reform; others were skeptical of the work and dismissed many of its rites as concoctions by Sung neo-Confucians, lacking roots in the Classics. Indeed, Ch'eng I and Chang Tsai had conceived the descent-line system essentially as an institution for ancestor worship and made no attempt to ground their innovations in the Classics through rigorous research. Ch'eng I explicitly spoke of his scheme of ancestral rites as an inference from "principles of duties" (*i-li*) that he had comprehended.[60] Reinstating the descent-line principle in the ancestral rites was in accordance with "heavenly principle."[61] He was of the belief that "great worthies" (*ta-hsien*), having grasped the "principles," were qualified to reform and innovate rituals.[62] Whether the ancients had such rites did not matter, for the concrete rites change with time. Ch'eng I and Chang Tsai knew that their lesser descent-line principle departed from its Classical model in which it was subordinated to the Chou feudal structure. With the rise of Confucian purism and Classicism, however, the rituals prescribed in the *Family Rituals* came under attack for lacking Classical precedents.

Criticism of the *Family Rituals'* ancestral rites focused on a number of issues of lineage organization. First, the *Family Rituals'* rites followed the lesser descent-line principle. But the hereditary aristocracy had long since disappeared, and it was impossible to reinstate the descent-line system. Some scholars opposed the revival of the descent-line system precisely on the grounds that it depended on a hereditary system of political power.[63]

Second, as Ch'en Ch'üeh and his friends pointed out, the worship of the four immediate ancestors as stipulated in the *Family Rituals* originated as a prerogative of the feudal lords.[64] It was a transgression for ordinary officials to practice such a rite. Ch'en further disputed the parallel Ch'eng I drew between ancestral rites and mourning grades.[65] Third, the Classics provided no precedent for enshrining more than one generation in a temple; hence the worship of four ancestors in one hall was at variance with Classical practice. Fourth, according to Cheng Hsüan, in the Chou dynasty the right to worship the primogenitor *t'ai-tsu* (the first ancestor entitled permanently to offerings from descendants) was granted only to officials descended from the differentiated sons of feudal lords.[66] Taken together, these criticisms amount to an outright denial of the authenticity of the rituals in the *Family Rituals* and a rejection of its five-generation model of lineage organization.

Wan Ssu-ta's Defense of the *Family Rituals* Model

Many of the difficulties involved in following the rites of the *Family Rituals* were solved with the appearance of a treatise on the descent-line system by Wan Ssu-ta. Wan's essays were most welcome and yet destined to become highly controversial. Since 1667 Wan and many students of Huang Tsung-hsi had held periodic meetings for studying the Classics.[67] After his extensive notes on the *Spring and Autumn Annals* were consumed by a fire in 1673, Wan became committed to the investigation of nothing but ancient rituals.[68] He put together his most important essays on rituals in a volume entitled *Hsüeh-li chih-i* (Doubts regarding the study of rituals), a work completed in 1677.[69] This work contained a treatise entitled *Tsung-fa*, a study in eight parts, in which he attempted to provide justifications in Classical terms for most of the important ancestral rites stipulated in the *Family Rituals*.

Wan Ssu-ta argued that the descent-line system in the Chou dynasty was, in fact, an institution for ancestor worship independent of the hereditary aristocracy. The goal of this system of organization was the maintenance of cohesion among agnates outside the hereditary line of descent of the feudal lords. Since those sons who had no legal claim to hereditary offices would easily disperse and fall into poverty, it was appropriate to institute the descent-line system to maintain kinship cohesion. The system was therefore a supplementary and yet independent institution, rather than a subordinate system, of hereditary aristocracy.[70]

The mistaken conventional view of the descent-line system, Wan argued, originated in Cheng Hsüan's explication of passages in the Classics pertaining to that institution. In glossing the phrase *pieh-tzu wei tsu* in the "Sang-fu hsiao-chi" (Brief notes on mourning grades) and "Ta-chuan" (Great commentary) chapters of the *Book of Rites*, Cheng took the word *pieh-tzu* (differentiated sons) to mean a feudal lord's secondary sons by concubines (*shu-tzu*) who had no right to their father's fief and rank and accordingly were not entitled to worship their father. They became the first ancestors of their patrilines to be "differentiated" from the main line of the feudal lord. The main lines of descent of these differentiated sons were to become "great descent-lines" (*ta-tsung*). The descendants of the secondary sons of those in the great descent-lines would form "lesser descent-lines" (*hsiao-tsung*).[71]

A few points emerge from Cheng's explanation. First, all secondary sons of a feudal lord were "differentiated sons." As a matter of course, the descendants of feudal lords in the main line belonged to the great descent-line; those in secondary lines belonged to lesser descent-lines. The status of *tsung-tzu*—that is, the heirs of both great and lesser descent-lines in every generation—derived from the mere fact that they were descendants of secondary sons of a feudal lord. The descent-lines system began as a subordinate institution of the hereditary aristocracy. The implications of this view for the revival of the descent-line system are several. Reviving the hoary institution necessitated the resurrection of hereditary aristocracy, but this was impossible under the imperial political structure, for success demanded no less than a voluntary reduction of the emperor's power. Its implementation would also negate the purpose of the entrenched civil service examination and upset the principle of a meritocratic bureaucracy.

As noted above, despite the neo-Confucians' attempt to promote a modified form of the lesser descent-line system—a truncated model of the ancient institution—almost no one championed the idea of reviving the great descent-line system. The relationship posited by Cheng Hsüan between the descent-line system and the feudal political structure presented the greatest obstacle to any such attempt.

For Wan Ssu-ta, however, this was merely an illusory obstacle resulting from Cheng Hsüan's misunderstanding of the Classics. Wan disputed Cheng's comment on the meaning of *tsu* in the phrase *pieh-tzu wei tsu*. Cheng's error was to render *pieh-tzu* as sons by concubines.[72] Actually, *pieh-tzu* designated all sons other than the heir. Wan Ssu-ta held that government offices in the Chou dynasty were not hereditary. Except for the heir, the sons of feudal lords did not receive official appointments by virtue of their aristocratic status. Accordingly, they did not have the right to worship their father. For them, personal merit and ability rather than birth determined appointment. Having attained office, any descendant of a differentiated son was entitled to establish a temple to worship the latter as the first ancestor of a great descent-line (*ta-tsung*).

What qualified a person as the first ancestor of a great descent-line, that is, as the differentiated son? According to Cheng Hsüan and K'ung Ying-ta, being differentiated sons of a prince was the only qualification for becoming the first ancestor of a great descent-line, and all secondary sons were differentiated sons. But Wan contended that becoming the primogenitor of a great descent-line depended on the individual differentiated son's personal ability to attain the rank of great official (*ta-fu*). Those who succeeded would be permanently worshiped as the first ancestor by their descendants in the main line. These patrilines sired by differentiated sons with the rank of great official were great descent-lines and included all splintering lesser descent-lines of their progeny. The less successful differentiated sons who ascended no higher than the rank of officer (*shih*) were to become "displacable" ancestors of lesser descent-lines to be honored for five generations by their descendants in the main line.

The entire descent-line system, in Wan's perspective, rested on the principle of achieved status in the sense of official appointment procured on the basis of personal merit by the noble's secondary sons. More important, the distinction between great and lesser descent-lines reflected differences in official status. In brief, in Wan's view, the descent-line system of the Chou dynasty was independent of the hereditary aristocracy.[73] This exposition, if accepted, would lay to rest any objections to reviving the system because of the impossibility of resurrecting the hereditary aristocracy. There was no reason to reject the Sung neo-Confucians' call for the revival of the descent-line system.

The second issue central to ancestor worship and the great descent-line system concerned the worship of the first ancestor. As noted above, the main object of Chang Tsai and Ch'eng I was to implement the lesser descent-line model of kinship organization. Although Ch'eng I recommended an annual ceremony to honor the first ancestor, he did not mean a descent group should worship a real forebear. Despite Chu Hsi's disapproval, Ch'iu Chün's comments on the *Family Rituals*, though condemning the enshrinement of the first ancestor in the ancestral hall, conceded that an annual oblation to the first ancestor as recommended by Ch'eng I was acceptable.[74] Ch'iu tolerated the worship of the first ancestor because the ceremony was not a full-fledged ritual. The absence of a permanent tablet in the ancestral hall indicated a ceremony of a lower grade than that practiced by the feudal nobles and emperor. Even in the neo-Confucian tradition, the worship of the first ancestor was not supported by a rigorous argument based on the Classics, despite Hsü Heng's seminal attempt to find such a basis. Such an argument safely anchored in the Classics was formulated only in Wan Ssu-ta's treatise.

By reconstructing the temple system (*miao-chih*) recorded in the Classics, Wan was able to demonstrate that the worship of the first ancestor was a privilege granted to great officials (*ta-fu*). The "Wang-chih" (Kingly institutions) chapter of the *Book of Rites* contains a passage concerning the number of temples "officials" were entitled to erect. They had the right to establish three fanes: one to the *t'ai-tsu* (first ancestor), one erected to its left, and another to its right.[75] Although Chu Hsi was aware of this provision, his understanding of the descent-line system as dependent on hereditary office prevented him from treating the worship of the first ancestor as Wan Ssu-ta did. For conventional exegetes, including Chu Hsi, the right to worship the first ancestor derived from the operating system of hereditary aristocracy, which conferred the status of great descent-line heir along with hereditary rank and stipend. The abolition of the ancient aristocratic polity precluded the revival of not only the great descent-line system but also the ancestral rite of worshiping the first ancestor.

In Wan's view, the right of a descendant to worship the first ancestor derived not from his personal status but rather from the fact that he belonged to the main line of a descent group sired by a differentiated son who had attained the status of great official. The status of descent-line heir was based not so much on the attainment of office on the part of the descendant as on descent alone. What the great descent-line heir inherited was not so much the rank and emolument of the differentiated son, as the exclusive right to worship him as the first ancestor. Any first son descending in the main line from a differentiated son with the status of great official could worship the first ancestor whether he was official or not. This treatment of descent line as purely a system defining the rights of descendants made possible a new interpretation of the worship of the first ancestor. The rite did not owe its existence to the presence of a hereditary aristocracy, since no inheritance of office was involved.

The Quaternary System of Ancestral Rites

Wan Ssu-ta's Classical studies provided as much evidence for worshiping the first ancestor as for worshiping the four immediate ancestors. Conventional exegeses on ancient ancestral rites permitted great officials to worship ancestors for three generations. They were granted three temples, one each to enshrine their great-grandfather, grandfather, and father. Only under exceptional occasions were they allowed to sacrifice to the great-great-grandfather. As we have seen, Ch'eng I argued that the restriction against worshiping one's great-great-grandfather was incongruent with the "principle of duty," for every person from emperor to commoner had mourning obligations toward kin sharing the same great-great-grandfather. He recommended a universal system of worship of ancestors for four generations back from oneself. Even though Chu Hsi unequivocally pointed out that this was an innovation by Ch'eng I without precedent in Classical antiquity, this new scheme was further elaborated in the structure of the ancestral hall outlined in the *Family Rituals*.[76]

Few voiced opposition to this practice, perhaps because the mourning grades were widely followed. But in the early Ch'ing it was challenged as lacking roots in the Classics. Wan Ssu-ta alluded to such skepticism in his treatise,[77] but argued that in the Chou dynasty great officials had had the right to worship ancestors up to their great-great-grandfather. He admired Ch'eng I for his insightful recommendation that everyone should make oblations to ancestors as distant as the great-great-grandfather, but lamented his failure to provide evidence from the Classics for his view.[78]

According to K'ung Ying-ta's explication of a passage in the "Wang-chih" chapter, in the Chou dynasty only the king had seven temples; the nobles had five, the great officials three, and the officers one.[79] The temple system paralleled the institution of ancestral rites, with each temple lodging one generation of ancestor. The great officials were entitled to enshrine father, grandfather, and great-grandfather in three temples; the officer granted one temple could worship only his father.[80] This view assumed one temple did not enshrine more than one ancestor in each generation or in different generations, and on the basis of this exegetical tradition the ancestral rites of the Chou dynasty were inferred.

Wan Ssu-ta set out to show that the temples of the Chou royal house could enshrine more than one ancestor of the same generation and of different generations. The ancestral temples of the Chou king were arranged in alternating generational order (*chao-mu*) in two rolls; the temple for the first ancestor occupied the center, with three temples to the left constituting the *chao* generational roll, and three to the right the *mu* generational roll. Each ruler belonged permanently to either a *chao* or a *mu* generation. If the father was a *chao*, his successor-son would be worshiped in a *mu* temple, and his grandson in a *chao* temple.

This pattern of succession, however, represented the normal situation. If a ruler was followed on the throne by his brother, both would belong to a *chao* or to a *mu* generation. Confusion would arise if the rule of one temple for one ancestor were to apply. There might, for example, be two temples for the same *chao* generation but no temple for the *mu* generation. The symmetry would be upset. One way to circumvent asymmetry was to change the brother's classification in the *chao-mu* system. But this created a more serious problem. Since *chao-mu* was essentially a system to distinguish fathers and sons, changing the brother's generation would make him a son of his predecessor-brother. Since the "Wang-chih" chapter clearly stipulates a symmetrical arrangement of temples, in the case of a brother succeeding to the throne, on his death his tablet must have been housed in the same temple as that of his brother-predecessor. It was apparent even in the Chou dynasty, Wan reasoned, that there were occasions when one temple accommodated more than one ancestor in partitioned chambers.[81]

Wan proceeded to argue that even the lowest-ranking officers and commoners were allowed to worship their four immediate ancestors. They were differentiated only by the number of temples that they were entitled to build. Great officials had three temples: the middle one housed the first ancestor; the other two lodged the quaternary ancestors. The one to the left, the *chao*, was set up for the great-great-grandfather and the grandfather. The right one, the *mu*, was for the great-grandfather and the father. The officers and lower officials (*kuan-shih*) alike worshiped four generations in segregated niches in one temple. The commoners, although denied the right to establish a temple, were nevertheless allowed to tend their ancestors up to the great-great-grandfather.[82] Wan essentially treated

the temple system as a prerogative of officials. The number of temples
varied with rank. The worship of the four immediate ancestors was, however, a universal rite applicable to all regardless of status and the number
of temples one was entitled to build.

The conclusions Ch'eng I had reached through his comprehension of
the "principles of duty" were now firmly grounded in the Classics. Wan's
Classical scholarship had rendered a great service to the rituals created by
Ch'eng I, and his eloquent argument was so cogent that Huang Tsung-
hsi declared it would not be superseded.[83] Impressed by its compelling
treatment, Ku Yen-wu copied the entire treatise into his *Wu-ching t'ung-i*
(Concordances and differences in the Five Classics).[84] When Ch'in Hui-
t'ien compiled his colossal compendium on rituals, the *Wu-li t'ung k'ao*,
he noted with delight that Wan Ssu-ta's superb exposition of the Classics
provided proof for Ch'eng I's insightful approach to ancestral rites. What
Ch'eng I had arrived at by inference from the principle of mourning dress
was cogently borne out by Wan's research on the descent-line system, ancestral rites, and temple system.[85] Wan's explication of the temple system
for great officials and officers in the Chou dynasty was in Ch'in's view
definitive.[86] Ch'eng T'ing-tso (1691–1767), an admirer of the teachings
of Yen Yüan and Li Kung, found Wan's argument extremely convincing
and believed that the system of one temple with partitioned chambers to
house one's quaternary ancestry was practical.[87]

Wan's interpretation cleared away a great theoretical obstacle to the
descent-line system and grounded the universal duty to worship one's
four immediate ancestors in the Classics. The building of a lesser descent-
line ancestral hall enshrining one's quaternary ancestry now had the blessing of the Classics. Going a step further than his neo-Confucian predecessors, Wan provided a Classical sanction for the revival of the great
descent-line system (*ta tsung-fa*).

Wan Ssu-ta's interpretations of the descent-line system are significant in several ways. If the descent-line system was not integrally related
to the institution of a hereditary aristocracy, it could be establish privately without disrupting the political structure. Inasmuch as the status
of great descent-line heir depended on the primogenitor himself, whether
the former held office made no difference. Chinese literati who decided to
forgo a career in the government under the Manchu regime could practice
the institution if their first ancestor had been an official under the Ming or
previous dynasties. As suggested above, what is more important perhaps
is that the revival of the descent-line system provided an outlet for anti-

Manchu feelings and a source of consolation. To the generation of Chinese literati plagued by a deep sense of guilt for not laying down their life for the Ming dynasty, ancient rituals clearly took on special significance. The descent-line principle was one of the ideal institutions of the Chou dynasty, the golden age for the Chinese. These anachronistic institutions suddenly became the symbols of Chinese culture, something to be clung to as the greatest achievements of the Chinese people.

Mao Ch'i-ling's Criticism

The response to Wan Ssu-ta's new interpretation, though generally enthusiastic, was far from uniformly positive. Some scholars, for example, took issue with him over the impracticality of organizing a lineage by the descent-line principle in a world based on meritocratic recruitment to the bureaucracy rather than hereditary status. The strongest criticism of Wan Ssu-ta's treatises did come from a Ch'ing official, Mao Ch'i-ling, who had earned the lowest examination degree from the Ming government.[88] Ironically, it was the Ch'ing government that provided the institutional conduit through which Wan's new interpretations were transmitted to wider scholarly circles.

From 1679 on, scholarly exchanges were greatly facilitated by the special *po-hsüeh hung-tz'u* (Scholar of Grand Erudition) examinations. Successful candidates in this attempt by the K'ang-hsi emperor to placate the Kiangnan literati were assigned to the *Ming History* project.[89] In addition, officials such as Hsü Ch'ien-hsüeh made semiofficial support for scholarly research available. These networks of patronage brought together scholars from different regions.[90] In 1680 Mao Ch'i-ling made the acquaintance of Wan Ssu-t'ung. Mao was then a compiler for the *Ming History* project in Peking, having won the *po-hsüeh hung-tz'u* degree the year before.[91] There is little doubt that it was through Wan Ssu-t'ung that Mao learned of Wan Ssu-ta's writings on rituals.

Mao was the most disputatious scholar to attack Wan's treatise on the descent-line system, which he dismissed as far from conclusive.[92] Based on his own reading of the Classics, he insisted that the descent-line system was inseparable from the institution of aristocracy. In the Chou dynasty, only the second brother, who did not inherit the rank and fief, became the descent-line heir. There was only one great descent-line heir for each lord.[93] Mao's exposition differed from those of Cheng Hsüan and Wan

Ssu-ta as to the number of great descent-line heirs. Despite their differences, neither Cheng nor Wan held that each noble could have no more than one great descent-line heir. Mao took exception to the belief that a revival of the descent-line system was possible without resurrecting "feudal organization."[94]

The controversy stemmed from the ambiguous comments on the term *pieh-tzu* in the *Book of Rites*. More than one definition of *pieh-tzu* had been advanced in the long history of Classical studies.[95] Three meanings had generally been accepted since the Sung. The first originated in Cheng Hsüan's gloss of *pieh-tzu* in a passage in the "Sang-fu hsiao-chi" chapter of the *Book of Rites* as denoting "sons born to concubines" (*shu-tzu*).[96] *Shu-tzu* could also mean "various sons." In either case, Cheng thought the number of great descent-lines varied with the number of sons the feudal lord had.

Mao repudiated Cheng Hsüan's gloss of *pieh-tzu* as concubine's son. He pointed to the ancient rule that only the eldest son by the principal wife could perform a sacrifice to the ancestors. Clearly, under normal circumstances sons of concubines could not be *pieh-tzu*. The main purpose of the descent-line system was to distinguish sons by the principal wife from those born to concubines. The sons of concubines could enter the descent line only when no son born by the principal wife was available. Cheng's reading contradicted the very essence of the descent-line system.[97] The second meaning of *pieh-tzu* derived from the "Ta-chuan" chapter of the *Book of Rites*. There Cheng rendered *pieh-tzu* as sons of feudal lords living in a different domain.[98] In fact, this sense is derivative from the first for whether or not the sons of feudal lords remained in their own state, they were "differentiated sons" and would become the first ancestor of great descent-lines in either case.

Cheng's second gloss was equally unsatisfactory to Mao Ch'i-ling. According to K'ung Ying-ta, Cheng Hsüan had explained that the title *pieh-tzu* was applied as well to nobles' sons who took up offices in domains other than their father's. They themselves became first ancestors of great descent-lines. Mao questioned this because he could find no such usage in the Classics. He concluded that it resulted from a careless reading of Cheng's comment by K'ung. According to Mao, Cheng was attempting to illustrate the use of *tsu* in the phrase *pieh-tzu wei tsu*. In order to explain that *tsu* meant not ancestors in general but first ancestor, Cheng compared the usage to the case of nobles' sons who migrated to a different fiefdom and became first ancestors of their progeny there. K'ung failed to understand Cheng's analogy and mistook *wei tsu* (becoming ancestors) to be the corollary of moving to another state, hence making migration a second qualification of *pieh-tzu*.[99]

According to Wan Ssu-ta, the third meaning of *pieh-tzu* originated in Classical exegeses by Yüan neo-Confucians such as Ch'en Li (1252–1333) and Ch'en Hao (1261–1341).[100] To the Ch'ens, *pieh-tzu*, apart from the first and second uses, also designated commoners who became officials. This third meaning, Mao pointed out quite accurately, was an invention.[101]

Like Ch'en Ch'üeh, Mao embraced the traditional view that officers (*shih*) were granted the right to worship only their father for their rank qualified them to establish only one temple.[102] He maintained that the right to worship four generations in the temple did not reach below the great officials.[103] Mao was in effect challenging Ch'eng I's recommendation that everyone worship four generations. For Mao, this view was at variance with the principle of status differentiation. If everyone could worship four generations in the ancestral temple, how could the emperor distinguish himself from others?[104] He dismissed Ch'eng's idea as an invention without Classical precedent, although he conceded it was a good idea.[105]

Mao also disputed Wan's new interpretation of the number of generations lodged in one temple. Citing the "Chi-fa" (Methods of offering) chapter of the *Book of Rites*, he argued that "great officials," granted the right to establish three fanes, had no claim on worshiping their great-great-grandfather, as Wan had extrapolated.[106] In his suggestions for ancestral rites, Mao insisted that most people should honor only three generations of ascendants. The right to worship the great-great-grandfather was reserved for those with high official status.

Mao took a particularly great dislike to the *Family Rituals*, whose ceremonies were structured on the basis of the lesser descent-line principle, and severly criticized advocates of the descent-line system.[107] If this system could not be resurrected, neither could the rituals associated with it. Mao advised a friend against identifying the system with the five grades of mourning. The descent-line system required that the "heir" bear the heaviest ritual duties, which could deprive sons of their ritual obligations toward their natal parents. An adoptee who was a secondary son, for example, would have no ritual obligations toward his natal parents because of the need to elevate his adoptive parents over his own. For Mao, nothing was more absurd than applying the descent-line principle to mourning dress![108]

Other Critics of the Descent-Line System

Mao's profound Classical scholarship made a deep impression on Li Kung, the foremost spokesman for Yen Yüan's purist teachings. Li went to study with Mao in 1698.[109] No doubt, this decision was a result of his realization of the importance of Classical studies both in defending Yen Yüan's teachings and in the quest for canonical rites.

Quoting Mao's view, Li ridiculed those who aspired to restore the great descent-line system. Li insisted that in antiquity only the second son of a noble was made the great descent-line heir. The current practice of making the first son the descent-line heir violated this principle. Therefore, comparing the descent-line system to the current practice of establishing the lineal sons was misleading. More important, the status of descent-line heir in the Chou dynasty was accompanied by an inheritable office and rank. Inasmuch as there was no office and rank to bequeath, to speak of reviving descent-line system was absurd.[110]

Li, however, was by no means indifferent to the need for "unifying agnates" (*shou-tsu*). He recommended the building of "public lineage halls" (*kung-tz'u*) and delegating to lineage elders (*tsu-chang*) the ritual authority to direct ceremonials. The enshrined ancestors should begin with the first ancestor and not be confined to four generations as stipulated in the *Family Rituals*. Li, however, opposed the practice of establishing the first migrant ancestor or the first ascendant who became an official as the first ancestor unless the authentic original ancestor was unknown.[111]

Another critic of the idea of reviving the descent-line system was Wang Wan, an early Ch'ing *chin-shih* (1655) and a renowned essayist from Kiangsu.[112] Instead of drawing on the Classics for support, he pointed to the practical difficulties involved in reinstating the descent-line system. In his view, the descent-line heir in antiquity was a great official, who not only had a temple founded to honor his ancestors but also received a fief to provide for his scions. But the majority of contemporary descent-line heirs were plebeians with neither temple nor estate. How could they assume leadership in liturgies over kinsmen who possessed official rank? Furthermore, under the ancient descent-line system, property was held collectively. Surplus resources from individual households were returned to the lineage treasury, and funds for extra expenses were drawn from it. But in Wang's day it often happened that quarrels between father and son and among brothers over a pittance of wealth resulted in hostility, brawls, and even killings. Given such conditions, joint property was difficult to achieve even within a family. How much more difficult it would be to eliminate selfishness and to demand collectivization of all the properties of a kin group.[113]

Wang's last objection concerned mourning dress. In his view, mourning obligations ceased when a descent group branched off to form a separate unit.[114] But the great descent-line heir was distinguished by requiring agnates outside his five grades of mourning dress to mourn his death. This, Wang argued, was not stipulated in the Ch'ing Code.[115]

Gentry Status and the Descent-Line System

If we look at scholars' relationship with the Manchu regime, those who did not serve the Manchus tended to favor the *Family Rituals* model, and those who did tended to reject it. Chang Lü-hsiang and Lu Shih-i exemplify the first category; Mao Ch'i-ling and Wang Wan the second. This dichotomy cannot be pursued too far. Ch'en Ch'üeh's queries on the *Family Rituals'* prescriptions are noted earlier in this chapter, and some officials, generally affiliated with the Ch'eng-Chu school, followed the *Family Rituals* approach to lineage organization.

Hsü San-li, an official and an adherent of the Ch'eng-Chu school, deemed the descent-line system the foundation of all activities pertaining to ancestor worship. It was crucial not only to the structure and liturgy of the ancestral hall but also to the staff of the lineage organization. Unlike Lu Shih-i, who was concerned to make the descent-line system available to all regardless of status and wealth, Hsü stressed the attainment of official position (*kuei*) as the main qualification for the descent-line heir. He cited Classical sanction for his view from the *Classic of Filial Piety*, which spoke of the filial duties proper to great officials and officers in terms of their ability to retain their position in the government and of their devotion to performing sacrifices in the temple. Needless to say, this superficial exercise in Classicism could hardly be counted as serious scholarship. Of greater importance is that Hsü changed the qualification for descent-line heir from a biological status to the attainment of government position. In Hsü's view, this had the advantage of allowing agnates holding a government appointment to assume ritual leadership and to finance the construction of the ancestral hall as well as the regular expenditures entailed in the performance of liturgy.[116]

Hsü's criterion for the qualification of descent-line heir was representative of one version of the descent-line system practiced in the Ch'ing. Gentry subscribing to this view maintained that office was more important than genealogy to the operation of the descent-line system. Nowhere was this view justified more eloquently than in the writings of Li Kuang-ti.

Li deemed it impractical to revive the descent-line system outlined in the *Family Rituals* despite his devotion to the teachings of the Ch'eng-Chu school. To illustrate the difficulties involved, Li related the experiences of his own descent group in the Ming dynasty. Some members of the Li kin group had contemplated reviving the ancient descent-line system, but had encountered several obstacles. First, in high antiquity only the descent-line heir, who inherited his father's rank and emolument, was entitled to perform sacrifices to the ancestors. But since the system of inheritable office had long been abolished, no one qualified for this status. Second, in antiquity the status of descent-line heir was bestowed by the ruler, and generally all descent-line heirs were well-versed in rituals. In Li's times, some firstborns engaged in menial work, and they had neither knowledge nor experience of worship. As descent-line heir, they would be at a loss when called on to officiate in the liturgy. Third, the ancestors would feel humiliated to be tended by abjectly poor descendants. These difficulties had forced Li's forebears to resort to a system of alternating duty in monitoring worship.[117]

Li argued that changes in social conditions called for adjustments in ritual. The ancient rule that "secondary sons do not make sacrifice" should not be observed dogmatically because of its Classical origin. Instead, the rule that "only those receiving a government stipend make sacrifice" (*wu-lu pu-chi*) should be followed. Li suggested that only those who had attained office or examination degrees and were advanced in age should preside. Only when such persons were unavailable would the firstborn be made the descent-line heir and given authority over the conduct of ancestral rites.[118]

It is obvious that the descent-line systems advocated by Hsü San-li and Li Kuang-ti did not correspond with that in the *Family Rituals*. In their views, the status of descent-line heir should depend more on success in securing government office. They changed the qualification for descent-line heir from natal son in the lineal ancestry to possessor of gentry status. Where lineage leadership was concerned, Li wanted not so much to do away with the descent-line principle entirely as to subsume it under gentry control.

Apart from these objections raised by Confucian elite affiliated with the Ch'eng-Chu school, attempts to reinstate the descent-line system were criticized on the grounds that it would throw other rites into disarray. Li Fu (1675–1750), an important official and influential scholar inclined toward the teachings of Wang Yang-ming and Lu Chiu-yüan, scoffed at Wan Ssu-ta's idea that the descent-line system should be resurrected and other rituals be rectified accordingly.[119] For example, Wan opposed the common practice of appointing any surviving son as the director of funeral ceremonies in the absence of the first son. He suggested that the first son of the first son (the "first grandson," or *ti-sun*) officiate at the obsequies of his grandfather if he survived his father. Wan's argument derived substance from the descent-line system, which required the establishment of a descent-line heir vested with the exclusive right to worship ancestors. Since the first grandson was in the descent line, he, rather than a surviving uncle, should conduct the mortuary rites for his grandfather.[120]

Li Fu strongly disagreed with the method Wan proposed, for reasons similar to those of Mao Ch'i-ling. In the absence of heritable fiefs and offices, descent-line heirs had no means to command the respect and obedience of kindred. Li argued that neither the great descent-line system nor the lesser descent-line system could be rehabilitated.[121] Accordingly, he was disposed to condemn any attempt to bring rituals in line with the descent-line principle.

Li was particularly offended by exponents of applying the descent-line system to ancestral rites. As a worship system, the descent-line system called for centralization of ritual authority in the hands of the descent-line heir and relegated secondary sons to subordinate positions. For that reason, he ridiculed the *Family Rituals* for stressing the descent-line principle. He doubted that Chu Hsi himself had conducted all the ceremonies in accord with that principle.[122] In Li's view the best way to achieve greater kinship cohesion was to build lineage halls and compile genealogies.[123] In other words, he preferred an approach to lineage organization centered on an apical hall regardless of lineality.

Ritual Debate and the Study of Classical Antiquity

The controversy over the revival of the descent-line system continued well into the eighteenth century. References to the Classics became indispensable to any discussion of ancient ancestral rites. The noted *Spring and Autumn Annals* scholar Ku Tung-kao, and his good friend Yang Ch'un (1676–1753), for example, refuted arguments for reviving the descent-line

system by citing the Classics. Yang was wary of the consequences of a revival for the worship rights of each agnate. When Ku asked his opinion on
the Classical rule that "secondary sons do not make sacrifice," Yang drew
a distinction between the "family offering hall" (*chia-tz'u*) and the lineage
hall (*tsung-miao*). The contemporary family hall bore no resemblance to
the ancient lineage temple. Inasmuch as the family hall was a place for a
family to worship its ancestors, every agnate was entitled to erect one.[124]

He proceeded to explain that the ancient temple system had operated
in conjunction with a hereditary aristocracy and the descent-line system.
The descent-line heirs as a rule inherited office and emolument and were
able to shoulder ritual duties. With the disappearance of inheritable offices,
however, there was no assurance that the descent-line heir could procure
an office in the bureaucracy. But secondary sons often rose to high positions. The discrepancy in status and ritual authority rendered any attempt
to adhere to the descent-line principle meaningless.[125]

Revival of the descent-line system would also entail that the descent-
line heir officiate in the temple liturgy. But the temple was now nothing
more than a family shrine honoring several generations of ancestors. With
the descent-line principle in force, the descent-line heir would monitor the
ceremony regardless of the presence of senior kinsmen, and elders would
have to bow to a descent-line heir who was their junior. This would not
only affront the living but displease the deceased.[126]

Yang proposed that each agnate erect a family altar in his own house
and worship his four immediate ancestors. With each change in generation, those more distant than the great-great-grandfather would be displaced. Yang noted Mao Ch'i-ling's objection to the worship of four immediate ancestors, but he argued that in the Classics officials did have the
right to worship their great-great-grandfather. His source was the "Ta-
chuan" chapter in the *Book of Rites*, which recorded that officials could
obtain permission from the ruler to worship their great-great-grandfather
on "big occasions" (*ta-shih*). Cheng Hsüan had erred in commenting on
this passage by rendering *kan* as "empty" (*k'ung*) and hence *kan hsia* as
"worship all ancestors without temple." Yang took the word *kan* to mean
"request" (*ch'iu*), for "request to worship all ancestors in the temple."
"How absurd it would be to worship all ancestors in the wilderness when
there was a temple!" he commented. Yang further enlisted the support of
Ch'eng I's well-known argument on the mourning circle and ancestral
rites.[127] Yang was arguing against applying the descent-line system to ancestral rites within the mourning circle of five generations. It is ironic that

he adopted Ch'eng I's views on quaternary ancestry but rejected Ch'eng's attempt to rehabilitate the descent-line system.

Yang's friend Ku Tung-kao argued against the system in terms of historical changes. Arguing along the lines of Mao Ch'i-ling, Li Fu, and others, Ku insisted that the descent-line system had been an inalienable constituent of the "feudal polity." Without fiefs and the income emanating from them, it was beyond the means of the descent-line heir to keep his kin from falling into destitution. The material basis to carry out his main duty of unifying agnates no longer existed. Nor could he command respect and compliance when he had no claim to official rank bestowed by the emperor. Ku pointed to the numerous examples of secondary sons whose talents gained them high office and to as many cases of great descent-line heirs whose ineptitude drove them down the social scale. To press his case further, Ku cited the T'ang writer Liu Tsung-yüan's *Feng-chien lun* (On feudalism), a widely known critique of this anachronism. Liu ridiculed attempts to reinstate "feudal" institutions because of the uncertainty regarding the quality of the descent-line heir. The Chou rulers had adopted the descent-line system not because they favored the principle of heredity but because they had to reckon with circumstances. It was nothing but an institution that grew out of circumstances and was by no means intended as a sacred system to be emulated by future generations irrespective of changes.[128]

Although Ku expressed disdain for resurrecting the obsolete descent-line system, he committed himself to the current fad of "unifying kinsmen." Officials could practice an attenuated form of the descent-line system privately. This should not be a part of their bureaucratic functions. Those moved by the lofty ideal could put their resources at the service of their agnates, who would then look to them as the descent-line heir by virtue of their benevolence.[129]

The debate did not conclude with Yang Ch'un and Ku T'ung-k'ao. In the early eighteenth century, Yin Hui-i (1691–1748) and Wang Fu (1692–1759) argued that the descent-line system could be installed without reviving the institution of hereditary office.[130] To conclude this chapter, we need to take a closer look at the crux of the debate.

Wan Ssu-ta was arguing that there were two proper ways for kin groups to worship ancestors, both based on the descent-line principle. Agnates belonging to lesser descent-lines would worship ancestors as far removed as the great-great-grandfather. The scope of the lineage therefore did not reach beyond three collateral lines. The ancestral hall of the great descent-line would, in addition to the four immediate ancestors, house a first ancestor. The lesser descent-line systems, though descended from the same first ancestor, did not have the right to worship him. These types of halls were much less inclusive than the type of lineage hall preferred by Mao Ch'i-ling, Li Kung, and Li Fu. Its gravest disadvantage, in its opponents' view, lay in its adherence to the descent-line principle.

As conceived by Wan Ssu-ta, Ku Yen-wu, and Lu Shih-i, the descent-line principle was operative in ancestral rites and would strengthen kinship ties. This institution was to function with no connection to the larger political structure. It was meant to be a purely private ritual rooted in the Classics. A lineage so organized might serve scholars well when they had no concern about the position of officials within the lineage organization, but their attempts immediately alarmed those who served the Manchus.

Mao Ch'i-ling favored the building of a more inclusive lineage hall, without regard for descent-line principles. Since this type of hall was not based on the descent-line system, it did not encroach on the right of each individual, especially those holding government office, to worship his three immediate ancestors at home. The leader of the liturgical services to commemorate the first ancestor and the great-great-grandfather must be a high official.[131] Mao preferred lineage halls that enshrined ancestors even further removed than the great-great-grandfather. A greater generational depth allowed otherwise unrelated agnates to participate in the ceremonial. Mao's model can be distinguished from Wan Ssu-ta's by the inclusion of ancestors between the first ancestor and the great-great-grandfather; he recommended ten generations for a lineage hall.[132] Mao noted that the type of ancestral hall prescribed in the *Family Rituals* was not a common choice.[133] Like Li Fu, he regarded the worship of first migrant ancestor as a necessary accommodation to changing times. Both men favored the building of ancestral halls and the strengthening of kinship ties without reinstating the descent-line system.

These differences in reading the Classics contributed to a considerable degree to disputes over the proper way to organize a descent group. Beneath the conflict lay a more fundamental clash between bureaucracy and feudalism. The Classical descent-line system could not be revived in an age in which political power and wealth came with examination degrees and official status. Being a descent-line heir required leisure for education and liturgical observances. A descent-line heir with neither government office nor wealth could not be expected to assume leadership in a lineage. Only by enlisting the authority, power, and wealth of officials could loosely connected kin be assembled.

Ironically, as we saw in the last chapter, Ku Yen-wu and Lu Shih-i aspired to revive the descent-line system as an institution independent of the political structure of the state. Lu Shih-i even took pains to reduce to a minimum the expenses entailed by ritual performances. He hoped this would enable poor descent-line heirs to fulfill their obligations.[134] Their means for achieving their goal were, however, at odds with their desire to strengthen the status of the gentry class. Political power rested in the bureaucracy, and only those members of a descent group who were officials were in a position to command respect and hence the authority to organize their agnates. Li Fu pointed to the heart of the problem when he accused those insistent on practicing the descent-line system as "substituting a privately established descent-line heir for rank and office conferred by the kingdom [kuo]."[135] Without doubt, the apical lineage hall was a more flexible model for building lineages, despite considerable disputes over the proper way to organize a lineage. Small wonder that in the eighteenth century it proliferated at a rate so great as to alarm scholars.[136] In mid-nineteenth century, Li Yüan-tu (1821–87), a native of Hunan, noted that lineage halls had spread "throughout the whole realm under heaven."[137]

Unlike Wan Ssu-ta, scholars such as Mao Ch'i-ling and Li Fu did not justify what they advocated in terms of Classical studies. They, like many others, believed that ritual practice should be adjusted to accommodate change, but they were compelled to delve into the Classics for evidence to support their critique of the ritual innovations of Sung neo-Confucians. Without serious research, it would have been impossible to recognize the misinterpretations and abuses of the Classics they thought many Sung neo-Confucians and later scholars such as Wan Ssu-ta had committed. The need to clarify the ancestral rites and other rituals prompted many scholars to take up rigorous research in the Classics, especially those on rituals. Nonetheless, the descent-line system and the *Family Rituals* continued to inspire lineage building and to stimulate Classical scholarship in the early eighteenth century.

5

Ritual and the Classics in the Early Ch'ing

In Chapters 3 and 4, we saw how the battle over ancestral rites in relation to lineage organization was fought out in the interpretation of the Classics. In this chapter we shall probe further into the relationship between the emphasis on ancient ritual and the growing importance of historical studies of Classical antiquity.

Sung neo-Confucianists departed from previous Confucian traditions in many significant ways. They not only had a profound interest in metaphysical questions and the relation of the cosmos to humanity, but also reinterpreted the history of high antiquity by writing their own exegeses of the Confucian Classics. The revival of Ch'eng-Chu learning and the growth of Classicism in the K'ang-hsi and early Ch'ien-lung periods contributed to the upsurge of interest in Sung and Yüan exegetical scholarship. Those who esteemed Sung neo-Confucianism, however, were interested less in its teachings concerning cosmology and ontology than in its expositions on the Classics, especially on ancient rituals. The Classical past they resurrected was by and large the legacy of Sung-Yüan scholarship.

A study of this revival of Sung-Yüan classical scholarship not only demonstrates the waning interest in metaphysical discourse among adherents of Ch'eng-Chu learning but also illuminates the circumstances leading to the rise of the Han Learning school in the mid-eighteenth century. That school's attacks on Sung Learning and Chu Hsi's scholarship were aimed not so much at neo-Confucian metaethics as at the exegetical traditions forged by Sung and Yüan neo-Confucians. Adherents of the Han Learning criticized the exponents of Ch'eng-Chu learning partly for their continued endorsement of the mild textual skepticism they inherited from their Sung predecessors and partly for their critical stance vis-à-vis Han exegeses. Despite its iconoclastic potential, the textual skepticism of the Sung Learning as well as that of the K'ang-hsi period in general was directed only at the authorship and some parts of the Classics. It was by no means aimed at Confucianism as a belief system.

A review of trends in ritual studies will allow us to trace the course Classical studies took before the mid-eighteenth century. These trends will be examined under two headings: a detailed analysis of the divergent views on two great rites, *ti* (grand worship) and *hsia* (collective worship), which were as controversial as they were crucial to kinship rituals; and a review of the studies of a group of scholars who worked in the Bureau for the Compilation of the Three Ritual Classics, (San-li kuan), a government office for the compilation of commentaries on these Classics.

Ritual Studies Before the Mid-Eighteenth Century

The various attempts among the Confucian elite to reform rituals and to cement kinship bonds resulted in conflicting interpretations of ancient rituals. The study of rituals, largely neglected until the last decades of the Ming, was pursued increasingly as a serious scholarly effort, especially within the framework of Classical studies. Scholars committed to resurrecting Confucian rituals had to examine intensively the three ritual Classics, the *Rites of Chou*, the *Book of Etiquette and Decorum*, and the *Book of Rites*. As the K'ang-hsi period unfolded, Classical and ritual studies came to dominate scholarship. Increasingly in the early K'ang-hsi period ritual studies were characterized by a topical approach, eclecticism, and the prominence of Chu Hsi's ritual scholarship.

The Topical Approach to Ritual Studies

Writings on rituals in this period often took the form of treatises, essays, and notes on specific rituals. This topical format clearly arose from the need to clarify ritual practice. For example, Ch'en Ch'üeh and Chang Lü-hsiang wrote notes on miscellaneous rituals used in obsequies and ancestor worship. They were in particular noted for their attack on Buddhist rites.[1] Chang Lü-hsiang wrote extensive notes criticizing improper popular mourning and funerary customs.[2] To express his objection to the current practices of cremation and delays in burial to allow time to find an auspicious grave site, Ch'en wrote a treatise on the proper ways to construct a burial vault and to inter the dead.[3]

In his attempt to revive the descent-line system in ancestor worship, Lu Shih-i set down in 1667 his specific ideas in *Tsung-chi li* (Ancestral worship based on the descent-line principle).⁴ In his widely read *Ssu-pien lu chi-yao* (Selected records of reflections), he discussed various rituals, ranging from the imperial temple system to sacrifices to mourning grades to social deportment.⁵

Shen Yün, another student of Liu Tsung-chou and a good friend of Ch'en Ch'üeh, compiled a practical manual of obsequies entitled *Shih sang-li* (Funeral rites for scholars) to provide instructions for his students.⁶ Shen's friend Ying Hui-ch'ien (1615–83), also an admirer of Liu Tsung-chou, wrote a voluminous work on a wide range of rituals entitled *Li-hsüeh hui-pien* (Collection of ritual studies) in 70 *chüan*.⁷ Ying included illustrations of some ritual vessels in a separate *chüan*.⁸ Ying's colossal undertaking was, however, not so much an exegesis on the Classics as a compendium on rituals.⁹

Ku Yen-wu's contributions to Classical studies and thinking on statecraft are well documented, but not his concern for rituals and his scholarship in this area. Like Ch'en Ch'üeh and Chang Lü-hsiang, he censured Buddhist influence in popular practices.¹⁰ His interest and research on rituals are evidenced by his *Wu-ching t'ung-i* (Concordance and differences in the Five Classics) and *Jih-chih lu* (Records of daily learning). He copied verbatim essays by other scholars, including Wan Ssu-ta and Wang Wan, into the *Wu-ching t'ung-i*. The writings he found worthy of inclusion covered a wide range of rites such as the descent-line system and the most controversial rites, the *ti* and *hsia*.¹¹ In the *Jih-chih lu*, he wrote on such topics as mourning grades, adoption, burial, and lineage.¹² Correction of improper customs and social protocols were an important part of the *Jih-chih lu*, a work regarded as representative of Ku's statecraft thought.

Mao Ch'i-ling, the sophisticated polymath, produced several treatises on rituals. In many cases these challenged the prescriptions of the *Family Rituals*. As mentioned in Chapter 4, he wrote the *Ta-hsiao tsung t'ung-shih* to discourage the revival of the descent-line system. To meet the growing concern about proper rites, he wrote a manual on funerary and ancestral rites, wedding ceremonies, and the temple system.¹³ Apart from these practical writings, he wrote extensively on Classical rituals. In accord with contemporary practice, however, Mao left no systematic commentary on any one of the three ritual Classics despite his deep interest in scholarship on the subject.

Li Kung learned the importance of practicing proper Confucian rituals under Yen Yüan's tutelage. After he made the acquaintance of Mao Ch'i-ling, he promptly devoted himself to Classical studies. Li made no attempt to treat any of the ritual Classics fully. Instead, he completed in 1698 and 1699 a number of essays on temple structure and various sacrifices.[14] In addition, he wrote extensive notes on various ritual matters, which were published in a volume entitled *Hsüeh li* (Learning rituals).[15]

Wang Wan became interested in ritual studies after the demise of the Ming but did not produce a commentary on the entire text of any of the three ritual Classics. His collected writings contain many treatments of ancient and current ritual matters, however.[16]

Yen Jo-chü, Wang's formidable opponent, outwitted Wang in debates over whether the ancients studied mortuary rites while their parents were still alive. Like others, Yen was more concerned about rituals of a practical nature and wrote supplementary notes on mourning dress.[17]

Given this strong orientation toward practice, it is not surprising that throughout most of the K'ang-hsi reign, research on the three ritual Classics rarely took the form of annotations of an entire Classic, much less supplementary comments on exegetical works of previous times. The Classics were consulted for criteria of propriety. As discussed in previous chapters, in the early K'ang-hsi period a large group of scholars born in the first three decades of the seventeenth century committed themselves to studies of Classical rituals. Few, however, attempted a systematic annotation of the three ritual Classics as a purely scholastic exercise.[18] Chang Erh-ch'i and Wang Fu-chih (1619–92) were among the few who wrote a formal commentary to one or other of the ritual Classics.[19]

Although most privately produced books on the ritual Classics may have borne the name of the Classics, few produced before the 1750's were faithful to the textual order of the Classics. In his study of the *Book of Rites*, Wang Hsin-ching (1656–1738), a student of the noted neo-Confucian Li Jung, rearranged the order of its chapters. Wang's study was divided into three parts and opened with Confucius' remarks on rituals followed by the chapters on the "Great Learning" and the "Doctrine of the Mean."[20] This flexibility, characteristic of most works on Classical rituals, clearly suggested that scholars in this period did not consider themselves engaged in purely academic exercises.

As discussed in Chapter 4, Wan Ssu-ta wrote a long treatise on the descent-line system and many other rituals. His greatest works on ritual scholarship are *I-li shang* (Discussion of the *Book of Etiquette and Decorum*), *Li-chi ou-chien* (Casual notations on the *Book of Rites*, and *Chou-kuan pien-fei* (Clarifying errors in the *Rites of Chou*).[21] These collections of critical essays deal with specific issues in each Classic. His brother Wan Ssu-t'ung is better known for his contributions to the *Ming History* project, and his profound knowledge of ritual has remained largely unexplored.[22] He and many of his friends including Yen Jo-chü, Fang Pao (1668–1749), and Li Kung were deeply committed to ritual studies.[23] Wan Ssu-t'ung wrote a long essay on the temple systems of the major dynasties. In his studies of Ming history, he expressed his disapproval of the title the Chia-ching emperor adopted for his father, the incident that provoked the notorious Great Rites controversy.[24] Most of Wan's ritual studies are preserved in the *Ch'ün-shu i-pien* (Doubts about and criticism of various books).[25] He is also credited with compiling a magnum opus on the rites, *Tu-li t'ung-k'ao* (A comprehensive study of rituals), on behalf on Hsü Ch'ien-hsüeh, in 120 *chüan*.[26] It remained the most voluminous work on rituals until Ch'in Hui-tien produced his *Wu-li t'ung-k'ao* (Comprehensive study of the five categories of rituals), a compendium of rituals in 262 *chüan*. Neither work was meant to be a commentary to the Classics.

Sung-Yüan Scholarship and Eclecticism

The second characteristic of ritual research before the 1750's was the absence of a sharp differentiation of Sung scholarship and Han exegeses as two systems of hermeneutics based on diverse sets of intellectual and methodological premises. Classical scholarship in the early Ch'ing did not begin where Han scholars had left off but continued to thrive on the foundation laid by Sung, Yüan, and Ming scholarship. Neo-Confucianism since the Sung dynasty had developed a critical approach to the Classics and the post-Classical commentaries. The superiority of Han exegeses to the scholia of subsequent periods had yet to be established. To the contrary, although the writings of Cheng Hsüan and Hsü Shen (d. A.D. 120?), the author of the *Shuo-wen chieh-tzu*, were beginning to receive greater recognition, many scholars used them critically.

Before the mid-eighteenth century, when the wedge between Han and Sung exegeses was to be driven deeper, Cheng Hsüan and other Han scholiasts were less respected than Sung scholars.[27] The case of Wan Ssu-t'ung is representative. His Classical scholarship shows a general preference for Sung exegeses. In many cases Wan took Cheng Hsüan to task.[28] To him, Cheng's expositions on the Classics for the most part were a flight of imagination.[29] The intensity of Wan's diatribes against Cheng's scholarship brought protests from his contemporaries. When asked to account for his apparent partiality, he argued that the Han scholars' antecedence in time did not necessarily make their scholarship more credible. In his judgment, Ch'eng I excelled in grasping the meaning of the Classics and revealing the distortions of the Han scholars.[30] Wan Ssu-ta's friend Ying Hui-ch'ien also took the liberty of refuting Cheng Hsüan's commentaries on the Classics on rites.[31]

The idea that Cheng's learning did not deserve exceptional commendation continued to inform works on the three ritual Classics written before 1750; for example, Chiang Chao-hsi's (1666–1745) *Li-chi i-chang* (The meanings of the *Book of Rites* in chapters), Jen Ch'i-yün's (1670–1744) *Li-chi chang-chü* (*Book of Rites* in chapters and verses), and Fang Pao's *I-li shih-i* (Explanations of doubts about the *Book of Etiquette and Decorum*).[32] These scholars readily accepted explications by other exegetes. Even Mao Ch'i-ling, a leading critic of Ch'eng-Chu learning, did not appeal to Cheng Hsüan as the authority. In his appraisal of previous scholarship, he showed no great regard for Cheng's commentaries and much less for those of the T'ang exegete K'ung Ying-ta, which he took great satisfaction in denouncing.[33] (For his specific criticisms of Cheng Hsüan, see the discussion below of the controversy over *ti* and *hsia*.)

Despite their relatively critical stance toward the Han glosses, however, most scholars of the K'ang-hsi period did not dogmatically reject Han commentaries. Few dichotomized exegetical traditions into Han and Sung, as would be done increasingly after the mid–eighteenth century. There was, in fact, a growing recognition of the Han exegetes' expertise on ritual matters. Ku Yen-wu praised Chang Erh-ch'i for his efforts to revive Cheng Hsüan's scholium on the *Book of Etiquette and Decorum*. To Ku, Cheng was unmatched in his knowledge of ritual.[34] Even Lu Lung-ch'i, the universally acclaimed luminary of Ch'eng-Chu neo-Confucianism in early Ch'ing, found Cheng Hsüan more reliable than some T'ang and Sung scholars. Lu criticized K'ung Ying-ta and Chia Kung-yen for accepting Cheng Hsüan's views uncritically, but he found their complaisance commendable in comparison to that of other T'ang scholars such as Chao K'uang (fl. 770) and Tan Chu (d. 770), whose flights of fancy knew no bounds.[35] Lu strove to maintain a critical stance toward previous exegetical learning. He disparaged Cheng Hsüan's infatuation with spurious texts (*wei-shu*), but thought highly of his philological annotations.[36] Lu after all was a staunch believer in Chu Hsi, and despite Cheng Hsüan's high achievements, Chu Hsi was still the pre-eminent Classical scholar in Lu's mind.[37]

Chu Hsi and Ritual Scholarship

The third characteristic of ritual studies before the 1750's was the prominence given to Chu Hsi's teachings about ritual matters. Many works were in varying degrees inspired by either the *Family Rituals* or *I-li ching-chuan t'ung-chieh* (A general exposition of the Classic and commentaries on the *Book of Etiquette and Decorum*), an unfinished study by Chu. As we have seen, the *Family Rituals* stimulated both ritual practices and ritual scholarship and served as a primer for gentry attempts to establish family rituals.[38] Chang Lü-hsiang, for example, observed the rituals prescribed in the *Family Rituals* during the mourning for his mother.[39] Many of his friends, including Ch'en Ch'üeh and Wu Fan-ch'ang, followed in earnest most of its ritual instructions.[40]

As noted in previous chapters, the cultural symbolism of the *Family Rituals* resulted in its promotion by Chinese scholars serving the Manchus. Wei Hsiang-shu (1617–87), a native of Shansi, began to serve the Manchus as early as 1646.[41] He was committed to promoting the *Family Rituals* both privately and publicly. In 1684 he memorialized the K'ang-hsi emperor that the *Family Rituals* should serve as one of the models for a new system of rituals for all classes under the new regime.[42] Privately, he urged a friend to edit and publish the *Family Rituals* for the sake of upholding the moral order.[43]

In 1701 Sung Lao (1634–1710), in his capacity as governor of Kiangsu, printed the *Family Rituals* together with Ch'iu Chün's elaborate notes on etiquette, Sung's great-granduncle's ritual instructions, and Lü Nan's (1479–1542) *Ssu-li yüeh-yen* (Essential remarks on the four types of ritual.[44] Chu Shih's *I-li chieh-yao* (Essentials of the *Book of Etiquette and Decorum*) in 20 *chüan*, completed in 1719, was in essence a manual based on the *Family Rituals*.[45] In addition to other writings on rituals, Jen Ch'i-yün wrote the *Chia-li cho* (Deliberations on the *Family Rituals*), in all likelihood as a guide for practical rituals.[46] For most scholars, the *Family Rituals* was the point of departure in ritual practice and studies, despite criticism of its ideas.

The overwhelming influence of Chu Hsi's views on rituals, however, was not confined to the *Family Rituals*. His *I-li ching-chuan t'ung-chieh* prompted many grand projects for amassing information on rituals in the late seventeenth and early eighteenth centuries. The first such work was Hsü Ch'ien-hsüeh's *Tu-li t'ung-k'ao* (A comprehensive study of rituals), a colossal work in 120 *chüan*.

Hsü began studying rituals during his mourning for his mother in 1677.[47] With the help of Wan Ssu-t'ung, Yen Jo-chü, Ku Yen-wu, Chu I-tsun (1629–1709), and others, he was able to accumulate a formidable collection of information on mourning ceremonies and obsequies.[48] The original plan was a work devoted exclusively to the study of those rituals, but in 1694 at the suggestion of Chu I-tsun, Hsü decided to expand the work to incorporate other kinds of rituals.[49] He died before he could celebrate the completion of the new project, but the finished manuscript was printed posthumously as *Tu-li t'ung-k'ao* in 1696.[50]

The work was encyclopedic in conception. Its organization was partly modeled on that of Chu Hsi's *I-li ching-chuan t'ung-chieh*, grouping variant explications under each rite.[51] The work made extensive use of writings on rituals by contemporary scholars, including Chang Erh-ch'i, Wang Wan, Huang Tsung-hsi, Lu Yüan-fu (1617–91), Ying Hui-ch'ien, and those who helped Hsü with its compilation.[52] Like the *I-li ching-chuan t'ung-chieh* and most other important works on rituals of this period, the *Tu-li t'ung-k'ao* was not intended to be a commentary on any particular ritual Classics. It was undertaken largely in response to practical needs and cumulative inquiries into the theory and practice of rituals.

Hsü's model in turn prompted another and much grander project to compile a comprehensive account of ritual scholarship. Ch'in Hui-tien lamented that Chu Hsi's students Huang Kan (1152–1221) and Yang Fu had failed to complete Chu's *I-li ching-chuan t'ung-chieh*. During his mourning for a parent in 1747–48, Ch'in read Hsü's *Tu-li t'ung-k'ao* and commended it as compatible with Chu Hsi's original design. Ch'in and some of his friends agreed to collaborate on a new project, the *Wu-li t'ung-k'ao*, based on the models of the *Tu-li t'ung-k'ao* and *I-li ching-chuan t'ung-chieh*.[53] It took 38 years to complete.[54] Over the long period of the undertaking, Ch'in sought assistance from many scholars. Among them were Fang Kuan-ch'eng (1698–1768), a nephew of Fang Pao, and some younger scholars who were to attain prominence as Classicists in the second half of the eighteenth century, such as Wang Ming-sheng (1722–97), Tai Chen, Wang Ch'ang (1725–1807), and Ch'ien Ta-hsin.[55]

Whereas both the *Tu-li t'ung-k'ao* and the *Wu-li t'ung-k'ao* were accomplished by collective effort, Chiang Yung's *Li-shu kang-mu* (Outline of books on rites) was a result of the determination and industry of one person. This exacting undertaking, a work in 85 *chüan*, was written in emulation of the *I-li ching-chuan t'ung-chieh* and intended to bring Chu Hsi's work to a higher level of perfection in terms of organization.[56] Like the

Tu-li t'ung-k'ao and *Wu-li t'ung-k'ao*, this work was meant to be read not as a commentary on the ritual Classics but as a comprehensive scholarly reference work.

These encyclopedic works on rituals did not, however, serve the purposes of scholars who sought consistency in understanding Classical rites. As scholars probed deeper into the multilayered exegetical traditions, some realized that, for the most part, variations in the commentaries had generated conflicting expositions. More important, they discovered that through the mediation of the commentaries non–Confucian ideas had infiltrated the Classics. Anyone who depended on commentaries to unravel ancient rituals ran the risk of skewing Confucianism. An independent and historical approach to the Classics would be more productive, they felt. An analysis of the debate over the *ti* and *hsia* rites will demonstrate the increasing importance accorded knowledge of the general historical background as a basis for a more consistent understanding of ancient rituals.

The Debate over *Ti* and *Hsia*

The purist passion for true Confucian rites continued to inspire rigorous research on the Classics. As the attempt to restore the Classical rites and the effort to purge heterodox elements proceeded, historical empiricism became an essential component of Confucian purism. Scholars began to treat the Classics increasingly as ancient history, as sources for an accurate understanding of high antiquity.

Toward the end of the seventeenth century, ritual issues initially studied for practical reasons came to be tackled increasingly as historical and textual topics within the discipline of Classical scholarship. This increasing academic and historical orientation of Classical studies was made inevitable by the need to corroborate one's views on a specific rite. It became apparent that an accurate understanding of ancient ritual called for nothing short of a comprehensive study of all the rites related to those under discussion. As Wan Ssu-ta had cautioned, a fragmented approach to the Classics was of no avail. What was needed was a systematic and integrative reconstruction of rites as historical events. To do this, scholars had to piece together scattered information from the various Classics and to clarify ambiguities and explain away contradictions in the Classics.[57] Prompted by the purist quest, this approach necessarily fostered a critical spirit that not only challenged preceding exegetical traditions but also generated skepticism of some Classical texts. These strains were already apparent in the Classical learning of such scholars as the Wan brothers, Mao Ch'i-ling, and Li Kung, as will be borne out in the following discussion of *ti* and *hsia*.

These rites were two of the most controversial issues in Classical scholarship on ancestral rites. When early Ch'ing scholars disputed the proper rites for the ancestral hall, they invariably had to deal with the ancient practice of *ti* and *hsia*. For our purposes, the complex issues involved can be reduced to six questions. (1) Were *hsia* and *ti* the same ceremony? (2) If not, which was more important? (3) How often were they performed? (4) Was *ti* a ceremony undertaken to honor the first ancestor in the temple or to honor Heaven? (5) Was *ti* performed in the ancestral temple or in the open? (6) As a fiefdom, the Lu state had performed *ti*. Did the rulers of Lu transgress and exceed their status, or had they been granted the privilege by the Chou king? To answer these questions, Ch'ing scholars returned to the different exegetical traditions developed by scholiasts of the Han and subsequent dynasties.

There are three major explications of *ti* in Han exegeses. First, it was explained as a special ceremony, in addition to the regular rites (*shih-chi*), the Chou king undertook to worship his ancestors at a three- and/or a five-year interval. In his *Wu-ching i-i* (Different meanings of the Five Classics), Hsü Shen glossed *ti* as a ceremony held every three years, but in his widely read *Shuo-wen chieh-tzu* (Explaining writing and characters) he said it was held every five years. Despite the difference in time span, *ti* and *hsia* were the same rites for him. Hsü's view that *ti* and *hsia* are different names for the same rite was shared by other Han scholars, such as Liu Hsin (?–23) and Chia K'uei (30–101). Cheng Hsüan, in contrast, argued that *ti* was held every five years, in contrast to the *hsia*—a ceremony to honor all ancestors en masse—which was held every three years, and hence was less important.[58] Therefore, for Cheng the *hsia* differed from the *ti*.

Second, *ti* is also glossed as a "concluding ceremony" (*chung-ti*) performed at the end of the mourning period, in which the new king informed his deceased predecessor of the latter's new residence in the temple. Both Hsü and Cheng espoused this meaning.[59]

In addition to the first and second meanings, Cheng explained *ti* in yet another two senses: a ceremony to heavenly deities (*t'ien-shen*) held on a mound in the open; and a ceremony to earthly specters at the altar of Earth (*fang-tse*). Unlike the first two meanings, this third explication glosses *ti* as a sacrifice whose main object of worship was not a human ancestor in the temple. Under the influence of spurious texts, Cheng believed that the first ancestors of the founders of dynasties were sons of deities. He rendered *ti* as a sacrifice to honor the heavenly origin (*so tzu ch'u*) of the ruler's first ancestor. This *ti* was an exclusive prerogative of the Chou king. Since the principal object of worship was Heaven, ancestors of the king other than the first ancestor were not included in the ceremony. It is therefore not a "collective worship" (*hsia*) of the ancestors in the temples (*ch'ün-miao*).[60] Cheng glossed *ti* as such in most of his commentaries on the *Book of Rites*, the *Book of Etiquette and Decorum*, the *Book of Odes* and the *Analects*.[61] It was the last sense of *ti* that bore directly on the problem of worshiping the first ancestor in the lineage ancestral hall.

The Legacy of Neo-Confucianism and the Ch'ing Debate

The worship of the first ancestor and the collective worship of all ancestors emerged in early Ch'ing scholarly discourse as the two rites of paramount importance to lineage building. In his treatise on *ti*, Wan Ssu-ta made this connection explicit by drawing a parallel between *ti* and a descent group's worship of the first ancestor in conjunction with all other ancestors.[62] The need to discover the nature and historically accurate liturgical details of *ti* and *hsia* became acute.

As discussed in the preceding chapter, Ch'eng I was the first to advocate worship of the first ancestor in his seasonal worship schedule (*shih-chi*). Since, Ch'eng argued, all members of a descent group owed their existence to the first ancestor, he should be honored even though he was not enshrined in the ancestral hall. With Chu Hsi, this rite became associated with the ancient imperial rite of *ti*.[63] In addition, Ch'eng I proposed that a ceremony be held in the second month of spring in memory of all ancestors from the primogenitor to the great-great-great-grandfather. This came close to the ancient rite of *hsia*, a ceremony allowed only to aristocrats.[64]

To Chu Hsi, however, the oblation to the first ancestor recommended by Ch'eng I paralleled the *ti* ceremony, which only the king could perform.[65] In high antiquity, it had been the sole prerogative of the son of heaven and the nobility to worship a first ancestor further removed than the great-great-grandfather. Only officials who had done great service to the king could worship their great-great-grandfather. In brief, it was a transgression of status for officials to perform *ti*.[66]

Cheng Hsüan's inconsistent comments elicited criticism from Sung neo-Confucians. Chang Tsai disputed Cheng Hsüan's view that *ti* and *hsia* were held at intervals of three and five years. He suspected that they were performed annually.[67] Chu Hsi, in responding to a question regarding the nature of *ti* and *hsia*, criticized Cheng's expositions of these rituals as mutually contradictory.[68]

In the early Ch'ing, Cheng Hsüan's exegesis was attacked by scholars such as Wan Ssu-ta, Wan Ssu-t'ung, Ku Yen-wu, and Mao Ch'i-ling. All took exception to Cheng's exposition on *ti*, particularly to his distinction between *ti* and *hsia*. In Wan Ssu-ta's view, Cheng Hsüan's definition of *ti* as a grand ceremony held every five years and hence a lesser ceremony than *hsia* derived from the spurious *Li-wei*. *Ti* was not a special ceremony to honor the first ancestor exclusively but a "group worship" (*hsia*) for all ancestors in the temple.[69] *Ti* and *hsia* were different names for the same ceremony. Their identity rendered meaningless any question as to which was the greater ceremony.

Wan Ssu-ta also took exception to Hsü Shen's explanation. It was a mistake, Wan argued, to view *ti* as a rite held by the successor to the throne at the end of the three-year mourning period.[70] Wan concluded that *ti* was performed in the Chou dynasty to honor the first ancestor and all other ancestors in the temple.[71] His brother Wan Ssu-t'ung agreed and held Cheng Hsüan responsible for sowing confusion through his inconsistent explications of the term.[72] Wan went so far as to say that "in order to understand the nature of the *ti* rite, nothing is more important than to know the errors of Cheng Hsüan's exposition. Only then can the meaning of *ti* be discussed."[73]

According to Wan Ssu-t'ung, the true meaning of the *ti* had been lost amid the contradictory explications of Cheng Hsüan. He focused especially on Cheng's reading of *ti* as a ceremony to worship Heaven. Cheng's speculative comment had obfuscated the original purpose of *ti*, which was essentially an oblation by the ruler to honor and repay his ancestors. Wan's criticism of Cheng notwithstanding, he was aware that Cheng was a victim of the incredible mass of apocrypha (*wei-shu*) in circulation during the Eastern Han dynasty.[74] Once these views entered Cheng Hsüan's scholia, they became the orthodox references for these rites.[75] Cheng's gloss of *ti* went unchallenged until Chao K'uang of the T'ang dynasty. Chao pointed out that *ti* was a rite to honor a human primogenitor not Heaven.[76] Wan praised Ch'eng I for his insightful remark that *ti* designated the sacrifice a ruler made to commemorate the ancestor from whom the first ancestor of his descended.

The purist strain is discernible in the Wan brothers' critique of Cheng Hsüan's exegeses. It was apparent to them that the hazards of relying on commentaries were considerable. Through the mistakes of commentators, unorthodox ideas such as those in the spurious texts had been introduced into the Classics, subverting the authentic ritual of the sages. For Wan Ssu-t'ung, where *ti* and *hsia* were concerned, it was not so much the Sung glosses as the Han exegeses that had obscured the Classics: "These annotators of the Classics were entirely dependent on the spurious *wei-shu*, as have been those who institute rites. Therefore, ever since the Three Dynasties, there have been only apocryphal *wei-shu*, but no Classics." [77]

Critics of Wan Ssu-t'ung's partiality toward the Sung exegetical traditions argued that the Han scholars' explications were more reliable because they were closer than the Sung exegetes to Classical antiquity. Wan retorted that despite their temporal precedence the Han commentators had misread the texts. Worse were the liberties they took in passing on fictitious accounts. Only through the efforts of students in the T'ang and Sung periods had the genuine institutions of Classical antiquity been recovered.[78] The critical view of the Wan brothers was built on the exegetical tradition begun by Wang Su (d. A.D. 256) and continued by Chao K'uang and Ma Tuan-lin (1223–89). The charges hurled at Cheng Hsüan by many scholars followed a similar line of argument.[79] Wan argued that the Han scholars had betrayed the Classics by using doubtful sources as the basis for their expositions. In Wan's mind temporal proximity to antiquity did not in itself constitute an important criterion in choosing between Han and Sung explications, but this was to become a critical factor in the Han Learning scholars' categorical rejection of Sung scholarship.

The Wan brothers' approach to the Classics was one of direct reading independent of exegeses. Commentaries should be used only when the meaning of the text was abstruse. In contrast to the eighteenth-century Classicists' esteem for Han scholarship, the Wan brothers' position is particularly noteworthy but by no means exceptional. Wang Shih-p'eng (1112–71), in a treatise quoted verbatim by Ku Yen-wu, for example, prefigured the Wan brothers' rejection of Cheng Hsüan's view on the distinction between *ti* and *hsia*. In a comparison of the various references to *ti* in the *Spring and Autumn Annals*, the *Book of Odes*, and the *Analects*, Wang noted that the word appeared by itself; there were no references to *hsia* as a specific ceremony. It was only in the exegeses that *ti* became tangled with *hsia*. Wang, therefore, proposed dropping the idea that *hsia* was a specific ceremony. There were good grounds for this proposal, he contended.

[Since there are discrepancies between the Classics and the glosses], scholars should adhere to the Classics and reject [the meanings given in] the commentaries.

If one were to abide by the Classics, [one had to acknowledge that] there was *ti* in antiquity but no *hsia*. Not that there was no *hsia* in practice, but that *hsia* was a part of *ti* ceremony. . . . If the *Spring and Autumn Annals*, the *Book of Odes*, and the *Analects* were not the writings of the sages, the extrapolations put forth by scholars in the Han dynasty could not be displaced. But if these Classics were written by sages, how could I not believe in them and discard unorthodox views?[80]

Although Ku Yen-wu was quoting the ideas of Wang Shih-p'eng, the ideas could be taken to be his own. His attitude toward the Han exegetes was further evidenced by the fact that he accepted Wang Wan's judgment that half the *Book of Rites* was the arbitrary opinions of Han scholars.[81] Ku's approach to the Classics is representative of the scholars of the K'ang-hsi period. He placed no particular faith in the Han exegetes and believed that the Classics could be apprehended without the meddling of these scholars. In fact, the divergent views on ancient rites embraced by different scholars could in general be traced back to the exegetical traditions. The focus of the attack was on the commentators rather than on the Classics. Cheng Hsüan was blamed not only for misunderstanding the Classics but also for a more serious crime in the eyes of purists of the K'ang-hsi period— insinuating non-Confucian ideas into the Classics.

The Descent-Line System and the Meaning of *Ti*

Early Ch'ing scholars expressed dissatisfaction with Cheng Hsüan's exposition of *ti* and *hsia* from yet a different perspective. Lu Lung-ch'i, the celebrated master of the Ch'eng-Chu school, criticized Cheng Hsüan for his preposterous reading of *so tzu ch'u* as Heaven, hence of *ti* as dedicated to the supreme divinity.[82] Many attacks on this rendering were made by those who were concerned about lineage ancestral rites.

Lu Shih-i, who advocated the restoration of the descent-line system, also noted that the conflicts over the meaning of *ti* and *hsia* had deep roots in the inconsistencies characteristic of Han exegeses. He was of the opinion that these contradictions could be resolved only by appealing to "principles of duty" (*i-li*), an interpretive tactic that in effect bypasses Han scholars.[83]

Lu explained *ti* in light of the descent-line principle. A passage in the "Ta-chuan" chapter of the *Book of Rites* referred to a ceremony dedicated to the ancestor of the king's "first ancestor" (*t'ai-tsu*). But if the first ancestor was the most distant ancestor of the king, who then was this "ancestor"? Lu argued that this seemingly nonsensical remark could be understood only from the standpoint of the descent-line principle. The ancients valued nothing more than the descent-line institution, as attested by the fact that the Chou rulers worshiped Hou-chi, instead of King Kao as their first ancestor. Hou-chi must have been a secondary son of King Kao, or, in descent-line terminology, a differentiated son. They did not initially worship King Kao as their first ancestor because the Chou rulers were not yet kings and hence unqualified to worship an ancestor who was a king. Once the Chou rulers founded their own kingdom, they were allowed to do so, but they had to observe the descent-line principle that Kao was the first ancestor only of the main line established by his primary son. As the descendants of a secondary son, the Chou rulers could worship only Hou-chi as their first ancestor.[84] This explanation had the effect of placing the descent-line system above political authority and made it independent of changes in the political system.

By associating the descent-line rite with *ti*, Lu Shih-i by implication argued against Cheng Hsüan's conception of *ti* as worship of Heaven. Lu regarded *ti* as a pivotal rite in the descent-line system, a rite offered to human ancestors. His explanation did not achieve the rigor of the Wan brothers' arguments, but Lu's approach was adopted by Mao Ch'i-ling in his treatise on this rite and other related ceremonies.

Mao Ch'i-ling noted that the word *ti* was not used in the *Rites of Chou* and the *Book of Etiquette and Decorum*, but there were references to it under a different name.[85] When Li Kung inquired about the relation between the two rites, Mao drew no distinction between *ti* and *hsia* and listed three kinds of *ti* ceremony: (1) a grand ceremony (*ta-ti*) held every five years in memory of the father (*so tzu ch'u*) of the first ancestor of the royal line; (2) an auspicious rite (*chi-ti*) held to mark the end of the three-year mourning period when the new king introduced the tablet of the deceased king to the enshrined ancestry to be worshiped collectively along with the "displaced" ancestors (ancestors whose tablets were withdrawn from the temple to make room for more recent ones)—since this *ti* was essentially the concluding part of the royal obsequies, it took place only once after the inauguration of a new reign; and (3) a regular seasonal oblation (*shih-ti*) offered to ancestors recent enough to occupy a place in the temple.[86]

Mao followed Lu Shih-i's line of argument and attributed the failure to explain *ti* correctly to the lack of accurate knowledge of the descent-line system.[87] He credited Lu with the insightful explication of *ti* in terms of its relation to the descent-line principle. Like Lu, Mao believed that Hou Chi was a secondary son of Kao, thus confirming the centrality of descent-line principle in the Three Dynasties.[88] Elsewhere Mao connected the two more explicitly.

In *Ta-hsiao tsung t'ung-shih* (A systematic explanation of the great and lesser descent-lines), Mao explained *ti* and the descent-line principle in such a way as to make them interdependent.[89] This connection, to his regret, had been obfuscated by Cheng Hsüan's treatment of *ti* as a cere-mony to worship Heaven. In antiquity, the sacrifice to Heaven was called *chiao* not *ti*. Mao found two similar passages in the *Book of Rites* alluding to the connection between *ti* and the descent-line institution.[90] Both the "Sang-fu hsiao-chi" and "Ta-chuan" chapters contain the phrase *wang-che ti ch'i tsu chih so tzu ch'u* (the king worshiped the source from whom his ancestor descended). Cheng Hsüan had mistakenly read *so tzu ch'u* (the source from whom) as indicating Heaven. Mao argued that this expla-nation was out of place in a context that concerned establishing a great descent-line.[91] In his treatise *Chiao-she ti-hsia wen* (Questions regarding *chiao, she, ti,* and *hsia*), Mao explained the *chiao* rite and contrasted it with *ti*.[92] It was obvious that Cheng Hsüan's glossing of *ti* as worship of Heaven had rendered *ti* irrelevant to kinship organization and the descent-line institution. In contrast, Mao's discussion of *ti* as an offering to a human primogenitor had a direct bearing on contemporary lineage building.[93]

On *hsia*, Mao took a position similar to that of the Wan brothers. *Hsia,* he argued, was not a "designation" (*shih-ming*) for a particular ceremony but merely a generic name (*hsü-i*). There was no rite called the *hsia* in high antiquity. The view that *hsia* and *ti* were held every three and five years, respectively, was widely accepted in Han scholarly circles. It was found not only in the dubious apocrypha but also in the discussions of repu-table scholars such as Liu Hsiang (77–6 B.C.). Mao traced these putative rites to a comment in the *Kung-yang Commentary*. Under the second year of the Duke Wen of Lu, the *Spring and Autumn Annals* mentions a *ta-shih* (great event). The *Kung-yang Commentary* renders this as *ta-hsia* and glosses it as "a grand ceremony repeated every five years" (*wu-nien tsai yin chi*). This passage has often been cited since the Han dynasty as evidence for a three-year *hsia* and a five-year *ti*.[94]

Li Kung continued the attacks on Cheng Hsüan's inconsistent expli-cations of *ti*. Like most of his contemporaries, Li discredited Cheng's treatment of *ti* as a sacrifice made on a circular altar.[95] In *Ti-hsia k'ao-pien* (A critical study of *ti* and *hsia*), he agreed neither with Cheng Hsüan's nor with Wang Su's treatment of *ti* and *hsia*. In his view the controversy over which rite was more important arose from the misconception of treating *hsia* as a specific ceremony instead of a generic term for a collective sacri-fice to a number of forebears. As a rite honoring a group of ancestors, *ti* was a specific type of *hsia*. Although all ranks in antiquity performed oblations to a pantheon of forebears, only the king could worship the father (*so tzu ch'u*) of the first ancestor of the royal house. This rite was called *ti* to distinguish it from the *hsia* performed by all aristocrats and officials.[96]

The reasons why scholars in the K'ang-hsi period committed themselves to studying Classical rituals should be clear. Differences in interpretations of Classical rites had a direct bearing on the current attempts to build lineages based on two fundamental rites: the *ti* and *hsia* were the ancient precedents for the sacrifice to the first ancestor and for the collective sacrifice to all ancestors enshrined in the lineage hall.

The Rise of Historical Empiricism

Early Ch'ing scholars had no advantage over their predecessors in the desperate struggle with ambiguities, incongruities, and obscurities in the Classics. The debate over *ti* and *hsia* continued to rage unabated well into the first half of the eighteenth century and remained a great issue of dispute throughout the Ch'ing dynasty. It involved most scholars, and few experts on the Classics and ancient ritual abstained from comment.

Scholars came to realize that a fragmentary approach to specific rituals ran into difficulties. The understanding of one ceremony always entailed understanding of another. The nature of *ti* and *hsia* to a considerable extent depended on the meaning of other rites, such as *chiao* and *she*. What followed from this recognition was the need to study ancient rituals not as fragments but as an integral part of the history of the Chou dynasty.

One example of this process is Yang Ch'un, a good friend of Ch'i Shao-nan (1703–68) and Ku Tung-kao. Yang distrusted Cheng Hsüan's view of *ti* and questioned the idea that King Kao was the father of Hou Chi, the first ancestor of the Chou people.[97] If Chi was Kao's son, he would have been the elder brother of Yao. How was one to explain why Yao favored his protégé Shun as his heir rather than his virtuous brother?[98] Yang maintained that the distinction between *ti* and *hsia* stemmed from the fact that only the king could worship his first ancestor in addition to his four immediate ascendants (the *ti* ceremony). The feudal lords worshiped only the four immediate ancestors (the *hsia* ceremony). Cheng Hsüan was mistaken in believing *hsia* to be a more important rite than *ti*.

As Yang saw it, the polemics over these baffling issues arose from a confusion of the rite practiced in the state of Lu with that practiced in the Chou court.[99] This misconception had originated with the Han scholar Wei Yüan-ch'eng, who equated the presumptuous practice of *ti* by the state of Lu with the rite of the Chou king. Lu had appropriated the *ti*—the worship of the ancestor of the first ancestor—while it continued performing *hsia*, which it was entitled to do as a principality. From his knowledge of the rites of Lu, Wei concluded that the Chou king had practiced both *ti* and *hsia*.[100] Yang contended that *ti* and *hsia* were oblations practiced by the king and the feudal lords, respectively. The lords had no claim to extending their ritual veneration beyond their first ancestor and hence were barred from performing *ti*.

Yang's friend Ku Tung-kao, a noted historian of Classical antiquity, focused his study of these issues on the Eastern Chou period and devoted himself to a meticulous examination of the three commentaries on the *Spring and Autumn Annals*.[101] First, Ku took exception to Chao K'uang's accusation that Cheng Hsüan had embraced the apocrypha of the Han. In these dubious texts the conception of the first ancestor of the emperor was attributed to a mysterious sensing of a deity in Heaven (*kan-sheng shang-ti*). Chao contended that the *so tzu ch'u* must be the human father of the first ancestor, not a deity.[102] Seeking historical evidence for his view, Chao asserted that the first ancestor of the Chou house was Hou Chi and that his father, that is, his *so tzu ch'u*, was King Kao. For the state of Lu, the Duke of Chou was the first ancestor and King Wen the *so tzu ch'u*. This new explanation was accepted by Ch'eng I and eventually found its way into the commentary by Chu Hsi. Ever since, it has been a widely held view on the historical rite *ti*.[103]

Ku reviewed the three commentaries on the *Spring and Autumn Annals*, the *Book of Rites*, the *Classic of Filial Piety*, the *Analects*, and the *Doctrine of the Mean*, as well as their exegeses, but found no reference to sacrifices to the father of the first ancestor. Nor did Ku find any evidence for Chao's assertions about the worship of Kao by the Chou kings or the worship of King Wen by the Duke of Lu, even though Chao based his view in part on the *Kuo-yü* and the "Chi-fa" chapter in the *Book of Rites*. Ku also took exception to Cheng Hsüan's view regarding the site of the ceremony. It was farfetched for Cheng to explain *ti* in terms of a sacrifice conducted to honor the first ancestor's "supernatural father" (*kan-sheng shang-ti*) at the southern suburb (*nan-chiao*). The three commentaries without exception spoke of *ti* in the context of sacrifices in ancestral temples, not in the suburbs. Contrary to what Chao K'uang and Chu Hsi claimed, Ku argued that *ti* was a rite dedicated to all the enshrined ancestors (*ch'üan-miao*).[104]

There were many affinities between Ku and the Wan brothers regarding *ti* and *hsia*. Obliged as he was to criticize Cheng Hsüan, Ku did not agree with Wan Ssu-ta's exposition on these rites. His main disagreement concerned the meaning of the phrase *so tzu ch'u*. He was not convinced that it referred to the human father of the first ancestor. In this regard he accepted Cheng Hsüan's view that the referent of *so tzu ch'u* was Heaven. In Ku's view, Wan was misled by Chao K'uang, who blamed Cheng Hsüan for accepting ideas from the apocryphal literature.[105]

From the view of ritual performance, Ku pointed to two difficulties with Chao's gloss of *so tzu ch'u* as the "human father of the first ancestor." The first concerned the placement of the tablet representing the father of the first ancestor. No location was more prestigious than the center. The first ancestor already occupied this position, but where else could the tablet of his father be installed? Placing the father's tablet to the side would desecrate their relationship. Installing it on either side of the flanking generations (*chao-mu*) below the first ancestor would subvert the father-son relationship. In Ku's view, the predicament of the Wan brothers stemmed from their delusion that the Chou kings had performed *ti* to Kao. To be sure, their view was based on passages from the *Book of Rites*, the *Book of Etiquette and Decorum*, and the *Kuo-yü*, but these sources were much less dependable than the authentic statements of the sage-kings and of Confucius and Mencius.

For Ku, this error originated in Ssu-ma Ch'ien's (ca. 145–ca. 85 B.C.) *Records of the Historian* (*Shih-chi*), whose ideas had crept into the *Book of Rites* and the *Kuo-yü*. These texts were not to be trusted entirely, for they were no more than writings of Han scholars. If *ti* was a ceremony as the Wan brothers had conceived it, the *Book of Odes* and the *Book of History* should have mentioned it, but such references are nonexistent.[106]

Although entertaining some doubts about Cheng Hsüan, Ku found Wan Ssu-t'ung's criticisms of Cheng's scholarship too harsh. Despite the influence of the spurious texts, Ku argued, Cheng Hsüan was perfectly correct in treating *ti* as the worship of Heaven, from whom the first ancestor descended. All sovereigns had received the mandate from Heaven. Cheng's exposition was well substantiated by the *Book of Odes*. Ku, therefore, reaffirmed Cheng's rendering of *ti* as a ceremony to worship Heaven. His great point of contention with Cheng's comment concerned the place of the worship. Whereas Cheng considered *ti* a ceremony held in the southern suburb, Ku insisted that it was conducted in the ancestral temple. To Ku, Chao K'uang's rendition had obscured the meaning of the rite, and Chu Hsi's acceptance of it was a mistake.[107]

Eclecticism in Classical Studies

Ku Tung-kao challenged established views without discriminating between Han exegeses and Sung traditions. For him, both traditions erred. The inaccuracy and extrapolation characteristic of most glosses had created havoc in the Classics. No commentary could be compared to the Classics themselves.

Ku's position is reminiscent of Wan Ssu-t'ung's view. Wan was critical of both Han and Sung commentators. He felt deep scorn for the highly arbitrary manner in which Ch'eng I and his followers explained dates in the *Spring and Autumn Annals*. Ch'eng I believed that Confucius deliberately "invested the calendar with special meaning" and that calendrical terms had a special meaning other than their literal usage. Spring, for example, was used to mark not spring but winter![108] Wan argued that Confucius would never have violated the chronological facts in the Classic to suit his own purpose. Although Wan was somewhat skeptical of the authenticity of the text, he felt that the Sung neo-Confucians had gone too far in their distrust of the Classic and the commentary. Wan dismissed the views of neo-Confucians on the *Spring and Autumn Annals*, not excepting those of Ch'eng I and Chu Hsi, as preposterous.[109]

A respect for historical accuracy with the goal of transcending exegetical sectarianism was in the ascendant. Wan Ssu-t'ung, for example, insisted on a distinction between theory and history.

There is a difference between speaking about the principle of duty [li-i] and undertaking an examination of institutions [chih-tu]. Whereas the principles can be determined in ourselves, institutions must be verified against the past. They [Sung neo-Confucians] deny the accuracy of the remarks by the Chou people on the Chou institutions. But can we regard the imaginings of Sung scholars as facts [shih]?[110]

In a similar vein, Ku Tung-kao argued that the proper way to understand antiquity was to approach the Classics directly. Han exegeses were less reliable than the earlier three commentaries on the *Spring and Autumn Annals*. By the same token, the three commentaries were not as credible as the Classics themselves. Ku's criterion is noteworthy for its stress on temporal proximity to the golden age as a measure of reliability. His idea presaged in some measure an important methodological premise of the Han Learning movement.

Ku's eclectic attitude toward glosses not only was typical of his precursors, such as the Wan brothers and Mao Ch'i-ling, but also resembled that of his contemporaries. As noted above, Wan Ssu-t'ung, Mao Ch'i-ling, and Li Kung had freely assailed the Han and Sung exegetical traditions. Wan Ssu-t'ung was as critical of Cheng Hsüan as of Ch'eng I and Chu Hsi.[111] Nor did Mao Ch'i-ling and Li Kung feel obliged to discriminate Han from Sung expositions in their effort to expunge deformed teachings from the Classics. The notion that Sung and Han exegeses constituted disparate systems of expositions had yet to gain currency. Eclecticism continued to characterize the approach of most scholars born in the 1660's through the 1680's, such as Chu Shih, Fang Pao, Jen Ch'i-yün, and Wu T'ing-hua (1682–1755). These scholars were most active in the first half of the eighteenth century, a time when Han scholarship had not yet gained prominence in intellectual circles. The object of the purists' quest was original Confucianism. For them the distinction between Sung and Han scholarship had little relevance to recovering the authentic teachings of the sages.

It is clear from these examples that the first half of the eighteenth century did not view Cheng Hsüan's exegetical scholarship with the general esteem granted Sung scholarship, despite an undercurrent working in Cheng's favor. The attitude of the Wan brothers, Ku Yen-wu, Mao Ch'i-ling, and Lu Lung-ch'i contrasts sharply with that of the practitioners of the Han Learning school. While espousing a direct approach to the Classics and attacking both Han and Sung scholars, scholars of the K'ang-hsi period were generally partial toward the exegetical traditions forged by Sung neo-Confucians and highly critical of Han traditions. A limited degree of textual skepticism continued to characterize scholarship of this period as well.

Skepticism and critical methods, however, did not always serve the purpose of Confucian purism. As will be seen in the following discussion, there was a growing call for greater respect for the textual integrity of the Classics and an increasing emphasis on reliance on Han exegeses.

The Official Project on Rituals

The major trends and seminal changes in ritual studies in the late seventeenth and early eighteenth centuries can be observed by reviewing the academic credentials of a few scholars appointed to the Bureau for the Compilation of the Three Ritual Classics. The initiative for the founding of the bureau came from officials. The Ch'ien-lung emperor's approval of the plan could well have resulted from respect for his mentor Chu Shih, a trusted confidant of the Yung-cheng emperor and a tutor to the new emperor for many years.[112]

Upon his accession in 1735, Ch'ien-lung aspired to observe the three-year mourning in full.[113] The duty to work out a schedule and appropriate ceremonies fell upon the president of the Board of Rites, Wei T'ing-chen (1657?–1746).[114] Wei called upon Fang Pao, then the vice-director of the Bureau for the Compilation of Essays by Ch'ing Officials (Huang-Ch'ing wen-ying kuan). Fang drafted the ceremonial program Wei submitted to the throne. The program pleased Chu Shih, a friend of Fang since the early Yung-cheng period. Chu was anxious to see it accepted. When it was presented for deliberation, however, a congregation of high officials rejected it on the grounds that implementation would cause too much inconvenience. The proposal was dropped (it is preserved in Fang Pao's collected works as "Sang-li i" [A proposal for mourning ceremonies]).[115] The Ch'ien-lung emperor's attempt to perform the three-year mourning in full seems to have been more than a symbolic gesture. Despite objections from many officials, he continued to insist on observing it, until the empress dowager intervened.[116]

The Bureau for the Compilation of the Three Ritual Classics was founded in 1736. Its main objectives were to edit and compile commentaries to the three ritual Classics. The results were published as three *i-shu* (exegeses) in 1748: the *Ch'in-ting Chou-kuan i-shu* in 48 *chüan*, the *Ch'in-ting I-li i-shu* in 48 *chüan*, and the *Ch'in-ting Li-chi i-shu* in 82 *chüan*.[117] The new emperor appointed O-er-t'ai (1680–1745), Chang T'ing-yü (1672–1755), and Chu Shih as directors-general.[118] Fang Pao, then a vice-president of the Board of Rites and concurrently a grand secretary, was made vice-director of the bureau.[119] Other high officials such as Hsü Chou-t'ang and the Manchu scholar Hsü Yüan-meng (1655–1741) were appointed vice-directors of the bureau, but both were in their eighties and do not seem to have made any contribution.[120] Both Chu Shih and Fang Pao shared a great interest in rituals. Chu Shih, however, was unable to contribute substantially to the project, for he became seriously ill in October 1736 and died shortly thereafter.[121] Another vice-director, Yang Ming-shih (1661–1736), was in poor health and died at the end of the same year. Hence, the duty to set forth the editorial rules for the project devolved upon Fang Pao. (The officials in charge of these imperially sponsored projects were responsible for determining the editorial rules they followed.)

Fang enumerated seven rules for ordering comments on specific passages in the Classics: (1) *cheng-i* (correct meaning); (2) *pien-cheng* (correction of misrendered text); (3) *t'ung-lun* (general exposition); (4) *yü-lun* (supplementary comments not directly related to the text); (5) *ts'un-i* (preservation of differences; i.e., registration of disparate but defensible views); (6) *ts'un-i* (preservation of doubt; i.e., names of concrete artifacts that lacked dependable explanations were noted, and plausible conjectures were given); (7) *tsung-lun* (explication of the meaning of the entire sentence after each individual word had been clarified).[122] These rules were accepted by the bureau without modification as its general editorial principles.[123]

A number of features of the publications of the bureau are noteworthy. First, the rules regarding "preservation of doubt" and "preservation of differences" are indicative of the accommodating approach of the directors. The inclusion of variant views and the acknowledgment of uncertainties elevated the compilations to the level of serious scholarship. The editors selected annotations from a wide range of sources and cited any ancient text with information on rituals, including the writings of the "hundred philosophers," to help illuminate the text, without discriminating against them on the grounds of unorthodoxy.

Second, Sung and Yüan exegeses figured prominently in this compilation, but not without significant changes. The editors relied extensively on the commentary to the *Book of Etiquette and Decorum* by Ao Chi-kung of the Yüan dynasty. Ao, however, had rearranged the contents of the Classic. The bureau's *Exegesis of the Book of Etiquette and Decorum* utilized Ao's glosses, but the editors restored the original arrangement of the Classic. They also strictly observed Cheng Hsüan's distinctions in pronunciation between the Old Text and the New Text traditions. In dividing the text into chapters and sections, they for the most part duplicated Chu Hsi's divisions in the *I-li ching-chuan t'ung-chieh*. They adapted the diagrams of the temples and palaces in the *I-li shih-kung* (Illustrations of the buildings in the *Book of Etiquette and Decorum*) by Li Ju-kuei (fl. 1193),[124] and reproduced illustrations of ritual vessels and articles from Nieh Ch'ung-i's *San-li t'u chi chu* (Collected annotations on the illustrations of the three ritual Classics) and Yang Fu's *I-li t'u* (Illustrations of the *Book of Etiquette and Decorum*). All these were the works of Sung scholars with strong affiliations to the Ch'eng-Chu school.[125]

The same can be said of the *Exegesis of the Rites of Chou* in terms of eclecticism and the primacy of Sung exegesis.[126] Although Cheng Hsüan's explications are extensively cited, the explanations of many major institutions are dominated by Sung and Yüan traditions, which followed more the views of Wang Su than of Cheng Hsüan.[127] This preponderance of

Sung and Yüan scholarship is equally evident in the *Exegesis of the Book of Rites*. One of its editorial rules explicitly grants Ch'eng I's and Chu Hsi's views priority in cases of conflicting interpretation.[128] What distinguishes these works, however, is the absence of preference for any one exegetical work. The once-influential glosses of Ch'en Hao now stood on a par with other annotations.[129]

The relative prominence of Sung and Yüan scholarship should come as no surprise. A brief overview of the intellectual background of the editors of the three imperially sponsored works will make this clear.

Fang Pao met Wan Ssu-t'ung in 1691 in Peking.[130] The eminent historian counseled Fang to concentrate on Classical studies.[131] As discussed in Chapter 4, Wan Ssu-t'ung and his brother Ssu-ta in general preferred Sung to Han scholia and annotations.[132] Ritual learning in the late seventeenth century owed much to Sung and Yüan Classical studies, and the works of the Wan brothers and Fang Pao were no exception.

The limited skepticism and eclectic approach that characterized Classical studies in general and ritual studies in particular throughout the K'ang-hsi period can be found in Fang Pao's private work on the Classics. In an essay entitled "Tu *Chou-kuan*," (Reading the *Chou-kuan* [another name for the *Rites of Chou*]), written in 1696, his tone seemed to be set in defense of the overall authenticity of the Classic. He criticized Ou-yang Hsiu (1007–72) and Hu Hung (1105–55) for drawing parallels between the institutions described in the *Rites of Chou* and the policies and measures of the reformer Wang An-shih (1021–86). But in two essays written in 1714, he contended, as Wan Ssu-ta had, that some portions of the *Rites of Chou* were fabrications by Wang Mang (45 B.C.–23 A.D.).[133] In "*Chou-kuan* pien-wei" (Distinguishing the falsified [parts] of the *Rites of Chou*), his skepticism is unmistakable.[134] Although he followed Chu Hsi regarding the overall authenticity of the Classic, he expressed reservations about portions of it in his more systematic commentary on the Classic, the *Chou-kuan chi-chu* (Collected annotations on the *Rites of Chou*), a work he completed in 1720. The work's format of annotation was modeled on that of Chu Hsi, that is, citation without provenance.[135] Later when he was working in the Bureau for the Compilation of the Three Ritual Classics, he memorialized the throne about the "falsified" parts, possibly suggesting that they be excised.[136] Similar influences can be found in two other of his works: the *Li-chi shih-i* (Explanation of doubts about the *Book of Rites*) and the *I-li shih-i* (Explanations of doubts about the *Book of Etiquette and Decorum*). The former was completed in 1712 when he was incarcerated after being implicated in the notorious literary inquisition of Tai Ming-shih (1653–1713). He studied the *Book of Etiquette and Decorum* seven times and finished the last revision of his research only one month before he died in 1749.[137]

The bureau must have employed scores of scholars to work on the project, but only a few can be identified.[138] One scholar-official who contributed substantially was Jen Ch'i-yün, one of the original vice-directors.[139] He was as devoted to Chu Hsi's teachings as most of his colleagues in the bureau and lamented that Chu Hsi had died before writing a commentary to the ritual Classics. Before he became an official, Jen wrote a work entitled *Li-chi chang-chü* (*Book of Rites* in chapters and verses) in 1718. Despite its title, it was not a commentary on the Classic in the strict sense. Wu Ch'eng's *San-li hsü-lu* provided the basic textual organization for Jen's work. Both authors disregarded the original format of the Classic and rearranged it as they saw fit. Jen put "The Great Learning" and "The Doctrine of the Mean" first, an arrangement clearly indicating his partiality toward the Ch'eng-Chu neo-Confucian approach to Classical learning.[140]

Jen produced two great studies of ancient rituals: *Kung-shih k'ao.* (Study of buildings and rooms) and *T'ien-tzu ssu hsien lo k'uei-shih li*, a work on various ceremonies. Jen adopted an approach akin to that of Fang Pao.[141] Although he overrode previous commentaries, he drew upon them extensively and freely.[142] At times he sided with Cheng Hsüan, but sometimes he preferred the explications of Wang Su and neo-Confucian scholars such as Chin Lü-hsiang (1232–1303). For example, he rejected Cheng's explanation for Liu Hsin's and Wang Su's view that there were seven temples for the king even in the early Chou dynasty.[143] On the controversial *ti* and *hsia* issue, he strove to reconcile the variant views advanced by Cheng Hsüan, Tu Yü, and Chao K'uang.[144] Jen's eclecticism and "audacity" in expounding new ideas were noted with disfavor in the *Ssu-k'u ch'üan-shu* synopsis, but his commitment to rigorous verification was credited in the same breath.[145]

Wu T'ing-hua was another scholar who contributed significantly to the projects. As an official of the Grand Secretariat, he had impressed Chu Shih with his profound knowledge of the Classics. On the founding of the bureau, Chu wanted to recommend him as a compiler but died before he was able to submit the proposal personally. Fang Pao submitted the recommendation on Chu's behalf, and Wu was appointed to the position. Wu worked as a compiler in the bureau for ten years.[146]

Wu had reservations about the *Book of Etiquette and Decorum*, parts of which he suspected to be Han forgeries. Like Fang Pao, Wu took note of Chu Hsi's doubts.[147] In his view, the *Book of Rites* had similar defects. Most of it had been written by Han scholars, and its explications of rituals often proved incongruent with antiquity. He therefore suggested that the basic task of the bureau be the correction of transcription and printing errors, as well as of misrendered passages. As for the criteria for verification, he recommended that Classics other than those on rituals should serve as primary references and be given priority over commentaries and other materials. References to certain rituals in other Classics should be used as evidence. In the absence of such information, the meaning of the text should be "determined by reason" (*tuan i li*).[148]

Wu's critical stance toward scholarship on the Classics is apparent in his approach. Early in his education a teacher had impressed upon him the notion that commentaries were not always correct. One example his teacher cited was Cheng Hsüan, who used Han institutions to account for the rituals and institutions of the *Rites of Chou*.[149] Wu berated his predecessor Chang Erh-ch'i for unwarranted deference to Cheng's glosses. Nonetheless, Wu held Cheng's philological annotations in high esteem. For Wu, Chang was commendable for his confidence in Cheng Hsüan's philology but was guilty of stretching his faith beyond proper limits.

In his *I-li chang-chü* (*Book of Etiquette and Decorum* in chapters and verses), Wu showed no partiality toward Cheng Hsüan's glosses. He accepted explications freely taken from whomever he was convinced could illuminate the text. At times he opted for the views of Chu Hsi and other late scholars such as Ao Chi-kung and Wan Ssu-ta.[150] On one of the most important issues of ancestral worship—whether Chou officials (*ta-fu shih*) had the privilege of erecting tablets in their ancestral temple—Wu rejected Cheng Hsüan's and Hsü Shen's negative views. Wu, like Wang Wan, argued they had enjoyed this privilege.[151] But on the question of the length of three-year mourning, Wu found Cheng Hsüan's view of twenty-seven months closer to the Classical canon than that of Chu Hsi, who accepted the twenty-five months version Wang Su propounded.[152]

If Jen Ch'i-yün and Wu T'ing-hua had modest regard for Cheng Hsüan's scholarship, their colleague Chiang Chao-hsi had even less. Chiang was appointed a compiler when the bureau was created. He often engaged Fang Pao in argument over the authenticity of some chapters in the *Rites of Chou*. Fang had no qualms in rejecting any passage dealing with a ritual not mentioned in other Classics. Chiang wrote a work entitled *Li-chi chang-i* (Meanings of the *Book of Rites*, in chapters), in which he attempted to correct mistakes in the divisions of the text made by Cheng Hsüan.[153] He displayed no particular respect for annotations by Cheng or the T'ang exegete K'ung Ying-ta.[154] His works on other Classics continued to uphold Sung scholars such as Chu Hsi and Hu An-kuo (1074–1138).[155]

The prominence of Sung-Yüan scholarship was also evident among high officials who served as vice-directors of the bureau. In the seventh month of Ch'ien-lung's first year on the throne, Kan Ju-lai (1684–1739), another confidant of the Yung-cheng emperor, was appointed to a supervisory position. He was assigned the project on the *Book of Rites*.[156] Kan exalted the work of the Yüan scholar Wu Ch'eng, who had written extensively on ritual matters. His respect for Wu was so great that he memorialized the emperor in 1737 reaffirming that Wu deserved a place in the imperial temple dedicated to worthies.[157]

Emerging Trends in Ritual Studies

Although the compilation of commentaries at the Bureau for the Compilation of the Three Ritual Classics was largely under the sway of Sung and Yüan exegetical traditions, new trends were discernible at the margins of the field. Respect for the work of Cheng Hsüan was on the rise. To be sure, Cheng's expositions of the overall nature of specific rituals were often criticized in the *pien-cheng* (corrections) and *an* (comment) sections of the bureau's publications, but the importance of Cheng Hsüan's notes on ancient philology was beginning to gain wider recognition. The *Exegesis of the Book of Etiquette and Decorum*, for example, for the most part followed Cheng Hsüan's phonetic transcriptions and his notes on variant forms of characters.[158] The same can be said of the other two commentaries. Most of Cheng's explanations for names of articles were entered as the "proper meaning" (*cheng-i*); annotations by other scholars were attached for reference under the *ts'un-i* heading.[159] Thus, amid the general preference for Sung and Yüan exegetical scholarship, a strong undercurrent was in view that was to lead in the mid-Ch'ien-lung period to the Han Learning movement.

As mentioned above, most scholars in the bureau entertained varying degrees of doubt about the authenticity of portions of the ritual Classics. A minor group of scholars in the bureau had misgivings about the prevalent textual skepticism, however limited in scope it might be. Li Fu, an eminent official and influential scholar, was appointed vice-director of the bureau in the twelfth month of the first year of the Ch'ien-lung period.

He was assigned to the project on the *Book of Etiquette and Decorum*.[160] Fang Pao asked him to draft a list of basic references for the three ritual Classics. He enumerated 116 titles, mainly in the possession of families in Chekiang and Kiangsu provinces. The bureau at first followed the conventional practice of procuring texts by rewarding collectors who submitted works to be copied. This soon proved too expensive a process and, more important, too time-consuming.[161] Li then proposed to copy from the Ming collectanea *Yung-lo ta-tien* (Great compendium of the Yung-lo emperor) those works relevant to the project. The proposal was accepted in order to supplement efforts to procure books from the Lower Yangtze area.[162]

Li was among the few scholars who held the three ritual Classics in equal esteem. As noted above, scholars such as Fang Pao, Jen Ch'i-yün, and Wu T'ing-hua did not have full confidence in parts of these Classics, especially the *Book of Rites*. They shared the view that the three had different values. Following the tradition begun by Chu Hsi, many refused to treat the *Book of Rites* as a Classic and considered it a commentary written by Han scholars.[163] Chu Hsi said, "Generally speaking, of the three Classics on institutional rites, the *Rites of Chou* and the *Book of Etiquette and Decorum* are trustworthy; the *Book of Rites* is not to be taken for granted."[164] Such an appraisal inevitably undermined the *Book of Rites* relative to the other two.

Li Fu, however, took exception to this notion. In a letter to his colleagues in the bureau, he argued that many chapters of the *Book of Rites*, such as "Yü-tsao," "Ming-t'ang wei," "Chi-fa," and "Shen-i," were authentic records. It was erroneous to relegate the *Book of Rites* to the category of commentary. Besides, if it were downgraded on the grounds that some parts were doubtful, the other two ritual works should be downgraded as well. He cited Chu Hsi's remarks that the *Rites of Chou* had not necessarily been written by Duke of Chou, and that although the *Book of Rites* could not be accorded full credibility, its chapters were nonetheless writings by disciples of Confucius and Mencius. Hence, the *Rites of Chou* and the *Book of Etiquette and Decorum* had no more claim to authenticity than the *Book of Rites*. The most appropriate approach was not to discriminate against any particular Classic. In regard to the exegetical tradition, Li stressed the primacy of commentaries by Cheng Hsüan, K'ung Ying-ta, and Chia Kung-yen. Unless their remarks appeared to be farfetched, they should be accepted as correct. Li further pointed out that in advising his students on Classical studies, even Chu Hsi had underlined the paramount importance of the glosses by Cheng and Chia.

Li outlined some basic rules for editing the commentaries. First, the compilers should follow Chu Hsi's advice to adopt Cheng Hsüan's and K'ung Ying-ta's opinions on dividing the Classics into chapters and verses. Explanations and versions of events that were contradictory to Cheng's comments should be accepted only after deliberation. Second, Cheng's quotations from apocryphal texts were to be excluded. Third, inasmuch as the ritual Classics consisted primarily of records of institutional rituals, speculation about the symbolism of rituals (*fan-lun i-li chih shuo*) should be reduced to a minimum. Li reminded his colleagues that Chu Hsi regarded the concrete ceremonies and etiquette as the basis of moral principle (*i-li*). Once the performative structures of ritual were restored, the moral meanings would reveal themselves transparently. Li therefore recommended that stress be placed on institutions (*chih-tu*) and that discourse on moral meaning be avoided.[165]

A few points in Li's proposed rules warrant discussion. First, Li was a follower of the teachings of Lu Chiu-yüan and was partial toward the Wang Yang-ming school.[166] That he had to adduce Chu Hsi's view to buttress his own ideas clearly indicates his collaborators' predilections. Second, Li's belief in the primacy of the exegeses by Cheng Hsüan, K'ung Ying-ta, and Chia Kung-yen was not shared by his colleagues. His exclusive concern about "names and articles" (*ming-wu*) and the performative structure of ritual anticipated the position of such scholars as Hui Tung (1697–1758), Tai Chen, Ch'ien Ta-hsin, and Wang Ming-sheng. Third, Li denounced the notion that posited a distance between the moral meaning and the literal signification of rituals. Li's view was to become the point of departure for the rejection by the Han Learning school of a bifurcated approach to ritual studies.

Although Li's ideas are not representative of the thinking of the bureau, he was not alone in stressing Han glosses and the priority of understanding the concrete details of rituals. Shen T'ung (1688–1752) was one of the few who shared Li's attitudes. Shen failed to win the designation "scholar of erudition" (*po-hsüeh hung-ju*) and was appointed a compiler in the bureau.[167] He had studied with the famed Classicist Ho Ch'o (1661–1722) and the prominent official Chang Po-hsing (1651–1725).[168] Textual skepticism directed toward the Classics particularly disturbed Shen. The noted Sung scholar-official Ou-yang Hsiu had argued that the great number of officials listed in the *Rites of Chou* could not represent a faithful record of the Chou dynasty. The limited size of the Chou domain precluded the possibility of maintaining a government of such immense scale, for there would not have been sufficient government income. Many accepted Ou-yang's reasoning.[169]

In 1742, Shen began to write up his investigations of the emolument system of the *Rites of Chou*. He completed his task in the same year the three imperially sponsored commentaries to the ritual Classics were published.[170] His findings showed that there were enough stipendiary estates to reward the great number of officials listed in the *Rites of Chou*. Obviously, Shen was seeking to defend the Classics against the skepticism of many of his colleagues.[171] Despite minor divergences, Shen's overall attitude toward Cheng Hsüan's scholarship resembled that of Li Fu and his good friend Hui Tung, widely recognized as the founder of the Han Learning school.[172] But Shen was aware that his commitment to the scholarship of Cheng Hsüan and other Han exegetes was not as complete as that of Hui Tung. Accordingly, he felt no compunction against drawing freely from the writings of Chu Hsi and of his contemporary Fang Pao.[173]

Hui Tung's father, Hui Shih-ch'i (1671–1741), was another participant in the project who valued Han scholarship much more than that of subsequent scholars.[174] Six years after his dismissal from office in disgrace, Hui was reappointed in 1737 as a sub-reader at the Han-lin Academy and made a compiler of the Bureau for the Compilation of the Three Ritual Classics by the Ch'ien-lung emperor.[175] In his Classical studies, Hui put a premium on cross-verification by texts believed to have been written in and before the Han periods. He expanded the scope of references beyond the Classics and called writings conventionally dubbed heterodox into service in attempts to establish lexical meanings. Hui cited the work of Chuang-tzu, Hsün-tzu, Kuan-tzu, Mo-tzu, and Huai-nan-tzu without the slightest concern for the treacherous implications of their unorthodox ideas. In an apology for his unorthodox employment of Mo-tzu's writings, he stated that those texts were ancient history and were excellent sources for ancient philology. He treated them as neutral sources of information on Classical language and ancient history.[176] Hui made extensive use of Han writings, such as the *Shih-chi*, Chia I's *Yung-ching*, and the *Pai-hu t'ung*,[177] and frequently cited lexical information from Hsü Shen's *Shuo-wen chieh-tzu* and the commentaries by Cheng Hsüan and Chia K'uei (30–101).[178]

Hui distinguished himself from others by stressing the recovery of ancient pronunciations and lexical meanings. He was keenly aware of phonetic variations stemming from dialectical divergencies, discrepancies in character style, and the common practice of "borrowing" (*chia-chieh*) words to be used in a new sense. He held that knowledge of these linguistic developments was crucial to an accurate understanding of the Classics,[179] and he lamented the obscuring of Confucius' teachings as a consequence of the loss of ancient lexemes.[180] Without the ancient writings and commentaries by Han scholars, the Classics would be incomprehensible.[181] For him, Cheng Hsüan's knowledge of ancient philology was without peer.[182]

Hui's views on methodological matters resembled those of Li Fu, who considered the pursuit of moral meanings secondary in the study of Classical rituals. As Hui saw it, the main task was an accurate reconstruction of lexical references to concrete things and events in high antiquity. This preliminary work was indispensable:

> The Classics on rites were uncovered from the walls [of K'ung An-kuo's house]. Their language abounded in ancient characters and anachronistic pronunciations. The meanings of the Classics are retained in ancient lexemes [ku-hsün]. Only after the sound and the style of characters are identified can the sense be known. Therefore, ancient lexical meanings should never be tampered with.[183]

Hui was speaking of the proper way to read the Classics, a conscious endeavor to get at the basics of Classical studies. His stress on learning the ancient language reflected a recognition of the historical dimension of language itself. To render the Classics in terms of current usage could not but result in misunderstanding. His method aimed essentially at clarity at the lexical level. With pronunciation and hence literal sense determined, the meaning of the text would unfold itself; this would obviate the need for a higher level of integrative understanding, let alone interpretation. Hui's approach gained currency from his son Hui Tung's continued refining of his methods and theory of reading the Classics. Hui Tung's scholarship came to exercise a strong hold over scholars from the mid-eighteenth century on.

The breadth of Cheng Hsüan's knowledge of ancient language continued to win the admiration of younger scholars working in the compilation bureau, such as Hang Shih-chün (1696–1773). Nonetheless, Hang did not draw a sharp line between Han scholarship and Sung scholarship. He esteemed Li Kuang-ti and Chu Shih and lauded the latter as the specialist on ritual studies par excellence.[184] That he chose to compile a supplement to Wei Chih's Li-chi chi-shuo (Collected discussions of the Book of Rites) indicates that he was not yet committed to studying the Classics simply by depending only on Han exegeses.[185]

The scholars at the Bureau for the Compilation of the Three Ritual Classics were the best available at the time. Some of them were influential officials; others were prominent scholars. If they did not set the tone for

Ch'ing ritual studies, they were certainly representative of the many tendencies of ritual research in particular and Classical studies in general. The demarcation of approaches to the Classics into Sung and Han was emerging, but it had yet to dominate the intellectual scene. Both the private undertakings and the collaborative projects of these scholars illustrate the sway of Sung scholarship and its limited skepticism. But as noted above, textual skepticism in the K'ang-hsi period was aimed not so much at Confucianism as a belief system as at suspicious elements, whether textual or conceptual, in the Classics. The attacks on certain parts of the Classics should be understood as part of the Confucian purist movement's attempt to expunge heterodox ideas, to say nothing of fabricated texts claiming to have been written by the sages. The distrust of some portions of the three ritual Classics is but another example of the purist quest for authentic Confucian ritual.

Few scholars dedicated to Classical studies slavishly followed previous judgments. Scholarship did not develop in a vacuum but in a context of continuing debate and discussion. To the extent that understanding the Classics involved grasping the meaning of obligations (*i-li*), the works on rituals by Chu Hsi, Ch'en Hao, Wu Ch'eng, and Ao Chi-kung still carried more weight than commentaries by Han and T'ang exegetes. There was, however, in the writings of these early Ch'ien-lung scholars a movement to restore the paramount position of Han scholia. As the belief in the credibility of Cheng Hsüan's learning grew at the expense of Sung scholarship, the tide turned in the favor of Han scholarship, which became the main guide to the proper reading of the Classics.

From about the 1750's to the 1770's, the reputation of Cheng Hsüan as the most reliable savant on antiquity loomed larger and larger. The passion for Han scholarship eventually took on a life of its own. In due course, commentaries by Han scholars replaced Sung exegetical traditions as the correct interpretation of the sages' teachings. Eclecticism, skepticism, and the liberal approach that characterized Classical studies and ritual research before the mid-eighteenth century gradually gave way to an absolute faith in the textual integrity of the Classics and Han exegeses and a stress on the historico-philological approach. How did this happen? What forces brought about this revolt against Sung exegetical scholarship and the ascendancy of "purist hermeneutics"? In the Introduction to this book, I asked why Sung neo-Confucian scholarship, a form of intellectualism, came to be rejected by the Han Learning school. An answer will be attempted in the next two chapters.

6

Linguistic Purism and the Hermeneutics of the Han Learning Movement

By the mid–eighteenth century, the debate between supporters of the Sung-Yüan exegetical tradition and proponents of Han classical scholarship over lineage rituals, ancient history, and textual issues began to polarize Confucian discourse into Sung Learning and Han Learning. Adherents of the Ch'eng-Chu learning were losing ground to the vociferous and sophisticated attack of those who viewed Han scholarship as the more reliable interpretation of the Classics and denounced Sung scholarship for its sullied teachings. The currents of ritualism and opposition to heterodoxy continued to shape Classical studies, and they combined to work against Sung-Yüan scholarship. To purge Classical studies of Sung expositions, scholars with a purist bent developed a hermeneutics capable of both protecting the Classics from excessive skepticism and continuing the purification of Confucianism. This "hermeneutics of linguistic purism" distinguishes the Han Learning movement from earlier purist attempts.

A brief explanation of my reasons for choosing the term "hermeneutics of linguistic purism" is in order. The term "Han Learning" (*Han-hsüeh*) does not adequately characterize this intellectual movement. Scholars in this movement did not simply strive to revive what Han exegetes had written on the Classics; nor did they regard philology and textual research an end in itself. They sought to understand Confucian teachings on more solid grounds.[1] The other term commonly used to refer to this movement, "evidential scholarship" (*k'ao-cheng hsüeh*), is no more adequate, for it tends to overshadow the ethical underpinnings and the purist orientation of the movement's methodological premises. Although both terms are used in this study, for analytical purposes, "hermeneutics of linguistic purism" highlights the strong forces of ethical ritualism and opposition to heterodoxy that informed the Classical scholarship of these scholars.

By "hermeneutics," I mean the principles and methods of understanding the texts of the Classics. In the West the term traditionally designates the theory of Biblical exegesis.[2] As James M. Robinson points out, the Greek term *hermēneia*, generally translated "interpretation," embraces the aspects of speech, translation, and commentary.[3] All three involve understanding something obscure. As will be argued, these aspects of hermeneutics apply quite well to Chinese scholarship in the second half of the eighteenth century. Leading scholars in philological and exegetical studies, such as Tai Chen and Hui Tung, proceeded from the belief that Sung neo-Confucians had misconstrued the meaning of the Classics. Their task was to "recover" the original meaning of the Classics by exposing and expunging uncanonical elements. This purist impulse led most scholars to reject Sung scholarship categorically and embrace Han exegeses vigorously.

As will be shown, the usages and pronunciations of ancient Chinese posed problems of textual understanding. The problems of translating an ancient version of a written language into a more recent one parallel those of rendering comprehensible a foreign text. Unlike the neo-Confucians and many scholars in the K'ang-hsi period, linguistic purists rejected the idea that one could understand the Classics without the earliest commentaries. Language has its own history, and pronunciation and meaning change. Without commentators who knew Archaic Chinese and the history of Classical antiquity, the Classics could not be accurately understood.[4] *K'ao-cheng* scholars were convinced that rigorous philological and historical studies would enable the Classics to speak for themselves. Their scholarship, rather than that of the Sung neo-Confucians, therefore "spoke" for the sages.

A final, and not the least important, reason for choosing the term "hermeneutics" has to do with the subservient role of traditional hermeneutics in Biblical studies. Hermeneutics in Biblical studies is a means, not an end in itself. Similarly, in the present study, "hermeneutics," while entailing philological exercises and critical scholarship, also serves Confucian purposes. There is no question that the moral philosophy of the Sung neo-Confucians suffered immensely as philological studies advanced. As we shall see, however, the Han Learning scholars meant philological studies to reaffirm the core values of Confucian ethics. As a result, the metaphysical superstructure of neo-Confucian ethics crumbled, but the social ethics of Confucianism was reinforced. It cannot be overemphasized that the *k'ao-cheng* movement had a deep commitment to certain ethical beliefs and that its philological methods were meant not to be applied freely but to operate within certain ideological perimeters. Unlike many current theories of hermeneutics that aspire to be independent of theological purposes and universally applicable, the hermeneutics of linguistic purism upheld Confucianism as strongly as traditional Biblical hermeneutics has sustained Christianity.[5]

The hermeneutics of linguistic purism made it possible for the Han Learning scholars to harness philology. By identifying and purging the Classics of terms and usages that originated in heterodox texts, they could restrict the target of philological criticism to the exegetical level and hence seal off questions of the textual authenticity of the Classics. Instead they concentrated on attacking the Sung neo-Confucians for insinuating heterodox usages into Classical exegesis. It is this restrictive linguistic purism that distinguishes the Han Learning movement from the evidential scholarship of the K'ang-hsi period, which did not exempt the Classical texts from questions of authenticity. Even scholars who were not dogmatic adherents of Han scholarship practiced this hermeneutics.

The Han Learning movement embraced a spectrum of positions ranging from a general preference for Han exegetical scholarship to a dogmatic adherence to views of Han scholars. The Anhwei school of Tai Chen represents the former position, and the Han Learning school of Hui Tung of Soochow the latter.[6]

In order to explain the rise of the Han Learning movement, we need to know why the Ch'eng-Chu school, having enjoyed prominence since the mid-seventeenth century, came under fierce attack and gradually lost its credibility. In explaining the decline of Sung scholarship in relation to Han Learning, we shall also analyze the premises of this hermeneutics as a methodology developed largely to counteract the basic assumptions of Sung scholarship. What Confucian doctrines did the Han Learning scholars stand for? This question is directly linked to the question of why their beliefs gained currency at the expense of the Sung scholarship from the mid-eighteenth century on, a question to which we now turn.

The Waning of the Cultural Symbolism of Sung-Ming Rituals

As outlined in the preceding chapters, from the 1650's on scholars such as Ch'en Ch'üeh, P'an P'ing-ko, and later Yen Yüan and Li Kung mounted an all-out attack on neo-Confucianism. This radical strand of purism remained an undercurrent during the K'ang-hsi and early Ch'ien-lung periods because Sung Classicism was in the ascendant and the Classical rituals recommended by Sung scholarship were associated with the fallen Ming dynasty. As the Manchus consolidated their rule under the K'ang-hsi emperor in the last quarter of the seventeenth century, however, the appeal of the cultural connotations of Sung and Ming rituals began to evaporate.

A major factor in the dissolution of the symbolic association between Sung-Ming rituals and anti-Manchu sentiment was a significant change in Manchu policy toward the gentry, especially those of the Lower Yangtze area. Under the rule of the Oboi regency (1661–69), the Manchu court pursued a policy of self-aggrandizement, assuming the overbearing posture of a conqueror over the Chinese gentry. It was partly under this hostile rule that dissident gentry in the Lower Yangtze area were implicated in the large-scale persecution for tax delinquency in 1661. Anti-Manchu feelings remained intense even after all faults committed in and before 1662 were exempted from prosecution in 1663. The animosity toward and suspicion of the Manchus kept many southern literati away from the court, but the situation began to change in 1669 when the K'ang-hsi emperor assumed personal control of the Manchu government.[7]

The initial success of the Rebellion of the Three Feudatories (1673–76) made it all the more urgent to win over the Kiangnan dissidents. The K'ang-hsi emperor undertook initiatives to placate the alienated Confucian literati. His attempts included special examinations to attract the best scholars. The *po-hsüeh hung-tz'u* examinations, introduced in 1678, selected the best scholars for appointment to the *Ming History* project.[8] This policy did not win over diehard Ming loyalists, such as Ku Yen-wu or Huang Tsung-hsi, but these propitiative gestures did help allay the southern gentry's suspicion and hostility. Of the 50 who passed the special examination in 1679, 80 percent came from the southeastern provinces of Chekiang and Kiangsu.[9]

Under the rule of the K'ang-hsi emperor, the Confucians' loyalty to the Ming dynasty began to fade. Even though competition in the civil service examination may have begun to reach its pre-conquest level for the literati in the Lower Yangtze area, some younger scholars were able to find employment on the private staffs of officials assigned to a wide array of projects, including river conservancy, the reconstruction of the Grand Canal, the campaign against Wu San-kuei, and various literary undertakings.[10] Celebrated scholars like Yen Jo-chü, Ku Tsu-yü (1631–92), Liu Hsien-t'ing (1648–95), and Hu Wei enjoyed the patronage of Hsü Ch'ien-hsüeh, who was in charge of the imperial projects to compile the *Ming*

History and the *Comprehensive Geography of the Great Ch'ing (Ta-Ch'ing i-t'ung chih)*. This type of semiofficial patronage was one of the institutions behind the increasing professionalization of scholarship that was to emerge fully with the Han Learning movement.[11]

Another important factor eroding the political and cultural symbolism of Sung-Ming rituals was the patronage of the Ch'eng-Chu school and Chinese rituals by the Manchu regime under the K'ang-hsi emperor. The K'ang-hsi emperor's growing interest in the Ch'eng-Chu school rendered meaningless any nostalgic indulgence in Sung-Ming rituals as a means of symbolic resistance to the Manchus. Compared with the overbearing behavior of the Manchus under the Oboi regency, the K'ang-hsi emperor's attempts to seek greater cooperation from and understanding of the Chinese elite facilitated the rise of the Ch'eng-Chu school as the ideology of the new empire. The fusion of Manchu rule with the revived Ch'eng-Chu learning gathered pace in the late seventeenth century. In the 1680's and 1690's, the K'ang-hsi emperor developed trust in many staunch exponents of the Ch'eng-Chu school, including Lu Lung-chi, Hsiung Tz'u-lü (1635–1709), and Li Kuang-ti.[12] Even Li Kuang-ti's political rival Hsü Ch'ien-hsüeh favored Chu Hsi's teachings over those of Wang Yang-ming.[13]

The last twenty years of the K'ang-hsi emperor's reign saw a growing tendency to exalt Chu Hsi's teachings over other neo-Confucian persuasions. In 1712, an imperial rescript honored Chu Hsi by ordering his tablet to be placed in the main hall of the Confucian temple alongside those of the ten Confucian disciples. The emperor also ordered Li Kuang-ti to compile the complete works of Chu Hsi and the *Classified Remarks of Master Chu (Chu-tzu yü-lei)*. Chu's writings were printed in 1714 under the title of *Complete Works of Master Chu (Chu-tzu ch'üan-shu)*. The next year, in compliance with the K'ang-hsi emperor's order, Li compiled the *Essential Ideas of Human Nature and Principle (Hsing-li ching-i)*, a collection of writings of the Ch'eng-Chu school.[14]

The symbolic association between the Ming regime and Sung rituals disappeared as the Manchu government incorporated Chinese rituals on a grand scale. In 1684, the emperor commissioned the first edition of the *Collected Statutes of the Ch'ing Empire (Ta-Ch'ing hui-tien)*, whose section on rituals owed much to Ming precedents.[15] Hsü Ch'ien-hsüeh was appointed director-general of the project.[16] He also memorialized the throne that the Chinese practice of a three-year mourning period be imposed on Manchu officials.[17] That same year, Wei Hsiang-shu proposed the compilation of a protocol of rituals based on the *Family Ritual* and ceremonies used in previous dynasties.[18] The *Collected Statutes* was completed and printed in 1690.[19] Even so, some officials memorialized the K'ang-hsi emperor on the need, in addition to the *Collected Statutes*, to compile a more comprehensive manual of rituals, drawing on the *Family Rituals* and Ming practices.[20]

The cultural and political overtones of Sung-Ming rituals vanished as the Ch'eng-Chu school became the new orthodoxy of the Manchu regime. As anti-Manchu sentiment subsided during the last decades of the seventeenth century, the cultural and political attraction of Sung rituals gave way to the unabated purist quest for authentic rituals, a pressure, as we have seen in Chapters 4 and 5, heightened by heated debates over ancestral rites, imperial rituals, and institutions of the Classical age.

The removal of the psychological buffer against a full-scale onslaught on Sung neo-Confucianism allowed the purist logic to reach its conclusion. As we saw earlier, from the 1660's on critical scholarship had irremediably damaged the textual foundation of Sung cosmology and ontology. As a result, Sung scholarship had suffered enormously as many neo-Confucian texts were discredited as non-canonical. Nor were Sung traditions of exegeses immune from criticism leveled by such scholars as Li Kung and Mao Ch'i-ling.

Meanwhile the heated debates over such Classical rituals as the *ti* and *hsia*, the actual operation of the descent-line system, and the lineage temple system and its liturgy continued to rage. The more scholars immersed themselves in previous exegetical traditions, the more they became aware of the need to consult Han commentaries. Han exegeses received growing respect for their attention to philology and, more important, for their detailed explanation of the institutions and artifacts of high antiquity. Knowledge of these objects was essential to an accurate understanding of the performative structure of ritual, especially those pertaining to ancestral worship and kinship institution.

The radical purism exemplified by Ch'en Ch'üeh, Yen Yüan, and Li Kung now came to the fore and became the dominant trend until the mid-nineteenth century.[21] This purism threw adherents of Ch'eng-Chu neo-Confucianism on the defensive, for they were now criticized for embracing the perverted teachings of the Sung neo-Confucians. To purists such as Hui Tung and Tai Chen, the principal task was a continued purge of neo-Confucian distortion of the Classics and a battle against the current of textual skepticism in Sung scholarship, which had revived in the K'ang-hsi period.

The Decline of Textual Skepticism

As background for the discussion of the hermeneutics of linguistic purism, a word on an alternative approach to Classical studies—that of the neo-Confucians of the eighteenth century—is needed. Linguistic purists took as their object of attack the revived Classical traditions of Sung neo-Confucianism. Sung Classical traditions provided much more than a system of cosmology and ontology. They also offered different ways of punctuating and reading specific passages in the Classics. In this study, the term "neo-Confucian" continues to apply to those Ch'ing supporters of Sung neo-Confucian views on major issues in Classical studies and to their appraisals of the authenticity of passages in the Classics. These Ch'ing neo-Confucians, as pointed out in Chapter 2, notwithstanding a token interest in metaphysical issues, devoted themselves to the study of rituals and the Classics. They continued to esteem Ch'eng I and Chu Hsi for their "illuminating" expositions on Classical texts. Like the Han Learning scholars, scholars in the Ch'eng-Chu tradition were concerned with interpretive principles, for they continued to support and defend many Sung exegetical traditions. Their methodology can thus be called "neo-Confucian hermeneutics."

Sung expositors were suspicious of the Han commentaries and subscribed to a direct approach to the Classics. In order to establish their own interpretation of Confucianism, Sung neo-Confucians chose to focus on parts of the Classics and Confucian texts amenable to their concerns and interests in metaphysics and cosmology. Although they intended no impiety and remained committed to the core values of Confucianism, they felt the need to restructure the Confucian texts. In the light of a new structure of meaning, they not only cast doubt on the Classics but also freely rearranged their textual order. It was a common practice for them to change characters and to delete or add new words or phrases to the Classics.[22]

For example, the famed scholar-official Ou-yang Hsiu questioned whether the "Hsi-tz'u" and "Wen-yen" sections of the *Book of Changes* were authored by Confucius. Ssu-ma Kuang had similar doubts regarding the "Hsi-tz'u" section. Wu Yü and Chu Hsi expressed distrust of the *Old Text Book of History*. Wang Po (1197–1274) went a step further and changed the titles of its chapters.[23] Their incredulity led many to conclude that some of the Classics were apocryphal. No Classic had come down to the

Ch'ing scholars unchanged, including the crucial neo-Confucian text, the *Great Learning*.[24]

As discussed earlier, the K'ang-hsi revival of the Ch'eng-Chu school to a considerable extent was a resurrection of Sung Classical scholarship and skepticism. The critical scholarship of Wan Ssu-ta, Yen Jo-ch'ü, and Mao Ch'i-ling in various ways attests to the vitality of Sung scholarship in the early Ch'ing. But skepticism was a double-edged sword, and purism could afford to dispense only with non-canonical texts attached to the Classics by Sung neo-Confucians. Purists such as Yen Yüan and Li Kung had no reluctance in excising the "Diagram of the Great Ultimate" ("T'ai-chi t'u") and Sung neo-Confucian commentaries. But when skepticism fell on conventionally acknowledged Classics such as the *Old Text Book of History* and the *Rites of Chou*, Li Kung was prompt to defend their authenticity.

Li Kung's concern to combat textual skepticism became a major task of purists in the mid-eighteenth century committed to fighting textual skepticism and the legacy of the revived Sung and Yüan scholarship. In the 1730's a small segment of the scholars working in the Bureau for the Compilation of the Three Ritual Classics became alarmed by the ominous effects of skepticism in Classical studies. As noted in Chapter 5, scholars such as Li Fu, Shen T'ung, and Hui Shih-ch'i attempted to curb skepticism toward the Classics. They took the Han commentaries seriously and generally strove to explain and restore rather than to criticize the Classics themselves.

Unlike their predecessors in the K'ang-hsi period, purists from the mid-eighteenth century on had little interest in exposing the spurious elements of the Classics.[25] As Liang Ch'i-ch'ao noted, critical scholarship aiming at evaluating the authenticity of texts declined after the mid-eighteenth century and did not regain its vigor until the late nineteenth century.[26] Scholars in general developed an extreme respect for the original text of the Classics and seldom questioned the origins of the texts. The *Old Text Book of History* was the only Classic commonly denounced.

The revival of Han exegetical traditions helped to curb skepticism. Exegeses of the Later Han were generally reverent toward the Classics. Their objective was explication. To vindicate the Classics against the skepticism associated with Sung neo-Confucians was clearly a major task for the exponent of Han Learning Hui Tung. As Ch'ien Mu notes, with the growing influence of Hui Tung, the vigorous skepticism of the early Ch'ing gave way to "faith" in the Classics. Energy no longer went into exposing the doubtful parts of the Classics but into resuscitating Han commentaries.[27] Han exegetes had had few reservations regarding the authenticity of the Classics and devoted themselves to illuminating rather than to criticizing the Classics.[28] The revival of Han exegeses is a strong indication of the growing faith in the Classics and the decline of skepticism.

As noted earlier, the neo-Confucians regarded the *Rites of Chou* with doubt. Fang Pao argued that Liu Hsin had forged certain passages and chapters for political purposes and attributed them to the Duke of Chou.[29] To strengthen his point, Fang dismissed the "Ming-t'ang wei" chapter in the *Book of Rites* as a tract. To provide a precedent to legitimize Wang Mang's usurpation, Fang argued, Liu Hsin manufactured the story that the Duke of Chou had ascended the throne.[30] Fang Pao's view reiterated the beliefs of Sung scholars.[31]

Mao Ch'i-ling was known for his erudition as well as for a propensity to bend the Classics to serve his own purposes. One of the main reasons he cast doubt on the *Book of Etiquette and Decorum* was that the *Family Rituals* was in the main based on it. His animus against Chu Hsi led him to write a set of treatises criticizing the Classic.[32] Mao argued that the *Rites of Chou* was neither the writings of the Duke of Chou nor a real Classic, but did essentially present rituals of the Chou dynasty. Mao's seeming vindication did more harm than good to the Classic.[33] Li Kung, for one, felt obliged to refute his argument that ancient rituals had been lost by Confucius' time.[34]

In contrast to neo-Confucians such as Fang Pao, the Han Learning scholars attempted to counteract skepticism by reconciling the various inconsistencies present in the Classics. Hui Tung, for example, wrote a treatise to demonstrate the canonicity of the "Ming-t'ang wei" chapter. He argued that the sovereigns of high antiquity had performed a great variety of functions, including worship of Heaven and the ancestors, in the Ming-t'ang (the Hall of Illumination). For each particular function, the same structure was given a different name.[35] Therefore, the specifically diverse functions mentioned in other sources did not necessarily constitute contradictions and hence evidence of falsehood. He also rejected the attribution of the chapter to Liu Hsin.[36]

Like Hui Tung, Tai Chen was disturbed by the charges that the *Rites of Chou* was a forgery. In 1760 he wrote a letter to Jen Ta-ch'un marshaling evidence to prove the authenticity of disputed passages in the *Book of Rites* and the *Book of Etiquette and Decorum*. Like Fang Pao, Jen did not have complete faith in these Classics.[37] Fang Pao had argued that the "Sang-fu chuan" chapter contained insertions by Liu Hsin.[38] Jen Ta-ch'un had also made similar charges. Tai Chen cautioned him against such skepticism.[39] Tai also vigorously condemned the license with which Mao Ch'i-ling had challenged the Classics.[40] The purist objection to applying textual skepticism to the Classics themselves was remarkably similar in Li Kung and Tai Chen.

The tendency to revere the textual integrity of the Classics is equally evident in the work of another evidential scholar, Wang Chung (1745–94). Like Tai Chen, Wang was alarmed at neo-Confucian skeptical views. In order to refute Fang Pao's charge of spuriousness, Wang, in his essay "Textual Evidence Corroborating the *Rites of Chou*" ("*Chou-kuan* cheng-wen"), strove to substantiate that it was a work by the Duke of Chou.[41]

The Hermeneutical Principles of the Han Learning Movement

To purists like Tai Chen, the Sung neo-Confucians had not only subverted pristine Confucianism but also pervasively tampered with the textual order of the Classics. The critical edge of Classical research should now be directed against the Classical scholarship of Chu Hsi and Sung-Yüan neo-Confucians. In order to draw a line between "original" Confucianism and subsequent "perverted" expositions, the purists came to stress a set of methodological premises for understanding the Classics. These principles amount to the hermeneutical system of linguistic purism. In the development of this hermeneutical perspective of the Han Learning movement, Confucian purism reached its ultimate phase as an ethical system vigilantly guarding against the infiltrations of heterodoxy and textual skepticism.

The following discussion concerns not so much the detailed practice of this scholarship as the premises underlying its methodology and their relationship to ritualist purism. The ethical thought of the major figures of this trend—Tai Chen, Ling T'ing-k'an, and Juan Yüan—is the subject of the next chapter.

The Classics as the Source of Moral Truth

The basic belief of the Han Learning scholars that the moral truth (*i-li*, or the Way [*tao*]) transmitted by ancient sages, such as the Duke of Chou and Confucius, can be found in the Classics is the primary premise of purist hermeneutics. Ku Yen-wu's idea that "studying the Classics is studying principle" (*ching-hsüeh chi li-hsüeh*) was further elaborated by these scholars.[42] This rejection of the neo-Confucian claim that "principles" (*li*) are in the human mind had important implications for Classical studies.

According to Tai Chen, this neo-Confucian idea grants everyone the ability to attain "principle." If human beings are born with these principles, they do not need to study the Classics. This claim had opened the floodgates to subjectivism and heterodox interpretations. People often mistook personal opinions for "principles."[43] This subjectivism had nurtured Sung and Yüan neo-Confucians who rejected previous commentaries in favor of personal expositions based on direct reading of the Classics. They confidently made changes in the Classics according to the "principles" they perceived. This "speculative" approach was responsible for the perversion of Confucian texts by heterodox ideas.[44] Tai's antipathy toward the neo-Confucians' skepticism and their arbitrary changes in the Classics reveals his empirical spirit as much as his reverence of the Classics does. For instance, in 1761 in a letter to the renowned philologist Lu Wen-ch'ao (1717–95), he faulted Chu Hsi precisely for such mischievous desecrations.[45]

To re-establish pristine Confucianism, Tai Chen insisted that the Classics had to be made the only textual basis for any understanding of "principles and propriety." For Tai, "The Classics are the main sources of the 'Way and propriety' [*tao-i*]." He rejected the idea that "principles of duty" (*i-li*) could be grasped independently of the Classics.[46] Underlying this idea is the assumption that moral truths are not innate, but objectively independent of the mind and directly accessible only to the ancient sages.[47]

Tai's complex and sometimes contradictory ideas are tackled in detail in the following chapter. Suffice it to say here that in Tai's view the sages were better able to perceive and learn much faster and better than common men.[48] This authoritarian perspective enshrined the Classics as the ultimate source of morals. If the opinions of ordinary people, such as the neo-Confucians, contradicted the Classics, the Classics being the repository of sacred teachings, should be granted preference. The aura of sanctity that Han Learning scholars established around the Confucian Classics and their antiquity is best epitomized in Ch'ien Ta-hsin's remarks: "The Six Classics were edited by the sages. There would be no learning without the Classics. Learning the Way requires that one shows respect for antiquity; one will never understand the Way with disdain for antiquity."[49] The famed philologist Tuan Yü-tsai (1735–1815) echoed Ch'ien's view and averred that there was nothing that the Classics had not dealt with.[50]

Institutionalized Conduct as Morality

The second hermeneutical premise of most Han Learning scholars was the ritualist approach to the Confucian doctrine prevalent during the K'ang-hsi period. The ancient sages had expounded moral doctrines not in elusive principles or theories but in concrete ritual-institutions (*li*) and actual experience (*shih*). In other words, the Classics were the institutional and political history of the golden age of high antiquity. Hui Tung maintained that the moral truths of the ancient sages could be found only in their administrative institutions and their documents (*tien-chang chih-tu*) of the Classical age.[51] Unlike the neo-Confucians who "talked" and preached about moral principles in abstract terms, the sages practiced and institutionalized morality.

Chiang Fan (1761–1831), the author of the partisan documentary history of the school of Han Learning, *Kuo-ch'ao Han-hsüeh shih-ch'eng chi* (Records of the lineage of Han Learning of the present [Ch'ing] dynasty), found the Sung neo-Confucians culpable of abandoning the study of the ritual and institutions in their quest for moral truths.[52] Only through empirical study of the ritual-institutions and actual experiences of the sages could scholars attain authentic moral knowledge. The great patron and practitioner of linguistic purism Juan Yüan clearly considered "seeking truth in concrete matters" (*shih-shih ch'iu-shih*) the proper approach to Classical teachings about morality.[53]

This premise was closely related to the more general view that the Classics were the history of high antiquity. This view was by no means new. Liu En (1247–93) of the Yüan dynasty had stated that there was no distinction between the Classics and history in high antiquity.[54] This position was occasionally expressed in the K'ang-hsi period but became dogma only with the rise of the Han Learning movement. Yen Jo-chü, who in many ways set an example for subsequent research on the Classics, ridiculed Wang Wan for distinguishing the Classics from history even in the Three Dynasties. Wang had cited examples to show that history had been used to verify the events in the Classics. What he did not know, Yen pointed out, was that the Classics were the histories of the Three Dynasties. They became Classics only after Confucius had emended these ancient historical documents.[55]

Ironically the best articulation of the identity of ancient history and the substance of the Classics is to be found in the writings of a critic of evidential scholarship, Chang Hsüeh-ch'eng, whose views are too widely known to warrant discussion here.[56] Less familiar to modern students of this period are the ideas of Ts'ui Shu (1740–1816), who has been lauded for his allegedly iconoclastic approach to ancient history. In explaining the identity of the Classics and ancient history, he said, "The ways of the Two Emperors and Three Monarchs are identical. Therefore, in the Three Dynasties, there was no distinction between Classics and history. The Classics were their history, and history was what is known as the Classics today."[57]

The identification of the Classics as records of the governing experiences of high antiquity did not lower the status of these documents. On the contrary, this literature was regarded as unique and not to be treated as ordinary historical records. Even so, despite the sacred aura built around these ancient writings, the increasing stress on their historicity inevitably drew scholars to rigorous research on the historical aspects of the Classical age.

Investigation of Institutional History and Moral Knowledge

From the belief in the preservation of moral truths in these records of ancient institutions evolved some attitudes that came to characterize the scholarship of the Han Learning movement. It became apparent to these scholars that objectivity was essential to an empirical study of the past if the authentic principles of human order were to be retrieved. A scholar had a duty to avoid speculation and to seek moral principles through empirical investigation of ancient institutions and history (shih-shih ch'iu-shih). Tai Chen and others presupposed the possibility of reconstructing the past as objective history. Insofar as a scholar guarded against his own bias, the past would present itself exactly as it happened. This belief in a somewhat "empiricist" approach to history was evidenced by the high regard for the Tso Commentary to the Spring and Autumn Annals.

The growing emphasis on empirical investigation as opposed to the "empty talk" that critics charged characterized much of neo-Confucian scholarship discredited the Kung-yang Commentary and similar approaches to the Annals. For the purists, such utopian approaches to the Spring and Autumn Annals were comparable to the neo-Confucian indulgence in metaphysical speculations on human nature and the cosmos. These historically minded scholars insisted that the priorities of Classical studies lay in the empirical study of the facts and events described in the text. Any exposition not derived from such groundwork was unreliable. Hui Shih-ch'i prized the Tso and the Ku-liang commentaries as the most dependable exegeses on the *Annals* and denounced the "curious and strange opinion" of the *Kung-yang* gloss and Ho Hsiu's (129–82) annotation of it as far-fetched. The *Tso Commentary* surpassed the other two as a detailed record of events; the *Ku-liang* excelled in judgment.[58] Hui Tung wrote supplementary notes in six *chüan* to the *Ch'un-ch'iu chi-chieh* (Collected annotations on the *Spring and Autumn Annals*) of Tu Yü. In the preface, he named the *Tso Commentary* superior for its preservation of ancient style of writing.[59]

Lu Wen-ch'ao found the *Kung-yang Commentary* packed with preposterous projections.[60] As Ch'ien Ta-hsin pointed out, the *Kung-yang* argued that in the *Annals* Confucius had hidden his judgments on historical personages and events behind ordinary language. Only by mastering the complex esoteric "rules" (*li*) of the method of writing could one understand Confucius' intended judgments. To Ch'ien, the Classic praised the worthy and condemned the corrupt simply by stating the plain facts in ordinary language.[61] There was no need to search beyond the ordinary language for "hidden meanings" by speculating on the "methods of expression." Ch'ien's distaste for this theory was shared by many scholars of the time, including Hao I-hsing (1757–1825) and Shen Ch'in-han (1775–1831).[62]

This general commitment to the empirical investigation of the Classical language as an ordinary language is evident in the bibliographical notes of the *Ssu-ku ch'üan shu* (Complete library of the four treasuries).

With the secondary annotations, the meanings of the *Tso Commentary* can be made clear; when the meanings of the *Tso Commentary* are known, all the good and evil deeds that took place within the 242 years [of the *Spring and Autumn Annals*] will be verified. Those Confucians who indulge their imagination and speak arbitrarily of "blame and praise" can still refer to the *[Tso] Commentary* and find out their mistakes. Ever since Han and Chin times, [scholars] have depended upon the *Tso Commentary* for comprehending the Classic; since the Sung and Yüan, for purging speculative accounts. Great is the contribution of the *[Tso] Commentary* and the secondary annotations![63]

For the *Ssu-k'u* commentator, the *Tso Commentary* was the key to the history of the period covered by the *Spring and Autumn Annals*.[64] This approach to the *Annals* presupposed the objectivity of the historical knowledge that constituted the basis for understanding the moral principles of the sages. If moral knowledge could be learned only from history, the need to study the history of high antiquity was apparent.

The gradual rise of historical empiricism among scholars involved in the debates over the *ti* and *hsia* rites and over the descent-line system of the Classical age is also visible in the works of the famous historian of ancient geography Ku Tung-kao. In studying the *Annals*, Ku compiled many tables of events and data grouped by topic. He criticized Sung neo-Confucians, such as Ch'eng I, who insisted that one needed to pierce through the veil of common language to uncover hidden meanings.[65]

As the approach of purist hermeneutics became increasingly histori-cal, its critics found its preoccupation with trivia contemptible. There were works devoted exclusively to the study of the calendrical system, genealogies of clans, official titles and duties, various categories of ritual, and geographical names and locations.[66] In summarizing the contribution of Wang Ming-sheng, a famed scholar of empirical studies, Chiang Fan outlined the Han Learning scholars' basic position toward history.

[Wang's] *Shih-ch'i shih shang-ch'üeh* [Critical study of the seventeen dynastic histo-ries] in 100 chüan . . . examines the authenticity of events and compares biog-raphies for similarities and differences. Nothing is treated more thoroughly than geography, official positions, institutions, and the records of government. The only thing [he dislikes] is the evaluation of persons, for he believes that empty words are useless.[67]

Wang's belief in the transparency of moral judgment in correct his-torical knowledge is unmistakable. The *Ssu-k'u* commentator criticized the hermeneutical tradition on the *Annals* since the T'ang dynasty, which stressed a direct reading of the Classic independent of the three commen-taries. The result was an understanding based on personal extrapolation that utterly disregarded historical and linguistic facts. This exegetics, the commentators argued, was modeled after the *Kung-yang* and *Ku-liang* com-mentaries. The problem with this approach was that "if facts are dispensed with, how can [we] tell the right from the wrong? . . . The *Spring and Autumn Annals* has registered the events, and everyone is able to under-stand them."[68] The general penchant for facts and data inevitably led scholars to underline the importance of the *Tso Commentary*.

Until the late nineteenth century, the *Tso Commentary* was upheld as the most reliable and factual annotation of the *Annals*.[69] This historical ap-proach to the *Spring and Autumn Annals* partly explains why the *Kung-yang Commentary* did not receive the attention in the mid–eighteenth century as it would half a century later.[70]

No less is this true of the study of other Classics. In fact, as one modern scholar aptly puts it, the Classical studies of the eighteenth century were nothing but historical inquiries.[71] Classical studies had become a discipline of historical research on the idealized Three Dynasties, the repository of moral rules.

Han Exegeses and the Phonology of Archaic Chinese

The third principle of Han Learning methodology stresses the priority of Han exegetical works, especially those of the Later Han by Cheng Hsüan, Hsü Shen, Chia K'uei, and Ma Jung (79–166). This is a basic tenet with which the Han Learning scholars distinguished their work from New Text Confucianism and the Classical scholarship of the K'ang-hsi period. As discussed in Chapter 5, although Han exegeses steadily gained favor, scholars in general did not take them to be better than those of the Sung and Yüan. It was from this preference for Han glosses that the term "Han Learning" gained currency in the mid-eighteenth century.

Han exegetical traditions revived as a result of the growing understanding of the problems arising from ignorance of ancient phonetics. Ku Yen-wu is credited with stressing the need to avoid reading the Classics with current pronunciations.[72] Hui Shih-ch'i took pains to point out the intimate relationship between pronunciation and meaning of the Classical language (see Chapter 5) and criticized the T'ang scholar Chia Kung-yen for reading the Classics in the pronunciations current in his times, hence leading to misunderstanding.[73]

Hui Tung left a clear explanation of the reason for the preference for Han glosses. Hui blamed the Ch'in dynasty for burning and proscribing the Classics. Not until the Han called for a retrieval of the Classics were the Classics revived, but most of the rediscovered Classics were written in ancient characters of uncertain pronunciation. Even the most learned scholars did not find every word comprehensible. Nonetheless, knowledge of ancient language survived, thanks to the philological traditions based on the memories of scholars who outlasted the Ch'in dynasty. Therefore, the key to the meaning of the Classics lay in Han philological works.[74]

Tai Chen elaborated on Hui Tung's idea. For him, scholars who lived over a thousand years after the Chou dynasty could hardly understand the institutions and documents of the Classics. The structure of buildings, the pattern of clothing, the names of places, had changed with time. They could not be adequately understood without the Han commentaries' phonetic notations and glosses on the Classical language.[75] For Hui, Tai, and Tuan Yü-ts'ai, knowledge of ancient phonetics and paleography was essential to the correct reading of the Classics. Tai Chen reiterated Hui Shih-ch'i's idea that once the old meanings were known, the Classics would be understood, and so would the moral truths of the sages.[76] In a similar vein, Ch'ien Ta-hsin stressed the value of Han exegetical writings in view of the loss of original meanings of the Classics occasioned by the loss of philological knowledge.[77] It was apparent to these scholars that the pioneering works on Archaic Chinese of Cheng Hsüan and Hsü Shen were invaluable. This belief led to a closely related methodological principle—moral truth resided in the original literal meanings of the Archaic Chinese language.

The study of the archaic language and writing system moved to the foreground of Confucian discourse in the mid-eighteenth century as scholars became aware of the complex relationship between understanding the Classics and the linguistic properties of Archaic Chinese. Scholars such as Tai Chen noted that part of the problem stemmed from the polyphonemy (*i-tzu shu-yin*) and homonymy (*i-yin shu-tzu*) characteristic of the Chinese language.[78] Homonymy had given rise to the method of "borrowing" (*chia-chieh*) in transcribing speech sounds.

According to Tai Chen, the number of characters was relatively small in antiquity. In order to transcribe a speech sound that did not as yet have a written symbol, an existing character with a similar or identical sound was "borrowed" (*chia-chieh*). The character then acquired this derivative meaning in addition to its original meaning. This method was widely used in Archaic Chinese.[79] According to Tai, in antiquity, the method of adding a radical to a character to distinguish its new use had not yet been invented.[80] Each character therefore has at least an "original meaning" (*pen-i*) and a "borrowed meaning" (*chia-chieh i*). Since the written symbol remained unchanged, its original meaning is easily confused with the borrowed meaning. With the passage of time, the original meaning often passed into oblivion and the borrowed meaning survived. Since the Six Classics contained a large number of borrowed characters, ignorance of the original meanings of the characters and failure to distinguish "original meaning" from "borrowed meaning" inevitably results in misunderstanding.

For Tai Chen the Sung neo-Confucians' ignorance of these linguistic principles had led many of them to misread and cast doubt on the authenticity of the Classics. One notable example was the *Rites of Chou*. One piece of evidence that had led the Sung neo-Confucians and their Ch'ing followers, such as Fang Pao,[81] to regard parts of this Classic as a forgery by Liu Hsin is the passage concerning an official matchmaker (*mei-shih*), who was responsible for arranging marriages for the people. In spring this official would bring together (*hui*) the opposite sexes and allow those who were unable to put on a marriage ceremony to "run away" (*pen*). For Fang Pao this passage was evidence of forgery because it was impossible that the Chou court would have promoted debauchery by bringing men and women together and letting them mix freely and run away.[82]

Tai Chen argued that the Sung interpretation resulted from ignorance of the correct meaning of ancient language and ritual, from not studying the linguistic principle of borrowing in ancient etymology. The term *hui* originally meant "count" rather than "bring together" or "meet," a meaning the term acquired only in a later period. The word *pen* in the Classic meant not "run away" but the matching of men and women who could not afford a marriage ceremony. *Pen* therefore was an alternative method for marrying people without resources. This rendering removes the moralistic perspective and reveals the institutional aspect of the terms.[83]

The attempts to reconstruct the system of homonyms so that possible borrowings of speech sounds could be examined and verified would help in the recovery of the original pronunciations and hence the original meanings. Phonetic knowledge of the ancient writing system was therefore the key to a correct reading of the Classics.[84] For Tai Chen and Hui Tung, Han exegetical works provided the best knowledge of the ancient phonetic system.

Han scholars had not only provided phonetical and lexical notations on the Classics but also developed their own study of the linguistic characteristics of Archaic Chinese. Consultation of exegetical works by Han scholars therefore entails an adequate knowledge of the phonology and lexicography they had developed. This need explains why interest in lexical works such as the *Shuo-wen chieh-tzu* by Hsü Shen and the *Erh-ya* (Approach to elegance) came to occupy a central place in philological studies for the Han Learning scholars. For example, it is important to understand what Hsü Shen meant by *liu-shu* (six [types of] characters), a scheme he developed to classify the methods of character formation. In other words, the difficulties of understanding the Classics are further compounded by the urgent need to study Han philological theories and practices. For example, Tai Chen argued that *chuan-chu* (explain by a different term), one of the *liu-shu*, in fact meant "mutually explanatory" (*hu-hsün*); that is, the method of explaining the meaning of one character in terms of another with a similar or identical meaning.[85] These characters were synonyms. Tai argued that before his clarification the meaning of the method of *chuan-chu* developed by Hsü Shen had been lost for two thousand years.[86]

Tai Chen's student, the famed linguist Tuan Yü-ts'ai, further argued that Han scholars had developed a system of philological notations. In his *Study of Han Readings of the Rites of Chou (Chou-li Han tu k'ao)*, he enumerated three basic methods of notation used by Han exegetes; each clearly specified whether the commentator was making a phonetic notation, a lexical explanation, or a corrective comment.[87]

This preference for Han philological works was one of the principles of evaluation in the *Ssu-k'u ch'üan-shu* (Complete library of four treasuries) project. Classical exegeses written after the Han dynasty were less reliable because the scholiasts of the T'ang and Sung dynasties had not paid enough attention to the phonology of Han glosses. In a similar vein, Hu Ch'eng-kung (1776–1832), a great Classical scholar from Anhwei, explained why the T'ang and Sung commentaries were less trustworthy than the Han exegeses: "Master Mao [commentator on the *Book of Odes*] lived in the Ch'in dynasty, which was not remote in time from the Chou dynasty. Since the language, writings, names, and philology he knew had already become unknown to the scholars living in the Later Han, how much less would scholars of the T'ang and Sung dynasties know!"[88]

Small wonder that scholars displayed great interest in the lexical writings on the ancient language by Han scholars such as Hsü Shen. Hui Tung himself compiled his reading notes of Hsü Shen's *Shuo-wen chieh-tzu* in fifteen *chüan*.[89] After studying the *Shuo-wen chieh-tzu* for three years, Tai Chen concluded that it was necessary to study all the commentaries and secondary annotations of the Thirteen Classics to investigate the lexical meanings of the Classical language exhaustively.[90] For the same reason, the *Erh-ya* also received unprecedented attention. As Ch'ien Ta-hsin explained, "The Six Classics are there for the elucidation of the way. No one can comprehend the way without the knowledge of philology. [Anyone] who wishes to understand the meanings of the Classics has to begin with the study of the *Erh-ya*."[91] Ch'ien also valued Hsü Shen's *Shuo-wen chieh-tzu* for preserving the ancient phonetics and lexicography of the Three Dynasties.[92] This belief in the instrumental importance of the *Shuo-wen chieh-tzu* to a proper reading of the Classics was generally shared by those who devoted themselves to such linguistic studies.[93]

Given this cogent argument, the rapid growth of research on philology (*hsiao-hsüeh*), especially ancient phonology, into a respected discipline in the late eighteenth century is hardly surprising. Tuan Yü-ts'ai was one of the best scholars of ancient phonetics. Another of Tai Chen's students, Wang Nien-sun (1744–1832), and his son, Wang Yin-chih (1766–1834), achieved their reputations in the lexical study of Archaic Chinese.[94]

Ritual and Classical Studies

The Classics, like Confucianism itself, are not a monolithic tradition; rather, they consist of elements capable of manifold emphases and different directions of development. Historically the importance of each Classic varied with the concerns and problems confronting Confucians. The *Rites of Chou* was to Wang An-shih's reforms as the *Book of Changes* was to the speculations of the third-century A.D. philosophers Kuo Hsiang and Wang Pi. For Han Learning scholars, the focus of Classical studies continued to be *li*, ritual in the broadest sense, and the Classics that commanded their interest were those directly and indirectly concerning rituals. To be sure, they were seeking moral truths; as discussed earlier, they insisted that moral principles reside in *chih-tu* (ritual institutions). Insofar as the leading scholars were concerned, Classical studies were endeavors essential to the understanding of ancient rituals. The sages had established the structure of proper behavior in ancient institutions and the various rites, and the ancients cultivated morality by learning and practicing these rituals.

The ultimate concern of Han Learning scholars was aptly revealed in a critical remark made by Weng Fang-kang (1733–1818). In a letter to Ch'eng Chin-fang (1718–84), Weng explained why Tai Chen insisted on the empirical study of ritual institutions as the baseline for the quest of moral truths.

[Tai] said, "Moral truth [*tao*] must be grasped in ritual institutions and the knowledge of [ancient] things [*ming-wu*]." This makes sense only if he was referring to one or two things. . . . Is it possible to say that . . . the principles of loyalty and filial piety can be comprehended from [studying] the birds, animals, grass, and trees? . . . Can the *Analects* and the *Mencius* be approached as institutions and knowledge of things? Is it possible to study the *Classic of Filial Piety* as institutions and knowledge of things? What Tai essentially meant is the three rituals Classics.[95]

Weng's account is accurate and to the point. The intimate relationship between ritual and ancient institutions, to be sure, was not a new issue. In the early Ch'ing, Lu Lung-ch'i had pointed out the inextricable relationship between the two.[96]

The conviction that moral truths would become immediately transparent if ancient history were accurately understood attests that the classicists were seeking knowledge of ancient rituals, the only concrete rules of moral behavior they recognized. They were against abstract moral maxims such as sincerity and reverence. The catchphrase *shih-shih ch'iu-shih* essentially confined *shih* (affairs) to rituals and events with ritual information. Ling Shu (1775–1829), a distinguished scholar of the *Kung-yang Commentary*, summarized this idea in his remark "The very substance of *shih* is no more than ritual."[97] Chiang Hsiang-nan, who studied under Juan Yüan and Chiang Fan, underlined the perception behind evidential research when he said, "Confucianism should be called the learning of ritual [*li-hsüeh*], not the learning of principle [*li-hsüeh*]."[98]

The *Spring and Autumn Annals* and the Institutional History of the Chou Dynasty

The profound interest of the *k'ao-cheng* scholars in ancient ritual revealed itself in the focus of their studies on the *Spring and Autumn Annals*. As noted earlier, the *Tso Commentary* was valued for its details on institutions. Some early studies of the *Annals* concentrated on the clarification of ancient rituals, especially those of the Chou dynasty. Ch'ien Ch'eng-chih (1612–93) believed that the *Book of Odes* and the *Book of History* were like the *Annals* in their concern about ritual institutions, but the institutions mentioned in the two Classics had to be verified by studying the ritual Classics.[99]

Huang Tsung-hsi's student Wan Ssu-ta pioneered in the cross-verification of ancient rituals recorded in the *Annals* and the three ritual Classics. From his *Hsüeh Ch'un-ch'iu sui-pi* (Casual notes on the *Spring and Autumn Annals*) and Huang Tsung-hsi's letters in response to his questions about ritual, it is clear that Wan's central interest in studying the *Annals* was ancient rituals.[100] The same can be said of Mao Ch'i-ling, who saw rituals as the key to understanding the *Annals*.[101]

Han Learning scholars continued to emphasize the need to clarify ancient rituals in their research on the *Annals*. Hui Shih-ch'i investigated the *Annals* for this reason,[102] and Hui Tung approached the *Tso Commentary* in a similar way. In a postscript to Hui Tung's *Tso-ch'uan pu-chu* (Supplementary notes on the *Tso Commentary*), Shen Ch'in-han characterized the *Tso Commentary* as well as the *Kung-yang* and *Ku-liang* commentaries as exceedingly elaborate records of rituals.[103]

Attaining accurate knowledge of ancient ritual was a major concern of scholars who studied the three commentaries. As is well known, from the 1820's on the *Kung-yang* school increasingly addressed itself to current political affairs.[104] Eighteenth-century scholars delving into the *Kung-yang Commentary*, however, expressed no interest in seeking justifications for political changes. Ch'u Yin-liang (1715–90) compared the *Rites of Chou* with the *Kung-yang Commentary* for differences of rituals.[105] The famous *Kung-yang* scholar Liu Feng-lu (1776–1829) emphasized that Confucius wrote the *Annals* to express his censure against violations of rituals.[106] His student Ling Shu came to focus exclusively on the reconstruction of ancient ritual from the *Kung-yang Commentary*. He believed that the Classic's "grand meanings in subtle words" (*wei-yen ta-i*) could be made comprehensible through investigation by philological and phonetic methods.[107] Ling's pioneering work was further advanced by his student Ch'en Li (1809–69), author of an annotation on the *Kung-yang Commentary* in 76 *chüan* combining a concern for ancient ritual with philological interests.[108]

Not until the second decade of the nineteenth century did *Kung-yang* scholarship become associated with political reformism, but even the politically oriented strand was no more than one approach to the *Kung-yang Commentary*. Ancient rituals continued to be an important concern of such scholars as Ch'en Li and Ch'en Huan (1786–1863).[109] The *Ku-liang Commentary* was the least studied of the three commentaries. However, Ch'en Huan regarded it, too, as an important source for studying ancient rituals.[110] Hou K'ang (1798–1837), a good friend of the famed Ch'en Li (1810–82), examined the *Ku-liang* in order to collate the rituals recorded in the three ritual Classics.[111]

Cheng Hsüan and Ritual Studies

Classical scholarship of the Later Han dynasty displayed a marked attention to philological details.[112] That ancient rituals, including all forms of institutions, constituted the major area of studies for the Classicists is further explained by the ascendancy of Cheng Hsüan's exegetical scholarship. The growing interest in clarifying the pronunciation of ancient words and the terminology of ancient ritual from the outset presaged the revival of Cheng Hsüan's commentaries on the three ritual Classics. Cheng Hsüan is distinguished for his extensive knowledge of rituals and his exegetical comments. He was the only Han scholar to write commentaries on all three ritual Classics,[113] and his scholarship came to be synonymous with research on ritual. The noted T'ang commentator K'ung Ying-ta said, "Ritual is the learning of Cheng Hsüan."[114] Cheng's meticulous attention to philological clarity and details made his work indispensable to any empirical investigation of ancient ritual. The importance of his works was recognized by Chang Erh-ch'i, the Ch'ing scholar who first proclaimed

Cheng's commentary on the *Book of Etiquette and Decorum* the key to an understanding of that Classic.[115] Chang's name for his work on the Classic, *Punctuated Reading of Cheng Hsüan's Commentary on the Book of Etiquette and Decorum*, reveals his intention to clarify the text through painstaking efforts to separate it into meaningful sentences on the basis of Cheng's annotation. Ku Yen-wu praised Chang's book for emphasizing the clarification of textual meanings as a precondition for a general understanding of the principles of ancient ritual institutions.[116] Chang's approach and the connection Ku Yen-wu drew between textual clarity and the moral principles behind ancient institutions presaged the methodological premise of eighteenth-century Classical studies. It is hardly surprising that Ku's laudatory remarks were repeated by the *Ssu-k'u* reviewer.[117]

As the previous chapters show, the growing tendency to take rituals seriously had brought scholars into conflict over neo-Confucian rituals, and the quest for authentic ancient rituals gradually brought Cheng Hsüan's writings to the fore. The *Ssu-k'u* commentator reproduced Hui Shih-ch'i's cogent explanation why Cheng Hsüan's commentaries were the most reliable.

Cheng Hsüan lived in a time when the Chou dynasty was long gone. Hence, in his attempt to understand its institutions, he drew parallels between the institutions of the Chou dynasty and those of the Han. Now, our age is over 1,600 years away from the Later Han, and we can hardly know what he meant when he refers to something as [equivalent to] such a thing, such an event, such an office of his day. Not to mention differences of writing and pronunciation that have arisen in the transmission of learning and in the philological exegeses by Classical scholars.[118]

The *Ssu-k'u* commentator commended Hui Shih-ch'i's study of ancient ritual and pointed out that Hui's ultimate aim was to understand the principles of Chou institutions through a study of the Han institutions.[119] Cheng Hsüan's works were held in high regard because of his firsthand knowledge of the institutions of the Han dynasty, which were believed to be comparable to those of the Chou dynasty. The elevation of Cheng's scholarship reinforced two basic methodological principles of purist hermeneutics. First, it placed a premium on Han commentaries. From a historical standpoint, Han expositions on ancient rituals were more reliable because they were closer in time to the Chou dynasty.[120] Second, the moral principles (*i-li*) of the sages could be grasped only by means of empirical studies of these ancient institutions as recorded in the Classics.

This admiration for Cheng Hsüan was even reflected in building names. Wang Ch'ang named his study the Studio for the Learning of

Cheng Hsüan (Cheng hsüeh chai).[121] K'ung Kuang-sen (1752–86), a pioneer in reviving the *Kung-yang Commentary* on the *Annals*, requested an essay from the noted teacher and exponent of neo-Confucianism, Yao Nai (1732–1815) to celebrate the construction in his residence of the Hall of Emulating Cheng [Hsüan] (I Cheng t'ang).[122] Even scholars who were not part of the Han Learning school such as Yao Nai and the historian Chao I (1727–1814) recognized Cheng Hsüan's paramount position in Classical studies.[123]

Until 1530, Cheng Hsüan had been among those honored in the imperial temple for ancient worthies. But in that year Chang Ts'ung (1475–1539) proposed that Cheng Hsüan's tablet be removed on the grounds that his scholarship was not good enough to merit him a place among the worthies.[124] Cheng's exclusion continued until the Ch'ien-lung reign. As respect for Cheng grew, the call for his restoration to the imperial temple for ancient worthies gained more supporters. As early as 1685, Lu Lung-ch'i, a follower of the Ch'eng-Chu school, had questioned Cheng's disqualification.[125] A few years later, Chu I-tsun proposed to restore Cheng to the temple.[126] In 1724, the Yung-cheng emperor called for discussion of the question of Cheng Hsüan's restoration. The restoration finally came in 1753.[127]

Anti-heterodoxy and Philology

That Han philology served the purists well can be seen in their dogmatic preference for Han scholia. Apart from their chronological proximity to the Chou dynasty, the Han commentaries were regarded as superior in not having been exposed to Buddhist influence. The great patron and *k'ao-cheng* scholar Juan Yüan spelled out the ideological dimension of philological research.

The Classical scholarship of the Han dynasty should receive priority because of its closeness to the sages and worthies and because Taoism and Buddhism had yet to gain ascendancy. . . . Buddhist texts could not be understood without translation. Erudites of the Northern dynasties and the wise literati projected their arbitrary opinions into the Buddhist writings. . . . It was not that Confucianism was perverted by Buddhism, but that the reverse was true. . . . Therefore, I state that the reason why the Han exegeses are superior lies in their preceding the rise of Taoism and Buddhism.[128]

Here Juan Yüan was not so much defending Buddhism as explaining how Confucians were led to believe that there were parallels between Buddhism and Confucianism. In fact, he was dealing with a universal problem of cultural borrowing. In introducing Buddhism to the Chinese, the Buddhists had used ideas and terms familiar to the Chinese. As a result, Buddhism was "perverted" by the original meanings and associations of the Chinese terms. Chinese perceptions were imposed on Buddhist concepts.

Juan Yüan, however, was not concerned about the corruption of Buddhism. For him, the consequence of this borrowing process was the interjection into the Chinese language of alien notions and values. The terms chosen for translating Buddhist texts came to take on new meanings, which then became derivative usages of the Chinese characters and phrases. When the origins of these uses were lost to memory, ill-informed Chinese could point at the meanings derived from translating Buddhism as evidence that the Chinese themselves had developed ideas similar to those of the Buddhists. Juan and like-minded scholars were of the belief that from the Wei-Chin era on the Chinese language had been pervaded by Buddhist notions. The Classics therefore could not be properly understood without a thorough study of Archaic Chinese using Han exegeses. He therefore regarded philology as the best means to undermine the influence of Buddhism.[129] Juan Yüan's purist posture is unmistakable.

Criticism of heterodoxy was no mere token gesture on the part of the k'ao-cheng scholars. Most of them acted on their anti-Buddhist feelings. Of Chiang Fan's list of Han Learning scholars, a fairly large number articulated their antipathy to Buddhism. Ch'ien Ta-hsin criticized Buddhism for its extreme individualism and charged that it paralleled the teachings of the ancient exponent of egoism, Yang Chu.[130] Hung Liang-chi (1746–1809) pledged not to use Buddhist terms in his poetry.[131] Wang Chung refused to allow Buddhist ceremonies at his mother's obsequy and mourning.[132] Wang Yin-chih professed a strong dislike for Taoism and Buddhism.[133] Like Wang Chung, Ch'en Huan eschewed Buddhist ceremonies in his parents' obsequies.[134] Chu Yün and his student Wu I (1745–99) were unsparing in their attacks on Buddhism. When serving as a magistrate, Wu summoned all the Buddhist monks and nuns to his county yamen to enlighten them about the perversion of Buddhism. Chiang Fan claimed that these believers renounced their beliefs and returned home.[135] Wang Chung's antipathy to Buddhism was bequeathed to his son Wang Hsi-sun, who emulated Wu I's attempt to reduce the properties held by Buddhists as well as the number of worshipers.[136] Wang Chung's good friend Li Tun (1734–84) no less earnestly committed himself to ideological countermeasures against Buddhism.[137]

The opposition to heterodoxy of these scholars was echoed in the *Ssu-k'u ch'üan-shu*, generally considered the greatest achievement of the empirical scholarship of the late eighteenth century. Liang Ch'i-ch'ao, exaggerating only slightly, spoke of the *Ssu-k'u ch'üan-shu* Bureau as the citadel of Han Learning.[138] Of the 10,230 titles listed in the *Concise Annotated Catalogue of the Ssu-k'u ch'üan-shu*, only 25 are works by Buddhists and only 144 by Taoists. Thirteen of the Buddhist writings and 44 of the Taoist works were copied into the Imperial Library. Not one Buddhist scripture was included in the entire collection. Those Buddhist writings accepted were mainly biographies and records of Chinese Buddhist activities valued for their use as historical sources rather than for the wisdom they offered.[139]

This analysis of the hermeneutical principles of Han Learning has revealed an implicit critique of neo-Confucianism both for its approach to Classical studies and for its corruption by heterodox ideas. The ultimate concern of the Classicists of Han Learning pointed to the centrality of ritual in Classical scholarship. Its paramount importance in the purist thinking of these scholars will be better understood if we examine their views of human nature and moral cultivation. This will provide a fuller perspective on the special place of ritual in the ethics, especially the method of moral cultivation, of the Han Learning scholars.

7

Ritualist Ethics and the Han Learning Movement

The linguistic purism of Han Learning scholars was much more than a methodology. It represented an attempt to demolish the neo-Confucian interpretation of the Classics and Confucian ethics. Under the guiding principle of linguistic purism, philological and textual studies not only served as powerful weapons for excising heterodox ideas from the Confucian Classics but also as a sure ground for an ethical theory. This ethical system was founded on a monistic notion of human nature, a method of moral cultivation emphasizing the molding of behavior by pure Confucian rituals. These premises were clearly reflected, in varying degrees, in the ethical thought of the leading Han Learning scholars. Unlike their Sung and Ming predecessors, who philosophized ethics, these mid-Ch'ing scholars "philologized" their ethical views.

A close analysis of the ethical thought of Tai Chen, Ling T'ing-k'an, and Juan Yüan will demonstrate further that the philological and historical studies prominent in the latter half of the eighteenth century in great measure evolved in connection with a ritualist ethics. It is ironic that as the scope of classical scholarship expanded to include more specialized disciplines such as linguistics, astronomy, and mathematics, the ethical thinking of the evidential scholars remained restricted by ritual purism.

Many of the ethical beliefs and methods of attack on neo-Confucianism were anticipated by purists of the K'ang-hsi reign such as Yen Yüan and Li Kung.[1] Although the available evidence does not conclusively confirm Tai's exposure to their views, the following discussion will show that many of Tai's ideas, as well as those of Ling T'ing-k'an and Juan Yüan, resemble those of Yen Yüan and Li Kung.

Tai Chen: Mencius and Learning Propriety

Tai Chen, a towering figure in eighteenth-century evidential scholarship, professed that the main objective of his treatise on the teachings of Mencius was to cleanse the Sung neo-Confucian exposition from Confucian teachings, which had been pervasively vitiated by Buddhism.[2] Tai offered a reasonable historical explanation for the infusion of Buddhist modes of thinking into Confucianism. Great neo-Confucians such as Ch'eng I and Chu Hsi had not deliberately appropriated Buddhism. Rather, they were the victims of their own intellectual habits, for in their quest for truth they had immersed themselves in Buddhist teachings for a long time before returning to Confucianism.[3] Buddhist modes of thinking and Buddhist language had crept into their thinking and then found their way into their teachings on Confucianism. Tai Chen exonerated Ch'eng I and Chu Hsi of deliberate subversion of Confucianism, but he nonetheless felt obliged to demolish their corrupted teachings. Tai's view about the source of heterodox elements in Sung neo-Confucianism is reminiscent of that of Yen Yüan and Li Kung.

Yen Yüan had pointed out the Buddhist dualism implicit in neo-Confucian ontology.[4] With Li Kung he castigated the Sung neo-Confucian program of moral cultivation based on this dualistic ontology. Similarly, Tai Chen saw in this dichotomized notion of principle and "material force" or "physical force" (ch'i) the basis of the neo-Confucian view of human nature that led to a method of moral cultivation stressing suppression of appetites and feelings (ch'ing).[5] Such a negative view of human appetites, Tai Chen argued, was essentially a logical extension of the Buddhist polarization of "physical force" (hsüeh-ch'i) and "mind-intellect" (hsin-chih).[6] Because of this dualism, neo-Confucian teachings exalted principle as real nature and condemned "physical force" for the impulsive outbursts of the desires. Translated into a theory of government, this demand for the renunciation of desires inevitably slighted the basic needs of the subject.[7]

In a way reminiscent of the ideas of Yen Yüan and Li Kung, Tai Chen argued that Classical Confucianism never conceived "principle" and "physical force" as distinct entities.[8] In the writings of Mencius, Tai found textual evidence for a monistic notion of human nature. Mencius had clearly stated that human nature consisted of nothing but "physical force" and "mind-intellect."[9] The idea of a "nature of principle" (i-li chih hsing), as opposed to physical nature, was fallacious.[10] Hence the corporeal aspects of human existence should not be degraded. The virtues of humanity, duty, ritual–propriety, and wisdom could not be sought outside desires.[11] In fact, the human ability to improve morally and intellectually hinged upon the mind, which consisted of nothing but physical force. Tai Chen argued that human nature, in terms of its ability to learn, was essentially good.[12] Except for the sages, all had to learn to expand the intellect. Even those less endowed would become "enlightened" if they persisted in seeking moral knowledge (*wen-hsüeh*).[13] It was in this sense that Tai Chen spoke of the goodness of human nature (*hsing shan*).

Unfortunately, ordinary people tend to give free rein to their desires out of selfishness (*ssu*).[14] Dissipation is the main cause of evil and chaos in society. Indulgence in gratification of bodily appetites arises primarily because of selfishness, which stems from the lack of knowledge of the principle of propriety. Selfishness and ignorance (*pi*) of propriety are the gravest problems of humankind.[15] Tai's maxim "moral qualities grow from learning" (*te-hsing tzu yu hsüeh-wen*) captures the inextricable relationship between morality and learning.

Insofar as moral conduct is concerned, the most important knowledge is the "absolute" (*pu-i*) yet "differentiated rules" (*fen-li*) in things, which are accessible to human beings through the intellect. They are universally acceptable or acknowledged "truths." Without common consent, "principles" are nothing but personal opinion.[16] But how can universal agreement on the propriety of principles be secured? To Tai, agreement was possible only if it had been instituted as ritual propriety by the sage-kings and was readily available for verification. Like all Confucians since the Sung, by "principles" Tai mostly referred to the principles of duty. The most important principles relevant to humans were those of ritual.

Rituals are the rules and the laws of heaven and earth; they are the perfect rules, only those who understand heaven will know them. Etiquette, ceremonies, measures, and regulations are the rules that the sages perceive in heaven and earth, and they institute them as the standard for the myriad generations to come. Rituals are established to govern the feelings of all people, either to sanction against excess or to encourage those who fall short of the standard.[17]

Although Tai Chen insisted that everyone is equally capable of learning ritual propriety, he regarded the sages as extraordinary persons who could "understand heaven" and were so perfect in their judgment and moral conduct that they were able to determine the propriety of rituals for the common people. The sages lived in the Three Dynasties, however, and their teachings on ritual propriety are preserved in the Classics. As Tai said, "The Classics are the main sources of the Way and propriety [*tao-i*]." He therefore rejected the idea that moral truths (*i-li*) could be grasped independently of the Classics.[18] Underlying this idea is the assumption that moral truths are not ingrained in the mind but were historically instituted in high antiquity.

In Chapter 6, I mentioned in passing that Tai's ideas are very complex and sometimes contradictory. We shall see why this is so. In the *Verification of the Literal Meanings of the Mencius* (*Meng-tzu tzu-i shu-cheng*), Tai argues against Hsün-tzu's idea that only the sages had access to ritual propriety. Everyone, according to Tai, is born with the intellectual abilities to ponder and learn ritual propriety. The only reason why the common people learn from the sages is because of the latter's extraordinary wisdom. The sages simply were better endowed and hence able to perceive and learn much faster and better than others.[19] The common people might take longer and have to make much more effort, but by virtue of their inborn intellect they can perceive ritual propriety without the sages. Implicit in this position is an autonomous approach to morality denying the sages' monopoly over moral truths. Tai, however, insisted that moral truths cannot be grasped without the Classics.[20] His belief in the Classics as the repository of moral truths enshrines the Classics as an authoritative, ultimate source of morals. When conflict arises regarding morality between the Classics and common people, which includes the neo-Confucians, the Classics are the final authority. The authoritarianism in Tai's ethics is obvious when compared with Wang Yang-ming's and Li Chih's stress on the autonomy of the individual's moral will.

In the final analysis, despite Tai Chen's criticism of Hsün-tzu's conception of human nature, their ethical ideas were comparable in their stress on "eliminating erroneous ideas" and the strong authoritarianism inherent in their notion of moral cultivation. In fact Tai's fellow student Ch'eng Yao-t'ien (1725–1814) acutely pointed out the parallels between the teachings of Hsün-tzu and those of Tai Chen.[21] Ch'eng had misgivings about Tai's stress on *ch'u-pi* (eliminating erroneous ideas) and *ch'ü-ssu* (eradicating selfishness). Tai's ethics underscored extirpation of bad conduct and ideas rather than developing the good inherent in humans.[22]

Despite his criticisms of Hsün-tzu, Tai evidently did not believe that all people shared an intrinsic ability to perceive moral truths independently. Nonetheless, he insisted that everyone had the ability to learn and understand moral truths in terms of the proper rules of behavior. The main duties of the Confucian were to ascertain these moral rules in the Classics and teach them to the common people.

Ling T'ing-k'an: Hsün-tzu and Ritualist Ethics

The most eloquent exponent of the ritualist ethics of the *k'ao-cheng* scholars was Ling T'ing-k'an. He epitomized his understanding of Confucianism in the statement: "The Way of the sages is only ritual propriety." [23] Hu Shih aptly called Ling's ethical teachings a "philosophy of ritual." [24] Hu, however, did not recognize the strong parallels between Tai Chen's views on ethics and those of Ling T'ing-k'an. [25] The importance of Ling's ethical philosophy has not received the proper attention.

Despite the contemporary stress on Han exegetes, Ling did not believe that the term *Han-hsüeh* (Han learning) accurately characterized the Classical studies of his times. He had misgivings about the increasingly fragmented textualism that was obscuring the purist goal of seeking the original Confucian teachings. [26]

Ling's ethical view cannot be understood without reference to his anti-heterodox stance. Like Ch'en Ch'üeh, P'an P'ing-ko, Yen Yüan, and Li Kung, Ling condemned all versions of neo-Confucianism as Ch'an Buddhism. [27] Despite the efforts of his predecessors in the K'ang-hsi period to extirpate Buddhist elements from neo-Confucian teachings, Ling continued to criticize them as heterodox. He felt that the attempts of scholars like Ku Yen-wu, Mao Ch'i-ling, and Tai Chen to purify Confucian teachings left something to be desired. [28] However severe their strictures might be, they were no more than internal strife among contending factions of neo-Confucians.

For Ling, even Tai Chen had not completely weaned himself from Buddhist influence. He found vestiges of Buddhist ideas in Tai's major critique of neo-Confucianism, the *Verification of the Literal Meanings of the Mencius*, which began with an exposition of the meaning of the term "principle" and discussed "elementary learning" (*hsiao-hsüeh*) in terms of "substance-function" (*t'i-yung*) and other language similar to the teachings of the Ch'eng-Chu school. According to Ling's study, the *t'i-yung* dyad was prima facie evidence of Buddhist dualism. It had been profusely employed in Sung neo-Confucian exegeses of Confucian Classics. [29]

Li Kung had criticized the neo-Confucian term *t'i-yung* and rejected it as a concept impregnated with Buddhist dualism, but he did not formulate

a philological argument to advance his case.[30] Ling, however, traced the
t'i-yung concept to the Ch'an Buddhism introduced by Bodhidharma.[31] In
the *Analects*, the word *yung* (function) never appears in conjunction with
the character *t'i* (substance). Only in neo-Confucian writings were the
two characters used as a term and applied liberally in explaining Confucian ideas. What the neo-Confucians had been expounding, Ling argued,
was nothing but Ch'an Buddhism, which had gained a hold on Chinese
scholars in the T'ang dynasty.[32] What is important here is not so much the
accuracy of Ling's philological research as his anti-heterodox stance. With
one stroke he swept all neo-Confucianism persuasions into the category
of heterodoxy.

Ling further disputed the idea that the Sung neo-Confucians excelled
in articulating the moral truths (*i-li*) of the Classics whereas Han scholars knew no peer in their knowledge of ancient institutions and regulations (*chih-shu*).[33] This stricture could also have been aimed at Tai Chen,
who entertained such a view when he was 32.[34] Those who agreed with
Tai Chen did not realize that any attempt to approach moral truths as
abstract principles, as the neo-Confucians did, was a practice of Ch'an
Buddhism.[35]

Ling's discontent with Tai Chen's incomplete purge of Buddhism notwithstanding, he held Tai in high regard and continued to ponder the
issues of human nature and desire along the lines set forth in Tai's philo-
sophic writings. Unlike Tai Chen, however, he did not attempt to refute neo-Confucian dualism at any length. In fact he wrote sparingly on
philosophical issues, for he, like most Han Learning scholars, dismissed
theoretical formulations as personal speculation. His basic ethical position
was that it is a deviation from Confucianism to speak of human nature
independently of ritual propriety.[36]

Ling's interest in ritual was evident as early as 1792, the year he completed the first draft of his monumental study on the *Book of Etiquette and
Decorum*, which was an attempt to enumerate the general rules underlying
all the rituals recorded in that Classic.[37] In 1802 he put forth in a more
coherent manner a monistic conception of human nature. His famous "On
Returning to Ritual Propriety" ("Fu-li lun") represents his purist effort
to formulate a cogent reinterpretation of the main goals of Confucian
ethics.[38]

Contrary to the neo-Confucian notion, Ling maintained that human
nature is anything but principle (*li*). Ling had deep disdain for this term.
The neo-Confucians who had appropriated the term to discuss human

nature had done violence to Confucianism by substituting a Buddhist notion for Confucian teachings. For Ling, principles are abstract and elusive and incapable of verification.[39] They are useless for moral cultivation because people mistake their own personal opinions for principles and assume them to be the absolute truths.[40]

Ling understood human nature essentially in terms of physical endowment. According to Ling, the human being is constituted of "material force" (ch'i) and "five elements" (wu-hsing) and comprises senses and faculties of the body. The individual is in perfect balance (chih-chung) before feelings, emotions, and desires arise.[41] In Tai Chen's favorite term, these are "blood-forces" or "physiological forces" (hsüeh-ch'i). The perfect balance is easily upset in either direction when feelings and desires arise,[42] but human desires are not essentially evil or the opposite of true nature. They are necessary for the nourishment of the human body and need to be controlled rather than extirpated. Ling reduced the desires to "likes and dislikes" (hao-wu).[43] When the senses encounter the external world, feelings of "like or dislike" emerge. As these feelings develop out of physiological reactions, they are unreasoned and tend to run either to excess or to insufficiency; the balance of human nature is disturbed as a result.[44]

To "restore" (fu) the balance, ritual propriety is required to keep the expression of feelings and desires at an appropriate level. Ling did not employ the term "restoring nature" in the neo-Confucian sense of retrieving something lost or blurred by human desires. Since human nature is not principles embedded in the mind, it cannot be discovered by introspection. For Ling, the balance is frequently disrupted, and constant effort is needed to maintain it. In theory, the balance as it exists before the emergence of feelings and desires is irrelevant since the latter constantly arise in response to internal impulses and external stimuli. What matters is the balance achieved during their expression. When the feelings and desires are expressed and satisfied in accord with ritual propriety, human nature is restored to its harmonious state. For Ling, this is the basic teaching of Confucianism on moral cultivation.[45]

For Ling, the Confucian method of self-cultivation is not a personal undertaking and cannot be done in isolation. It is a far cry from the Buddhist or Taoist methods for achieving spiritual liberation or physical immortality, let alone the introspection exercises of neo-Confucians. Moral qualities must be acquired in the context of inter-human relationships. Rituals that reinforce Confucian social ethics such as filial piety, loyalty to the monarch, and the notion of social hierarchy govern the conduct of people of all stations.[46] The authoritarianism of Ling's ethics is unmistakable in his explanation of why people should be taught to abide by proper rules of behavior rather than to seek to understand principles. Those who are not taught how to conduct themselves by developing habits of proper behavior must use their own judgment in dealing with society. They must depend on their understanding of principles. This impromptu manner of social interaction always results in improper conduct.[47] Ling's argument parallels that of Tai Chen in its stress on developing proper habits through constant drill in clearly defined patterns of behavior.

With respect to principles, Ling went a step further than Tai Chen in systematically applying the hermeneutical rules of linguistic purism to neo-Confucianism. Whereas Tai Chen still spoke of ritual propriety in terms of "ordering principle" (t'iao-li), Ling simply jettisoned the term li and designated optimal rules as ritual propriety. According to his study, the *Analects* never use the word li (principle), but make numerous references to ritual propriety.[48]

Despite his commitment to philological evidence, Ling's interpretation of Classical ideas sometimes was based more on ideological than on philological grounds. Moreover, his argument is valid only if one confines Confucian teachings to the *Analects*. As Tai Chen's critique showed, the *Book of Changes* and the "Record of Music" ("Yüeh-chi") in the *Book of Rites by the Senior Tai* did employ the term "principle."[49] Ling's abhorrence of the term and his preoccupation with ritual propriety prompted him to disregard philological evidence, which he claimed to be the touchstone for evaluating the purity of the teachings advanced by neo-Confucians. Fang Tung-shu (1772–1851), in an impassioned apology for neo-Confucian usage of the term "principle," pointed out that it was used in the "Yüeh-chi" and that Ch'eng I owed his notion of the equation of principles and human nature to Cheng Hsüan's commentaries.[50] If Cheng Hsüan was to be trusted because of his extensive knowledge of the Classical language and ritual, why were Ch'eng I and the Sung neo-Confucians to be excoriated for distorting Confucian teachings? They were in fact liable only to the charge of not rejecting Cheng Hsüan's interpretation.

In ritual propriety Ling saw the essence of Confucianism. On its basis he presented his own interpretation of Confucianism. Unlike Tai Chen, who regarded Mencius as the most faithful student of Confucius, Ling gave the laurel to Hsün-tzu. As discussed above, Tai Chen in many ways was closer to Hsün-tzu than to Mencius. At least, his stress on eliminating erroneous ideas and learning ritual propriety as a major means of "expanding" one's initial sense of goodness resembles Hsün-tzu's dependence on ritual propriety for "attaining" (*wei*) good nature. Both teachings underline the exteriority of the knowledge of ritual propriety and the need for human exertion, whether it be "expansion" of an innate sense of the good or "regulation" of natural impulses. In a preface to a eulogy of Hsün-tzu, Ling T'ing-k'an wrote: "The writings of Hsün-tzu record nothing but the lost texts of ritual propriety, expound their profound meanings. . . . Mencius always explained *jen* in terms of duty [*i*], whereas Hsün-tzu spoke of *jen* in conjunction with ritual propriety. . . . [Without ritual propriety] *jen* is as elusive as it is incomprehensible."[51] In the knowledge of ancient ritual propriety, Hsün-tzu surpassed Mencius.[52]

Hsün-tzu's teachings had long been discredited for his theory of "evil nature" (*hsing-o*). Neo-Confucians shared with their predecessors a strong disapproval of Hsün-tzu's view of human nature. Ling's perspective on Hsün-tzu serves to undermine the neo-Confucian exaltation of Mencius, and his reinterpretation of Hsün-tzu was clearly an attempt to appraise anew the overall doctrine of Confucianism.[53]

Ling re-examined some critical passages and concepts in the *Four Books*. The *Doctrine of the Mean* and the *Great Learning* were important sources of neo-Confucian ethics and metaphysics, but for Ling, they were no more than expositions on ritual propriety.[54] Since the rise of Sung neo-Confucianism, the doctrine of vigilance in solitude (*shen tu*) had been understood as a method of spiritual cultivation and parallels had been drawn between it and the Buddhist and Taoist practice of quiet-sitting. Ling argued that neo-Confucians who practiced quiet-sitting and introspection had read Buddhist and Taoist ideas into the text. He agreed that the term involved introspection but contended that it referred to ritual propriety as used in the *Doctrine of Mean* and the *Great Learning*. In solitude one should watch whether one's conduct was properly cultivated according to ritual propriety.[55]

The term *ko-wu* (investigation of things) had elicited much debate between adherents of the Ch'eng-Chu tradition and the followers of the Wang Yang-ming school. To Ling, however, the explanations of both schools were mere speculations, if not distortions of the original meaning. In a letter to Ch'ien Ta-hsin, he argued that *wu* (things) could not refer here to anything other than ritual propriety. If it meant things in general, a lifetime would not suffice for the study of all things. *Ko-wu* is equivalent to *ko-li* (investigation of ritual propriety). Not just the investigation of things but also "sincerity in intention" (*ch'eng-i*), "rectification of mind" (*cheng-hsin*), and "self-cultivation" (*hsiu-shen*) require ritual propriety.[56] Hence to speak of the Way as separated from ritual propriety was both elusive and unreliable: "The way of sages is based on ritual propriety, which is what they see as real. The way of heterodoxy renounces ritual propriety, and its teachings are mere speculations without substance."[57]

Like Tai Chen, Ling regarded the knowledge of ritual propriety as external to ordinary humans; the sages' nature was so balanced that no external rules were required. Ordinary people and scholars alike, however, had to learn ritual propriety so that their feelings and desires could be kept in balance and their nature be restrained (*chieh-hsing*).[58] Like all Han Learning scholars, Ling regarded the Classics as the repository of absolute ritual propriety. It is not surprising that he regarded the *Book of Etiquette and Decorum* as paramount among the Classics. He spent thirty years trying to comprehend the rules he believed to be the absolute moral truths by which the sage-kings designed the ritual and institutions of high antiquity. Like Chiang Yung and Hang Shih-chün, he hoped to discover the common principles or rules underlying all the rituals.[59] In his view, the greatness of the Duke of Chou was unmatched; without him, there would have been no institutionalization of "human ethical relations" (*jen-lun*).[60]

Even though both Tai Chen and Ling T'ing-k'an stressed the role of learning ritual propriety in developing good character, their ideas differed subtly. Tai was still concerned about "principles," about the need to come to grips with the meaning of "propriety" through the exercise of intellect. Ling, by contrast, tended to put a premium on practice and the molding of behavior through repetitive action. Put differently, Tai still believed in discussion of the symbolic domain of ritual, whereas Ling came to stress the performative side of ritual. As Ling envisioned it, the perfect society of the Three Dynasties was made possible because everyone from the sovereign to the lowest subject was bound by ritual propriety, and no one went against it. Everyone gradually restored their balanced nature without knowing it.[61] The advantage of ritual as the means for cultivating good conduct lay in its exteriority as well as its demand for uniform compliance. Despite his suspicion of personal bias, Tai Chen was optimistic enough to believe that universal agreement on the propriety of rules could be attained by exercise of the human intellect. By contrast, Ling had little faith in the possibility that everyone would agree on universal principles.

Lurking behind Ling's thinking was a strong distrust of the common people's ability to perceive propriety without help. What they could offer were mostly personal opinions. If scholars sought principles of moral cultivation through their intellect, the worthies would go to extremes whereas the obtuse would fall short of the proper standard.[62] At one point, Ling even said that if the sages set out to seek principle, they could possibly mistake their personal opinions (ssu-hsin) for principle, a fear that Tai Chen shared. Hence sages chose to depend on ritual propriety as the guide to the restoration of nature.[63] For Ling, scholars should study canonical rituals both for methods of cultivating their own morals and for teaching the common people how to discharge their duty. Like many purist ritualists, Ling personally practiced what he understood to be the teachings of the *Book of Etiquette and Decorum*.[64]

Juan Yüan: Tseng-tzu and Philology

The ritualist ethics espoused by Han Learning scholars was further clarified by Juan Yüan, whose reinterpretation of Confucianism was increasingly couched in terms of linguistic evidence. Despite the monistic view of human nature and the conviction of the validity of historico-philological approach to the Classics that he shared with Tai Chen and Ling T'ing-k'an, Juan arrived at a Confucian ethics with a scope even narrower than that of his predecessors.

The expunging of non-Confucian ideas continued unabated. Juan Yüan shared with Tai Chen and Ling T'ing-k'an a strong aversion toward Buddhism and Taoism. As noted in Chapter 6, he argued cogently for the methodological principle of temporal proximity central to linguistic purism. Because of his persistent criticism of the enormity and ubiquity of the impact of Buddhist and Taoist ideas on Confucianism, he made it a matter of principle to depreciate post-Han commentaries and exegeses of the Classics.[65]

Juan Yüan's purist approach to Confucianism is conspicuously reflected in his philological arguments for his ethics and in his criticism of Ling T'ing-k'an. He felt that Ling's theory of moral cultivation was influenced by Taoism. Despite the efforts of Tai Chen and Ling T'ing-k'an, Confucianism remained vitiated by remnants of heterodox notions.

Juan esteemed Ling for his treatise *On Returning to Ritual Propriety*, but he had misgivings about Ling's term *fu-hsing* (restoring nature). He argued that the phrase did not appear in the Confucian Classics,[66] but was a term employed by the Taoist Chuang-tzu, who had denounced culture and learning as erosions of human nature. (Juan is here echoing Tai Chen's criticism of Chuang-tzu's disparagement of learning.)[67] Such an anti-intellectualist attitude informed the influential "On Retrieving Nature" of the T'ang scholar Li Ao (772–841), whose thinking in this regard presaged the neo–Confucian concept of human nature.[68] By means of philological deduction, Juan discovered that the ancients spoke only of "regulating nature" (chieh-hsing), never of "restoring nature."[69] Confucius instructed Yen Hui only in "returning to ritual propriety" (fu-li), not in restoring nature.[70]

Juan Yüan's theory of human nature owed much to Tai Chen, but he tended to be more consistent in fashioning his ideas in the form of philological arguments. He found that the word hsing (nature) was seldom used in early Chou writings.[71] It first appeared in the Book of History and was made up of the character "life" (sheng) and "mind" (hsin) and hence meant "blood forces" (hsüeh-ch'i) and "mind-intellect" (hsin-chih).[72] Since human desires grow out of feelings (ch'ing) and are inalienable elements of human nature, it is a mistake to exclude them from considerations of human nature. Besides, the desires themselves are not evil, for humans are born with a physical being and must satisfy their basic bodily appetites.[73] To corroborate his argument, Juan assembled many passages and notes by Han scholars such as Cheng Hsüan and Hsü Shen.

The Shuo-wen says, "Nature is the yang force of man; hence human nature is good. Feelings are the yin force along with desires [yü]." Hsü [Shen]'s explanation is the ancient meaning. . . . Feelings are a part of nature; they are not something independent of or in contrast to nature. Cheng [Hsüan] explained the words wu (things) and tse (rules) in terms of nature, which includes feelings. Cheng's view is the old meaning before the Han period.[74]

Hsü's definitions could be interpreted as a dualistic conception of human nature. His notion of human nature was an important one in the Han and was infused with the idea of yin-yang. In fact, Hsü was influenced by the second century B.C. philosopher Tung Chung-shu, who perceived a bifurcation of nature on the one hand and feelings and desires on the other.[75] Juan, however, was either unaware of or indifferent to this possibility.

Juan Yüan clearly knew that in equating life (sheng) with nature (hsing), he was endorsing the heterodox teaching of Kao-tzu, whose theory of human nature Mencuis had rejected. Juan therefore argued that Kao-tzu's mistake lay not so much in identifying life with nature as in confusing human nature with animal nature.[76] For Juan, human beings are distinguished from animals by their innate goodness.

The very physical constitution of human beings demands the satisfaction of various appetites of the senses as well as the desire for leisure (an-i). Juan, like Tai Chen and Ling T'ing-k'an, saw desires as natural impulses with a life of their own. If unchecked, they would run to extremes, resulting in immorality and social chaos. Therefore, bodily appetites need restraint.[77] In the "Chao-kao" chapter of the *Book of History*, the Duke of Chou's exhortation to his younger brother, Juan found the first occurrence of such a teaching in the term *chieh-hsing* (restraining nature).[78] Unfortunately, most people are not intelligent enough to limit their desires voluntarily. As explained in the *Doctrine of the Mean*, those who are perfectly intelligent simply let their nature run its course and keep their bodily appetites within limit without the aid of learning (*tzu ch'eng ming wei chih hsing*). On the other hand, the obtuse need to be taught the proper way to control their desires (*tzu ming ch'eng wei chih chiao*).[79] Juan echoed Ling T'ing-k'an's view in his remark that everyone has to learn ritual propriety in order to "restrain" nature. *Chiao* (teaching) refers to the "six rituals" (*liu-li*) that the official for education taught subjects so they could cultivate their nature.[80] The need to "restrain nature" is what the *Doctrine of the Mean* refers to in the passage "To cultivate the way is teaching" (*hsiu tao chih wei chiao*) and what the *Great Learning* calls "self-cultivation" (*hsiu-shen*).[81]

Juan Yüan's idea of self-cultivation is best spelled out in his philological treatise on the meaning of *k'o-chi fu-li* (restraining oneself in order to return to ritual propriety). Ch'eng I had interpreted *k'o-chi* as the suppression of selfish desires (*ssu-yü*). According to Juan, Ch'eng's exposition was philologically unsound. Juan argued that *chi* in the next phrase *wei jen yu chi* (to perform *jen* depends on oneself) could not possibly be translated "selfish desires." *Chi* simply meant oneself as opposed to other persons. Specifically, *k'o-chi* involved the bringing of oneself in line with ritual propriety in matters of seeing, hearing, speaking, and bodily movement, and thus into the state of *jen* with others.[82]

By stressing the realizing of *jen* in relation to others, Juan was taking aim at the neo-Confucian rendition of *jen* as the essence of mind. For Juan, mind and *jen* are not identical. If the mind itself is *jen*, one need not learn or practice ritual propriety, nor is it necessary to realize *jen* in relation to other human beings.[83] Such an interpretation would certainly grant *jen* to neo-Confucians, who contemplated *jen* in their minds.[84] Hence, what Mencius called the sense of sympathy as *jen* is no more than the beginning (*tuan*). This frail beginning needs to be developed and realized in concrete human action (*jen chih shih-shih*).[85] There is no *jen* without human endeavor.[86] It was obvious to Juan that *k'o-chi* meant self-cultivation through the practice of rituals.[87]

Juan's interpretation of *jen* also departed from that of Tai Chen, who used the term more in the sense of the quality (*te*) of the cosmos and the human mind. For Tai, *jen* designates nature's endless reproduction of life as well as the human virtue of helping others to complete their lives and to continue reproducing lives.[88] Juan Yüan would not agree that *jen* could be the virtue of the cosmos. Whereas Tai spoke of *jen* as an interior quality of the mind, Juan Yüan tended to stress the exterior relational dimension. Hence, for him moral development cannot be sought independently of human relationships.

Juan Yüan's view of self-cultivation is closer to Ling T'ing-k'an's than to Tai Chen's. In stressing *shih-shih* (concrete actions, thing or event) and conduct (*hsing*), Juan showed his preference for practice over intellect. This predilection was pronounced in his reappraisal of the relative importance of the Confucian Classics. Like most other scholars, Juan was never systematically consistent in his writings. Sometimes, he regarded the *Spring and Autumn Annals* and the *Classic of Filial Piety* as the most important texts;[89] at other times, he gave primacy to the *Analects* and the *Classic of Filial Piety*.[90] The exceptional status he accorded the *Classic of Filial Piety* was unmistakable. As a staunch purist, he believed in the validity of the earliest sources. He did not dispute that the teachings of Tzu-ssu and Mencius were in tune with those of Confucius, but, unlike Tseng-tzu, they had received no personal instruction from the sage himself. The ten essays by Tseng-tzu preserved in the *Book of Rites by the Senior Tai* were, together with the *Analects*, among the only extant writings by Confucius' disciples. For Juan Yüan, Tseng-tzu's teachings on filial piety even surpassed those of Mencius in their pure reproduction of Confucius' teachings.[91] He went so far as to say that "the way of Confucius lies nowhere other than in the *Classic of Filial Piety*."[92] Hence, those who commit themselves to the teachings of Confucius must begin with the writings of Tseng-tzu.[93]

Ritual propriety and filial piety eventually became the two pillars of Juan Yüan's ethical thinking. They also represent for him a proper combination of the doctrines of the Duke of Chou and those of Confucius. Whereas the Duke stressed restraining nature by ritual propriety, Confucius' teachings on filial piety epitomized the essence of moral obligations.[94] Juan Yüan seemed to take delight in the term *chieh-hsing*; the phrase so perfectly epitomized his idea of self-cultivation that he named his study the Chieh-hsing chai (The studio of restraining nature) and himself Chieh-hsing chai lao-jen (The old man of the studio of restraining nature).[95] His notion of human nature and self-cultivation had a great impact on his students in the Ku-ching ching-she, the academy he administered in Hang-chou, and the Hsüeh-hai t'ang, founded by him in Canton.[96]

I conclude this chapter with an evaluation of the ethical beliefs of the Han Learning scholars by Fang Tung-shu, who believed that Sung neo-Confucians had contributed more to the explanation of the Classics and hence had a prior claim on Confucian truths. "In the present, the Han Learning scholars prohibit the quest of principles and instead depend exclusively on rituals as the instrument of teaching. What they call rituals are nothing but the names of things, institutions that are recorded in the commentaries and annotations written by scholars of later times [i.e., the Han period]."[97] Fang's remark is by and large an accurate description of the Han Learning scholars' ritualist ethics, which was, as the preceding analysis shows, enmeshed in their historico-philological methodology. From the viewpoint of purist hermeneutics, the history of Confucian ethics since the Han was a process of deplorable subversion by unorthodox teachings; the best one could hope for was an accurate reconstruction of the archaic rules of human conduct.

From Tai Chen through Ling T'ing-k'an and Juan Yüan, there was a continuous intellectual attempt employing philological arguments to cleanse Confucianism of "Buddhist" and "Taoist" influences. These thinkers attempted to dismantle Sung neo-Confucian ethics, which they believed to be uncanonical, and sought to reinstate a monistic notion of human nature embracing feelings and desires. In addition to this linguistic purism was a tendency in their ethical thinking to emphasize conformity to external authority, which significantly undermined the intellectual autonomy essential to their evidential scholarship. They grounded ethics in Classical philology and the institutional history of the Classical age. Their own ethical values therefore tended to be historically bounded. Paradoxically, Tai Chen's ethical writings exhibit both a strong intellectualism and an implicit authoritarianism. Tai's intellectualism became attenuated amid the increasing demand for "seeking facts in things and events," which degenerated further into textualism and sometimes a fetish of antiquity.

The preceding remarks do not do justice to the contributions of the Classicists in the areas of ancient philology and the institutional history of high antiquity. It is not the objective of this study to discuss and honor the achievements of their empirical research, or to document its negative effects on Sung moral philosophy. Elman's excellent study serves that purpose well. His focus on the refined methods of research clearly demonstrates that these scholars' vigorous investigations did contribute to the understanding of ancient history.[98] My purpose here, however, is to bring out their purist commitment to Confucian ethical values.

We have seen that Ling T'ing-k'an did not follow Cheng Hsüan faithfully in regard to explaining principle. This is one example that shows philology was not applied freely. When it came to such important issues as principle and human nature, the *k'ao-cheng* scholars chose to ignore Cheng Hsüan's expertise. The philological expositions of Tai Chen, Ch'ien Ta-hsin, and Juan Yüan often deviated from the respect for philological evidence they professed when discrediting Sung neo-Confucian explanations and heterodox notions.[99] This inconsistency is best explained in terms of purist ritualism. We must distinguish their contributions in the areas of ancient philology and institutional history from the ethical convictions that motivated their scholarship. The failure to see the discrepancy between their method and their purpose has given rise to the puzzling questions raised in the Introduction of this study.

In the hands of Ling T'ing-k'an and Juan Yüan, ethical theory came even more to emphasize behavioral conformity. Despite divergent views on the relative importance of the Classics, they concurred on the critical role of ritual in moral development. Unlike their predecessors in the K'ang-hsi period, they did not accept Sung neo-Confucian rituals and interpretations of the Classics.

The Han Learning scholars never revived the Han exegetical traditions in their entirety,[100] but their study did lead them to understand the paramount importance of Hsün-tzu. In their attempts to redefine Confucianism, they came to shed new light on his writings. Tai Chen's criticism of Hsün-tzu notwithstanding, his position on the dynamic nature of moral development and his ritualism were reminiscent of the latter's views. Ling T'ing-k'an actually exalted Hsün-tzu above Mencius. The relative status of Mencius in the thinking of the Han Learning scholars continued to decline.[101] Based on seemingly solid philological study and the application of the principle of temporal proximity, Juan Yüan concluded that Yen Hui and Tseng-tzu were the most reliable sources of Confucian teachings.

With respect to the relation of the individual to society, the ethics of the Han Learning scholars, no less than that of their Sung neo-Confucian predecessors, strongly favored the subjection of the individual to uniformly instituted rules of conduct. Instead of stressing individuality in moral development, as radical thinkers did in the late Ming, they extolled the submission of the individual to authority, whether paternal or institutional. They began their critique of neo-Confucianism by condemning the latter's indulgence in speculation and introspection. Paradoxically, the intellectualism that characterized their methodology served an ethical position that stressed individual submission to external authority.

8

Ritualism and Gentry Culture: Women and Lineage

The rise of the Han Learning movement after the mid-eighteenth century did not undermine the gentry's commitment to building lineages as a local institution for promoting Confucian ethics and maintaining social order. The ritualist ethics of the Han Learning scholars in most cases served to enhance the gentry's effort to promote the ancestral cult and the cult of women's purity—two of the most important values on their cultural agenda. A discussion of Wang Chung's criticism will show the mounting pressure for women to conform to the cult of women's purity. As the criteria of the scholarly communication of the eighteenth century required, Wang's criticism had to be presented as ritual and Classical studies based on philological evidence.

Wang Chung: Philology as Social Criticism

Wang Chung was an active *k'ao-cheng* scholar. He received patronage from high officials such as Pi Yüan (1730–97) and Chu Yün (1729–81).[1] He was one of the few *k'ao-cheng* scholars who combined Classical studies with social criticism. In his hands philology became a powerful weapon for ridiculing social follies.

Wang was among the few who had a more sophisticated understanding of language. He noted that language sometimes was not to be understood literally. He argued, for example, that words such as *san* and *chiu* do not always mean "three" and "nine." In some contexts *san* means "for a long time," and *chiu* "infinite." By rendering *san* as "a long period of time," Wang advanced a different interpretation of a phrase in the *Analects* concerning the obligation of a filial son not to go against the will of his deceased father (*san-nien wu kai fu chih chih*). According to Wang, this phrase does not mean that the son should live according to his father's wishes for at least three years after his death; rather, it simply means that the son will be regarded as filial if he continues to uphold his father as a model for a long time.[2] Further, Wang argued that a son should respect his father's will because it corresponded with the Way, not simply because it was his father's.

Wang's reading can be regarded as a challenge to paternal authority. In reinterpreting the Classic, he ridiculed previous scholars and his contemporaries for misreading it and hence rendering conformity to paternal authority an absolute duty of the son whatever the propriety of the father's conduct. Moreover, Wang's interpretation could point to a hypothetical challenge to the idea of the three-year mourning period. If the phrase *sannien* means only "a long period," the three-year mourning period a son was obliged to observe for his parents may be understood to mean that one does not have to mourn for three years but for a period of time.[3] To mourn an oppressive and uncaring father for three years would be contrary to one's feelings and no more than a hypocritical gesture.

The Han Learning movement had revived the Classical notion of the complementary relationship between husband and wife. The marital relationship should be one of "affection, partnership, and shared responsibility."[4] Through his scholarship, Wang Chung revived Classical notions of women's status. Fang Pao had argued that it was in accord with ritual propriety not to install tablets for women in the family shrine. In contrast, Wang Chung argued that the ritual status of a mother equaled that of a father. In high antiquity wives had enjoyed the same status as husbands since they were also represented by tablets in worship rites. Culling the Classics, Wang Chung found several passages that clearly suggested women were represented by tablets in ancestor worship in high antiquity.[5]

Wang Chung also expressed deep concern for the mounting pressure for women to endure suffering in order to conform to notions of faithful widowhood and the duty of betrothed girls to remain unmarried if their prospective husband died. Several of his essays on ritual question the growing cult of women's purity. He was greatly disturbed by the glorification of death and suffering in the name of ritual propriety. The deaths of two unmarried girls to preserve fidelity to their betrothed prompted him to criticize the practice by delving into the Classics. He argued that the ancient sage-kings had discouraged excess in observing rituals. Death resulting from extreme grief or from suicide was at odds with the purpose of ritual, which was created to give people a way to release emotion without damaging their health. For a betrothed girl to grieve herself to death after her fiancé died was, according to Wang's research, acting contrary to ritual. It was also a violation of ritual for a betrothed girl to marry into her fiancé's family as a widow. To his dismay, such chaste young women actually believed that they were acting according to ritual.

Critical to Wang's argument is the question of what counts as a marriage, and which rites mark the formal or proper bonding of a couple. For him the betrothal did not constitute the beginning of a conjugal relationship. It was only one of three steps in the marriage ritual, and it was by no means the core ceremony. Alluding to the Classics, Wang argued that the crucial rite was the groom's "personal reception of the bride" (*ch'in-ying*). A betrothed girl who had never been received personally by the groom had not yet become a wife. Suicide or a pledge to remain faithful to the deceased fiancé did not confer upon a girl the status of widow. She had no obligation toward her deceased fiancé and his family. Pledging fidelity to a deceased fiancé was at odds with propriety. Even more so was committing suicide in the name of faithfulness to the fiancé.[6]

By the same token, it was a breach of ritual if her parents and the fiancé's parents allowed the girl to marry into the family of her deceased fiancé and adopt a son as his heir. Even if the girl desired such an action or the parents mandated such a "marriage," everyone had the obligation to stop her and her parents.[7] Here again Wang Chung was upholding ritual as an authority above parental power, a point noted above in connection with his views on a son's duty to abide by the wishes of his deceased father. Wang discussed these matters from the broad perspective of the Three Bonds—the relationships between ruler and official, husband and wife, and father and son—stressing the personal relationship of the couple.

A woman's service to her husband resembles that of an official to his ruler. Ch'iu Fang and Hsüan Hsi committed suicide when their rulers were killed. This is the highest manifestation of loyalty. But if their rulers die a natural death in bed, even their personal attendants need not take their lives. A literatus who has never paid homage to a ruler but [when the ruler dies] wails and kills himself cannot be regarded as a loyal official.[8]

Wang Chung was implicitly challenging the idea that the relationship between ruler and official is as natural as that between father and son.[9] To be sure, the marital relationship and the ruler-official relationship were governed by rituals, but these relationships were legitimate only if established according to proper ritual. Illegitimate relationships created no obligations.

Wang Chung's essay is not an ordinary piece of evidentiary scholarship. It was prompted by his personal knowledge of two girls who remained celibate and faithful to their deceased fiancés. One of the girls was the sister of the celebrated poet Yüan Mei; the other was the maid of Wang's patron Cheng Hu-wen (1714–84).[10] Wang Chung was not challenging a social ethic practiced by only a few exceptional families. He was battling a practice common among gentry families. Wang's view provoked a scholarly debate that involved Chang Hsüeh-ch'eng, the noted historian.[11] Chang conceded that a refusal to remarry and suicide to show loyalty to one's fiancé were practices without any basis in the Classics or in the commentaries, but he believed that to condemn these practices as contrary to "the teaching of status" (*ming-chiao*) was a mistake.[12]

The Cult of Women's Purity

Although philology could be used as a weapon of social criticism, the ritualist approach to ethics tended to promote an uncritical attitude toward established norms and practices. An important instance of this tendency is the unprecedented growth in the number of chaste widows and of cases of suicide committed by betrothed maidens and widows in the Ch'ing dynasty.

The spread and growth of the cult of women's purity was itself a complex social phenomenon with variations over time and space. The cult had long been prominent in areas where Han culture was firmly entrenched. Scholars from Hui-chou prefecture in Anhwei had for centuries taken pride in its claim as the birthplace of Chu Hsi, and it was common to attribute the comparatively large number of chaste women the prefecture produced to the strong influence of the Ch'eng-Chu school there.[13] Having expressed his great esteem for the moral excellence of the chaste women of Hui-chou, Lu Wen-ch'ao, a scholar committed to philological and textual studies of the Classics, suggested that such an exceptional performance resulted from the influence of Chu Hsi's teachings.[14] There are indications, however, that the cult of female chastity was not particularly strong in Hui-chou under the Ch'ing compared with other regions.

According to T'ien Ju-k'ang, "the cult of female chastity and fidelity seems to have gained greater momentum during the Ch'ing Dynasty."[15] She county in Hui-chou, Anhwei, was outstanding for its exceptionally large number (770) of chaste widows in the Ming, but the growth of the cult in other provinces in the Ch'ing dwarfed that figure. In 1827 T'ao Chu (1779–1839), then governor of Kiangsu, in a proposal to commemorate chaste women in Wu-chin and Yang-hu counties of Ch'ang-chou prefecture, reported a total number of 3,018.[16] The number of chaste women from each of these two counties over 183 years is almost double that of She county for the entire Ming dynasty, a time span of 276 years.[17] In Wu-chin and Yang-hu, the candidates were so numerous that they could not be honored by the standard practice of building an arch for each woman. T'ao suggested instead a large arch bearing the names of all those women approved for receiving imperial honor. The Board of Rites accepted T'ao's innovation and ordered other governors to do likewise. During his tenure as governor of Kiangsu (1825–30), T'ao recommended a total of 9,084 chaste women for such an honor.[18] The number of chaste women recommended for commemorative arches continued to soar. In 1843 the Board of Rites had to restrict honors to those who committed suicide to preserve their chastity. The heirs of those who died a natural death were not entitled to a grant for building an arch.[19]

The dramatic increase in the number of chaste widows owed much to a change in the criteria for award. Since 1304 honorific insignia had been granted chaste widows who were over 50 and had been under 30 when their husband died. In 1723, the minimum age for the award was reduced to 40 and the required period of chastity to 15 years. In the early nineteenth century, widows who had remained unmarried for 10 years qualified for honorific insignia.[20] Another factor in the rapid increase in the number of faithful widows was the government's practice of seeking out women from poor families whose virtues would otherwise have remained unrecognized.[21] If the eighteenth century did not witness a dramatic increase in the number of chaste widows, there is little question that this century saw heightened concern on the part of the gentry to promote widow chastity by relaxing the criteria for award. Whether there was in fact a substantial increase in chaste widows is irrelevant compared with the change in attitude.

The growth of the cult of women's purity was to some extent a result of the gentry's attempt to extend its cultural construction of the relationship between the sexes to both lower levels of society and non–Han ethnic communities.[22] The strong incentive for betrothed maidens and the widows to decide against remarriage cannot, however, be explained exclusively in terms of the aura increasingly bestowed upon women's purity.

In the Canton Delta and some parts of Fukien and Kwangsi where "delayed transfer marriage" and "marriage resistance" were practiced, there were cases in which, upon hearing the news of the death of the fiancé, the betrothed women would rush to the fiancé's house and perform all the necessary rites before returning home. These women were reported in local gazetteers as faithful widows.[23] This kind of fiancée chastity, to be sure, is not Confucian in nature. In fact, in addition to cultural and economic motives, sectarian belief in female celibacy also provided religious grounds for marriage resistance among maidens.[24] But the point here is that the economic contribution of women, whether unmarried, married, or widowed, was important to family survival. Parents-in-law had a strong incentive against their widowed daughter-in-law's remarriage.

Finally, the growth of the cult cannot be explained without reference to the highly competitive social environment of the mid-Ch'ing period. The remarkable social mobility resulting from the revival of commerce in the mid-Ch'ing also made it an urgent task among the gentry families to differentiate their women's conduct from that of the lower social classes.[25] Greater competition in the civil service examinations may have contributed to the heightened concern for bringing the conduct of women of frustrated examination candidates in line with that of the gentry families.[26] Ch'ing scholars were particularly wary of the increase in literacy, especially among gentry women. They sought to restrict the use of literacy to promote greater conformity to women's roles as mothers and wives.[27] However, their efforts did not prevent women from putting literacy to different uses, such as writing poetry and reading vernacular novels.[28]

Scholars and the Cult of Women's Purity

As might be expected, Ch'ing scholars played an important role in promoting female chastity. Indeed, evidence for this role abounds. In the K'ang-hsi period, Yen Yüan and Li Kung, their attacks on neo-Confucian rituals notwithstanding, fully endorsed the idea of chastity and suicide committed in its name.[29] Both Lu Lung-ch'i and Mao Ch'i-ling, however, rejected the idea and specifically opposed the practice of chastity by betrothed maidens.[30]

The polarization of Confucian scholarship into Han Learning and Sung Learning in the mid-eighteenth century did not polarize attitudes toward the cult of female chastity along partisan lines. Naturally, many proponents of the Ch'eng-Chu school endorsed widow and finacée chastity. Scholars such as Weng Fang-kang and Ch'eng Chin-fang argued that chastity on the part of a betrothed maiden was commendably in accord with the rules of propriety.[31] The towering figure of evidential research Tai Chen, expressing his regard for a chaste widow, commented that widows who refused to remarry and were willing to bear the wretched consequences of widowhood, including death, had attained the highest virtues of humanity (*jen*) and duty (*i*).[32] Tai's eulogy is reminiscent of the oft-quoted statement of Ch'eng I that a widow dying of hunger was a matter of little account, but remarriage, which would desecrate her chastity, was a serious matter. Many scholars roundly castigated Ch'eng I for this statement, but he was no more blameworthy than the many Ch'ing scholars who continued to praise such martyrdom. Under the influence of a ritualist approach to moral norms, leading scholars like Tai Chen who were otherwise distinguished for their criticism of Sung neo-Confucian ethics gave full consent to the idea and practice of female chastity.

Chi Yün, the chief editor of the *Ssu-k'u ch'üan shu* and a champion of Han Learning, espoused chastity with no less enthusiasm. The Ch'ing code did not honor those women who died while resisting sexual assault. Chi Yün submitted a memorial arguing that these victims were too weak to resist the rapists but their will to preserve chastity was no less than those who died successfully preventing their rape. They therefore deserved commemoration as much as those who succeeded in blocking the assault.[33] This proposal was equally important to Chiang Fan, a diehard Han Learning scholar, who deemed Chi's proposal important enough to be included in his intellectual biography of Chi.[34] The commendations of chastity expressed by such proponents of Han Learning as Chi Yün and Chiang Fan call into question the hypothesis that the Manchu state and the Ch'eng-Chu school were responsible for such a heightened puritanical idea of morals.[35]

Scholars whose intellectual vista transcended the narrow dichotomy between Sung Learning and Han Learning displayed similar convictions regarding female chastity. Lu Wen-ch'ao, a devoted scholar of Classical and philological studies who did not engage in polemics against Sung neo-Confucianism as a matter of principle, expressed admiration for fiancé chastity.[36] Chuang Ts'un-yü (1719–88), a pioneer in the study of the *Kung-yang Commentary*, held fiancées who pledged loyalty in deep regard.[37] Chiao Hsün, a versatile scholar with few peers in Classical learning, wrote a short treatise defending the propriety of fiancée chastity.[38] Hu Ch'eng-kung, a scholar devoted to nonpartisan Classical studies, considered arguments condemning fiancée chastity as a breach of propriety because of the absence of explicit rules in the Classics objectionable.[39] Li Chao-lo (1769–1841), an important leader of the Ch'ang-chou school in the nineteenth century, criticized Wang Chung for endorsing the sixteenth-century Ming scholar Kuei Yu-kuang's censure of fiancée chastity.[40] Even though scholars' attitudes toward fiancée chastity might be ambivalent,[41] few objected to the idea and practice of widow chastity.

It is clear from these examples that ideological affiliation cannot explain the different positions of scholars concerning the idea of chastity and the common practice of suicide committed in its name. What is especially noteworthy for this study is that Han Learning scholars did not consistently challenge established moral norms promoted by Sung neo-Confucians. Despite the discord over the proper approach to the Classics and the accurate reconstruction of ancient rites and institutions, scholars of diverse ideological affiliations helped promote conformity with external norms, whether they believed them to be canonical or neo-Confucian in origin. The next issue to be considered here is how the obsession with female chastity was reflected in the lineage leaders' attitude toward women.

Lineage and Widow Chastity

It was in the interest of scholars involved in lineage activities that their female relatives maintain a good reputation by strictly observing all rules of proper behavior. Misbehavior that violated norms of women's purity disgraced the entire descent group of which the scholars were members. By the same token, a commemorative arch bestowed by the imperial government on a chaste widow or maiden brought honor to the entire lineage.

Women were at a disadvantage in the patriarchal lineage not just because of their inferior status but also because of stereotypes of female behavior. Women were considered the major source of domestic conflicts. Most lineage regulations enumerated and warned against certain types of misbehavior by women, especially in their relations with their husband's family members.[42] On the other hand, Ch'ing lineages in general encouraged and rewarded women of moral excellence, especially chaste widows. Lineage rules reflected a general commitment to supporting widows. To help them remain unmarried, proceeds from lineage estates were used to support them and their dependent minors.[43] Some lineages pledged punishment for kinsmen who attempted to appropriate the properties of widows.[44] Occasional support notwithstanding, there was strong prejudice against widows who remarried. One who did so would be expelled from the lineage, and in many cases her name would be removed from the genealogy.[45] Some lineages forbade marriage with widows.[46] Although the lineage rules provide no information as to how effectively they were enforced, the attitudes and expectations of the lineage leaders were unmistakable.

Although the lineage played an important role in promoting widow chastity, the lineage was not a uniformly oppressive institution for women. The cult of female chastity undoubtedly conjures up unpleasant images of women suffering from suppression of emotional needs and denial of intimate relations with a living spouse. From the perspective of power relations, however, the cult of female chastity offered a widow greater ritual authority and control over her own family. Unlike an unmarried girl, a widow could, in the name of remaining faithful to her deceased husband, resist attempts to put her on the market as a concubine. As head of her own household, a widow could utilize the lineage to maintain and enhance her status. Jerry Dennerline has demonstrated that widows took a great interest in setting up charitable estates for their husband's lineage.[47] A lineage with charitable estates could underwrite the education of a widow's sons and provide support for the family. Her daughters, if married into a family with access to lineage charitable funds, would not be forced to remarry. Although the lineage in the Ch'ing strengthened partiarchal authority, widows enjoyed a greater role in preserving the patriline.

But chastity could take a great toll. It had become such a sacred virtue that voluntary and forced suicides were committed in its name. When a widow committed suicide in honor of her deceased husband or out of resistance to forced remarriage, lineage leaders would request the right to erect a *p'ai-lou* (commemorative arch) from the government.[48] The protective policies of many lineages as well as the imperial insignia made it desirable for widows to commit themselves to chastity, at least nominally. Some may have found it emotionally rewarding to be honored as moral exemplars. Those who headed a household could, moreover, enjoy a considerable degree of control over children and property. The belief in widow chastity was so pervasive in Kwangtung that in one case bandits attempted to absolve themselves of their molestation of a bride on the grounds that she was a remarried woman.[49] A recent study cites at least one case suggesting that the ideal of female chastity was not confined to literati families but was influential also at the lower levels of society.[50]

Under Ch'ing law widows enjoyed greater protection from forced remarriage. The T'ang and Ming legal codes gave her parents and grand-parents the right to arrange a remarriage. The Ch'ing Code, however, took away that right and specified 80 strokes for the widow's parents and grandparents if they arranged a second marriage against her will.[51]

Under the Ch'ing regime chastity acquired so much sanctity that it prompted actions bordering on absurdity. Chastity became a virtue earned not just by the sexual conduct of a woman but also by her efforts to maintain a good reputation. From the eighteenth century on, cases of a woman committing suicide after hearing obscenities or after being verbally abused multiplied. The Ch'ing Code included precedents (*li*) prescribing harsh punishments for the sexual harrasser. Whether the insulting remarks were merely overheard by a woman who later committed suicide, or made in her presence, or reported to her by a third person, the offender was held responsible and subject to punishment.[52] It is permissible to argue that the growth of the cult of female chastity gave Ch'ing women some legal protection against harrassment.

The status of women under the Ch'ing dynasty is a complex subject requiring further research. Since the May Fourth movement students of the subject have in particular condemned neo-Confucianism, especially the teachings of Ch'eng I and Chu Hsi, for promoting widow chastity and thereby inflicting such profound tribulations on women. But the question we need to ask is why with the rise of the Han Learning school, which criticized Sung neo-Confucianism for its puritanical ethics, the cult of female chastity seems to have reached new heights. True, those engaging in empirical studies constituted only a small segment of the gentry, and the majority were under the sway of the Ch'eng-Chu school. As noted above, however, scholars of all persuasions supported the cult of female chastity. If we move away from the Han versus Sung perspective and consider both the effects of the multiplication of lineages and the prevailing purist ritualism, the increasing puritanism and the unprecedentedly large number of chaste women reported in local gazetteers can be explained. Lineage rules in general attest that the belief in female chastity and its various puritanical expressions transcended the narrow dichotomy of Sung and Han Learning.

This brief discussion of lineage rules in relation to control of members' conduct supports the argument that purist ritualism nurtured a gentry less tolerant of non-Confucian values and highly concerned with conformity to Confucian socio-ethical values. This Confucian elite had come to stress the principle of patriarchy in social action and strongly influenced the functions of lineages. The proliferation of lineages in the Ch'ing dynasty strengthened the social status and authority of the gentry, who were thus able to exert greater control over their kin and, with the resources and organization provided by the lineage, over their local community as well. To be sure, the actual power of the gentry varied greatly.

The Gentry and Lineage Building

It is time to consider the relationship between purist ritualism and lineage development during the Ch'ing dynasty. Recent scholarship has considerably advanced our understanding of the complex temporal and regional variations in lineage development in Late Imperial China and alerted us to the need to take into account ecological and social differences in the formation of lineages.[53] These local variations notwithstanding, it is possible to detect a general trend in the gentry's participation in lineage building.

Chapters 3 and 4 analyze why scholars in the K'ang-hsi period took such an interest in strengthening kinship bonds and how the debates over the meaning of the descent-line system and the structure and liturgy of the ancestral temple were related to this goal. The following discussion covers the involvement in lineage affairs of the same scholars, especially eminent Classicists, treated in the previous chapters.

Despite the great variety in lineage organizations and practices, most lineage leaders in the eighteenth and nineteenth centuries concurred on the desirability of some institutions: a freestanding ancestral hall, a genealogy, corporate estates, and occasionally a lineage school. For our purposes, the scholar's role in the preparation of the lineage's genealogy is especially noteworthy.

To be sure, the writing of a genealogy does not presuppose the existence or the founding of a lineage, but it could serve as the first step in that direction.[54] A genealogy not only provided a documentary history (substantiated or manufactured) of a descent group but also maintained a list of nominal members who could be turned into an active corporate group when other institutions such as an ancestral hall or a sacrificial estate were founded.

Genealogy was an old genre of writing in China, but the Ch'ing period witnessed a proliferation in their number.[55] All genealogies establish a pedigree descended from an ancestor, often a "first ancestor."[56] The writing of genealogies therefore involved issues of ancestor worship and the much-debated descent-line system of high antiquity. This is where scholars contributed most to the evolving lineage organizations.

K'ao-cheng Scholars' Participation in Lineage Building

A great number of celebrated Ch'ing literati are known to have written genealogies for their own lineages either single-handedly or in collaboration with kin members, including Ch'ien Ch'ien-i, Ku Yen-wu, Chang Lü-hsiang, Huang Tsung-hsi, Lü Liu-liang, Wan Ssu-ta, Wang Yüan (1648–1710), P'u Sung-ling (1630–1715), Hsü Fang (1622–94), Weng Fang-kang, and Yao Nai.[57] Here a few examples of genealogies by renowned evidential research scholars will suffice.

Amid all his endeavors in the field of Classical scholarship, the polymath Tai Chen also took part in lineage building. He complained that the genealogy of his patriline had not been revised for more than a hundred years, and he undertook to revise and expand it. He traced his descent group over twenty centuries back to a great descent-line headed by a secondary son of a prince of the Sung feudatory in the Spring and Autumn period. His understanding of the qualifications of the great descent-line head resembled that of Mao Ch'i-ling, who argued that there had been only one great descent-line head among the secondary sons of a prince.[58] From this first ancestor, Tai reconstructed the pedigree of his own lineage. The genealogy was completed in 1773, three years before he completed the final revision of the *Verification of the Literal Meanings of the Mencius*.[59]

Lu Wen-ch'ao regarded the genealogy as an institution that provided kinship cohesion beyond the five degrees of mourning relations. Lu attempted to compile a genealogy for his kin group but was unable to complete it because of his official duties. The genealogy was eventually completed by a junior kinsman in 1791. Lu took great pleasure in writing a preface to commemorate the occasion.[60]

The case of Chi Yün, chief editor of the *Ssu-k'u ch'üan-shu* and a fervent promoter of Han Learning scholarship, is particularly revealing. Chi took the compilation of his genealogy seriously. His commitment to keeping a good record of his patriline was manifested in his lengthy explanation of the rules for entering biographical data.[61] Chi's method became a model for subsequent genealogies.

Ch'ien Ta-hsin's descent group did not have a lineage hall until his father proposed to build an ancestral hall in 1761 and undertook to compile a genealogy.[62] The proposal was made seven years after Ch'ien Ta-hsin passed the *chin-shih* examination.[63] The liturgy of the hall was in the main taken from the *Family Rituals by Master Chu*.[64] Like many other scholars of his time, Ch'ien wrote commemorative essays for his lineage hall and penned several prefaces to the genealogies of other lineages. In these writings, he expressed approval of the building of ancestral halls devoted to a first migrant ancestor even though the institution of first migrant ancestor was not canonical in origin.[65] Perhaps Ch'ien had to bow to his father's wish despite his complaint about the unreliability of Sung scholarship.

Ch'ien Ta-hsin's relative Wang Ming-sheng was a less renowned historian but he pursued Han scholarship with no less enthusiasm than did Ch'ien. He especially valued the special services the lineage could render the gentry. Commemorating the founding of a corporate estate to support a school for his lineage, Wang praised the institution as most beneficial in producing gentry.[66]

Wang Ch'ang, a celebrated paleographer of inscriptions on stones and bronze vessels, founded a lineage hall in 1781 to honor a first migrant ancestor, who, he argued, was qualified to be treated as the founder of a great descent-line. Attached to the lineage hall was a school and a library to be supported by 500 *mou* of corporate estates Wang personally donated.[67]

The father of Juan Yüan built a lineage hall with his own funds.[68] Juan Yüan's successful official career prompted his father to urge him to erect an official ancestral temple (*chia-miao*) in Yang-chou. The building was constructed in 1803–4.[69] In 1840 Juan Yüan himself completed a revised genealogy of his lineage.[70]

Sun Hsing-yen (1753–1818), one of the many scholars Juan Yüan helped, was an admirer of Han scholarship. Juan appointed him director of the Chi-shan Academy in Shao-hsing in 1800 when Juan was serving as governor of Chekiang.[71] Sun took the initiative to found a lineage hall in Nanking in memory of his first ancestor, who had earned a high military office for his contribution to the founding of the Ming regime. Sun even requested a commemorative essay from Yao Nai.[72]

Not unlike Sun, Ling T'ing-k'an was concerned about the loss to memory of the various patrilines descended from a first migrant ancestor who settled in Hsi county in Anhwei. In 1797 he began to compile a genealogy including all patrilines descended from that first ancestor.[73]

All these scholars were classified by Chiang Fan as accomplished students in the Han Learning tradition. Clearly their devotion to the study of ancient rituals were relevant to current concerns for kinship solidarity. This strong interest in building lineages through writing and revising genealogies, erecting ancestral halls, and founding corporate estates was shared by scholars in the eighteenth and nineteenth centuries regardless of ideological persuasion.

Chang Hsüeh-ch'eng (1738–1801), a critic of Tai Chen's indulgence in Classical studies and an eminent theorist of historical method, expressed no less anxiety over the long lapse of time since the last edition of the genealogy of his descent group.[74] Chang had long taken to heart the duty to compile a genealogy of his lineage.[75] He treated genealogical writings as seriously as other genres of historical writing and regarded them as basic sources for local history.[76] Chang shared the common belief that it was proper to build a lineage hall devoted to a first ancestor so that a descent group could pay homage to ancestors en masse.[77] Chang came from a large and powerful lineage in Chekiang with a strong tradition of scholarship and government service. By Chang's time, the existing ancestral hall was overcrowded, with the tablets of ancestors piling up in the hall. To solve the problem of supernumerary tablets, he proposed that the names of ancestors in different groupings be engraved on a large plaque instead of continuing the old method of setting up a separate tablet for each individual.[78]

The cases presented here indicate the role scholars of diverse ideological affiliations played in building lineages in the Ch'ien-lung and Chia-ch'ing period. Such evidence needs to be viewed in the general context of the Confucian elite's role in lineage leadership. Chapters 3 and 4 analyze how leading scholars of the K'ang-hsi period engaged in ritual reforms and how differences in reading the Classics spawned conflicting interpretations of ancient rituals. By dint of their knowledge of ancient rituals, many scholars came to have a controlling say in their lineages, even though there were other ways in which the gentry dominated lineages.

Gentry and Lineage Leadership

The importance of the gentry in building lineages cannot be overemphasized. Their activities in this regard warrant further study. For our purposes a brief discussion of the various roles of the Confucian elite suffices. Kung-chuan Hsiao notes that lineages under the Ch'ing regime were "normally promoted and dominated by the gentry."[79] This privileged group performed many functions crucial to the operation of lineages and provided not only the ideological justification for organizing lineages but also the theoretical and practical guidelines for many essential institutions, such as the ancestral hall, the descent-line system, genealogical records, and corporate estates.

It is not surprising that officials and degree-holders were strongly represented in lineage leadership. They were given special honors in liturgies both as worshipers and as ancestors. The elite, with its knowledge of proper rituals, was crucial to the performance of the elaborate rites of ancestor worship.[80] As noted in Chapters 3 and 4, the correct way to organize a lineage and conduct ancestral rites were subjects of enormous concern to scholars.

Lineage rules unmistakably favored degree-holders and officials in assigning liturgical and administrative duties.[81] As we saw in Chapter 3, officials were inclined to make government office the qualification for the chief officiant in ancestral rites, that is, for the descent-line head. Scholars such as Hsü San-li, Li Kuang-ti, Mao Ch'i-ling, and Ku Tung-kao insisted that officials and degree-holders should have precedence over kinsmen regardless of natural descent-line status and age.[82] More important, their degrees and official status sheltered the lineage from extortion by clerks and runners and, depending on their rank, gave them access to different levels of political influence.

Clearly, those among the gentry who not only contributed large amounts to the lineage but also possessed political influence had the power to determine the rules of its operation. When Fang Pao, for example, established lineage rules for his own patriline, he specified that the holder of the highest official rank or degree would officiate at ceremonies in the lineage hall.[83] Yin Hui-i made the same rule when he built an ancestral hall and corporate estates for his lineage.[84]

The special status the gentry enjoyed in the lineage can be seen in the privileges many lineage rules accorded them. Degree-holders received larger amounts of sacrificial meat in accordance with rank. A *chü-jen* degree and an office enabled a lineage member to have his tablet admitted into the ancestral hall without a fee.[85] Some lineages rewarded successful candidates in the civil service examinations with amounts ranging from 80 taels for attaining the highest honor at the palace examination to 2–10 taels for the lowest degree.[86] By formulating the lineage rules and influencing the selection of lineage managers, the gentry were able to legitimize their special status and interests. Some lineage rules even included admonitions against harming members who were degree-holders, officeholders, or wealthy. Such members of the gentry had the ability to protect and bring prosperity to the entire lineage.[87]

The Confucian elite had always played an important role in compiling genealogies.[88] As Kung-chuan Hsiao notes, lineages with genealogical records always had a large body of degree-holders as members.[89] The lower number of literati in north China yielded a small number of genealogical records.[90] Officials and degree-holders were in a better position to provide the necessary financing for the compilation and printing of the genealogy. Their literary skills as well as the respect they commanded among their kinsmen were also indispensable to such an undertaking.

Genealogies were no small literary exercises. The ability of the gentry to cull the Classics for canonical principles placed them at an advantage. Lineages with a large membership required full-time efforts by many scholars to compile and print their records. The huge funds necessary for such an undertaking sometimes were obtained when the lineage elders were powerful enough to levy a tax on each household for the compilation and printing of the genealogy.[91] The role of the gentry in keeping genealogical records is demonstrated by the case of Liu Jung (1816–73), a famous leader of the Hunan army during the Taiping rebellion. Although over 10,000 kinsmen lived in the vicinity, the descent group did not have a genealogy until Liu Jung took the initiative in 1856.[92]

The possession of a literary education and economic resources naturally elevated the gentry above other social classes in the contest for controlling the lineage. Recognizing the importance of the gentry in lineage building and management is, however, not to slight the equally important contributions of merchants. The strong lineages of Hui-chou in particular attest to the importance of commercial wealth in lineages. The Hui-chou merchants funded the compiling and printing of genealogies, the building of large ancestral halls, and the setting up of lineage estates.[93]

There were lineages free from gentry control and lineages only partially controlled by the gentry. There were instances in which poor tenants in the lineage organization violently resisted demands from their wealthy kinsmen for rent arrears.[94] But in general the gentry had a firm hold on lineage leadership, and their willingness to help maintain order and peace in the local community was essential to maintaining hegemony.

Lineage and Social Order

The omnipresence of lineages in Kiangsi prompted some officials such as Ch'en Hung-mou (1696–1771), in his capacity as governor of that province (1742–43) to utilize lineages to help maintain local order. The lineage elders (*tsu-chang*) were authorized to punish violators of Confucian norms and laws.[95] The governor-general of Chekiang and Fukien made a similar proposal in 1775. Another was submitted by a provincial official in 1789. But the Ch'ien-lung emperor was suspicious of lineage chiefs and rejected the idea of granting them the power to punish kin.[96] As secret society activities increased in Kiangsi, however, the court ordered lineage chiefs and the gentry in the province to oversee the conduct of their kin and, in effect, serve as local watchmen for the court.[97]

Ku Yen-wu's and Lu Shih-i's proposals that lineages should be organized to supplement the state in the task of administration were no longer just an ideal. As the lineage-building movement gathered momentum in the eighteenth century under the great pressure of population growth, an increasing number of descent groups, especially in central and south China, began to organize into lineages, making such a vision practical. By the mid-nineteenth century, lineages with ancestral halls were ubiquitous in central and south China.[98] Some scholars concerned with statecraft suggested that lineages help maintain social order at the local level.

Lineage: Statecraft and Liturgical Governance

Early nineteenth-century Confucians of diverse ideological backgrounds saw lineages as an effective solution to many problems. Chang Hsüeh-ch'eng, for example, shared the view of other scholars that lineage charitable estates were filling a gap in welfare left by the imperial government.[99] Hung Liang-chi, an extremely versatile scholar, argued for more lineage control of social conduct; this would reduce the administrative burden on the state.[100]

But lineages could serve purposes other than those sanctioned by Confucian idealism. Instead of being stabilizing institutions at the local level, lineages could create abominable social problems. Lineages were so widespread in such provinces as Fukien and Kwangtung that lineage feuds became a major form of collective social violence.[101] In the wake of the 1681 revocation of the coastal evacuation, descent groups in Fukien and Kwangtung found better organization essential to survival and success in scrambling for land and control of resources.[102] From the mid-Ch'ing on, lineage feuds increased in frequency as conflicts for control of market towns and natural resources intensified.[103] Such armed affrays among lineages, however, did not convince the gentry or the Manchu government to take strong measures against lineages, although the Classical scholar Ch'en Shou-ch'i (1771–1834) thought that lineage feuds could be reduced by increasing official control over the lineages themselves.[104] It was difficult for the Ch'ing government to ban the lineage, thanks to the strength of the Confucian ideology from which the kinship institution derived its legitimacy.[105]

In the statecraft thought of the nineteenth century, lineage organization became an extremely important element in the discourse on "liturgical governance," which was a major focus for solutions to problems of local society. Chang Hai-shan (1782–1821), a scholar with an eclectic bent,[106] argued that the pao-chia system based on residence and neighborhood was not reliable for defense. He believed that the descent-line system had the advantage of appealing to mutual feelings among kindred. As a kinship institution, the descent-line system was the best agency to carry out some functions of local government, such as collecting taxes, policing neighborhoods, dispensing relief to the needy, settling disputes among kinsmen, and promoting social ethics. People otherwise loosely associated could be "gathered together" (chü) under the leadership of the descent-line heirs.[107]

In the Tao-kuang period, among scholars concerned with practical statecraft problems, there was a strong belief in the potential of lineages as supplementary institutions of local government. Such famed scholars of the Kung-yang school as Kung Tzu-chen (1792–1841) and Wei Yüan (1794–1856) were of the opinion that lineages were essential to social stability. In order to solve the problem of land distribution, a fundamental source of social unrest, Kung set forth in 1823 a land-tenure system based on the principle of the descent-line. He called for a redistribution of land among the "descent-line heads [both great and lesser] of the peasants" (nung-tsung); the resulting economic security should provide the foundation for a just and stable society.[108] Kung's ideas were too radical to appeal to the Confucian elite. His good friend Wei Yüan advanced a more moderate alternative. A year after Kung's proposal, Wei Yüan, in praising the founding of a charitable estate, suggested that the court restore the great descent-line system so that at the local level several hundred lineages throughout China could keep order and support social dependents.[109]

The growing interest in enlisting lineages to assist the local administration was not a flight of imagination on the part of its exponents. From mid-Ch'ing on, in various places in Kiangsu, Chekiang, and Kwangtung, some lineage leaders collected taxes from the entire lineage in order to avoid extortion by clerks and runners.[110]

The important role of the lineages in maintaining social order and in supplementing the state apparatus was to a considerable extent borne out by the Opium War and the Taiping Rebellion. Frederic Wakeman has documented the importance of lineage involvement in the militia movement against the British during and after the Opium War. During the 1840's and 1850's, lineages and the militia in Kwangtung were "mutually intermingled."[111]

Philip Kuhn has shown that the lineage provided one of the basic organizational structures of local militarization.[112] Powerful lineages responded rapidly to the threats from the Taipings by raising militia from among their membership even before the Manchu court gave permission to enlist the help of the newly raised temporary forces in quelling the Taipings.[113] When Tseng Kuo-fan organized his new force in Hunan, lineage ties constituted the basic principle at the lower echelons.[114] As Kuhn aptly puts it, the Taiping rebellion "brought lineage into play on the lower levels of militarization in Central China just as chronic interlineage conflict had in the case of South China."[115] What is more important for subsequent social and political developments is that militarization in the mid-nineteenth century reinforced kinship solidarity and enabled lineage leaders to exert greater control over their community.[116] This trend was to persist into the Republican period.[117]

Conclusion

When Ku Hsien-ch'eng and K'ao P'an-lung rebuilt the Tung-lin Academy in 1604, the stage was set for a major reorientation of Confucianism—the rise of Confucian ritualism in the scholarly circle centered in the Lower Yangtze area. We have examined this intellectual movement in the areas of ethical thought, Classical learning, and lineage discourse from the seventeenth through the early nineteenth centuries. Ritualism emerged as the common framework in which the Chinese literati re-examined their role in relation to the Confucian heritage, the imperial state, and the common people.

Confucianism Redefined

The ritualist re-orientation of Confucian thought was already evident in the ethical thought of the Tung-lin leaders. Ritualism in the late Ming first evolved as part of the revival of Ch'eng-Chu neo-Confucianism. Scholars were attracted to the ritual scholarship of Chu Hsi and the ethical thought of Chang Tsai. The ritual and Classical studies of the K'ang-hsi period developed in the shadow of Sung and Yüan exegetical traditions. As the Han Learning movement gathered momentum in the mid-eighteenth century, linguistic purism prevailed, and Cheng Hsüan and other Han exegetes came to replace Chu Hsi as the authority on ancient ritual and exposition of the Classics. With the rediscovery of Hsün-tzu's ritualist philosophy and his crucial role in the shaping of the Han Classical tradition, the theoretical re-orientation of Confucianism was completed.

If the Confucianism of the Sung and Ming periods was the "learning of principle," or "the learning of the mind-and-heart," the Confucianism of the Ch'ing, at least down to the early nineteenth century, was the "learning of ritual." Ling T'ing-k'an epitomized this learning in the statement "The Way of the sages is nothing but [observing] rituals."[1] This conception of the quiddity of Confucianism was echoed by Tseng Kuo-fan (1811–1872), the famous Confucian statesman, who argued that the common ground on which Han and Sung Learning rested was ritual.[2]

Confucian Literati and the Imperial State

The Tung-lin leaders' desire for greater involvement of the imperial state in maintaining the cultural order was to a considerable extent attained under the Ch'ing. That a close relationship between the Confucian literati and the imperial state had been re-established can be seen in the K'ang-hsi emperor's attempt to restore the supremacy of Confucianism by making Ch'eng-Chu learning the imperial orthodoxy. Greater control over the examination system also helped restrict the ways in which the Classical tradition could be interpreted in the eight-legged essays. The system of rewarding the gentry with official appointments and numerous local privileges for their services and normative compliance was re-established. The gentry could count on the Manchu state to support their superior status within the social hierarchy. It hardly needs mentioning that tension between the Manchus and the Chinese continued to be a problem of the imperial government throughout the Ch'ing dynasty.

Nevertheless, a close relationship between the Confucian literati and the imperial state can be seen in the new pattern of patronage by the Manchu government and officials. The powerful current of ritualism evolved in connection with the imperially sponsored Bureau for the Compilation of the Three Ritual Classics and the semiofficial patronage of ritual research by such high bureaucrats as Hsü Ch'ien-hsüeh and Ch'in Hui-t'ien. The bureau and the network of patronage became the arena where the competition between two approaches to the Confucian tradition was fought out. The polarization of Confucian discourse into Han Learning and Sung Learning in the mid-eighteenth century to a certain extent took place in an institutional context directly and indirectly linked to the state. The triumph of the Han Learning movement also bore the stamp of the Ch'ien-lung emperor's patronage in the grand *Ssu-k'u ch'üan-shu* project.

The ascendancy of ritualism also contributed significantly to the growth of the lineage-oriented ancestral cult, which helped reshape the relationship between the imperial state and the gentry at the local level. Even though there were regional variations in the distribution of gentry and the relative strength and variety of lineages, I would venture to suggest that with the proliferation of lineages under the Ch'ing, the local power of the gentry and the non-gentry elite was greatly enhanced. Unlike the gentry in the late Ming who depended primarily on horizontal networks of personal ties to officials or eunuchs, the gentry under the Ch'ing had deep roots in local society. An important source of their power came from the control of lineages. Unlike academies in the early Ch'ing and ordinary religious organizations, the lineage as a social organization was unequivocally sanctioned by the Confucian value of kinship. Shrouded in Confucian language, the lineage was able to provide the gentry with an institution through which they could increase their power at the local level without risking charges of sedition by the imperial state. The gentry now had at their disposal an institution with a variety of means—financial, ideological, and psychological—to make use of their kinsmen in the name of maintaining moral order. By invoking the honor and authority of the ancestors, they were able to mobilize kinsmen to further personal as well as communal goals. Kinsmen could be mobilized in struggle over control of land and markets. Lineages also provided the gentry with a convenient structure for organizing local militia for self-protection. To be sure, ultimately, the power of the gentry under the Ch'ing was still derived from the authority of the imperial government. But during times of social and political turmoil, they could fall back on their own lineages for immediate protection. Nevertheless, the closeness of their interests to those of the imperial government had made it desirable for them to support the existing regime.

The Gentry and the Common People

Both the revival of the Ch'eng-Chu learning in the K'ang-hsi period and the ascendancy of the Han Learning movement in the eighteenth century were gentry attempts to reassert their elitist role in the social hierarchy. Their method for communicating values shifted from didacticism to ritualism. Scholars no longer reached out to the people through unstructured public meetings or social organizations such as the populist lectures of the late Ming; rather, they approached the people through the family, the lineage, and the bureaucracy. Ritual provided them with a common ground to legitimate their dominance in these realms. They assumed the role of ritual experts who engaged in research on ancient ritual. Their deliberations on the symbolic domain of ritual were not open to the common people. Rather, they taught them how to align their conduct with proper ritual rules in the family and in lineage halls. Whereas they reserved to themselves the intellectual duty of pondering the symbolic meanings of ritual, they assigned to the common people the duty to observe ritual.

In the late Ming and early Ch'ing peasant rebellions and urban riots, the gentry witnessed the social and political implications of the late Ming idea that the common man could become a sage if he became enlightened about his innate knowledge of the Confucian precepts. The attempt to enlighten the common people by engaging them in discussions about the validity of Confucian precepts resulted only in the subversion of the Confucian teachings by heterodox ideas and in the degrading of the gentry status. The attack on the idea of principle and on public lecturing first by Ch'en Ch'üeh, Yen Yüan, and Li Kung and later by the Han Learning scholars indicates both the gentry's disappointment with the didactic method of popular mobilization and the growth of distrust toward the common people.

The following remarks by Li Kung are revealing of this abhorrence of the "discussion of principles" (chiang-li): "The common people can be told to follow, not to know [why they should do so]. Confucians of later times have often engaged the common people in discussions of "principle" and of the reasons for the principles so that the common people can be inspired. But the common people become more difficult and stubborn."[3] Li was referring to the public lecturers of the late Ming who sought to mobilize the common people by involving them in discussing Confucian precepts that were presumably innate in all.

Tai Chen may not have shared Li Kung's view when he criticized the practice of justifying the taking of life in the name of principle,[4] but Chiao Hsün clearly shared Li Kung's distrust of open discourse between the gentry and the common people. Like Tai Chen, he derided the neo-Confucian notion of principle. Chiao Hsün expressed disdain for litigation in which the parties insisted on their own reason or principle. He upheld ritual as the most effective method of promoting social harmony. According to him, ritual reinforced people's social station and was conducive to resolving conflicts. In contrast, the resort to reason only provoked disputes.[5] It is difficult to determine whether the Ch'ing scholars' ritualist approach to social relations encouraged the desired patterns of behavior among the common people. The gentry's emphasis on proper ceremonies and correct behavior to be promoted by lineages did, however, result in a different relationship between the gentry and the common people.

Confucian Ritualism and the Reform of Gentry Culture

The ritualist re-orientation of Confucianism under the Ch'ing provided the framework within which the gentry sought to redefine its own culture in "pure" Confucian forms. With the rise of Confucian ritualism and purism, the boundary between the gentry and the common people became more clearly defined. The syncretic movement of the late Ming represented not so much a new fervor for philosophical synthesis as the result of a necessary compromise the public lecturers and gentry activists had to make in order to engage the common people in a mutually comprehensible dialogue. Ritualism and purism had discredited accommodating attitudes toward popular values and sentiments. The best minds among the gentry in the Ch'ing withdrew from participating in and creating novels and plays; these activities were redefined as cultural pursuits not worthy of the Confucian literati. The literati's intellectual energy was expended primarily in ritual research, Classical learning, textual criticism, phonetic studies, and other subjects of scholarly interest. Patronage of drama shifted mostly to merchants.

The institutional focus of the gentry's reform centered upon the family, the lineage, and the state. The growth of the cult of female chastity, the ancestral cult in the form of lineage, the punctilious observance of hierarchical relationships, and the exaltation of the ritual authority of the Classics constituted a cultural reform movement aimed at re-establishing the gentry's dominance in the family as fathers and husbands, in the lineage as local leaders, and in their public capacity as officials, and in their intellectual capacity as ritual experts and guardians of the past.

The rise of ritualism and the Han Learning movement, however, did not result in the society the gentry envisioned. Research on the Classical heritage did not recover a clear and uniform image of the sacred past. The revival of competing hermeneutical traditions of the Han and Sung periods provided the Confucian literati with rich symbolic resources to articulate their social and political visions. Philology and ritual scholarship became powerful weapons of social criticism. Views not based on serious philological and ritual research could hardly command attention.

Ch'ing ritualism not only marks a significant point of departure in the history of Confucian thought, but also was a powerful force with which the Chinese in the late nineteenth and early twentieth centuries had to come to terms. Since the late eighteenth century, China had suffered from chronic problems of rebellion, population pressure, and many symptoms of dynastic decline. The quest for solutions to these pressing problems prompted the revival of interest in conventional statecraft knowledge and criticism of the futility and anachronism of *k'ao-cheng* scholarship. Although by the mid-nineteenth century, philological research had lost its appeal, ritualism remained an important approach to Confucianism. Hsün Tzu continued to be regarded as the foremost Confucian in transmitting the Confucian Classics and ancient ritual. Confucius was upheld only as the curator of ancient institutions created by ancient sage-kings. These views became the targets of attack by the reformist-oriented Kung-yang school of New Text Classicism in the late nineteenth century. In advancing his New Text version of Confucianism, K'ang Yu-wei (1858–1927) traced corruption in the interpretation of Confucian tradition to Hsün Tzu, who "put a premium on arid ritualism, jejune scholasticism, and inhibitory authoritarianism."[6] T'an Ssu-t'ung (1864–98), K'ang's follower, condemned ritualism and all subsequent persuasions of Confucianism as the legacy of Hsün Tzu that had for centuries restrained and oppressed the Chinese people.[7] The vehement attacks on the "doctrine of ritual" (*li-chiao*) during the New Culture movement of the 1920's attest to the impact of Ch'ing ritualism on both the Confucian tradition and Chinese society at large. The widespread ritual symbols—arches erected to commemorate chaste widows and freestanding ancestral halls—that dotted the Chinese landscape now became the abominable legacy the Chinese strove to disown.

Ch'ing Classicism in Comparative Perspective

To conclude this study, it may be useful to view Ch'ing Classicism from a comparative perspective. The Classicism of the early and mid-Ch'ing periods has been compared to the European Renaissance of the fifteenth and sixteenth centuries. Benjamin Elman compares the Ch'ing Classicists to the great humanists of the European Renaissance such as Lorenzo Valla (1407–57) and Desiderius Erasmus (1466–1536) in terms of their quest for "linguistic clarity, simplicity, and purity." The Renaissance classicists were as much committed to moral reform as the Ch'ing philologists. In addition, both the European and Chinese classicists were "scholarly iconoclasts."[8]

Indeed, some aspects of Ch'ing Classicism resemble the humanist movement of the Italian Renaissance. As we have seen, underlying the vigorous philological endeavors of the Ch'ing Classicists was a commitment to the core of Confucian ethics. The leading humanists of the Italian Renaissance were no less committed to Christianity. For example, Francesco Petrarch (1304–74) was initially known in Italy not as a great poet but as a master of Latin and a moralist.[9] Lorenzo Valla advocated "an alliance between faith and eloquence."[10] His notes on the New Testament are an attempt to apply philological methods to the study of the Scriptures.[11]

Erasmus' edition of the Greek New Testament can be viewed in the same light. In his attacks on scholastic theology, Erasmus upheld the authority of the Bible and the Fathers of the Church. According to Paul Kristeller, "the attempt to combine the study of theology with an elegant Latin style and a thorough knowledge of the Greek and Latin classics characterizes not only many Italian humanists and Erasmus, but also Melanchthon, Calvin, Hooker, and the early Jesuits."[12]

These parallels between Ch'ing Classicism and Renaissance humanism are interesting and to some degree justified. However, it is also useful to explore the contrasts between the two movements. To be sure, both the Renaissance humanists and the Ch'ing Classicists were philologists devoted to the recovery of classical antiquity. But from the very beginning, the Ch'ing Classicists and the Italian humanists set their minds on different concerns.

Kristeller points out the problem of equating Italian humanism with the rise of the classical movement. Such a notion neglects the medieval roots of Italian humanism—the tradition and practice of the professional *dictatores*. The Italian humanists were heirs to the medieval rhetoricians. With the notable exception of Petrarch, Boccaccio, and Erasmus, many humanists served as secretaries to princes or cities; others were teachers of humanities in secondary schools and universities. The humanists studied the classics for models of speech, rhetorical skills, and writing techniques.[13]

In contrast, Han Learning scholars had little interest in studying the grammar, phonetics, and semantics of Archaic Chinese to improve their writing abilities. In fact, Tai Chen was criticized for despising those who treated writing skills as a branch of serious learning that required training and devotion.[14] The Han Learning scholars did not undertake philological endeavors to improve their speaking skills. Whether they were working studiously to prepare themselves for the civil service examinations or serving as officials, eloquent speech was not considered an important skill. Whereas training in rhetoric and writing skills benefited the humanists professionally, Ch'ing Classical scholars in general saw no immediate utility in learning literary skills except for those required for writing the "eight-legged" examination essays. Their intellectual energies were totally consumed by their attempt to reconstruct the ancient model of social order and its patterns of behavior. Even later when some came to see the need for such skills, their interest was guided by a formalist approach. They preferred the parallel prose of the Han and Wei periods.[15]

Whereas the Italian humanists displayed a great interest in producing drama and other forms of literature in the vernacular, Ch'ing Classicists were hostile to vernacular novels and plays. Many great classical scholars of the Italian Renaissance were renowned poets and great prose writers. In contrast, only a few Ch'ing Classicists devoted themselves to refining their writing skills or theorizing about poetry and prose. Hardly any developed a passion for writing vernacular novels and drama.

The strong anti-heterodox sentiment and persistent purism of the Ch'ing Classicists were absent in Renaissance humanists, most of whom, according to Kristeller, were eclectic.[16] The humanists revived the different schools of Greek philosophy; the Ch'ing Classicists made philosophizing a taboo.

Finally, the strong ritualism and its connection with Classicism were not found in Renaissance humanism. The humanists were committed to "expressing the concrete uniqueness of one's feelings, opinion, experiences, and surroundings."[17] The exaltation of individuality in Renaissance arts, literature, and thought stands in sharp contrast with the Ch'ing Classicists' attempt to align the individual with what they believed to be the universally applicable patterns of conduct—rituals. Ritual promotes uniformity, not expression of individuality. The Ch'ing scholars' abhorrence of personal opinions and divergent patterns of behavior contrasts markedly with the attitudes of Renaissance humanists.

Reference Matter

Notes

For complete author names, titles, and publication data for the works cited here in short form, see the Bibliography, pp. 281–314. In this work, volume and page numbers are separated by a colon, chüan and page numbers by a period. The following abbreviations are used in the Notes:

CHWS	Wan Ssu-ta, *Ching-hsüeh wu-shu*
CJHA	Hsü Shih-ch'ang, *Ch'ing-ju hsüeh-an*
CSLC	*Ch'ing-shih lieh-chuan*
CSTHW	Mao Ch'i-ling, *Chiao, she, ti, hsia wen*
CTCL	Wang Chien, ed., *Chu-tzu chia-li*
CTYL	Chu Hsi, *Chu-tzu yü-lei*
DMB	Goodrich and Fang, eds., *Dictionary of Ming Biography*
ECC	Ch'eng I and Ch'eng Hao, *Erh Ch'eng chi*
ECCP	Hummel, ed., *Eminent Chinese of the Ch'ing Period*
HCCSWP	Ho Ch'ang-ling and Wei Yüan, *Huang-ch'ao ching-shih wen-pien*
HHWC	Mao Ch'i-ling, *Hsi-ho wen-chi*
HLCI	Wan Ssu-ta, *Hsüeh-li chih-i*
HSS	Ch'ien Mu, *Chung-kuo chin san-pai-nien hsüeh-shu shih*
JCL	Ku Yen-wu, *Jih-chih lu*
KCCHLC	Li Huan, ed., *Kuo-ch'ao ch'i-hsien lei-cheng*
KTLSWC	Ku Yen-wu, *Ku T'ing-lin shih wen chi*
LTCS	Liu Tsung-chou, *Liu-tzu ch'üan-shu*
MJHA	Huang Tsung-hsi, *Ming-ju hsüeh-an*
MTCK	Li Fu, *Mu-t'ang ch'u-kao*
MTPK	Li Fu, *Mu-t'ang pieh-kao*
PCC	Ch'ien I-chi, *Pei-chuan chi*
PTCL	Mao Ch'i-ling, *Pien-ting chi-li t'ung-su p'u*
SKCS	*Ssu-k'u ch'üan-shu*
SKTY	*Ssu-k'u ch'üan-shu tsung-mu t'i-yao*
SSCCS	Juan Yüan, *Shih-san ching chu-shu*
STP	Yen Yüan, *Ssu-ts'un p'ien*
TCLCSL	*Ta-Ch'ing li-ch'ao shih-lu*

THTTS   Mao Ch'i-ling, *Ta-hsiao tsung t'ung-shih*
WYMCC   Wang Shou-jen, *Wang Yang-ming ch'üan-chi*
YCSC   Juan Yüan, *Yen-ching shih chi*
YYHSCC   Chang Lü-hsiang, *Yang-yüan hsien-sheng ch'üan-chi*

Introduction

1. Ying-shih Yü ("Some Preliminary Observations") traces the rise of *k'ao-cheng* scholarship to the inherent tension within neo-Confucianism and to the swing of the pendulum from the moralism of Wang Yang-ming to the intellectualism of the Ch'ing scholars.

Benjamin A. Elman's *From Philosophy to Philology* shows the importance of official and semiofficial patronage and of libraries in the rise of evidential research scholarship in the Lower Yangtze areas. In *The Emperor's Four Treasuries*, R. Kent Guy analyzes the complex relationship between the state and scholars in his study of the *Ssu-k'u ch'üan-shu* project, which served the interests of both the Manchu court and the scholars. John Henderson in *Development and Decline* devotes five chapters to a detailed discussion of the criticism of cosmological perceptions in Ch'ing scholarship. On-cho Ng offers an extensive study of the *ch'i* ontology of Ch'ing thought.

2. Yü Ying-shih, "Some Preliminary Observations"; Elman, *From Philosophy to Philology*, pp. xix–xxi, 6, 32, 54–55.

3. Wakeman, *The Great Enterprise*; idem, "China and the Seventeenth-Century," pp. 15–23.

4. Here I follow Kwang-ching Liu ("Orthodoxy") in using "orthodoxy" to mean the core values of the socio-ethics of Confucianism, which was common to both Han Confucianism and neo-Confucianism in the late imperial period. In this study "neo-Confucianism" is used in a sense broader than *Tao-hsüeh*. It refers to three developments in Confucian thought in the Sung period: the metaphysical innovations, the new exegeses of the Confucian Classics, and the new ritual traditions. The first has been adequately studied by Wing-tsit Chan, Wm. Theodore de Bary, and others. For the best study of neo-Confucian rituals, especially the *Family Rituals by Chu Hsi*, see Ebrey, *Confucianism*. The Classical scholarship of Sung neo-Confucians that is not directly related to metaphysical issues has received the least attention. As we shall see, the revived Ch'eng-Chu learning in the K'ang-hsi period focused more on Classical scholarship and ritual studies than on metaphysics.

5. Ko; S. Mann, "Widows"; Zurndorfer, "*Han-hsüeh*."

6. S. Mann, "Widows"; Zurndorfer, " 'Constant World.' " As the cult grew, widow homes were established in urban centers in the second half of the eighteenth century to support and protect widows from forced remarriage. These homes proliferated rapidly after the Taiping rebellion (Leung, "To Chasten the Society"; see also Kai-wing Chow, "Scholar," pp. 301–2).

7. For the growing irrational exaltation of female chastity, see the articles in

the special issue on women in Qing period China in *JAS* (46, no. 1), esp. S. Mann, "Widows"; and V. Ng. See also Feng Erh-k'ang, pp. 311–15; and Waltner.

8. Ch'en Ch'üeh, p. 519; Wang Li-ch'i, *Yüan Ming Ch'ing*, pp. 256–58; Furth, pp. 24–25; Ropp, pp. 47–48.

9. See J. H. Smith, "Lü Kun's New Audience"; Widmer, "Xiaoqing's Literary Legacy"; and idem, "The Epistolary World."

10. Ropp, p. 48; McMahon, pp. 66–68; Furth, pp. 24–25.

11. Yagisawa, pp. 32–36; J. Hu, p. 16.

12. Those who held high offices include the famous scholar Ch'iu Chün, president of the Board of Rites and a grand secretary; Yang Shen, secretary of the Han-lin Academy; Wang Tao-k'un, vice-president of the Board of War; and Wang Shih-chen, president of the Board of Punishment (Yagisawa pp. 32–36).

13. Tanaka Issei ("Social and Historical Context," p. 143) argues that the Ming elite appropriated popular plays and transformed them into literary dramas; cf. J. Hu.

14. After its creation, K'un-ch'ü became the dominant form of drama enjoyed by the educated (Mackerras, *The Rise*, p. 30); Strassberg, pp. 131–32, 357–58n37. The early Ch'ing had such great dramatists as K'ung Shang-jen and Hung Sheng. Their works, however, marked the end of the golden age of Chinese drama in the Ming. For a discussion of K'un-ch'ü in the early Ch'ing, see Strassberg, p. 360n38.

15. Literati drama in the Ming, especially K'un-ch'ü, required not only "immense learning," but "great knowledge of music" (J. Hu, p. 61).

16. Ch'en Lung-cheng (1585–1645) noted with disapproval that in his time it was common for gentry to train young maids and servants to perform drama for private entertainment (Wang Li-ch'i, *Yüan Ming Ch'ing*, p. 171).

17. Mackerras, "The Drama," pp. 92–93, 96. K'un-ch'ü continued to be patronized by salt merchants in Yangchou until the late eighteenth century. It declined seriously in the nineteenth century (Mackerras, pp. 54–65, 61–63, 108). By the Tao-kuang period (1821–50) K'un-ch'ü became so stereotyped and unpopular in Peking that whenever it was performed in between plays of local dramas, the audience took the opportunity to go to the restroom (Hsü K'o, vol. 10, 78.5a).

18. Tanaka Issei, "Shindai"; idem, "Social and Historical Context," p. 143; Mackerras, "The Drama," p. 98.

19. Aoki, p. 478. Hegel, "Distinguishing," p. 130.

20. Wang Li-ch'i, *Yüan Ming Ch'ing*, pp. 4–14, 261, 267. According to Tanaka Issei ("Social and Historical Context," pp. 143–60), even in the sixteenth century different ranks of operatic troupes catered to different levels of audience—local market towns, small villages, and lineages. Plays sponsored by wealthy lineage leaders, rich merchants, and officials were more conservative in content. And lineage-centered drama was "probably the most conservative."

21. Wang Li-ch'i, *Yüan Ming Ch'ing*, pp. 283, 315.

22. For sanctions against vernacular novels, see McMahon, pp. 66–68.

23. Hegel, *The Novel*, p. 223. Richard Shek (p. 123) has noted that many of the redactors, editors, and commentators of such classic novels as the *Water Margin*, the

Golden Lotus, and *Journey to the West* were holders of high degrees and prominent literary and intellectual figures. Their involvement in the promotion of popular literature clearly indicates their "conviction in the worthiness of the undertaking."

24. Such edicts and official rescripts appeared in 1652, 1663, 1671, 1687, 1701, 1709, 1713, 1723, 1724, 1727, 1728, 1735, 1736, 1738, 1762, 1799, 1802, 1810, 1813, 1824, 1834, 1851, 1852, 1868, and 1881 (Wang Li-ch'i, *Yüan Ming Ch'ing*. pp. 23–84; see also Yü Cheng-hsieh, 9.269–70).

25. Wang Li-ch'i, *Yüan Ming Ch'ing*, pp. 37, 48, 68, 70, 78–79.

26. Ibid., p. 49. See also Yü Chih, 11.5a–11a, 11.12a–14b.

27. Both the *Ta-Ch'ing lü-li* and *Ta-Ch'ing hui-tien* had specific regulations against the organizers of public performances of drama and against officials who failed to enforce the rescript (Wang Li-ch'i, *Yüan Ming Ch'ing*, pp. 18–21, 39).

28. *Hsüeh-cheng ch'üan-shu* was authored by Wei Chin-hsi and *Mu-ling chi-yao* by Hsü Tung (1792–1865) (Wang Li-ch'i, *Yüan Ming Ch'ing*, pp. 23–24, 41–42).

29. The first censorship board was created in 1780 to screen dramas for seditious contents (Guy, *Emperor's Four Treasuries*, pp. 191–92).

30. Wang Li-ch'i, *Yüan Ming Ch'ing*, pp. 95–115, 307; Ku Kung-hsieh, *shang*.40b.

31. For discussion of the philological scholarship of Yang Shen and Hu Ying-lin, see Lin Ch'ing-chang, chaps. 3 and 6.

32. Wang Li-ch'i, *Yüan Ming Ch'ing*, p. 226.

33. Ch'ien Ta-hsin, 17.250.

34. Wang Li-ch'i, *Yüan Ming Ch'ing*, p. 236.

35. Liang Chang-chü (1775–1849; p. 134) mentioned that few among his contemporaries had not read *The Dream of the Red Chamber* (*Hung-lou meng*), *The Water Margin* (*Shui-hu chuan*), *Journey to the West* (*Hsi-yu chi*) and *The Romance of the Three Kingdoms* (*San-kuo chih*). On the popularity of local drama, see Tanaka Issei, "Social and Historical Context."

36. Li Wen-chih, pp. 304–6; Kung-chuan Hsiao, *Rural China*, pp. 342–43; Hui-chen Wang Liu; Beattie, *Land and Lineage*, pp. 120–22.

37. Meijer; Elvin, pp. 150–51. For the increasing rigor in enforcing the law for offenders in forced remarriage of widows in the Ch'ing Code, see Hsüeh, pp. 295–97.

38. As Elman (*From Philosophy to Philology*, pp. 96–112) has convincingly demonstrated, the growing "professionalization of scholarship" in the Lower Yangtze region in the Ch'ing period was aided by supportive institutions, including official and semiofficial patronage. Scholars were able to pursue academic research under the auspices of the government, officials, and merchants.

39. Chan, "*Hsing-li ching-i*"; de Bary, *Message*, chaps. 4–5. De Bary's study focuses on one aspect of the revived Ch'eng-Chu orthodoxy. De Bary does not address the revival in the K'ang-hsi period of the exegetical tradition forged by Chu Hsi; nor does he deal with rituals.

40. The purist intellectual impulse has been noted by a long line of scholars on Ming-Ch'ing thought. Many scholars use the term *fundamentalism* to denote such

an impulse, but since the term is heavily charged with contemporary associations, I use "purism" in this study. For a discussion of the purist strain under the rubric "fundamentalism," see de Bary, *Message*, chaps. 4–5 *passim*. For Elman (*From Philosophy to Philology*, pp. 45–48), this "fundamentalism" of the "return to antiquity (*fu-ku*) movement" in the late Ming and early Ch'ing sought to reaffirm "the original texts and doctrines of classical Confucianism." Lynn Struve ("Ambivalence and Action," p. 335) also finds the term "fundamentalist" useful in reference to Yen Yüan's rejection of both the Sung and Ming notion of moral cultivation. See also S. Mann, "Scholasticism," p. 34.

41. As we shall see, the attack by Han Learning scholars was not limited to the *Tao-hsüeh* (Learning of the Way) strand, or the Ch'eng-Chu orthodoxy, of Sung neo-Confucianism. Although a strong interest in metaphysical issues and a concern for doctrinal lineage mark such proponents of *Tao-hsüeh* as Chou Tun-i (1017–73), Ch'eng I (1033–1107), Chu Hsi (1130–1200), and others off from other Sung neo-Confucians, their interest in ritual and their approach to Classical learning bring them closer to such contemporaries as Wang An-shih (1021–86), Ssu-ma Kuang (1019–86), and Shih Chieh (1005–45). For a discussion that treats the *Tao-hsüeh* movement as only one of many intellectual currents in the Sung, see Bol, pp. 27–31; see also Tillman.

42. For a discussion of the term *syncretism*, see Berling, *Syncretic Religion*, chap. 1. But as used in this study, the term does not include what Berling calls "unconscious borrowing." The term *borrowing* itself presumes a conscious act of taking something one knows one does not possess. Syncretism is to be distinguished from eclecticism, which is the unsystematic, not always conscious *use* of ideas and practices from other religious and intellectual traditions. But to stress "pattern of selectivity," "intention of borrowing," and reconciliation of ideas and practices is to underscore *conscious* efforts on the part of the syncretist (see ibid., pp. 4–13).

43. The literature on the definition and functions of the gentry as well as its relationship with the imperial state and with other social classes such as merchants is enormous, as is the controversy over these issues. For general discussions, see Chung-li Chang; Ping-ti Ho; and T'ung-tsu Chü, chap. 10. For discussions of the greater fusion of the gentry with the merchants and the rapid expansion of the gentry's role as managers and of the gentry's functions and status in the nineteenth century, see Rankin, *Elite Activism*; and S. Mann, *Local Merchants*, chaps. 2, 5–7.

44. J. Watson, "The Structure," p. 3.

45. Ebrey, *Confucianism*, p. 8.

46. For a discussion of the range of rituals in the Ch'ing, see R. Smith, "Ritual," p. 284. See also Schwartz, *The World*, p. 22.

47. Schwartz, *The World*, pp. 79–82.

48. Ibid., p. 68.

49. For a discussion of the concept of *jen*, see ibid., pp. 75–85. For a discussion of the meaning of *jen* in pre-Confucian discourse and in the *Analects*, see Lin Yü-sheng, "The Evolution."

50. *Analects* 12.1.

51. Confucius said: "Respectfulness, without the rules of propriety, becomes laborious bustle; carefulness, without the rules of propriety, becomes timidity; boldness, without the rules of propriety, becomes insubordination; straightforwardness, without the rules of propriety, becomes rudeness" (*Analects* 8.2, trans. Legge).

52. Schwartz, *The World*, p. 72.

53. Hsiao Kung-chuan, *Chung-kuo cheng-chih*, p. 100.

54. Ch'en Fei-lung, pp. 17–22; Chang Hsi-t'ang, "Hsün-Tzu"; Hsü Fu-kuan, "Han- hsüeh," pp. 7–8, 22–25.

55. Wang Hsien-ch'ien, 2.30–44.

56. Ibid., p. 8. For a discussion of Hsün-tzu's ideas on ritual as an important means of government, see Hsü Fu-kuan, *Chung-kuo*, pp. 450–59.

57. Wang Hsien-ch'ien, p. 31.

58. K. C. Liu, "Socio-ethics," p. 53*n*1.

59. K. C. Liu, "Socio-ethics."

60. For a discussion of the general importance of ritual in Ch'ing China, see R. Smith.

61. Bloch, pp. 178–81.

62. Ibid., p. 181.

63. For a discussion of the meanings invested in the popular goddess T'ien Hou by various local groups and the imperial state, see J. Watson, "Standardizing the Gods," pp. 292–324. I owe the term "superscription" to Prasenjit Duara ("Superscribing Symbols," pp. 778–95).

64. This distinction between "symbolic domain" and "performative domain" is based on the work of James L. Watson ("Standardizing the Gods"). Watson distinguishes the "ideological domain" and "performative domain." I substitute *symbolic* for *ideological* because the meanings of ritual, unlike ideology, are not components of a proposition.

65. Ritual in this study does not denote formalized irrational and superstitious patterns of behavior as opposed to "rational" behavior. On the other hand, it is not used as an equivalent of religion, even though religious rituals were important in Late Imperial China.

66. Bloch, p. 182.

Chapter 1

1. For a general discussion of late Ming social and economic changes, see Rawski, "Economic and Social Foundations"; Brokaw, pp. 4–13; and Zurndorfer, *Change*, pp. 105–21.

2. In Hui-chou prefecture, Anhwei, a place known for the importance of its wealthy merchants in the Kiangnan and national economy, contracts specified rent payment in silver beginning in the Ching-t'ai reign (1450–57) (Li Jo-yü, p. 43). This special arrangement might have been a result of the new government

policy requiring roughly 15 percent of the total land tax from Nan Chihli and six Provincial Administration Commissions (*pu-cheng-shih ssu*)—Chekiang, Kiangsi, Hukuang, Kwangtung, Kwangsi, and Fukien—be paid in silver (T'ang Wen-chih, pp. 137–39; Chao I-feng, pp. 56–57). For discussions of the importance of silver in the late Ming economy, see Atwell, "Notes on Silver"; Chao I-feng; and Wakeman, "China."

3. Liang Fang-chung; T'ang Wen-chih, pp. 290–316; Fu I-ling, *Ming-tai Chiang-nan*, pp. 2–6.

4. Chao I-feng, p. 63.

5. Atwell, "Notes on Silver," p. 30*n*59; Wakeman, "China."

6. For the interregional circulation of commodities, see Fu I-ling, *Ming-tai Chiang-nan*, pp. 6–20; and Wu Ch'eng-ming, pp. 162–63, 227–39. Wu, however, underrates the role of overseas trade in the expansion of the domestic economy. See Atwell, "Notes on Silver," pp. 3–8.

7. Fu I-ling, *Ming-tai Chiang-nan*, pp. 229–32; Hsi, pp. 30–33; Fan, pp. 66–86; Huang P'ei-chin, pp. 210–22.

8. Hsü Hung, p. 23; Wu Tan-ko.

9. Ch'en Ch'üeh, p. 395; Wu Jen-an, p. 40; Wu Chin-ch'eng. For a discussion of Fukien gentry engaged in trade, see Lin Li-yüeh, "Min-nan shih-sheu."

10. Yü Shen-hsing, 4: 39.

11. *JCL* 13.27a.

12. Fu I-ling, *Ming-tai Chiang-nan*, pp. 32, 40, 50; Hsü Hung, p. 23; Han Ta-ch'eng, "Ming-tai kao-li-t'ai tzu-pen," p. 349.

13. For a discussion of urban life in Honan, see Wang Hsing-ya.

14. Wiens, "Social Change," p. 23.

15. Chang Hsien-ch'ing, "Ming-tai shen-chin"; for land concentration in the late Ming, see Oyama.

16. Wiens, "Social Change," p. 23; Wu Han, p. 4.

17. Officials opposed labor service on the grounds that an edict of 1377 exempted them from all corvée. But the edict was superseded by an edict of 1380, which clearly demanded the payment of regular corvée from the officials (Chang Hsien-ch'ing, "Ming-tai kuan-shen," pp. 165–69). A similar decree was issued to clarify the requirement of the gentry to pay the regular corvée (Wiens, "Social Change," p. 23; see also Fu I-ling, *Ming-tai Chiang-nan*, p. 51). For a discussion of gentry manipulation of tax registers and the problem of tax evasion, see Dennerline, "Fiscal Reform," pp. 94–95.

18. Chang Hsien-ch'ing, "Ming-tai shen-chin," pp. 32–33. For a discussion of widespread commendations, see Wu Tan-ko, pp. 13–14; and Chu-ko Chih, pp. 474–75. For T'ang's biography, see *DMB*, pp. 1252–56.

19. For a discussion of desertion of land, see Han Ta-ch'eng, "Ming-tai shang-p'in," pp. 55–59. Most of the surcharges had been converted to payment in silver by the Wan-li reign (see Wang Yu-ch'üan, p. 168).

20. Following McDermott, bondservant here is treated as a legal status. For a discussion of different types of bondservants, see McDermott, pp. 680–85; Wiens,

"Lord and Peasants," pp. 4–8; Tanaka Masatoshi, pp. 192–93; Chu-ko Chih, pp. 472–77; Hao, pp. 107–13; Han Ta-ch'eng, "Ming-tai shang-p'in," pp. 87–93.

21. McDermott, p. 681; Tanaka Masatoshi, p. 113.

22. J. H. Smith, *Action*, pp. 127–30.

23. Chao I, 34: 495–96; Wu Tan-ko, pp. 13–14.

24. N. Wu, "T'ung Ch'i-ch'ang: The Man," p. 72.

25. Sakai, p. 353.

26. N. Wu, "T'ung Ch'i-ch'ang: The Man," pp. 57–63.

27. Wu Han, pp. 14–16.

28. Of the 129 good officials, 114 served before or during the Cheng-t'ung reign (1436–50), ten from the period between 1450 and 1521, and only five after 1522. These three periods lasted 81, 72, and 122 year, respectively. The ratio of good officials per annum is 1.4 for the first period, 0.13 for the second, and 0.04 the late Ming (Hsü Hung, p. 31).

29. Quoted in Araki, p. 59.

30. For a sophisticated discussion of the transformation of social relations in the city of Chia-ting in Kiangsu, see Dennerline, chap. 3. The breakdown of local communities was widespread in the most commercialized areas in Kiangnan and south China. See also Tong, pp. 151–53.

31. Dennerline, *Chia-ting Loyalists*, p. 90. Although Dennerline's study focuses on Chia-ting city, the social change he presents was common in the commercialized areas in Kiangnan.

32. Without an examination degree or official status, wealthy families were easy prey to covetous magnates (see Wu Tan-ko, pp. 9–13). To be sure, this was not peculiar to the late Ming, but official status became particularly important in times of increasing lawlessness.

33. As Nelson Wu ("T'ung Ch'i-ch'ang: The Man," p. 72) has noted, from the 1560's on, "there was not a single position without someone trying to obtain it through some illegal means, and there was not a single office not offered for sale."

34. Lü K'un observed that in his time "when the tenants ask for help, the landlords ask for higher interest" (J. H. Smith, *Action*, p. 24; see also Weins, "Lord and Peasants," pp. 12–16).

35. McDermott, p. 685.

36. J. H. Smith, *Action*, pp. 131–32.

37. Brokaw, chap. 2.

38. The translation of the title is taken from Berling, "Religion and Popular Culture," p. 188.

39. Ibid., pp. 201–7, 213–15.

40. Plaks, chap. 1 and pp. 504–5.

41. J. H. Smith, *Action*, pp. 150–51. For discussions of urban riots, see Fu I-ling, *Ming-tai Chiang-nan*, p. 100–111; Yuan; Tanaka Masatoshi; and Hsieh Kuo-chen, pp. 209–36.

42. According to a 1565 report, the White Lotus sect had built 45 temples and

attracted 10,000 followers in the province of Hopei alone (J. H. Smith, *Action*, p. 23).

43. Ibid., p. 126. For discussions of the community compact, see Ch'en K'o-yün, pp. 44–49; and Wang Yin-lan.

44. E. Ch'ien, *Chiao Hung*, pp. 2–21.

45. Langlois and Sun; Farmer, pp. 123–25; Taylor, pp. 128–39.

46. Cf. Edward Ch'ien (ibid., pp. 26–29), who objects to the view that the growth of syncretism in the late Ming resulted from imperial patronage and argues that it evolved as a reaction against the Ch'eng-Chu orthodoxy.

47. Ebrey, *Confucianism*; for a discussion of the importance of Buddhism in the gentry culture of the late Ming, see Brook, "Gentry Dominance."

48. For detailed studies of printing in the Ming period, see Chang Hsiu-min, pp. 334–507; and Kwang-tsing Wu.

49. For a description of innovations in printing technology under the Ming, see Needham et al., sect. 32, pp. 175–83. See also Kwang-tsing Wu, pp. 212–14.

50. McDermott, pp. 693–94; Sakai, pp. 331–38.

51. Johnson, pp. 53–61.

52. Peterson, *Bitter Gourd*, pp. 32–33.

53. Hung-lam Chu ("Debate") warns against treating the popularity of Wang Yang-ming's teachings as merely a result of the intellectual power of his new ideas. Exponents and supporters of Wang's teachings were not able to gain imperial recognition until 1584.

54. *WYMCC* 7.65. De Bary ("Individualism," pp. 151–52) notes that Wang always discussed "innate knowledge" in relation to traditional moral virtues.

55. Wang Yang-ming, *Ch'üan-hsi lu* 3.76.

56. Although Huang Tsung-hsi (*MJHA* 32.62) attempted to exonerate Wang Yang-ming from the charge of corrupting Confucianism by singling out Wang Chi and Wang Ken as the disciples to blame for stretching their teacher's ideas beyond the boundaries of Confucianism, these two disciples did not depart far from basic Confucian ethics.

57. Hou, p. 995.

58. Asked about the difference between Confucianism and Buddhism, Wang said, "Don't look for identities and differences in Confucianism and Buddhism; seek to learn only the truth" (*WYMCC* 7.55). For an account of Wang Yang-ming's interest in Buddhism and Taoism in his youth, see Wei-ming Tu, *Neo-Confucian Thought*, pp. 42–47, 55–79.

59. Wang Yang-ming, *Instructions for Practical Living*, p. 220.

60. Quoted in Araki, p. 46.

61. Edward Ch'ien (*Chiao Hung*, pp. 26–29) views the syncretic movement among neo-Confucians essentially as a reaction against the Ch'eng-Chu school.

62. Although syncretism is not always a religious phenomenon, its driving force in sixteenth-century China was, for the most part, religious and moralistic. For a discussion of the definition of syncretism as a religious category, see Berling,

Syncretic Religion, chap. 1. For a discussion of the syncretic tendency shared by Confucians, Taoists, and Buddhists, see Shek, pp. 71–82.

63. Chün-fang Yü, pp. 64–66, 101–37; Berling, *Syncretic Religion*, pp. 46–61; Brokaw, pp. 72–95; de Bary, "Individualism," pp. 175–76. See also Yang T'ien-shih, *T'ai-chou hsüeh-p'ai*.

64. Chün-fang Yü, p. 228. Yü further points out that lay Buddhism was able to flourish from the late Ming on because it did not seek to break with the social system. It therefore survived and continued to flourish in the Ch'ing dynasty. In fact, the strength of lay Buddhism in the late Ming derived from its active support of Confucian ethics. But lay Buddhism lost ground among leading scholars for most of the Ch'ing period when Confucian purism emerged as the dominant force in intellectual developments. Lay Buddhism was not rejuvenated until the latter half of the nineteenth century.

65. Ibid., p. 227. See also Berling, *Syncretic Religion*, pp. 59–60.

66. To demonstrate his point, Han-shan Te-ch'ing wrote commentaries on the *Great Learning*, the *Doctrine of the Mean*, and the *Spring and Autumn Annals* (Sung-peng Hsü, p. 156).

67. Berling, *Syncretic Religion*, p. 58.

68. Sakai, p. 346; Brokaw, p. 105.

69. Sakai, pp. 347–62.

70. Brokaw; Chün-fang Yü, pp. 101–6.

71. Brokaw; Chün-fang Yü, pp. 116–17, 120–24; J. H. Smith, *Action*, pp. 203–6.

72. Brokaw, p. 107.

73. For an insightful discussion of the idea of viewing morality as a form of capital that requires management, see Berling, "Religion and Popular Culture," pp. 208–16.

74. Sakai, pp. 341–42, 361–62.

75. Berling, *Syncretic Religion*, pp. 73–78.

76. Ibid., p. 196.

77. Ibid., pp. 81–83.

78. Ibid., pp. 204–17.

79. Ibid., p. 236. Lin Ch'ao-en, like Wang Ken, had made himself a *san-kang wu-ch'ang i* (gown of the Three Bonds and Five Constant Virtues). His cap was a *san-kang chin* (Three Bonds cap) and his shoes *wu-ch'ang lü* (Five Constants shoes); see Shek, p. 71.

80. Liu Tsung-chou, *Liu Chi-shan chi* 2.31a–b.

81. Wang Ken, 3.10a, 4.6a, 5.3a.

82. In acknowledging Wang Ken's role in spreading the teachings of Wang Yang-ming, Huang Tsung-hsi (*MJHA* 32.62) alluded to Wang's great popularity. Wang Ken had as many as 480 followers. About 80, or 16 percent, were officials. These are not exact numbers (Yang T'ien-shih, *T'ai-chou hsüeh-p'ai*, pp. 78, 89; see also de Bary, "Individualism," p. 171).

83. Wang Ken, 4.5b–6a; Yang T'ien-shih, *T'ai-chou hsüeh-p'ai*, pp. 28, 42.

84. Yang T'ien-shih, *T'ai-chou hsüeh-p'ai*, p. 104.

85. J. H. Smith, *Action*, pp. 49–50.

86. Yang T'ien-shih, *T'ai-chou hsüeh-p'ai*, pp. 107–8.

87. Liang Ju-yüan, p. 70.

88. Hou, p. 999.

89. Dimberg, pp. 49–50; de Bary, "Individualism," pp. 177–81.

90. Ho's eventual arrest and execution probably had more to do with the hostility of local authorities in Hukuang province than with the animus of the grand secretary Chang Chü-cheng, traditionally the villain of the piece; Ho's activism sometimes led him into direct conflict with the authorities and conventional practices (Dimberg, pp. 51–54).

91. Despite the presence of some quasi-Buddhist ideas in Ho Hsin-yin's thinking, he did not seek a union of the Three Teachings as other members of the T'ai-chou school did. Dimberg (pp. 102–3, 143–48) argues that Ho's view of personal cultivation remained essentially Confucian. He also stresses that in Ho's social and political philosophy the five basic Confucian human relationships continued to be vital.

92. Ibid., pp. 83–85.

93. *MJHA* 35.4–50, 36.64–74. Berling, *Syncretic Religion*, pp. 51–52.

94. *MJHA* 36.67; *DMB*, p. 272.

95. *MJHA* 36.67–74.

96. Chün-fang Yü, pp. 82–83.

97. De Bary, "Individualism," p. 192; *DMB*, p. 809.

98. Hou, pp. 1039–45; de Bary, "Individualism," pp. 192–93; *DMB*, pp. 809–11.

99. Hou, pp. 1065–66.

100. De Bary, "Individualism," pp. 197–99.

101. Ibid., p. 211.

102. Li Chih, *Fen-shu*, pp. 31, 92, 99, 218–20.

103. Ibid., pp. 96–99.

104. Ibid., pp. 16–18, 31, 87.

105. *Ming-teng tao-ku lu*, cited in Hou, pp. 1046–47.

106. Ibid., p. 1073.   107. Li Chih, *Fen-shu*, pp. 48–49.

108. Li Chih, *Tsang-shu*, p. 544.   109. Li Chih, *Fen-shu*, p. 4.

110. Kuan Chih-tao, 2.59a–60a.   111. Chu Kuo-chen, 16.9a–b.

112. Quoted in de Bary, "Individualism," p. 178.

113. Berling (*Syncretic Religion*, p. 224) has pointed out that Hsieh's accusation, if accurate, would mean either that Lin's disciples had deviated from his own teachings or that these practices represented only a sidestream of Lin's religion because Lin personally condemned those practices.

114. Officials of the fourth rank and above had the privilege of making a deposition on their performance and having the emperor decide on any change in their position. Those of the fifth rank and below were evaluated by the Board of Personnel (Lin Li-yüeh, "Ming-mo," p. 276).

115. Ibid., pp. 258–73.

116. Ibid., pp. 276–83.

117. Busch, pp. 27–33. Kao P'an-lung and Ku Hsien-ch'eng were degraded in 1594 (Hucker, p. 142).

118. Ch'ien I-pen (1539–1610) of Wu-chin was degraded in 1592; Yü K'ung-chien (*chin-shih* 1580) of Chin-t'an, An Hsi-fan (1564–1621) of Wu-hsi, Hsüeh Fu-chiao (*chin-shih* 1589) of Wu-chin, and Ku Yün-ch'eng (1554–1607) of Wu-hsi were either degraded or dismissed in 1593.

119. See, e.g., Ku Hsien-ch'eng, *Hsiao-hsin chai* 11.3a.

120. Ku Hsien-ch'eng might have welcomed people to the lectures with no discrimination. But he did not advocate lecturing among the common people as Wang Ken, Yen Chün, and Ho Hsin-yin did. See the strict regulations for assembly at the Tung-lin Academy (Kao T'ing-chen, 2.13a–14b).

121. According to Hucker's (pp. 158–59) statistics, of the 153 Tung-lin partisans, 140 (91 percent) were *chin-shih*. According to Lin Li-yüeh ("Ming-mo," pp. 134–35), 278 (92 percent) of the 300 partisans had earned the *chin-shih* degree. Both studies point to the upper-gentry composition of the Tung-lin membership.

122. Of the 25 persons mentioned by Huang Tsung-hsi in the *Ming-ju hsüeh-an* as followers of Wang Ken, only 11 (44 percent) had earned the *chin-shih* degree (Busch, p. 47; de Bary, "Individualism," p. 173). Yüan Ch'eng-yeh gives a much larger figure and identifies about 80 officials among Wang Ken's followers. They, however, constituted only 16 percent of the total of 480 T'ai-chou school members. These are not exact numbers, however (Yang T'ien-shih, *T'ai-chou hsüeh-p'ai*, pp. 78, 89).

123. A distinction should be made between the Tung-lin Academy and the political movement centered around the academy. As a political phenomenon, the Tung-lin movement was more inclusive in terms of intellectual affiliations than the scholarly circle of the Tung-lin Academy. Some associates and friends of members of the Tung-lin Academy were not hostile toward heterodox teachings, notwithstanding their common conviction regarding elitist moralism. Tsou Yüan-piao (1551–1624), a leader of the political movement, was noted for syncretic tendencies in his thinking. He was on good terms with Lin Chao-en (see Berling, *Syncretic Religion*, p. 84). He seems, however, never to have attended the scholarly gatherings at the academy despite his political associations with Ku Hsien-ch'eng and Kao P'an-lung (*DMB*, p. 1313). Another example is Ch'ien Shih-sheng (1575–1652), who not only admired Yüan Huang but patronized the printing of Buddhist scriptures and the construction of Buddhist pavilions (Brook, "Gentry Dominance," p. 228).

124. Wang Chi, 1.17a–19b.

125. Ibid., 1.1a–3a.

126. Tang Chün-i, "Liu Tsung-chou's Doctrine," pp. 305–6; see also idem, "Development," p. 116.

127. Busch, pp. 84–85.

128. E. Ch'ien, *Chiao Hung*, p. 5.

129. See, e.g., Ku Hsien-ch'eng, *Hsiao-hsin chai* 4.3a–4a, 10.4a, 14.1a–2a, 15.9a–b, 16.8a–9a, 18.3a; idem, *Ching-kao ts'ang-kao* 2.21a–b, 5.47a–b, 6.3a–b; Ku Yün-ch'eng, 3.7b, 3.18a–b; Kao P'an-lung, *Kao-tzu i-shu* (SKCS) 3.54b–55a, 8.16a–b, 8.35a–37a, 9A.16a–b; Liu Tsung-chou, *Liu Chi-shan chi* 4.24b–26b, 6.34b–35b, 8.21a; and Feng Ts'ung-wu, 1.14b–16a, 1.17b–20a, 1.33a–39b, 1.59a–60a.

130. See Ku Hsien-ch'eng's preface to Fang Pen-an's *Hsin-hsüeh tsung* in Ku's *Ching-kao ts'ang-kao* 4.32b.

131. Ku Yün-ch'eng, 3.7a–9b.

132. Ibid., 3.19b.

133. K'ao P'an-lung, *Kao-tzu i-shu* (SKCS) 3.53a–55b.

134. Greenblatt, pp. 121–22. Timothy Brook ("Gentry Dominance," pp. 127–28, chap. 9) stresses that the lay Buddhist movement was "primarily a gentry phenomenon" found throughout China but with a higher level of activities in the Lower Yangtze area.

135. *MJHA* 58.59; McMorran, pp. 427–31.

136. Liu Tsung-chou, *Liu Chi-shan chi* 6.12a; Busch, pp. 47–48; McMorran, p. 425.

137. Ku Hsien-ch'eng, *Ku Tuan-wen kung i-shu* 3.5.

138. *MJHA* 60.5–6.

139. De Bary, "Individualism," p. 192.

140. Ku Hsien-ch'eng, *Hsiao-hsin chai* 3.6a.

141. Busch, pp. 86–91.

142. Hucker, p. 161.

143. *MJHA* 58.57. Ku Hsien-ch'eng, *Ching-kao ts'ang-kao* 6.9a.

144. Greenblatt, p. 97.

145. Kao P'an-lung, *Kao-tzu i-shu* (SKCS) 8A.12a–b.

146. Feng Ts'ung-wu, 1.44a.

147. Busch, pp. 90–91.

148. Ibid., pp. 76–86; Hucker, pp. 143–47.

149. Ch'eng I and Chu Hsi had long recognized that the Buddhists, like the Neo-Confucians, were devoted to subjective moral (spiritual) cultivation or mind-cultivation—*ching i chih lei* (be reverent so as to rectify one's internal life). They pointed out, however, that Buddhists stopped at mind-cultivation, whereas Confucians had to cultivate behavior in conformity with ritual propriety (*i i fang wai*) (Ch'ien Mu, *Chu-tzu hsin hsüeh-an*, 3: 491–96).

150. *MJHA* 60.5–6.

151. Ibid., 58.81.

152. Busch, pp. 130–32.

153. Chang Tsai, p. 23. For a discussion of the centrality of ritual in Chang Tsai's theory of moral cultivation, see Kai-wing Chow, "Ritual."

154. Chang Tsai, p. 29.   155. *LTCS*, vol. 1, 7.1b–2a, 13.31a.

156. Ibid., vol. 1, 1.5a–b.   157. Ibid., vol. 3, 13.30a.

158. *HSS*, p. 14. Ku Hsien-ch'eng began as a follower of Wang Yang-ming and later attempted to incorporate Chu Hsi's teaching of "investigation of things"

in the process of moral cultivation. Kao P'an-lung, a staunch admirer of Chu Hsi, came to adopt Wang Yang-ming's view regarding establishing one's moral position before beginning the investigation of things. See Busch, pp. 97–102, 116–17, 121–30.

159. De Bary ("Neo-Confucian Cultivation," p. 202) has noted that in their attempt to harmonize the teachings of Wang Yang-ming and Chu Hsi, Kao P'an-lung and Liu Tsung-chou, as well as avowed followers of the Wang Yang-ming school, saw in ritual the basis of integrating subjective and objective morality.

160. *MJHA* 59.97.

161. Ibid., 60.15.

162. "Nien-p'u," in *LTCS* 40.9b–10a.

163. Ibid., vol. 3, 13.30a.

164. Ibid., vol. 1, 1.2a–11a; "Nien-p'u," 40.4b–5b. For a detailed discussion of Liu's *Manual*, see Brokaw, pp. 121–38.

165. Yü Ying-shih, "Ts'ung Sung Ming," pp. 87–115.

166. Yü Ying-shih, "Ch'ing-tai ssu-hsiang," pp. 143–49.

167. *MJHA* 60.4.

168. Atwell, "From Education to Politics," p. 347.

169. Quoted in ibid., pp. 345–46.

170. Yü Ying-shih, "Ch'ing-tai ssu-hsiang," pp. 60–63.

171. *MJHA* 41.58.

172. *Ch'ing-shih kao*, p. 1470.

173. *MJHA* 41.56–58, 64.

Chapter 2

1. For some of the Ming military officials who surrendered to the Manchus before 1644, see Roth, pp. 31–32. For those Ming officials and degree-holders who joined Li Tzu-ch'eng and his Shun regime, see Wakeman, "Shun Interregnum," pp. 53–64. During the Southern Ming period (1644–62), numerous Ming officials, both civil and military, surrendered and collaborated with the Manchus (Beattie, "The Alternative"; Struve, *Southern Ming*, pp. 31, 48–49, 56–59, 65–67, 97–99, 115, 142–43, 193, 154).

2. Wakeman, *Great Enterprise*, pp. 420–22, 646–50, 653; idem, "Loyalism," pp. 55–60.

3. Chang Mu, 3: 228; *KTLSWC*, p. 60.

4. *KTLSWC*, p. 32. The preface was probably written in 1657 when Ku first met Chang Erh-ch'i.

5. *JCL* 13.5a.

6. Tai Chün-jen.

7. For a discussion of the upsurge of Chinese culturalism, see Langlois.

8. Peterson, "From Interest to Indifference," p. 82.

9. "Preface," *MJHA* 1.

10. *MJHA* 62.67; Tang Chün-i, "Liu Tsung-chou's Doctrine," p. 320.

11. "Preface," *MJHA* 1.

12. See Struve, "Huang Zongxi in Context," p. 94.

13. Ch'üan Tsu-wang, 11.136–37.   14. *MJHA* 62.55–56.

15. Ch'en Ch'üeh, p. 466.   16. Ibid., p. 442.

17. "Preface," *MJHA*.   18. Ch'en Ch'üeh, p. 386.

19. Chiang Fan, *Kuo-ch'ao Sung-hsüeh, shang.* 2b–3a.

20. Sun Ch'i-feng, 13.443.

21. Ibid., 14.472. When his parents died, Sun practiced ancient rituals during the mourning period (see T'ang Pin, *hsia.* 52).

22. *KTLSWC*, p. 195.

23. For discussion of the practice of self-indictment and confession of wrong-doings in the late Ming and early Ch'ing, see Pei-i Wu, pp. 16–38.

24. Ts'ung Hsiao-p'ing, pp. 272–83.

25. *ECCP*, pp. 548–49.

26. *HCCSWP* 3.165.

27. *CJHA* 3.11a. Ch'en Ch'üeh (p. 186) entertained similar ideas with respect to the view that Classical rituals were "heavenly principles" that could not be changed.

28. "Nien-p'u," in *YYHSCC* 24a–b.

29. Chang Tsai, p. 264.

30. "Preface" by Li Ts'ung-chuan, in *YYHSCC* 1a.

31. *KTLSWC*, pp. 32, 108–10, 118–119.

32. Ibid., pp. 32, 195.

33. *KTLSWC*, pp. 32, 109, 141, 195; *JCL* 7.32–33.

34. *KTLSWC*, pp. 141, 195, 197.

35. Ibid., p. 60.

36. Wang Fu-chih, *Ssu chieh*, p. 19.

37. Wang Fu-chih, *Ssu-wen lu*, p. 27.

38. Wang Fu-chih, *Ssu chieh*, p. 1; idem, *Ssu-wen lu*, p. 27.

39. During his formative years, Wang was influenced by friends and teachers close to the intellectual stance of the Tung-lin leaders (McMorran, p. 141). For Wang's philosophical thought, see Black.

40. Ch'ien Mu, *Chu-tzu*, 2: 140–41, 172.

41. Ibid., 2: 140–51.

42. Quoted in Ching, p. 281. For the importance of reverence in Chu Hsi's method of cultivation, see Ching; and Ch'ien Mu, *Chu-tzu*, 2: 298–335.

43. *HCCSWP* 1.93–94.   44. Ibid., 1.94.

45. *CTYL* 42.2330.   46. *CJHA* 3.11a–b.

47. Hsü Ch'ien-hsüeh, "Fan-li," *Tu-li t'ung-k'ao*. Wan was as devoted to ritual studies as he was to the *Ming History* project (Struve, "Early Ch'ing Legacy," p. 94).

48. *CSLC* 68.36b.

49. *CJHA* 58.3a–4b.

50. Ma T'ai-hsüan, p. 36; see also Wan Ssu-t'ung's son's Preface to *Tu-li t'ung-k'ao*.

51. Ch'in Hui-t'ien, "Fan-li" 1b.

52. Huang Tsung-hsi, *Nan-lei wen-ting* 1.10.
53. Struve, "Early Ch'ing Legacy," p. 94.
54. Ch'üan Tsu-wang, 11.136.
55. Ch'ien Ta-hsin, 28.353–54.
56. For Wan Ssu-t'ung, see Struve, "Early Ch'ing Legacy," p. 94. For Wan Ssu-ta, see *CJHA*, *chüan* 34.
57. Peterson, "Life," p. 127.
58. Chan, "*Hsing-li ching-i*," p. 553; Yü Ying-shih, "Ch'ing-tai ssu-hsiang," p. 147.
59. *KTLSWC*, p. 141.
60. Ch'üan Tsu-wang, 12.144. Ku Yen-wu (*KTLSWC*, p. 59) pointed out that the term *li-hsüeh* (study of principles) originated with Sung neo-Confucians. He believed that the study of principles in antiquity was based on the study of the Classics. Ku condemned contemporary *li-hsüeh* as nothing but Ch'an Buddhism.
61. *ECCP*, p. 547.
62. Chang Po-hsing, *Cheng-i t'ang wen-chi* 8.103–4.
63. *ECCP*, p. 547.
64. Ibid.
65. Chang Po-hsing, *Cheng-i t'ang wen-chi* 8.103.
66. As stressed in the preceding chapter, we cannot treat the rejection of Sung neo-Confucianism by Classicists after the mid-eighteenth century merely as a continuation of the general repudiation of metaphysical discourse in the early Ch'ing. The K'ang-hsi period attack on neo-Confucian metaphysics was not an indiscriminate condemnation of neo-Confucianism. Many condemned Ming scholars for neglecting the Classical scholarship of Sung neo-Confucians. Ku Yen-wu's (*JCL* 1.2b–5b) view was typical of that of his contemporaries. Commenting on Chu Hsi's exegesis on the *Book of Changes*, he said that the task of the scholars who hoped to understand the *Book of Changes* was to revive the commentaries by Ch'eng I and Chu Hsi.
67. Ch'en Ch'üeh, p. 442.
68. Ibid., pp. 442, 466–67.
69. *HSS*, pp. 40–41.
70. Ch'en Ch'üeh, p. 552.
71. Ibid., p. 563.
72. Ibid., pp. 552–61, 585–86.
73. In fact, Ch'en (ibid., p. 601) showed no interest in partisan polemics and denied he was a follower of Wang Yang-ming.
74. Ibid., pp. 567–621.
75. *HSS*, pp. 50–51.
76. Ch'en Ch'üeh, pp. 444–46, 474, 560.
77. *HSS*, pp. 51–55, 66, 69.
78. Ibid., pp. 65–66.
79. Li Kung, *Shu-ku hou-chi* 13.162; *HSS*, p. 67.
80. Liang Ch'i-ch'ao (pp. 155–56) explained the general lack of interest in P'an's teachings among scholars in Chekiang in terms of Huang Tsung-hsi's great reputation in that area. Liang failed to consider the rejuvenated strength of the Ch'eng-Chu school even in Chekiang. As has been mentioned, many leading ex-

ponents of the Ch'eng-Chu school were natives of Chekiang. Scholars such as Chang Lü-hsiang, Lü Liu-liang (1623–83), and Lu Lung-ch'i had no sympathy with the teachings of Wang Yang-ming.

81. Henderson, p. 158; Huang Tsung-hsi, *Nan-lei wen-yüeh*, in *Li-chou i-chu hui-k'an* 4.5b–6b; Pi Hsi-jui, *Ching-hsüeh t'ung-lun* 1.27–28; *ECCP*, p. 336.

82. Pi Hsi-jui, *Ching-hsüeh t'ung-lun* 1.28.

83. See the preface by Wan Ssu-t'ung in Hu Wei, *I-t'u ming-pien* 6.35–36, 43–45; Pi Hsi-jui, *Ching-hsüeh t'ung-lun* 1.27–28, 30–31; Liang Ch'i-ch'ao, p. 71; Henderson, p. 158; and *ECCP*, p. 336.

84. Li Kung, *Ta-hsüeh pien-yeh* 3.5b; idem, *Chou-i chuan-chu* 1a; Feng Ch'en 4.13a–b. See *HSS*, p. 216.

85. *HSS*, pp. 241–45.

86. Elman, "Philosophy (*i-li*)," pp. 182–89, 192–98.

87. Ibid.

88. For examples of Sung Confucians' highly critical approach to the Classics, see Yeh Kuo-liang.

89. Liang Ch'i-ch'ao, p. 71.

90. *HSS*, pp. 256–57; Liang Ch'i-ch'ao, pp. 102–3.

91. Wang Mou-hung, 1.1a–8b.

92. Elman, "Philosophy (*i-li*)," pp. 208–11.

93. Ch'ien Mu (*HHS*, pp. 232–33) has pointed out that Yen Jo-chü took exception only to Chu Hsi's understanding of concrete things and place-names. His regard for Chu's expositions of ethical principles remained unshaken.

94. Li Kung, *Shu-ku hou-chi* 9.106–7.

95. Li Kung, *Ta-hsüeh pien-yeh*.   96. Liang Ch'i-ch'ao, p. 253.
97. Ibid.   98. Ibid., pp. 1–10.

99. Cf. Tu Wei-ming, "Yen Yüan," pp. 511–35, esp. pp. 518, 525.

100. Ibid., p. 518.

101. Li Kung, *Yen Hsi-chai nien-p'u*, *shang*. 11a–b.

102. The authorship of this work has been disputed. The Ch'ing scholar Wang Mou-hung disparaged it as counterfeit. Wang's view was endorsed by the *Ssu-ku ch'üan-shu* commentator. But Hsia I (1789–1871) came to the work's defense. See Ch'ien Mu, *Chu-tzu*, 2: 165–77. See also Ebrey, *Chu Hsi's Family Rituals*, p. xiv.

103. Lü Liu-liang, 8.18b–19a; Appendix, 13b; *CJHA* 49.12a–13a.

104. *MTPK* 24.10a–b. For Li Fu's negative view of Buddhism, see "Seng-fo tzu shuo," in *MTPK* 9.1b–2b.

105. This situation is suggested in Huang Tsung-hsi's protest against discrimination against Wang Yang-ming in the *Ming History* project (see *Nan-lei wen-ting ch'ien-chi* 4.4b–7a, in *Li-chou i-chu hui-k'an*).

106. Chang Lieh, pp. 628–91, 693.

107. Lu Lung-ch'i, *Lu Chia-shu hsien-sheng wen-chi* 1.10–15. See also Chan, "Hsing-li ching-i," pp. 551–52.

108. Yen Yüan, *Hsi-chai chi-yü* 6.452, 455; idem, *Ssu-shu cheng-wu* 2.8b.

109. Yen Yüan, *Hsi-chai chi-yü* 3.436; *STP*, p. 75.

110. *STP*, pp. 44, 60.

111. Yen Yüan, *Hsi-chai chi-yü* 6.452.

112. *STP*, pp. 50–51.

113. Yen Yüan only learned of the teachings of Kao P'an-lung in a letter from Tiao Pao (*Hsi-chai chi-yü* 3.437).

114. *HSS*, p. 75.

115. Yen Yüan, "Preface to *Wei-chui chi*," *Hsi-chai chi-yü* 1.429. However, Yen admired Chang Tsai's doctrine of teaching morality through learning and practicing ritual. For Yen, Chang and Hu Yüan (993–1059) were the only two followers of authentic Confucianism among the Sung scholars. Despite Yen's attack on Ch'eng-Chu neo-Confucianism, he was moving in similar direction with other scholars in reviving Chang Tsai's ethical teachings.

116. *STP*, pp. 10–11.

117. Ibid., pp. 17–18, 53.

118. Ibid., pp. 30–34.

119. Yen Yüan himself practiced quiet-sitting until 1668 (ibid., p. 139).

120. Ibid., p. 45.

121. Ibid., pp. 31–32.

122. Yen recognized his affinity with Chang Tsai (*Hsi-chai chi-yü* 3.10b; *STP*, p. 48.

123. *STP*, pp. 118–19. See also note 143 to this chapter.

124. Ibid., pp. 111–22.   125. Ibid., pp. 66, 93.

126. Ibid., p. 101.   127. Ibid., p. 67.

128. For a view of Yen Yüan's thought as anti-intellectualist, see Yü Ying-shih, *Li-shih yü ssu-hsiang*, pp. 138–39.

129. Li Kung, *Shu-ku hou-chi* 11.135.

130. *CSLC* 66.56b–57a.

131. Wang Yüan, 8.134.

132. Li Kung, *Shu-ku hou-chi* 4.40.

133. Li Kung, *Yen Hsi-chai nien-p'u, hsia*.48a.

134. *STP*, 4: 101.

135. Li Kung, *Shu-ku hou-chi* 13.171.

136. Ibid., 11.136.

137. Li Kung, *Yen Hsi-chai nien-p'u, hsia*.44b–45a.

138. *HSS*, pp. 208–10.   139. Feng Ch'en, 3.36b–37b.

140. Ibid., 3.37a–b.   141. *HSS*, pp. 208–10.

142. Feng Ch'en, 3.44a.

143. *Hsiang san-wu* (three kinds of learning for a village) referred to *liu-te* (six virtues), *liu-hsing* (six proper behaviors), and *liu-i* (six arts). The six virtues were wisdom (*chih*), benevolence (*jen*), sagehood (*sheng*), duty (*i*), loyalty (*chung*), and harmony (*ho*). The six proper behaviors were filiality (*hsiao*), friendship (*yu*), affinity (*yin*), neighborliness (*mu*), trust (*jen*), and sympathy (*shu*). The six arts were ritual (*li*), music (*yüeh*), archery (*she*), chariot-driving (*yü*), writing (*shu*), and mathematics (*shu*) (Yü Ying-shih, "Ch'ing-tai ssu-hsiang," pp. 141–42). It is not

clear what *liu-fu san-shih* mean in the Old Text school even though *liu-fu* and *san-shih* figure as separate terms in the Classics.

144. Wan Ssu-ta, *Chou-kuan pien-fei* 1a; Fang Pao, pp. 17–21.

145. Li Kung, *Shu-ku hou-chi* 4.36–37.

146. Ibid., 9.106–7; Feng Ch'en, 3.12a–13a; Wan Ssu-t'ung, 1.14a–19b. See *HSS*, pp. 206–8.

147. Li Kung, *Lun hsüeh* 1.4a–7a.   148. *CJHA* 56.14a–15a.

149. Li Kung, *Lun hsüeh* 1.4a–7a.   150. *HSS*, p. 217.

151. Li Kung, *Ta-hsüeh pien-yeh* 2.5b–7a.

152. Li Kung, *Shu-ku hou-chi* 2.18–19.

153. *STP*, p. 45.

154. Yen Yüan, *Ssu-shu cheng-wu* 6.14b.

155. Li Kung, *Lun-yü chuan-chu wen* 2b.

156. Yen Yüan, *Ssu-shu cheng-wu* 4.5a–b; *STP*, pp. 10–11. Yen (*Chu-tzu yü-lei p'ing* 17b) also pointed out that Lu Chiu-yüan had criticized Chu Hsi's reading of *k'o chi*.

157. *STP*, p. 78; Yen Yüan, *Chu-tzu yü-lei p'ing* 1a–b.

158. Li Kung, *Shu-ku hou-chi* 13.162.

Chapter 3

1. Skinner (pp. 17–21) estimates that by the mid-nineteenth century effective administration of China and its population of 425 million required nearly 10,000 subprovincial governments. But there were only about 1,300 units in the 1850's (Tung-tsu Ch'ü, p. 2).

2. For an elaboration of Weber's concept of liturgies in the study of the merchant's role in local government in Ch'ing China, see S. Mann, *Local Merchants*, chaps. 2 and 5. While borrowing Weber's concept, I do not share his view that the dependence on liturgical governance was an obstacle to the development of capitalism in China and other non-European countries. See Weber, *Theory*, pp. 228–33, 310–18; and idem, *Religion of China*, pp. 74–78, 91–95.

3. Although Duara's study concerns primarily the early twentieth century, the social organizations and networks he discusses under the term *cultural nexus* constitute the arenas where the gentry and other local elites of the Ming and Ch'ing periods established their legitimate leadership. For details, see Duara, *Culture*, chap. 1.

4. See especially Dennerline's *Chia-ting Loyalists* for the social connections of the Chia-ting elite.

5. See the essays, especially the "Introduction," in Esherick and Rankin.

6. Sakai; Brokaw; J. H. Smith, *Action*.

7. J. H. Smith, *Action*, pp. 67–72; idem, "Benevolent Societies," pp. 311–13; Wakeman, *Great Enterprise*, pp. 628–29. For a discussion of the increasing gentry role in irrigation and river conservancy in Kiangsi beginning in the late fifteenth century, see Wu Chin-ch'eng, pp. 37–54.

8. J. H. Smith, *Action*, pp. 67–73.

9. Ibid., pp. 71–72.

10. J. H. Smith, "Benevolent Societies," pp. 312–13.

11. Ibid.; *DMB*, p. 174.

12. Leung, "Ming-mo Ch'ing-ch'u," pp. 59–61.

13. J. H. Smith, "Benevolent Societies," pp. 318–23, 328–29.

14. Ibid., p. 317.

15. Cited in ibid., p. 320. Joanna Handlin Smith (ibid., pp. 317–19, 328–29) discusses the rise of this new type of charitable organization from the perspective of increasing merchant wealth and the emotional satisfaction of making charitable donations. There is no question that merchant wealth explains why privately funded charitable institutions other than those supported by Buddhists flourished, and emotional satisfaction is an important motivation for giving to charity. But, as Smith has shown, for Ch'en Lung-cheng and Kao P'an-lung the fundamental purpose of "benevolent societies" was the promotion of Confucian values. They viewed them as alternatives to Buddhist charitable organizations. It is therefore equally tenable to argue that Confucian purism was behind the founding of these institutions, which combined moral persuasion with alms giving.

16. J. H. Smith, *Action*, pp. 47–51.

17. As early as 1544, Cheng Tso, a retired official in Hsi county, Anhwei, organized a village compact in his community to defend against riotous tenants and bondservants. Cheng's model was later adopted by other members of the gentry in their attempt to resist the Japanese pirates who in 1555 ventured as far inland as Hui-chou. See Ch'en K'o-yün, pp. 45–46.

18. J. H. Smith, *Action*, pp. 47–51, 198–99.

19. To be sure, patrilineal lineages were not the only important social organization in Ming-Ch'ing China. See Sangren.

20. Freedman, p. 8. Harriet Zurndorfer ("Local Lineages," pp. 32–33) in a study of the Fan lineage in Hui-chou from the ninth to the sixteenth century shows that the lineage was founded by the descendants of a common ancestor who himself did not set up any institution resembling a lineage. The studies by Rubie Watson ("Creation," pp. 66–99; *Inequality*) and David Faure (*Structure*, pp. 65–67, 149–63) clearly demonstrate that lineages in the New Territories of Hong Kong were created regardless of the primordial existence of groups of kinsmen living in a locality. For a discussion of lineage building since the mid-Ming in Kwangtung, see Inoue Tōru.

21. Commenting on Hilary Beattie's study of the T'ung-ch'eng lineages, Patricia Ebrey ("Types") argues convincingly that the lineage paradigm Maurice Freeman formulated on the basis of anthropological studies in Kwangtung and Fukien could not be applied indiscriminately to lineages in other parts of China. She suggests that the type of lineages developed in T'ung-ch'eng was of a different order. Keith Hazelton (pp. 165–67) also attempts to delineate the differences between what he calls "Lower Yangtze" lineages and "Kwangtung" lineages. See also the Introduction jointly written by Ebrey and James Watson in *Kinship Orga-*

nization. There is no question that lineages of the Lower Yangtze type had more degree-holders in the leadership echelon than did lineages of the Kwangtung type, but gentry leadership was important in both types. Gentry influence could be denied only by ruling out holders of lower degrees, many of whom had access to political influence.

22. Ebrey, "Early Stages," pp. 16–56.

23. In her study of the Fan lineage of Hsiu-ning county, Zurndorfer ("Local Lineages," pp. 45–46) argues that by the end of the fourteenth century, the Fan descent group had become a lineage: they performed ancestral rites and sacrifices to the memory of the common ancestor, compiled periodic editions of the group's genealogy, and maintained some form of common property. But they did not have an ancestral hall, which, as I shall argue, was the most important institution of lineages in central and south China in the Ch'ing period.

24. See note 21 to this chapter; Cohen; and Duara, *Culture*, chap. 4.

25. Cohen's study does not cover the Ming period, but the Ming situation would not have been very different from the Ch'ing with respect to the size of lineage and the resources available to the lineage leaders. See Cohen; and Duara, *Culture*, chap. 4.

26. For a discussion of the origin and development of the charitable estates of Fan Chung-yen's clan, see Twitchett.

27. For some examples in the Sung, see Hymes, pp. 129–30. For examples in the late Ming, see Hsü Fang, 3.11a.

28. Li Wen-chih, pp. 280–82.

29. Falsification of family names either by consent of the master or by concoction of descent was common in the late Ming. The practice of conferring the master's family name on bondservants was already widespread by the mid-fifteenth century in Soochow. See Oyama, pp. 10–12.

30. Dennerline, *Chia-ting Loyalists*, pp. 138–41.

31. Ch'ien Ch'ien-i, 27.11b–13a.

32. Zurndorfer, *Change and Continuity*, pp. 142–43.

33. McDermott, p. 700.

34. Dennerline, *Chia-ting Loyalists*, pp. 99–103.

35. Wang Pi, *shang*.50a–51a, *hsia*.56b; Yang T'ien-shih, *T'ai-chou hsüeh-p'ai*, pp. 88–89.

36. Yang T'ien-shih, *T'ai-chou hsüeh-p'ai*, p. 136.

37. Dimberg, pp. 43–47.

38. Liang Ju-yüan, p. 69.

39. Dimberg, p. 47.

40. Kao P'an-lung, *Chia-hsün*, in *Kao-tzu i-shu*, 10B.18b.

41. *Kao-tzu nien-p'u*, in Kao P'an-lung, *Kao-tzu i-shu* 36a.

42. *DMB*, p. 742.

43. *LTCS*, vol. 6, *Nien-p'u*, 40A.28a, 46a–b.

44. Ibid., 40A.46a.   45. Ibid., 40B.3a–b.

46. Ibid., 40A.49a–b.   47. Ibid., 40B.1b.

48. Ibid., 40B.4b–5b.

49. Ch'iu Chün (see note 12 to Introduction), in his comments on the organization of the chapters of *Family Rituals*, deemed it appropriate to begin the book with the section on descent-line principle (quoted in Wang Chien, 1.35b–36a). Wang Pi (1.39a–43a) was perhaps one of the few who attempted to organize his kin by the descent-line principle, but his understanding of the meaning of the term is not clear. For the popularity of Chu Hsi's *Family Rituals*, see Ebrey, *Confucianism*, chap. 7; idem, Introduction to *Chu Hsi's Family Rituals*; and Brook, "Gentry Dominance," p. 272.

50. Many scholars and officials associated with the Tung-lin movement displayed an interest in the *Family Rituals*. Before converting to Christianity in 1612, Yang T'ing-yün (1557–1627) was a sponsor of the rebuilding of the Tung-lin Academy (Gernet, p. 42). He was serving in Soochow as a censor concurrently in charge of educational affairs in 1605 when he wrote a preface for a reprint of the *Family Rituals* (*ECCP*, p. 894; Kao T'ing-chen, 17.3a). Yang was included as a scholar who had contributed to expansion of the *Family Rituals*. The other edition (1701) of the *Family Rituals*, by Wang Chien, has two prefaces: one by the grandfather of Fang I-chih (d. 1671?), Fang Ta-chen (?–1631), then a censor discharging duties as a salt tax commissioner for Chihli and Chekiang; the other by Chou K'ung-chiao (fl. 1604), then the governor Nan Chihli, a close friend of Ku Hsien-ch'eng and Kao P'an-lung, and a regular attendant at conferences of the Tung-lin Academy (*ECCP*, p. 232; *CTCL*, preface; Beattie, *Land and Lineage*, pp. 40–41).

51. For an analysis of the various seventeenth-century attacks on excessive centralization of political power in the court, see Hsiung Ping-chen.

52. *KTLSWC*, pp. 100–102.

53. Ibid., pp. 153–54.

54. Ibid.

55. *JCL* 9.15–16; trans. from de Bary, *Sources*, 2: 556.

56. For discussions of the origins of autocratic rule of the Ming imperial system, see Mote, pp. 24–29; and Dardess, *Confucianism*.

57. *KTLSWC*, pp. 12–17.

58. Kuhn, "Local Self-Government," p. 264.

59. Guy, "Development," p. 99.

60. *KTLSWC*, p. 13.

61. Dennerline, "Fiscal Reform," pp. 110–11.

62. *ECCP*, p. 327. See also Kessler, "Chinese Scholars," p. 188.

63. *JCL* 22.17b–19a.

64. Wakeman, "Localism," pp. 71–73.

65. Willard J. Peterson ("Life," pp. 214–15) assigns the date of 1657 to a preface Ku wrote for Chang Erh-ch'i's *I-li Cheng-chu chü-tu*. In that year Ku first met Chang, but Chang did not finish this work until 1670. Ku confided to Wang Wan in 1663 that he came to realize the prime importance of ritual only after he was over fifty (i.e., after 1662). It seems unlikely that the preface, which already shows Ku's conviction in this regard, was written in 1657. Ku visited Chang again in 1675 and

made a copy of the *I-li Cheng-chu chü-tu* for a library he was to build in Shansi that year. This was five years after Chang completed his work and twelve or so years after Ku himself awakened to the importance of rituals. See also *KTLSWC*, p. 60; Chang Mu, 2.218, 3.254; and Chang Erh-ch'i, Preface, *I-li Cheng-chu chü-tu*.

66. Chang Mu, p. 209; *KTLSWC*, pp. 107–8.

67. Chang Mu, p. 227.

68. *KTLSWC*, pp. 100–102.

69. *JCL* 6.14a–b.

70. For a good discussion of the descent-line system in the Chou dynasty and its prototype in the Shang, see Wang Kuei-min, pp. 30–50.

71. Ebrey, *Chu Hsi's Family Rituals*, pp. xxi–ii, 8–10.

72. But as the next chapter will show, the connotations of the term expanded in the Ch'ing period to mean more than the conventional sense of the biological "main line." The criterion for naming the heir of a "descent-line" *tsung* was not invariably biological; often the possession of official rank or examination honors outweighed genealogical considerations.

73. *JCL* 6.14b–15a.

74. *KTLSWC*, p. 109.

75. Kuhn, "Local Self-Government," p. 264.

76. *KTLSWC*, p. 109.

77. Ibid., p. 93.

78. To be sure, Ch'ing literati continued to write and print didactic materials such as morality books and moral ledgers to promote Confucian values. Only the specific form of didacticism—public lecturing—declined in the Ch'ing. Brokaw (p. 26) also notes the decline of original works of moral ledgers in the eighteenth century.

79. Tanaka Masatoshi; Tsing Yuan; Fu I-ling, *Ming-tai Chiang-nan*, pp. 100–111; Parsons; Von Glahn, pp. 292–93.

80. Feng Ch'en, 5.8a.

81. *KTLSWC*, p. 109; Chang Mu, p. 261.

82. *KTLSWC*, p. 109. Hsü Fang (1622–94; 5.10b–11b), a scholar known for his painting, entertained a similar view on the relation of "big families" to the security of a dynasty.

83. *JCL* 13.38a.

84. Lu Shih-i, 18.402.

85. Ibid.

86. *KTLSWC*, p. 13.

87. Lu Shih-i, 18.402.

88. Ibid., 10.382.

89. Ibid.

90. As will be discussed in greater detail in Chapter 4, the rules of most kinship organizations did not favor the hoary institution of the descent-line system, that is, the distinction of a natural main patriline as the core of the kin group.

91. Lu Shih-i, 21.409–10.

92. Ibid., 10.382.

93. Ibid., 10.381.

94. Ibid., 10.382.

95. Lu Shih-i (10.381) noted the great expenses required to practice the ceremonies of the *Family Rituals*.

96. *CTCL* 1.35b–36a.

97. Ch'en Ch'üeh, p. 195.

98. Chang Lü-hsiang, 18.9a–10a. Although by the mid-seventeenth century lineages with an ancestral hall of some sort were quite common in Hui-chou and T'ung-ch'eng in Anhwei and, perhaps in some areas of Kiangsi and Kwangtung as well, they were far from as ubiquitous in most provinces in south China as they would become in the nineteenth century.

99. *HCCSWP* 66.2416. For Chai's biography, see *KCCHLC*, 395.17a–24a.

100. *Ming T'ai-tsu shih-lu*, in *Ming shih-lu*, p. 1473. For the structure of the hall for officials, see *Ta-Ming hui-tien* 95.1a–10b.

101. Fang Hsiao-ju, 16.9b–10b.

102. *Hsü wen-hsien t'ung-k'ao* 86.3559; Lung Wen-pin, 10.168–169.

103. See Wang Tao-k'un, 21.20b–23a, 67.15b–17b.

104. Ch'iu Chün, 17.25b–26a.

105. Li Kuang-ti, *Jung-ts'un chi* 21.824.

106. Chang Lü-hsiang, 18.9a–10a.

107. Ibid.   108. Ch'en Ch'üeh, pp. 190–92.

109. Ibid., pp. 192–94.   110. Ibid., p. 196.

111. Ibid., pp. 196–98.   112. Ibid., p. 186.

113. Ibid., p. 195.

114. Chang Lü-hsiang, 10.10b–11a.

115. Ibid., 3.20a, 21.8a; Ch'en Ch'üeh, p. 142.

116. Chang Lü-hsiang, 32.13b–14a.

117. *CJHA* 5.25a–b; Chang Lü-hsiang, 11.6a–b.

118. Chang Lü-hsiang, 11.6a–7b.

Chapter 4

1. Ebrey is among a few who has written on the neo-Confucian theory of kinship; see, e.g., "Early Stages," pp. 35–39, 51. Hsien-chin Hu's pioneering work on the Chinese descent group gives only brief notice to the role of Sung neo-Confucians in shaping ancestral rites and kinship organization; see pp. 26–28.

2. Ebrey, "Conception," pp. 229–32.

3. The Chou king had the exclusive right to attend to more than five ancestors; the maximum limit varied with exegetical traditions. According to the Han commentator Cheng Hsüan's (127–200) exposition, the Chou king had five temples. Wang Su (d. A.D. 256), however, insisted that the Chou ruler had had seven. For a general discussion of the differences, see Wechsler, pp. 128–32.

4. According to Cheng Hsüan and the T'ang commentator K'ung Ying-ta (574–648), only on special occasions such as war were great officials granted the right to worship their great-great-grandfather, who was otherwise left uncommemorated. This exposition is based on a remark in the *Kung-yang Commentary*; see K'ung, p. 1506.

5. *ECC*, pp. 163, 167, 286.

6. *ECC*, p. 167.

7. *CTYL* 90.2317–18.

8. *ECC*, p. 179.

9. *ECC*, pp. 179–80.

10. Li Kuang-ti, "Chia-miao chi-hsiang li-lüeh," in *HCCSWP* 66.2403–5.

11. Su Shih, lamenting the abolition of the system of hereditary ranks and fiefs, suggested that the lesser descent-line system be resuscitated but conceded that the great descent-line system was an impossibility (Ch'in, 145.17a–b; see also Chi Ta-k'uei, in *HCCSWP* 58.2137–41).

12. Ssu-ma Kuang and Chang Tsai recommended the inclusion of ancestors up to the great-grandfather in the ancestral hall. Chang Tsai (p. 261) observed that ancient officials were not granted the privilege of worshiping their first ancestor (*t'ai-tsu*) and did not recommend its practice.

13. This translation follows the sense in Ch'eng I's writing (*ECC*, p. 240). Ebrey's ("Early Stages," p. 38) rendering of the term *shih-tsu* as "the first to have descendants in the line" is affected by subsequent usage. Ch'eng I did not unequivocally render the term in this sense.

14. *ECC*, p. 240.

15. Ibid.

16. *CTYL* 90.2318. Ch'eng I appears not to have equated *ti* with the worship of the first ancestor. He regarded *ti* as a ceremony appropriate only to an emperor and as a service undertaken to honor more than one ancestor in addition to the ancestor from whom the present emperor descended (*ECC*, p. 167).

17. Li Kuang-ti, *Chu-tzu li-tsuan* 4.709–10; *CTYL* 90.4809–11.

18. What *shih-chi* means here is not clear from the text (*CTYL* 90.4809). Yet its scope of meaning is wide enough to embrace both the first to attain office and the first to settle in a new locale.

19. See Ebrey, "Early Stages," p. 39.

20. Ebrey (ibid., p. 29) argues that the deeper consciousness of kinship fostered by offerings at graves during the Ch'ing-ming festival was crucial in the development of the descent group in Late Imperial China.

21. Hymes, pp. 113–33.

22. Ibid., p. 128.

23. Chang Po-hsing, *Chin-ssu lu* 9.255; idem, *Hsiao-hsüeh chi-chieh* 5.358.

24. Chan, "Chu Hsi and Yüan Neo-Confucianism," pp. 213–14.

25. Hsü Heng, 5.181–82.

26. K'ung, pp. 1495, 1508, 1335.

27. Ibid., p. 1335; Hsü Heng, 5.181–82.

28. As early as the eleventh century, Ch'en Hsiang-tao (1053–93) had defined three similar categories of *pieh-tzu*: feudal lords' secondary sons with high office, those who came from a different fiefdom, and high officials arising from the commoner (*min-shu*) stratum. But it is not clear whether he developed this usage independently of or in response to changing social reality, for it was not mentioned in connection with the building of a temple for a first ancestor. See Ch'in, 145.432.

29. Hsü Heng's debt to Ch'eng I is evident. His essay was written to com-

memorate worship conducted in the newly erected hall at the winter solstice, the time Ch'eng I assigned to the worship of the first ancestor. See Hsü Heng, 5.181–82.

30. In the late thirteenth century, Cheng Yung of the famous Cheng communal family of Chin-hua in Chekiang encountered similar difficulty with the *Family Rituals'* four-generation model. Cheng Yung found it necessary to enshrine nine generations of progenitors after the first ancestor. See Dardess, "Cheng Communal Family," pp. 48–50.

31. The temple in question was not a family shrine built according to the precepts of the *Family Rituals* but a lineage hall, for Hsü Heng (5.182) recorded a consensus on enshrining in the hall all kinsmen who had held office, in addition to the first ancestor.

32. See, e.g., Ch'iu, 17.30b–31a; and Lo Lun's (1431–78; 4.2b–4b) essay written to celebrate the founding of an apical ancestral hall.

33. Ebrey, "Early Stages," p. 39.

34. Chu Hsi's knowledge of the ancient temple system was in line with tradition in this regard; see *CTYL* 90.2298.

35. For Ch'eng I's advice to worship the first ancestor, see Chang Po-hsing, *Chin-ssu lu* 9.255; and idem, *Hsiao-hsüeh chi-chieh* 5.358.

36. Chu Hsi duly recognized these rites when he incorporated them into his own unfinished work on family rituals; see *CTYL* 84.4532, 89.4712, 90.4799, 4840.

37. Hu Kuang, 18.405, 21.466. See also *DMB*, p. 628.

38. Chan, "*Hsing-li ching-i*," pp. 569–70.

39. Hu Kuang, *chüan* 18–21.

40. Jung, *Ming-t'ai*, p. 2; Chan, "*Hsing-li ching-i*," p. 545; Ebrey, *Confucianism*, p. 152.

41. Chu Hsi (*CTYL* 89.4713, 90.4799) frowned on the financial drain involved in carrying out Ssu-ma Kuang's recommended ceremonies. Ironically, Lü K'un ("Chi-li" in *Ssu-li i* 3b) in the Ming found the rites recommended by the *Family Rituals* equally undesirable in terms of spending. Lu Shih-i's attempt to curtail expenses for ancestor worship of his lineage is noted in Chapter 3.

42. *DMB*, pp. 589–90. Liu Chi (1311–75) also took part in its compilation (*DMB*, p. 934).

43. Hsü I-k'uei, 6.171–72.

44. *Ming T'ai-tsu shih-lu*, in *Ming shih-lu*, vol. 4, 8.1473; Lung Wen-pin, 10.168.

45. Su, 7.510.

46. Ch'iu, 17.25b.

47. Huang Huai, 35.4b.

48. See comments in *CTCL*, "T'ung-li" 43b–44b.

49. Fang Hsiao-ju, 16.9b–10b.

50. See, e.g., Chang Mou, p. 717; the K'o (1449) and Lin (1465) lineages in Fukien, mentioned in Ch'iu, 17.24a–26a, 28b–31a; and the case of T'eng Yüan-hsi (1529–93) in Chang Hsüan, 5.402.

51. For the issues involved, see C. T. Fisher; Chang Hsien-ch'ing, "Ming Chia-ching"; and Meng Sen, pp. 218–54.

52. Hsia took exception to Chu Hsi's apology for abandoning the worship of first ancestor. For him the parallel Chu Hsi drew between the worship of first ancestor and the ancient imperial *ti* rite was fallacious. Whereas *ti* was a grand rite held only every five years, the ceremony Ch'eng I suggested was an annual event, and the offerings did not match the *ti* in terms of scale and grandeur. Chu Hsi's anxiety was beside the point, according to Hsia.

53. For the text of Hsia Yen's memorial, see Teng, vol. 5, 74.449; or Shen Ch'ao-yang, vol. 2, 5.458–59. See also Lung Wen-pin, 10.168–69; and *Hsü wen-hsien t'ung-k'ao*, vol. 16, 86.3559.

54. Wang Tao-k'un, 67.15b–17b, 69.18a, 72.9a–b.

55. Hsü I-k'uei, 6.12b–13a.

56. Hao Ching (1558–1639), quoted in Ch'in, 109.9a.

57. Annotation in *CTCL* 1.35b–36a.

58. Huang Tsung-hsi, *Ming-i tai-fang lu*, in *Huang Tsung-hsi ch'üan-chi*, pp. 13–14.

59. The compilation of the *Ta-Ch'ing hui-tien* was not commissioned until 1684 and was completed in 1690 (*ECCP*, p. 805). In 1684 Wei Hsiang-shu (3.69–70) memorialized the K'ang-hsi emperor to propose the compilation of a ritual compendium for the Ch'ing dynasty, which would draw on official works on rituals published by previous dynasties as well as on the *Family Rituals*. Ch'en Tzu-chih, a native of Chekiang, in a memorial submitted to the K'ang-hsi emperor in 1687, echoed Wei's request. Ch'en suggested that in the compendium ritual prescriptions for commoners be based on the rites of *Family Rituals* (*HCCSWP* 54.1977–78; *KCCHLC* 134.5404).

60. *ECC*, pp. 167, 245.

61. Ibid., p. 242.

62. Ibid., pp. 156, 236.

63. Wang Wan was among those who opposed the resurrection of the descent-line system; see *HCCSWP* 58.8a–b.

64. Ch'en Ch'üeh, p. 196.

65. Ibid., p. 197.

66. Chang Ching-ming, pp. 52–53.

67. Wan Ssu-ta's son gave the year 1666 as the beginning of the Club for Studying the Classics; in *I-li shang* Wan himself gave 1667 as the first year of the club's existence. See Wan Ssu-ta, *Li-chi ou-chien*, appended biographical essays, 3a; and *I-li shang*, appendix 3b. Ono Kazuko gives 1658 as the beginning of the club. Rituals were important topics of study for the club (Inoue Susumu, p. 238).

68. Wan Ching, "A biography," in Wan Ssu-ta, *Li-chi ou-chien* 3a–b.

69. Ying Hui-ch'ien's (1615–83) preface to this work is dated 1680. But Huang Tsung-hsi had written a preface for this work in 1677 (*Nan-lei wen-ting, Chien-chi* 1.10–11).

70. In Wan's words, "tsung-fa pu i shih-chüeh" (the descent-line system does not depend on hereditary rank; *HLCI* 2.460).

71. K'ung, pp. 1335, 1495, 1507–8; *HLCI* 2.457. The term *pieh-tzu* is not found in documents or archaeological relics (see Wang Kuei-min, p. 31).

72. K'ung, p. 1495.

73. *HLCI* 2.456–58.

74. In *CTCL* 1.43b–44b.

75. K'ung, p. 1335.

76. *CTYL* 90.4808.

77. *HLCI* 2.458.

78. Ibid., 2.458–59.

79. K'ung, p. 1335.

80. Ibid., p. 1506.

81. *HLCI* 2.448–50.

82. Wan Ssu-ta, *Li-chi ou-chien* 2.288–89.

83. *KCCHLC* 413.26a–b.

84. Ku Yen-wu, *Wu-ching t'ung-i, hsia.*13b–33b. Ku also included Wan's essay on the enshrinement of brothers in the same temple (ibid., 34a–36a). However, Tseng Chao (3.20a–22b), a student of Juan Yüan (1764–1849), noted with regret that even polymaths like Ku were misled by Wan's argument.

85. Ch'in, *chüan* 109 (pp. 610–12).

86. Ibid., 109.7b–8b.

87. Ch'eng T'ing-tso, appended essays, 1.5a–b.

88. *ECCP*, p. 563.

89. Kessler, "Chinese Scholars," pp. 191–92.

90. Elman, *From Philosophy to Philology*, pp. 100–103.

91. *K'ang-hsi ti yü-chih wen-chi* 8.12b–13b.

92. A note appended to the end of Mao's *THTTS* (p. 52) alludes to what Mao wrote to refute Wan's ideas.

93. Ibid., p. 48.

94. *PTCL* 2.2a.

95. See Ch'in, 145.430–39.

96. K'ung, p. 1494.

97. *THTTS*, p. 49.

98. Ibid., p. 1508.

99. Ibid. Mao's argumentativeness is nowhere revealed as clearly as in his views on this issue. Despite his criticism of K'ung for faulty reading, he elsewhere advocated the worship of the first migrant ancestor and invoked Kung's exposition for support (see *PTCL* 1.10a).

100. *HLCI* 2.456.

101. *THTTS*, p. 49.

102. Ch'en Ch'üeh, pp. 196–97.

103. *HHWC*, p. 757.

104. Mao Ch'i-ling, *Miao-chih che-chung* 2.4b–5a.

105. *PTCL* 1.8b–9a.

106. *HHWC*, p. 200; *PTCL* 1.9a; see also Mao Ch'i-ling, *Miao-chih che-chung* 2.4b–5a.

107. *HHWC*, pp. 163, 165.

108. Ibid., pp. 163–66.

109. *HSS*, pp. 206–14.

110. Li Kung, *Hsüeh-li* 4.726.

111. Ibid.

112. Wang Wan served as a department director in the Board of Punishments before he was implicated in the Tax Clearance Case of 1661. He later took part in the special *po-hsüeh hung-tz'u* examination and was appointed a compiler in the Han-lin Academy. Like Mao Ch'i-ling, he was invited to assist in the compilation of the *Ming History* (*ECCP*, p. 840; *K'ang-hsi ti yü-chih wen-chi*, vol. 1, 8.154–55).

113. *HCCSWP* 58.8a–b.

114. Here it is not clear what Wan means by *chüeh-tsu* (termination of the lineage). But it seems that he was speaking of the five-generations model.

115. *HCCSWP* 58.2149–50.

116. Ibid., 58.2150.
117. Li Kuang-ti, *Jung-ts'un chi*, 21.823–24.
118. Ibid., 21.823–26.   119. *MTPK* 9.5b–7b.
120. *HLCI* 2.467–70.   121. *MTPK* 9.6a–7b.
122. *MTCK* 24.12b–15a.   123. Ibid.
124. Yang Ch'un, 10.9a–12a.   125. Ibid.
126. Ibid.   127. Ibid.
128. *HCCSWP* 64.2362–63.   129. Ibid., 64.2361–63.
130. Yin, 4.36; Yu Lung-kuang, 2.13a–b.
131. *PTCL* 2.8b–9a.
132. Ibid., 1.18a, 2.5b.
133. *HHWC*, p. 757.
134. Lu Shih-i (10.381) noted the great expenses required to practice the ceremonies of the *Family Rituals*.
135. *MTCK* 24.13b.
136. Lu Yao (1723–85) observed with disgust that in Kiangsi it became a fad to establish apical lineage halls dedicated to a questionable original ancestor and a large number of ancestors. He recommended a model based on the *Family Rituals*, but he included a first ancestor, which was in fact the system defended by Wan Ssu-ta. See *HCCSWP* 66.2416–20.
137. Sheng, 73.1323–24.

Chapter 5

1. Ch'en Ch'üeh, pp. 179–180, 188–89, 281, 387; Chang Lü-hsiang, 18.10b–11b.
2. Chang Lü-hsiang, 18.1a–12b.
3. Ch'en Ch'üeh, pp. 476–505.
4. This work, begun in 1640, remained in rudimentary outline until Lu Shih-i resumed writing it in 1667 (Ling Hsi-ch'i, 10a, 47b–48a). The *Tsung-chi li* seems to have been lost, but Lu's general ideas are preserved in notes in his *Ssu-pien lu* (10.381).
5. Lu's remarks on these rituals can be found in the section called "Chih-p'ing" (Peace and order); *Ssu-pien lu* 21.408–12.
6. Ling Hsi-ch'i, 42b–43a; Ch'üan, 13.155; Ch'en Ch'üeh, pp. 97, 114, 118–19.
7. Ch'üan, 12.152–54.
8. Ying's illustrated work on ritual vessels is "Li-chi t'u-shuo" (*CJHA* 16.2a). According to *SKTY* (pp. 502–3) Li-hsüeh hui-pien was a work of 70 *chüan*, but *CJHA* (16.2a) has 63 *chüan*.
9. *SKTY*, pp. 502–3.   10. *JCL* 15.20a–23a.
11. Ku Yen-wu, *Wu-ching t'ung-i*.   12. *JCL*, *chüan* 5, 6, 14, 15, 23.
13. Mao Ch'i-ling, *Sang-li wu-shuo* (My exposition of funeral rites); *San-nien fu chih k'ao* (A study of three-year mourning dress); *Hun-li pien-cheng* (Clarification of proper wedding ceremonies); *Chiao, she, ti, hsia wen* (Questions regarding *chiao, she, ti,* and *hsia*); all in *Miao-chih che-ch'ung*. See *SKTY*, pp. 444–45, 498–501.
14. His great works include *Tsung-miao k'ao-pien* (A critical study of temple

systems), *Chiao-she k'ao-pien* (A critical study of *chiao* and *she*), and *Ti-hsia k'ao-pien* (A critical study of *ti* and *hsia*); see Chang Hsi-t'ang, "Yen-Li chu-shu k'ao," p. 132.

15. Li Kung, *Hsüeh-li*, pp. 719–731.

16. Wang Wan, 25.33.

17. Yen Jo-chü, *Sang-fu i-chu*, in *Ch'ien-ch'iu cha-chi* 4.1a–17b, 6.6a–8b, 12b–14a, 49a–b.

18. To the list of those discussed in this section, we need add only Huang Tsung-hsi, Hsü San-li, Lu Lung-ch'i, Wan Ssu-ta, and Wan Ssu-t'ung. Many more names could be added. Suffice it to say here that they wrote treatises and essays on rituals but none attempted a strictly annotated commentary on the entire text of any one of the ritual Classics.

19. Chang Erh-ch'i's *I-li Cheng-chu chü-tu* (Punctuated reading of Cheng Hsüan's commentary on the *Book of Etiquette and Decorum*) in 17 *chüan* was exceptional among early Ch'ing works on ritual. It is perhaps the only major effort in the K'ang-hsi period to revive Cheng Hsüan's exegeses on the *I-li*, stressing ancient pronunciations and accurate division of the text into meaningful units. Wang Fu-chih was exceptional for his devotion to producing many systematic commentaries on the Classics. His ritual scholarship crystalized in *Li-chi chang-chü* (*Book of Rites* in chapters and verses), a work comparable to Chang's work on the *I-li* in its commitment to full annotation. But whereas Chang's work was largely a faithful effort to exalt Cheng's scholium, Wang's commentary was essentially a personal reading of the *Li-chi* without particular reference to a specific exegetical tradition. No special homage was paid to Cheng Hsüan or to other Han exegetes. One other distinctive feature of Wang's book is the lack of citation.

20. Wang's work is entitled *Li-chi hui-pien* (A collection of writings on the *Book of Rites*); see Tang Chien, 10.359. This work stood very low in the evaluation scheme used by the *Ssu-ku ch'üan-shu*'s editors, which stresses fidelity to the original textual organization of the Classics; see *SKTY*, p. 487.

21. In *CHWS*.

22. Lynn Struve ("Early Ch'ing Legacy," p. 94) notes that late in Wan Ssu-t'ung's career he devoted himself to the study of ritual.

23. For the scholarly exchanges between Yen and Wan Ssu-t'ung, see Yen Jo-chü, *Shang-shu* 8.54a–b, 56b–57b, 59b–60a.

24. Wan Ssu-t'ung, 4.30a–b, 12.10a–b, 14a–15b. For a discussion of the Great Rites Controversy, see C. T. Fisher.

25. Wan Ssu-t'ung, *chüan* 3, 4, 7.

26. *ECCP*, p. 310.

27. See the section on the *ti* ceremonies below.

28. Wan Ssu-t'ung, *chüan* 1–6.   29. Ibid., 6.2b.

30. Ibid., 6.20a–b.   31. *SKTY*, pp. 502–3.

32. Ibid., pp. 484, 486; SKCS, vol. 103.

33. *SKTY*, p. 482.

34. *KTLSWC*, pp. 32–33, 109.

35. Lu Lung-ch'i, *Tu-li chih-i* 1.72. For K'ung Ying-ta, Chia Kung-yen, Chao K'uang, and Tan Chu, see McMullen, pp. 73–105.

36. Lu Lung-ch'i, *Tu-li chih-i* 1.72–73.

37. Chang Po-hsing, "Preface to *Tu-li chih-i*," in *Cheng-i t'ang wen-chi* 8.103–4.

38. On the gentry use of the *Family Rituals* as a manual, see Brook, "Gentry Dominance," p. 272; and idem, "Funerary Ritual." On the writing and printing of variant versions of the *Family Rituals* in the Ming and Ch'ing, see Ebrey, *Confucianism*, chaps. 7 and 8.

39. *PCC* 127.10b.

40. Chang Lü-hsiang, 33.24a. 3.34a–35a; Ch'en Ch'üeh, pp. 58, 278.

41. *ECCP*, pp. 848–49.

42. Wei Hsiang-shu, 3.70–71.

43. Ibid., 6.188.

44. *ECCP*, pp. 689–90; Preface to *CTCL*.

45. *SKTY*, p. 503.

46. Hsiao I-shan, p. 450. The title of the same work is given in *CSLC* (68.33b) as *Jen-shih chia-li cho*.

47. *ECCP*, p. 310.

48. See the prefaces by Chu I-tsun and Hsü's son in Hsü Ch'ien-hsüeh.

49. See the Preface (dated 1691) by Chu I-tsun in ibid.

50. See the Preface (dated 1691) by Hsü's son in ibid.; *ECCP*, p. 310.

51. Hsü Ch'ien-hsüeh, "Fan-li"; see also the prefaces by Chu I-tsun and Hsü's son; and *SKTY*, pp. 410–11.

52. See the bibliography in the beginning sections of the *Tu-li t'ung-k'ao*.

53. Ch'in, Preface; *SKTY*, p. 440.

54. *ECCP*, pp. 167–68. The project began before 1747 (Ch'in, Preface).

55. Fang Kuan-ch'eng's preface to Ch'in; Chiang Fan, *Kuo-ch'ao Han-hsüeh* 3.1a, 4.1b, 5.8a.

56. Chiang Yung, pp. 43–44.

57. *HLCI* 1.23a–24b.

58. In his *Ti-hsia chih* (Records of *ti* and *hsia*), Cheng Hsüan explained the ancestral rite *hsia* as a grand collective worship in which the king made sacrifice to all the displaced ancestors (*t'iao-chu*) and ancestors currently installed in the temples (Li Yün-kuang, p. 598).

59. The Classical sources for the first two meanings of *ti* are two commentaries to the *Spring and Autumn Annals*: the *Tso Commentary* has *ti* as a concluding ceremony; the *Kung-yang Commentary* has *ti* and *hsia* as three-year and five-year rites. The other source Cheng Hsüan cited for *ti* and *hsia* as different rites is the apocryphal *Li-wei* (Weft of rites). See Wan Ssu-t'ung, 6.4a, 7a–b; Ts'ui Shu, pp. 504–5; Huang Yung-wu, pp. 499–500, 502; and Hu P'ei-hui, p. 412. For a detailed schedule of Cheng Hsüan's *ti* and *hsia* ceremony, see Li Yün-kuang, pp. 597–98; for a critique of Cheng's schedule, see Wan Ssu-t'ung, 6.2b–3a.

60. *SSCCS*, pp. 1495, 1506; *HLCI* 1.21b–22a; Wan Ssu-t'ung, 6.1a–b; Ts'ui Shu, p. 509.

61. Wan Ssu-t'ung, 6.1a–b.
62. *HLCI* 1.24b.
63. *CTYL* 90.2229; 2318.
64. In fact, Chu Hsi's students referred to Ch'eng I's spring worship as *hsia*, by which he meant worshiping more than one ancestor in the same ceremony (*CTYL* 87.2258, 90.2318–19).
65. *CTYL*, 87.2229; Ma Tuan-lin, 101.920. According to Ts'ui Shu (pp. 500–504), the idea that *ti* was the exclusive privilege of the king resulted from a misreading of a statement in the *Book of Rites*.
66. *CTYL* 87.2256–59; 90.2313.
67. Quoted in Hu P'ei-hui, p. 413.
68. *CTYL* 87.2236–37. Ts'ui (p. 509) also criticized Cheng Hsüan for his confusing glosses.
69. *HLCI* 1.20b–21b.
70. Tu Yü (222–84) subscribed to Hsü's view; see ibid., 1.22a.
71. *HLCI* 1.22a.   72. Wan Ssu-t'ung, 6.1a–b.
73. Ibid., 6.2b.   74. Ibid., 6.10a, 11a–12b.
75. Ibid., 6.11b.
76. To Wan Ssu-t'ung's regret, Chao espoused the erroneous view that *ti* was not a collective ceremony to honor all ancestors (ibid., 6.13a–b).
77. Ibid., 6.19a.
78. Ibid., 6.20a–b.
79. See, e.g., Chiao, "Chi-li," in "San-li pien-meng," *shang*.12b–13a.
80. Ku Yen-wu, *Wu-ching t'ung-i, shang*. 40b–41b.
81. Ibid., *shang*. 47a–b; Wang Wan, 6.3a–b.
82. Lu Lung-ch'i, *Tu-li chih-i* 2.75, 4.79, 5.82.
83. Lu Shih-i, 21.408.   84. Ibid., 21.410.
85. *CSTHW*, p. 399.   86. Ibid., pp. 397–400.
87. Ibid., p. 398.
88. Ibid., p. 398. In this case both Lu and Mao took exception to the "Chi-fa" chapter of the *Book of Rites* and to the *Kuo-yü*, which considered Kao the remotest ancestor that the Chou people worshiped. According to Ts'ui Shu (p. 507), it was a mistake to treat Hou Chi as Kao's son. Early sources attributed this assertion to the *Kuo-yü* and "Chi-fa," but a careful reading shows that these writings did not make that connection.
89. *THTTS*, p. 50.
90. For the two passages, see *SSCCS*, pp. 1495, 1506.
91. *THTTS*, p. 50.
92. *CSTHW*, pp. 396–97.
93. Ibid., pp. 397–400.
94. *SSCCS*, p. 2267; see also *CSTHW*, p. 398.
95. Li Kung, *Chiao-she k'ao-pien* 1.8a.
96. Li Kung, *Ti-hsia k'ao-pien* 1a–3a, 7a.
97. Yang Ch'un, 10.3a–4b. For an account of the origin of this, see note 88 to this chapter.

98. Yang Ch'un, 10.3a–4b.

99. Yang was perhaps influenced here by Wan Ssu-ta, "T'i-hsia i-shih," in *HLCI* 1.26a–28a.

100. Yang Ch'un, 10.6b–7a.

101. Ku owed much of his interest in this Classic to his uncle, Hua Hsüeh-ch'üan, and his mentor, Kao Yu, a grandson of Kao P'an-lung (*PCC* 129.1b–2b, 131.25a–26b).

102. Ku Tung-kao, 15.24a–25b.

103. Ibid., 15.20a–b. For an excellent critique of this position, see Ts'ui Shu's *Ching-chuan ti-ssu t'ung-k'ao*, in *Ts'ui Tung-pi i-shu* pp. 507–12.

104. Ku Tung-kao, 15.20a–23a.   105. Ibid., 15.24a–25b.

106. Ibid., 15.25b–27a.   107. Ibid., 15.28a–29b.

108. Wan Ssu-t'ung, 5.3a–4b.   109. Ibid., 5.5a–9a.

110. Ibid., 5.2b.

111. See, e.g., ibid., 5.1a–9a, 6.1a–19a.

112. Kahn, pp. 155–63. Chu Shih is not listed as a grand councilor to Yung-cheng in Ch'ien Shih-fu (1: 136), but Pei Huang (pp. 144–49) suspects that he was.

113. *Kao-tsung shih-lu*, pp. 152–53, in *TCLCSL*. For discussion of Ch'ien-lung's filial devotion to his mother, see Kahn, chap. 5.

114. Ch'ien Shih-fu, 4: 3280.

115. Fang Pao, pp. 583–86, 882.

116. *Kao-tsung shih-lu*, pp. 152–53, 172, 183–85, 191–92, in *TCLCSL*.

117. *SKTY*, pp. 379–80, 395–96, 422.

118. *PCC* 102.9a–11a.

119. According to Fang Pao's chronological biography, he was a vice-president, whereas biographical essays written by Lei Hung and Shen T'ing-fang report that Fang was a president. The information given by Lei and Shen is either mistaken or a deliberate exaggeration (*PCC* 25.19b–22b).

120. Shen T'ung, *Kuo-t'ang chi* 6.5a–6a; *MTCK* 33.22b.

121. Fang Pao, p. 690; *ECCP*, p. 189.

122. Fang Pao, pp. 564–65.

123. See *SKTY*, pp. 379–80, 395–96, 422.

124. This work by Li had been attributed by mistake to Chu Hsi (*SKTY*, pp. 389–90).

125. Huang Pai-chia and Ch'üan, 69.29b, 36a.

126. *SKTY*, pp. 379–80.

127. See, e.g., the explanation of *ti* in *Ch'in-ting Chou-kuan i-shu* 22.587, 591.

128. *Ch'in-ting Li-chi i-shu*, p. 3.

129. *SKTY*, p. 422.

130. Fang Pao, p. 869.

131. Ibid., p. 332; see also Ch'üan, 17.203.

132. For his diatribes against Cheng Hsüan's exegeses, see Wan Ssu-t'ung, *chüan* 1–6.

133. Fang Pao, pp. 17–21.

134. Ibid., pp. 16–17.

135. Ibid., pp. 83–84; *SKTY*, p. 382.

136. Fang's memorial is mentioned in a letter written by Wang Mou-hung; see Wang Mou-hung, 10.16b.

137. Fang Pao, pp. 857, 888. *SKTY*, pp. 425–26, 400.

138. One of the known compilers for the official ritual project not treated in the present study is Hu Chih-wei, whose participation is mentioned by Yüan Mei (14.6a).

139. According to Li Yüan-tu's (80.1a–2b) account, Jen received the appointment in 1736, but *CSLC* (68.33a) gives 1743.

140. *SKTY*, pp. 486–87.   141. SKCS, vol. 109.

142. *SKTY*, pp. 402–6.   143. Jen, *Kung-shih k'ao*, p. 809.

144. Ibid., pp. 832–33.   145. *SKTY*, pp. 403, 405.

146. *CSLC* 68.26b.   147. Wu T'ing-hua, p. 457.

148. *PCC* 102.9a–11a.   149. Ibid.

150. See, e.g., Wu T'ing-hua, pp. 292, 297, 305, 430, 431.

151. Ibid., p. 456.

152. Ibid., p. 457; see *CTYL* 89.4736 for Chu Hsi's view.

153. *KCCHLC* 418.12609–11.   154. *SKTY*, p. 484.

155. Ibid., p. 629.   156. *MTPK* 34.15a–b.

157. *KCCHLC* 72.3856–57.

158. *SKTY*, pp. 395–96; SKCS, vols. 106–7.

159. SKCS, vols. 98–99, 124–26.

160. *CSLC* 15.7b.

161. *MTPK* 34.15a–16a.

162. *MTCK* 43.17a–18b, 21a–22b; *MTPK* 34.15a–16a; see also Hang, 4.17a–18a.

163. *CTYL* 84.4540.   164. Ibid., 86.4574.

165. *MTPK* 34.12a–13b.   166. *HHS*, pp. 269–85.

167. *CSLC* 68.34b.

168. Shen T'ung wrote a biographical essay of Ho, and Chang Po-hsing's instructions on personal integrity impressed him deeply; see Shen T'ung, *Kuo-t'ang chi* 11.8a–14a.

169. Su Shih and Su Ch'e elaborated on Ou-yang's view, and attacks on the *Rites of Chou* spanned the Sung period; see Yeh Kuo-liang, pp. 97–107, 151.

170. Shen T'ung, *Kuo-t'ang chi* 5.13b–14a.

171. Although he placed great trust in Cheng Hsüan's annotations, he took issue with Cheng on occasion. The *Ssu-ku* commentator regarded Shen's scholarship on the rites the best next to that of Hui Tung's father, Hui Shih-ch'i (1671–1741), but criticized Shen for deviating occasionally from Cheng's explication (*SKTY*, pp. 382–89).

172. Shen T'ung, *Chou-kuan, shang.* 678; idem, *Kuo-t'ang chi* 8.5b–6b.

173. Shen T'ung, *Chou-kuan, shang.*674; *chung.*694, *hsia.*704, 709, 711.

174. *Ch'in-ting Chou-kuan i-shu*, p. 3.

175. Hui was accused of appointing an educational official in Kwangtung, a

decision that in his capacity as educational commissioner he had no right to make (*ECCP*, p. 356).

176. For quotations from *Chuang-tzu*, see Hui Shih-ch'i, 2.434–35, 13.633, 638; from *Hsün-tzu*, 1.389, 6.514, 7.520, 8.535, 9.554, 10.589, 11.608, 14.657; from *Kuan-tzu*, 4.468, 8.542, 9.566, 9.568, 10.574, 13.637, 13.639; from *Mo-tzu*, 8.535, 12.624; and from *Lü-shih ch'un-ch'iu*, 11.599, 14.656.

177. Hui Shih-ch'i, 4.456, 7.516, 7.520, 7.523, 8.551, 10.587, 11.610.

178. Ibid., *passim*.

179. See ibid., esp. 1.400, 4.468–69, 6.507, 8.548–49, 11.598–600, and 13.646.

180. Ibid., 12.619.

181. Ibid., 9.567–568.

182. Ibid., 1.411, 2.419–20, 3.449, 5.490, 6.512.

183. *CJHA* 43.13a–b.

184. Hang, 4.17a–18a.

185. Ibid.

Chapter 6

1. Yü Ying-shih, "Some Preliminary Observations," pp. 110–15.

2. For the history of hermeneutics, see Robinson, pp. 1–7; and Palmer, pp. 34–40.

3. Robinson, pp. 1–7.

4. "Archiac Chinese" refers to the Chinese language of the Chou and Ch'in periods. For the differences between "Archiac Chinese" and "Ancient" Chinese in contemporary phonetic analysis, see Ting, pp. 1, 63–72.

5. For a discussion of the major theorists of contemporary hermeneutics such as Hans-Georg Gadamer, Emilio Betti, and Paul Riceour, see Bleicher.

6. To be sure, even Hui Tung sometimes rejected Cheng Hsüan's explanation; see, e.g., *Ming-t'ang ta-tao lu*, p. 665.

7. Kessler, "Chinese Scholars," pp. 179–200. The gradual dissipation of anti-Manchu feelings should not be mistaken for the disappearance of tension between the Manchus and the Chinese, especially in the imperial bureaucracy. For discussion of different aspects of the Manchu-Chinese tension after the K'ang-hsi reign, see Kessler, *K'ang-hsi*; Spence, *Ts'ao Yin*; and S. Wu.

8. Kessler, *K'ang-hsi*, pp. 81–90, 158–61.

9. Ibid., pp. 192–94.

10. Struve, "Ambivalence," pp. 324–56.

11. For the professionalization of scholarship, see Elman, *From Philosophy to Philology*, pp. 101–3.

12. *ECCP*, pp. 308–9, 474–75, 547–48, 709–10.

13. De Bary, *Message*, Chap. 5; Elman, *From Philosophy to Philology*, p. 102.

14. Chan, "Hsing-li ching-i," pp. 543, 555–56.

15. *CSLC* 10.7a; *ECCP*, p. 805.   16. *PCC* 20.20b.

17. Ibid.   18. Wei Hsiang-shu, 3.70–71.

19. *ECCP*, p. 805. The Manchu government promulgated a legal code as early as 1646, but it was nothing more than a replica of the Ming code and was not enforced (Chang Chin-fan et al., p. 434).

20. *HCCSWP* 54.5a–6a.

21. Current scholarship does not recognize such a connection between the Yen-Li school and eighteenth-century purist ritualism. Ch'ien Mu (*HSS*, p. 218) speaks of an immediate decline of the Yen-Li school after the death of Li Kung. But as we shall see, both the attacks on Sung neo-Confucianism and the ethical beliefs of Yen Yüan and Li Kung bore a strong resemblance to those of Tai Chen and his followers.

22. Pi Hsi-jui, *Ching-hsüeh li-shih*, p. 264; Ch'ü Wan-li, pp. 17–19.

23. Yeh Kuo-liang, p. 7–9, 49–51, 60–62. See also James T. C. Liu, pp. 85–99; and Ch'eng Yüan-min, pp. 762–85.

24. See Yeh Kuo-liang; Chan, "Chu-hsi chi hsin-ju-hsüeh," pp. 20–22; and Elman, "Philosophy (*i-li*)," pp. 184–86.

25. Ts'ui Shu (1740–1816) was unusual in the eighteenth century for his persistent effort to uncover doubtful aspects of the Classics. The lack of attention given his scholarship by his contemporaries clearly indicates the mood of his colleagues.

26. Liang Ch'i-ch'ao, p. 253.

27. *HHS*, p. 320.

28. *HHWC*, p. 583.

29. Fang Pao, pp. 16–21.

30. Ibid., pp. 3, 26–30.

31. According to Yeh Kuo-liang (pp. 97–105), 31 Sung scholars rejected either all or portions of the *Rites of Chou*. Of the 31, no fewer than 12 charged that Liu Hsin had forged the text. Among the illustrious scholars who rejected the *Rites of Chou* were Ssu-ma Kuang, Hu Hung, and Su Ch'e (1039–1112).

32. Pi Hsi-jui, *Ching-hsüeh t'ung-lun*, pp. 52–53.

33. *HHWC*, pp. 220–21.

34. Li Kung, *Lun hsüeh* 1.4a–7a.

35. Hui Tung, *Ming-t'ang ta-tao lu*, 1.1–3, 28–31.

36. Ibid., 1.11.

37. Tai Chen, *Tai Chen chi*, p. 177.

38. Fang Pao, pp. 24–25.

39. Tai Chen, *Tai Chen chi*, pp. 177–81.

40. Ibid., p. 181.

41. Kai-wing Chow, "Scholar and Society," pp. 310–11; Wang Chung, *Jung-fu hsien-sheng i-shu*, *Lei-pien* 2.10a. See also Chang Shun-hui, *Ching-tai Yang-chou*, pp. 95–96. According to Pi Hsi-jui (*Ching-hsüeh t'ung-lun*, p. 51), Wang Chung did not prove his case.

42. Ch'ien Mu (*HSS*, pp. 134–39) traces the idea to Ch'ien Ch'ien-I (1582–1664). Ho Yu-sen (pp. 188–90) points out this was not Ku's exact utterance, but it nonetheless epitomizes his idea.

43. Tai Chen, *Tai Chen chi*, pp. 267–69.

44. Ibid., pp. 166–68, 175, 187–88.

45. Ibid., p. 63.

46. Ibid., pp. 191–92, 213–15.

47. Ibid., p. 268.

48. Ibid., pp. 298–304.

49. Ch'ien Ta-hsin, 24.350.

50. Tuan, 6.14b.

51. Tai Chen, *Tai Chen chi*, p. 214. Ts'ui Shu, who had little contact with the best-known and most active scholars of the Han Learning movement, expressed similar ideas; see Ts'ui, p. 395.

52. Chiang Fan, *Kuo-ch'ao Han-hsüeh* 1.1b.

53. *YCSS, san-chi* 5.12a.

54. T'ang Yü-yüan, pp. 145–46.

55. Yen Jo-chü, 6.57–58.

56. Chang Hsüeh-ch'eng, *Wen-shih t'ung-i*, p. 2. See Nivison, pp. 60–62, 201–3. For an interpretation of Chang's notion as a response to Tai Chen's Classicism, see Yü Ying-shih, *Lun Tai Chen*, pp. 45–53. For an analysis of this view from the perspective of Chang's statecraft thought, see Kai-wing Chow and Liu, pp. 123–35.

57. Ts'ui, p. 20.

58. *CJHA* 43.13b–14a.

59. Hui Tung, *Ch'un-ch'iu Tso chuan pu-chu*.

60. Lu Wen-ch'ao, 8.115.

61. Ch'ien Ta-hsin, 2.17–20.

62. *CSLC* 69.13b; *CJHA* 135.21a–b.

63. *SKTY* 26.3.

64. Ibid., 26.1–3, 29.62, 70, 72, 81–83.

65. *CJHA* 56.2a–4b; see *ECC*, pp. 583–84, 1086–125, for Ch'eng I's views.

66. *SKTY* 29.69–70, 73–77, 80.

67. Chiang Fan, *Kuo-ch'ao Han-hsüeh* 3.1b.

68. *SKTY* 26.1.

69. Ts'ui Shu, lauded as perhaps the most "scientific" historian of traditional times, shared this view (see Ts'ui, p. 401).

70. To be sure, before the early nineteenth century, there were scholars interested in the *Kung-yang Commentary*; see Elman, *Classicism*.

71. Liu I-cheng, p. 119.

72. Tuan, 6.13a.

73. Ch'ien Ta-hsin, 38.601.

74. Hui Tung, *Chiu-ching ku-i*, pp. 1, 163. See also Ch'ien Ta-hsin, 24.348.

75. Tai Chen, *Tai Chen chi*, p. 191.

76. Ibid., pp. 200, 214; Tuan, 8.5b.

77. Ch'ien Ta-hsin, 15.208.

78. Tai Chen (*Tai Chen chi*, pp. 55–56) provides a few examples of polysemic characters. The character *i* in the term *hsi-i* (lizard) was borrowed to mean "change." The character *hsiang* (elephant) was borrowed to mean "symbolize."

79. Ibid., pp. 73, 200.

80. Ibid., p. 73.

81. Fang's view was shared by Wang Mou-hung (10.16b).

82. Fang Pao, pp. 20–21.

83. Tai Chen, *Tai Chen chi*, pp. 13–15.

84. Knowing the initials of characters would make it easier to find their meanings by applying the method of "mutual explanation" (ibid., pp. 55, 106–7).

85. Tai Chen (ibid., pp. 55, 73–75) is criticizing Ku Yen-wu for explaining *chuan-chu* in terms of change in sound, rather than in meaning. His student Tuan Yü-ts'ai (8.3b) also accepted Tai's definition. The view of Tai and Tuan represented one of several explanations of *chuan-chu* (see Chou, pp. 55–58).

86. Tai Chen, *Tai Chen chi*, pp. 73–75, 77.

87. Tuan, 1a–2a.

88. *CJHA* 138.1b.

89. Hui Tung, *Hui-shih tu Shuo-wen chi*.

90. Tai Chen, *Tai Chen chi*, p. 183.

91. Ch'ien Ta-hsin, 33.526.

92. Ibid., 27.413–14.

93. In a preface to the *Shuo-wen chieh-tzu*, Chu Yün expressed the same idea regarding its crucial importance to the comprehension of ancient language; see Chiang Fan, *Kuo-ch'ao Han-hsüeh* 4.9b.

94. See Chang Shun-hui, *Ch'ing-tai Yang-chou*, pp. 52–75.

95. Weng, 7.20b–21a.

96. Lu Lung-ch'i, *Tu li chih-i*, pp. 408–9.

97. *CSLC* 69.39a.

98. *CJHA* 158.35a.

99. *YSCC, hsü-chi*, 2.63.

100. *CJHA* 34.1a; Huang Tsung-hsi, *Nan-lei wen-ting, chien chi* 4.1a–2a; idem, *Nan-lei wen-yüeh* 4.48a–49a, in *Li-chou i-chu hui-k'an; SKTY* 31.4.

101. *SKTY* 29.69.

102. *CJHA* 43.12b.

103. Ibid., 135.21a–22a. Lu Pao-ch'ien (pp. 251–54, 268) points out that Liu Feng-lu (1776–1829) and Ling Shu in their study of the *Kung-yang Commentary* also focused on rituals.

104. For a study of the influence of the *Kung-yang* school on Kung Tzu-chen's (1792–1841) statecraft thought, see Kai-wing Chow, "Ts'ung k'uang-yen," pp. 303–18. For an analysis of the complexity of the development of the Kung-yang school, see Lu Pao-ch'ien, pp. 221–69; and Elman, *Classicism*.

105. Chiang Fan, *Kuo-ch'ao Han-hsüeh* 2.13b. For an explanation of the roots of the New Text school in terms of scholarly traditions in Ch'ang-chou, see Elman, "Scholarship and Politics," pp. 63–80; and idem, *Classicism, passim*.

106. *CJHA* 75.6a–7b.

107. Ibid., 131.2a–3b. Yang Hsiang-k'uei (p. 351) notes that Ling differed from Liu in his emphasis on rituals.

108. *CJHA* 131.12a–13a.

109. Ch'en Huan studied the *Kung-yang Commentary* in order to retrieve lost rituals (ibid., 148.2a–b, 14a–b). His student Yang Yin (1819–96) continued to study the rituals mentioned in the *Kung-yang*. Even Kang Yu-wei's (1858–1927) mentor, Liao P'ing (1852–1932), considered ritual the crucial criterion in evaluating

the relative strengths of the three commentaries; see Chang Shun-hui, *Ch'ing-tai Yang-chou*, pp. 536, 628.

110. *CJHA* 148.2a.

111. *CSLC* 69.56b.

112. Pi Hsi-jui, *Ching-hsüeh li-shih*, pp. 75–77, 89.

113. Ch'en Li, 15.227.

114. Ibid.

115. *KTLSWC* 2.32–33.

116. Ibid., 2.32.

117. *SKTY* 20.106.

118. Ibid., 19.93.

119. Ibid.

120. Chiang Fan, *Kuo-ch'ao Han-hsüeh* 2.2b.

121. Tai Chen, *Tai Chen chi*, pp. 224–25.

122. Yao Nai, pp. 164–65.

123. Ch'en Li, 15.236.

124. Wang Li-ch'i, *Cheng K'ang-ch'eng*, pp. 339–43.

125. Ibid., p. 343.

126. Ibid., p. 340.

127. Ibid., pp. 341–42.

128. Preface, in Chiang Fan, *Kuo-ch'ao Han-hsüeh* 1a.

129. *YCSC*, *i-chi* 11.13a–14b; *san-chi* 5.12a.

130. *CSLC* 68.43a.

131. Chiang Fan, *Kuo-ch'ao Han-hsüeh* 4.16a.

132. Wang Hsi-sun, 32b.

133. Wang Hsi-sun, *Wang-shih hsüeh-hsing chi*, Wang Chung, 3.7b.

134. *CJHA* 148.14b.

135. Chiang Fan, *Kuo-ch'ao Han-hsüeh* 4.13a.

136. Wang Hsi-sun, *Ts'ung-cheng lu*, *chüan* 4, in Wang Chung.

137. Chiang Fan, *Kuo-ch'ao Han-hsüeh* 7.4a.

138. Liang Ch'i-ch'ao, p. 22.

139. *SKTY*, "Fan-li," pp. 5, 145.24–36, 147.68–96. See also the biography of Chi Yün, chief editor of the reviews of the collection, in *ECCP*, pp. 121–22. This bias against Buddhism in the *Ssu-k'u* collection does not suggest a lack of interest in Buddhism among the Manchu rulers. See Naquin and Rawski, p. 20; for the Yung-cheng and Ch'ien-lung emperors, see Pei Huang, pp. 42–49; and Spence, pp. 121–23.

Chapter 7

1. Hu Shih (pp. 22–26) suggested that Tai Chen could have come under the influence of Yen Yüan. Chang Shun-hui (*Ch'ing-tai Yang-chou*, pp. 4–8), however, insists that there was no connection between Tai Chen and the Yen-Li school.

2. Tai Chen, *Tai Chen chi* pp. 165–76.

3. Ibid., p. 290.

4. *STP*, pp. 17–18. This dualistic notion of human nature, though especially prevalent in the Ch'eng-Chu school, did not remain unchallenged within the wide spectrum of neo-Confucian persuasions. In fact, exponents of the Ch'eng-Chu

school such as Hsüeh Hsüan (1389–1464), Ts'ao Tuan (1376–1434), and Lo Ch'in-shun (1465–1547), had been critical of the dualism implicit in Chu Hsi's view on human nature, and the late Ming witnessed a growing attack on ontological dualism. See T'ang Chün-i, *Chung-kuo che-hsüeh*, p. 473; Bloom; and Chung-ying Cheng, pp. 469–503.

5. Tai Chen, *Tai Chen chi*, pp. 279–81.

6. Ibid., p. 285.

7. Ibid., p. 328.

8. Hu Shih, p. 51; Liang Ch'i-ch'ao, pp. 118–19.

9. Tai Chen, *Tai Chen chi*, pp. 296–97.

10. Ibid., p. 271.   11. Ibid., pp. 272–73.

12. Ibid., p. 276.   13. Ibid., pp. 272–73.

14. Ibid., p. 285.   15. Ibid., p. 296.

16. Ibid., p. 267.   17. Ibid., p. 318.

18. Ibid., pp. 191–92, 213–14.   19. Ibid., pp. 298–301.

20. See Chapter 6.   21. HSS, p. 358.

22. Ch'eng Yao-t'ien, *Lun hsüeh hsiao-chi* 26b, in *Tung-i lu*.

23. Ling T'ing-k'an, *Chiao-li t'ang* 4.1a.

24. Hu Shih, p. 109.

25. Hu Shih, p. 115.

26. Ling T'ing-k'an, *Chiao-li t'ang* 23.7a–10b.

27. Ibid., 24.16b, 16.4a–5a.   28. Ibid., 16.5b–6b.

29. Ibid.   30. Li Kung, *Shu-ku hou-chi* 13.164.

31. Ling T'ing-k'an, *Chiao-li t'ang* 16.4a–6b.

32. Ibid., 16.4a–5a.

33. Ibid., 16.6b.

34. Hu Shih, p. 24.

35. Ling T'ing-k'an, *Chiao-li t'ang* 16.6b.

36. Ibid., 24.17a.

37. Ling T'ing-k'an, "*Li-ching shih-li* hsü" (Preface to *Study of the rules of the Book of Etiquette and Decorum*), 3a–4a, in *Ling Chung-tzu i-shu*.

38. *Chang Ch'i-chin*, 3.7a.

39. Ling T'ing-k'an, *Chiao-li t'ang* 4.7a–b.

40. Ibid., 4.8b–9a.   41. Ibid., 4.1b, 16.2b.

42. Ibid.   43. Ibid., 16.1a–2b.

44. Ibid., 16.1a.   45. Ibid., 4.6a.

46. Ibid., 4.5a–b.   47. Ibid., 4.6a.

48. Ibid., 4.7a.   49. Tai Chen, *Tai Chen chi*, p. 265.

50. Fang Tung-shu, 2.46–47.

51. Ling T'ing-k'an, *Chiao-li t'ang* 10.2a.

52. Ibid., 10.1b.

53. To be sure, Ling T'ing-k'an was only one among a few who were keenly aware of the exceptional role of Hsün-tzu in the transmission of ancient rituals and Classical learning. According to Wang Chung, Hsün-tzu was the principal source of Han Classical learning. Hsün-tzu's contribution to the shaping of the under-

standing of Classical ritual and hence the Confucian heritage was unmatched; see Kai-wing Chow, "Scholar and Society," pp. 303–4. Other Ch'ing scholars who espoused a more favorable reappraisal of Hsün-tzu's role in Classical scholarship include Lu Wen-ch'ao, Yen K'o-chün (1762–1843), and Ch'en Huan; see Lu Wen-ch'ao, 10.141–142; and *CJHA* 119.10b–13a, 148.7b–8b.

54. Ling T'ing-k'an, *Chiao-li t'ang* 16.3b, 7a–9b.

55. Ibid., 16.7a.

56. Ibid., 24.16a. Ling's view in this respect was not entirely original. Ku Yen-wu (*JCL* 6.18b–19a) had suggested that *wu* refers to basic human virtues as well as to ritual propriety.

57. Ling T'ing-k'an, *Chiao-li t'ang* 4.8a.

58. Ibid., 4.1b, 4.7a., 16.11a–b; idem, "Li-ching shih-li hsü" 3a–4a, in *Ling Chung-tzu i-shu.*

59. Ling T'ing-k'an, "Li-ching shih-li hsü" 3a–4a, in *Ling Chung-tzu i-shu.*

60. Ling T'ing-k'an, *Chiao-li t'ang* 5.7a.

61. Ibid., 4.3a.

62. Ibid., 24.16a.

63. Ibid., 4.8b–9a.

64. Ling T'ing-k'an, *Ling Chung-tzu i-shu,* 1: 3a–4a.

65. Juan Yüan, Preface, in Chiang Fan, *Kuo-ch'ao Han-hsüeh* 1a.

66. *YCSC, i-chi* 3.123–24.

67. Tai Chen, *Tai Chen chi,* p. 279.

68. *YCSC, i-chi* 3.123–24.

69. Ibid., 10.1b–3a.

70. Ibid., 10.15a. *Chieh-hsing* is a term Ling T'ing-k'an sometimes opted for. See the preceding section.

71. *YCSC, i-chi* 10.6a–b.

72. Ibid., 10.23b–24a.

73. Ibid., 10.21b.

74. Ibid., 10.12b–13b.

75. Hsü Fu-kuan, *Liang Han ssu-hsiang,* pp. 399–402.

76. *YCSC, i-chi* 10.23b–24b.

77. Ibid., 10.1b–3a.

78. Ibid., 10.5a; see also *YCSC, hsü chi* 4.14b.

79. *YCSC, i-chi* 10.19b–20a.

80. Ibid., 10.23b.

81. Ibid., 10.3a, 10.23b.

82. Ibid., 8.6b–8b.

83. Ibid., 8.21a.

84. Ibid., 8.6b–8b.

85. Ibid., 9.1a–2a.

86. Ibid., 9.9a.

87. Ibid., 8.9b–11b.

88. *Tai Chen chi,* pp. 316–17.

89. *YCSC, i-chi* 2.15a, 11.1a–b.

90. Ibid., 2.18a–19b, 11.1b–2a.

91. Ibid., 11.14b.

92. Ibid., 2.18a.

93. Ibid., 2.12b–13b.

94. Ibid., 4.4a–5b.

95. *YCSC, hsü-chi,* p. 1.

96. See, e.g., "Hsing-ching shuo" (On nature and feelings) by Hsü Yang-yüan and Hu Chin, in Juan Yüan, *Ku-ching ching-she,* pp. 257–63.

97. Fang Tung-shu, p. 62.

98. Elman, *From Philosophy to Philology.*

99. Hsü Fu-kuan, "Han-hsüeh," pp. 14–16.

100. Ibid., pp. 11–12.

101. Chiao Hsün was unique despite his agreement with many methodological cal premises of the Han Learning scholars. Mencius still occupied a very important position in his thinking. Chiao did not think that moral truths had been exhaustively enumerated in the Classics, which to him were no more than the rules and institutions of the past. The Classics were therefore not to be taken as sources of absolute truths. Moreover, Chiao insisted that personal insight or subjective understanding (*hsing-ling*) was essential to Classical studies; see Chiao, *Tiao-ku chi* 10.144–45, 13.212–14.

Chapter 8

1. Ch'en T'ieh-fan, pp. 67–78.

2. Wang Chung, *Shu hsüeh*, "Inner Chapters" 1.3a–b, in *Jung-fu hsien-sheng i-shu*.

3. In fact, none of the views on the meaning of *san-nien* literally requires three full years of mourning.

4. S. Mann, "Grooming a Daughter," pp. 207–12.

5. Wang Chung, *Shu hsüeh*, "Inner Chapters" 1.13a–14a, in *Jung-fu hsien-sheng i-shu*.

6. Ibid., 2.14a–15a.

7. Ibid., 2.14b–15b.

8. Ibid., 2.15a.

9. The challenge to the idea of treating the ruler-minister relationship as a natural bond can be traced back no earlier than Pao Ching-yen of the Wei-Chin period. Ho Hsin-yin in the late Ming and T'ang Chen in the early Ch'ing had a similar idea. On T'ang Chen, see Hou et al., 5: 302.

10. Wang Chung, *Shu hsüeh*, "Inner Chapters" 2.15b, in *Jung-fu hsien-sheng i-shu*.

11. Nivison, pp. 261–62.

12. Chang Hsüeh-ch'eng, *Wen-shih t'ung-i*, pp. 204–8.

13. Yeh Hsien-en, pp. 205–6. Much research still needs to be done before one can explain the exceptionally large number of chaste women in Hui-chou. Katherine Carlitz (p. 139) suggests that the cult of female virtue was closely related to the strong lineages of Hui-chou. Virtuous women helped to boost the prestige of lineages.

14. Lu Wen-ch'ao, 4.49.

15. T'ien, p. 126.

16. Wei Hsiu-mei, *T'ao Chu*, pp. 190b–92a.

17. T'ien Ju-k'ang (p. 39) citing the *Ku-chin t'u-shu chi-ch'eng*, gives the number of chaste women during the Ming dynasty as 35,829. For the Ming figure for She county, see ibid., p. 46.

18. Wei Hsiu-mei, *T'ao Chu*, pp. 190b–192a; *Ch'in-ting Li-pu tse-li* 48.1b.

19. *Ch'in-ting Li-pu tse-li* 48:4b; *Ch'in-ting ta-Ch'ing hui-tien*, vol. 13, 404.15b–16b.

20. In 1871 the period required for receiving the award was further lowered to six years for all deceased widows (Elvin, pp. 123–24).

21. Ibid., p. 133.

22. In "Where Were the Women?," Helen Siu demonstrates that marriage resistance in Kwangtung under the Ch'ing was a result of the long process of the encroachment of Han culture upon the local form of marriage.

23. Ibid. A new economic incentive for continuing the practice of marriage resistance in Shun-te county of Kwangtung in the nineteenth century was sericulture, which made possible economic independence for local women. For a discussion of the meaning of "delayed transfer marriage," see Stockard, chap. one; see also Topley, pp. 251–52.

24. Siu, pp. 245–59.

25. S. Mann, "Grooming a Daughter," p. 206.

26. For this line of argument, see T'ien.

27. S. Mann, "Grooming a Daughter," pp. 213–15; see also Rowe. For a detailed discussion of Chang Hsüeh-ch'eng's view of education for women, see S. Mann, "Classical Revival."

28. Rankin, "Emergence," p. 42; S. Mann, "Classical Revival."

29. Yen Yüan, Hsi-chai chi-yü 5.84.

30. Lu Lung-ch'i, Tu-li chih-i 2.17; Ropp, p. 130.

31. Weng, 10.17b–18a; Ch'eng Chin-fang, 3.11a–b.

32. Tai Chen, Tai Chen chi, pp. 257–59.

33. Lai, pp. 60–68.

34. Chiang Fan, Kuo-ch'ao Han-hsüeh 6.2a–b.

35. V. Ng, pp. 57–69.

36. Lu Wen-ch'ao, 4.50–51, 31.419–20.

37. Yao Ch'un, 16a–17b. For a detailed study of Chuang's scholarship, see Elman, Classicism, chap. 5.

38. Chiao Hsün, Tiao-ku chi 8.111–12, 18.303–4.

39. HCCSWP, hsü-pien 69.27a–28b.

40. Li Chao-lo, 6.19b–20a.

41. Wang Fu (Ts'an Tu-li chih i 1.23a), for example, was ambivalent whether the practice accorded with ritual propriety.

42. Hui-chen Wang Liu, pp. 84–89.

43. Ibid., pp. 90–93; Taga, pp. 518, 522, 525, 528, 530, 533, 536, 544, 549, 551, 553, 817; Li Wen-chih, p. 306; Hu Hsien-chin, appendix 58; Fang Pao, pp. 768–69; Dennerline, "Marriage."

44. Taga, p. 800. Jonathan Spence (pp. 70–73) shows that there was considerable pressure on widows to remarry, which sometimes resulted in suicide. For discussion of widow remarriage and forced remarriage in Ming-Ch'ing times, see Waltner, pp. 129–46, 137–41. It is reasonable to assume that remarriage was quite common, especially among the lower classes; see Feng Erh-k'ang, pp. 317–18.

45. Taga, pp. 821, 820, 825; Meskill, p. 149. This was not always the case. Some genealogies still registered widows who remarried (Waltner, p. 144; Eberhard, p. 135).

46. Taga, p. 553; Hui-chen Wang Liu, p. 233.

47. Dennerline, "Marriage."

48. The practice of granting commemorative arches to honor women who refused to remarry began in 1304 (Waltner, p. 132).

49. This case of 1727 was reported by Lan T'ing-yüan (pp. 88–92); Lan was magistrate of Chin-ning county in Kwangtung.

50. Sweeten, pp. 49–64. In his study of Ch'ing judicial cases, Jonathan Ocko (p. 217) suggests that "the chaste widow was truly a rarity." The sources Ocko used may have systematically understated the impact of the cult of widow chastity because they are primarily cases about widows who failed to remain chaste. In contrast, biographical essays written to honor chaste widows by the gentry tend to exaggerate the spread of the cult among the gentry.

51. Waltner, pp. 136–41.

52. These rulings were based on precedents from 1733 to 1821; see Meijer, pp. 289–304.

53. See the volume of essays on kinship organization edited by Patricia Ebrey and James Watson.

54. Meskill, p. 141.

55. In his study of the chronological distribution of genealogies, Taga (pp. 58–60) shows that 72.6 percent of all Chinese genealogies in Japan come from the Ch'ing dynasty. The study by Telford et al. (pp. 41–43) gives a similarly high percentage of Ch'ing genealogies. Of the 2,577 genealogies analyzed, 1.4 percent were produced before and during the Ming; 1,483 (57.2 percent) were Ch'ing; and 1,035 (39.9 percent) were compiled during the Republican period. Although Taga's figure for the Ch'ing period is lower than Telford's, the fact remains that only in the Ch'ing did genealogies become an important genre of writing. My own reading of Ch'ing sources also confirms their findings.

56. Telford et al., pp. 36–41.

57. Chang Lü-hsiang, 16.9a–10b; Hsü Fang, 3.11a; Taga, pp. 66, 162, 189, 341; Telford et al., p. 238; Yao Nai, 3.27.

58. Tai Chen, *Tai Chen chi*, pp. 215–16.

59. Taga, p. 357; *HSS*, pp. 328–31.

60. Lu Wen-ch'ao, 4.55–56.

61. Chi Yün, 8.34b–41a.

62. Ch'ien Ta-hsin, 21.303–4, 50.767–68.

63. *ECCP*, pp. 152–53.   64. Ch'ien Ta-hsin, 50.763–64.

65. Ibid., 21.302–4, 26.395–99.   66. Li Wen-chih, p. 318.

67. Wang Ch'ang, 37.10b; see also his *Nien-p'u* in *Ch'un-jung t'ang chi, shang*, 25a–b.

68. It is not clear whether the building was done before Juan Yüan became an official. In all likelihood this was the case; see *YCSC, erh-chi* 2.6a–8b.

69. Ibid., 2.11a–12b.

70. Telford et al., p. 74.

71. *ECCP*, p. 676.

72. Yao Nai, 14.179–80; Kai-wing Chow, "Discourse."

73. Chang Ch'i-chin, 3.5a; Ling T'ing-k'an, *Chiao-li t'ang*, 27.12a–13a.

74. Chang Hsüeh-ch'eng, *Chang-shih i-shu* 13.53a–b.

75. Ibid., 29.79b–81a.

76. Ibid., 13.46b, 14.19b, 24.17b–18a.

77. Ibid., 23.54b.

78. Ibid., 23.57a–58a. For a detailed discussion of Chang's views on reforming lineage practices, see Kai-wing Chow, "Ordering Ancestors."

79. Kung-chuan Hsiao, *Rural China*, p. 330; see also Hui-chen Wang Liu, p. 99.

80. Hui-chen Wang Liu (p. 119) examines the lineage rules given in a group of 151 genealogies printed between 1912 and 1936. Her study shows the crucial role of the Confucian elite in ritual performance.

81. Taga, pp. 718, 798, 826; see also Wang Ssu-chih, p. 162.

82. See Chapter 4.

83. Fang Pao, pp. 764–65.

84. Yin, 4.34–49.

85. Kung-chuan Hsiao, *Rural China*, p. 331.

86. Hui-chen Wang Liu, p. 128; Taga, pp. 796–97.

87. Taga, pp. 702, 723; Yeh Hsien-en, p. 175.

88. In his study of the Wu lineage of Hsiu-ning in Anhwei, Keith Hazelton (pp. 150–51) notes a correlation between office holding and genealogy compilation. In a study of two unrelated descent groups bearing the same surname, Susan Naquin ("Two Descent Groups," pp. 220, 227, 234) shows that despite the different means these two groups used to maintain their power, there was a similar bias in their genealogies in favor of the professionally successful lines. Efforts to organize lineage typically came from the gentry; see Woon, pp. 33–35, chaps. 5 and 6.

89. Kung-chuan Hsiao, *Rural China*, pp. 333–34.

90. Taga, pp. 61–64; Hui-chen Wang Liu, pp. 119–20; Woon, pp. 31–32.

91. The method of raising funds for compiling a genealogy by imposing a tax on each lineage member could work only when the lineage organizers already had enough power and authority to do so. From the early Ch'ing on, the lineages in T'ung-ch'eng county of Anhwei began to finance genealogies by this method (Beattie, *Land and Lineage*, pp. 119–20).

92. Kuo, pp. 89–90.

93. Yeh Hsieh-en, pp. 47–51; Chang Hai-p'eng et al., pp. 303–17.

94. Wang Ssu-chih, pp. 176–77.   95. *HCCSWP* 58.11b.

96. Tso, p. 107.   97. Ibid., p. 108.

98. Sheng, 73.1323–24, 1337–40. A similar trend can be seen in the increase in the compilation of genealogies and the creation of lineage estates (Taga, pp. 58–59). The mid-Ch'ing period saw a sustained increase in large lineage estates. See, e.g., the Hui-chou lineages studied by Yeh Hsien-en (pp. 46–51). Dennerline's study ("Marriage," pp. 190–94) of the charitable land of the lineages in Wu-hsi points to the eighteenth century as the beginning of a sustained growth in charitable estates. See also Kung-chuan Hsiao, *Rural China*, chap. 8.

99. Li Wen-chih, p. 297.

100. Hung, 10.258–59.

101. Lamley, "Lineage and Surname Feuds"; Wakeman, *Strangers*, pp. 111–12; T'an Ti-hua, "Lüeh-lun Ch'ing-tai."

102. For the effects of the coastal evacuation on lineage development in Hsin-an county, Kwangtung, see R. Watson, "Creation," pp. 79–81; see also idem, *Inequality*, chap. 2. For the situation in Fukien at the same period, see Lamley, "Lineage and Surname Feuds," p. 265.

103. Lamley, "Lineage and Surname Feuds," p. 267; T'an Ti-hua, "Lüeh-lun Ch'ing-tai."

104. Li Wen-chih, p. 303.

105. According to Lamley ("Lineage and Surname Feuds," pp. 271–75), although the epidemic outbreaks of inter-lineage armed feuds in eastern Kwang-tung and southern Fukien posed serious threats to stability of local communities, the Manchu court and the officials did not attempt to pacify belligerent lineages.

106. Wei Yüan, pp. 342–43.   107. *HCCSWP* 58.1a–2a.

108. Kung Tzu-chen, pp. 49–55.   109. Wei Yüan, pp. 502–3.

110. Li Wen-chih, p. 315; Yeh Hsien-en and T'an, pp. 1–4. For a discussion of lineages' rent- and tax-collecting roles, see Chang Yen, "Ch'ing-tai Chiang-nan"; and idem, "Ch'ing-tai tsu-t'ien," pp. 216–17. See also Dennerline, "Marriage," p. 187.

111. Wakeman, *Strangers*, pp. 112–15. Wakeman (pp. 111–15) argues that the militia movement both strengthened the gentry's leadership role within lineages and promoted class consciousness. After 1845 the conflict of class interests was to damage the kinship solidarity that bound the landlords and the peasants together.

112. Kuhn, *Rebellion*, pp. 77–82.   113. Ibid., pp. 106–9, 138–39, 152.

114. Ibid., p. 147.   115. Ibid., p. 80.

116. Ibid. For an example of the impact of militarization during the Taiping re-bellion and the subsequent strengthening of the kinship organization in K'ai-p'ing county, Kwangtung, see Woon, pp. 47–48.

117. Kuhn, "Local Self-Government," p. 293. In a study of the changes among the Chekiang elite in the early twentieth century, R. Keith Schoppa (pp. 48–51) has noted that the lineage structure continued to provide institutional strength for some powerful lineages and allowed them to dominate their local society while adapting to changing needs. The Kuan lineage in K'ai-ping studied by Yuen-fong Woon (chaps. 5–6) showed a similar pattern during the 1911–49 period.

Conclusion

1. Ling T'ing-k'an, *Chiao-li t'ang* 4.1a.

2. *HSS*, pp. 585–89; Kwang-ching Liu, "Education."

3. Li Kung, *Nien-p'u* 5.8a, in *Yen-Li ts'ung-shu*.

4. Tai Chen, *Tai Chen chi*, pp. 268–69. Tai's rejection of "principle" may be related to his personal suffering (see Chapter 7).

5. Hu Shih, pp. 125–26.

6. Hao Chang, *Chinese Intellectuals*, p. 64.

7. T'an Ssu-t'ung, pp. 334–37.

8. Elman, *From Philosophy to Philology*, p. 3. Both Liang Ch'i-ch'ao and Hu Shih regarded Classical learning and philological scholarship as an intellectual movement resembling the European Renaissance. Yü Ying-shih (*Li-shih yu ssu-hsiang*, pp. 88–89) takes exception to such a comparison.

9. N. Mann, p. 6.

10. Kristeller, *Renaissance Thought*, p. 78.

11. Based on his reading of the Greek text, Valla criticized the errors in Jerome's Vulgate (ibid., pp. 78–79; Kristeller, *Eight Philosophers*, p. 25.

12. Kristeller (*Renaissance Thought*, pp. 70–91) points out that the humanists of the Italian Renaissance contributed to Christianity by translating Greek patristic literature into Latin and that the writings of the Latin Church Fathers, especially Augustine, continued to exercise a strong influence on all theologians and other writers, including Bruni, Valla, Erasmus, and Vives. See also Gilmore, p. 205.

13. See Kristeller, *Renaissance Thought*, chaps. 1, 5.

14. Chang Hsüeh-ch'eng, *Wen-shih t'ung-i*, p. 337.

15. Ironically, this training was stressed by the critics of Han Learning scholars—scholars who continued to defend the Ch'eng-Chu learning after the mid-eighteenth century. The T'ung-ch'eng school was especially emphatic about the need to impart the Confucian doctrine in a wide range of genres. See Kai-wing Chow, "Discourse"; and Huters.

16. Kristeller, *Renaissance Thought*, pp. 21–22. George Sarton (pp. 56–57) points out the anti-Arabic sentiment in Renaissance thought.

17. Kristeller, *Renaissance Thought*, p. 20.

Bibliography

The following abbreviations are used in the Bibliography:

CHWS   Wan Ssu-ta 萬斯大, *Ching-hsüeh wu-shu* 經學五書
HJAS   *Harvard Journal of Asiatic Studies*
JAS   *Journal of Asian Studies*
KHCPTS   Kuo-hsüeh chi-pen ts'ung-shu 國學基本叢書 (Taipei: Hsin-hsing shu-chü)
SKCS   Ssu-k'u ch'üan-shu 四庫全書 (Taipei: Shang-wu yin-shu-kuan)
SPPY   Ssu-pu pei-yao 四部備要 (Taipei: Chung-hua shu-chü)
SPTK   Ssu-pu ts'ung-k'an 四部叢刊 (Taipei: Shang-wu yin-shu-kuan)
SSCCS   Juan Yüan 阮元, ed., *Shih-san ching chu-shu* 十三經注疏
TSCCCP   Ts'ung-shu chi-ch'eng ch'u-pien 叢書集成初編 (Shanghai: Shang-wu yin-shu-kuan)
TSCCHP   Ts'ung-shu chi-ch'eng hsin-pien 叢書集成新編 (Taipei: Hsin wen-feng ch'u-pan-she)
YLHP   *Yen-Li hsüeh-p'ai yen-chiu ts'ung-pien* 顏李學派研究叢編 (Hong Kong: Ta-tung t'u-shu)
YLTS   *Yen-Li ts'ung-shu* 顏李叢書 (Taipei: Kuang-wen shu-chü)

Aoki Masaru 青木正兒. *Chung-kuo chin-shih hsi-ch'ü shih* 中國近世戲曲史 (A history of modern Chinese drama). Tr. Wang Ku-lu 王古魯. Hong Kong: Chung-hua shu-chü, 1973.

Araki Kengo. "Confucianism and Buddhism in the Late Ming." In Wm. Theodore de Bary, ed., *The Unfolding of Neo-Confucianism*. New York: Columbia University Press, 1975.

Atwell, William S. "From Education to Politics: The Fu She." In Wm. Theodore de Bary, ed., *The Unfolding of Neo-Confucianism*. New York: Columbia University Press, 1975.

―――. "Notes on Silver, Foreign Trade, and the Late Ming Economy." *Ch'ing-shih wen-t'i* 3, no. 8 (Dec. 1977): 1–33.

Beattie, Hilary J. "The Alternative to Resistance: The Case of T'ung-ch'eng,

Anhwei." In Jonathan D. Spence and John E. Wills, Jr., eds., *From Ming to Ch'ing: Conquest, Region, and Continuity in Seventeenth-Century China*. New Haven: Yale University Press, 1979.

————. *Land and Lineage in China: A Study of T'ung-ch'eng County, Anhwei, in the Ming and Ch'ing Dynasties*. Cambridge, Eng.: Cambridge University Press, 1979.

Berling, Judith. "Religion and Popular Culture: The Management of Moral Capital in *The Romance of the Three Teachings*." In David Johnson, Andrew J. Nathan, Evelyn S. Rawski, eds., *Popular Culture in Late Imperial China*. Berkeley: University of California Press, 1985.

————. *The Syncretic Religion of Lin Chao-en*. New York: Columbia University Press, 1980.

Black, Alison Harley. *Man and Nature in the Philosophical Thought of Wang Fu-chih*. Seattle: University of Washington Press, 1989.

Bleicher, Josef. *Contemporary Hermeneutics: Hermeneutics as Method, Philosophy and Critique*. London: Routledge & Kegan Paul, 1982.

Bloch, Maurice. *From Blessing to Violence: History and Ideology in the Circumcision Ritual of the Merina of Madgascar*. Cambridge, Eng.: Cambridge University Press, 1986.

Bloom, Irene, trans. and ed. *Knowledge Painfully Acquired: The "K'un-chih chi" by Lo Ch'in-shun*. New York: Columbia University Press, 1986.

Bol, Peter K. *"This Culture of Ours": Intellectual Transitions in T'ang and Sung China*. Stanford: Stanford University Press, 1992.

Brokaw, Cynthia J. *The Ledgers of Merit and Demerit: Social Change and Moral Order in Late Imperial China*. Princeton: Princeton University Press, 1991.

Brook, Timothy. "Funerary Ritual and the Building of Lineages in Late Imperial China." *HJAS* 49 (1989): 465–99.

————. "Gentry Dominance in Chinese Society: Monasteries and Lineages in the Structuring of Local Society, 1500–1700." Ph.D. dissertation, Harvard University, 1984.

————. "The Spatial Structure of Ming Local Administration." *Late Imperial China* 6, no. 1 (June 1985): 1–55.

Busch, Heinrich. "The Tung-lin Shu-yüan and Its Political and Philosophical Significance." *Monumenta Serica* 14 (1949–55): 1–163.

Carlitz, Katherine. "The Social Uses of Female Virtue in Late Ming Editions of *Lienü zhuan*." *Late Imperial China* 12, no. 2 (Dec. 1991): 117–48.

Chan, Wing-tsit [Ch'en Jung-chieh 陳榮捷]. "Chu Hsi and Yüan Neo-Confucianism." In Hok-lam Chan and Wm. Theodore de Bary, eds., *Yüan Thought and Religion Under the Mongols*. New York: Columbia University Press, 1982.

————. "Chu Hsi chi hsin-ju-hsüeh chih ta-ch'eng" 朱熹集新儒學之大成 (Chu Hsi's completion of neo-Confucianism). In idem, *Chu-hsüeh lun-chi* 朱學論集 (Collection of essays on Chu Hsi). Taipei: Hsüeh-sheng shu-chü, 1982.

————. "The *Hsing-li ching-i* and the Ch'eng-Chu School of the Seventeenth Century." In Wm. Theodore de Bary, ed., *The Unfolding of Neo-Confucianism*. New York: Columbia University Press, 1975.

Chang Ch'i-chin 張其錦. *Ling Tz'u-chung hsien-sheng nien-p'u* 凌次仲先生年譜 (Chronological biography of Mr. Ling T'ing-k'an). In Ling T'ing-k'an, *Ling Tz'u-chung i-shu* 凌次仲遺書 (Writings of the late Mr. Ling T'ing-k'an). An-hui ts'ung-shu, ser. 4. Anhwei, 1935.

Chang Chin-fan 張晉藩 et al. *Chung-kuo fa-chih shih* 中國法制史 (History of Chinese legal institutions). Peking: Chung-kuo jen-min ta-hsüeh ch'u-pan she, 1981.

Chang Ching-ming 章景明. *Yin-Chou miao chih lun kao* 殷周廟制論稿 (On the temple institutions of the Shang and Chou dynasties). Taipei: Hsüeh-hai ch'u-pan she, 1979.

Chang, Chun-li. *The Chinese Gentry: Studies on Their Role in Nineteenth-Century Chinese Society*. Seattle: University of Washington Press, 1955.

Chang Erh-ch'i 張爾岐. *I-li Cheng-chu chü-tu* 儀禮鄭註句讀 (Punctuated reading of Cheng Hsüan's commentary on the *Book of Etiquette and Decorum*). SKCS, vol. 102.

Chang Hai-p'eng 張海鵬 et al. *Ming-Ch'ing Hui-shang tzu-liao hsüan-pien* 明清徽商資料選編 (Selected sources on the Hui-chou merchants in the Ming and Ch'ing). Hofei: Huang-shan shu-she, 1985.

Chang, Hao. *Chinese Intellectuals in Crisis: Search for Order and Meaning, 1890–1911*. Berkeley: University of California Press, 1987.

————. *Liang Ch'i-ch'ao: Intellectual Transition in China, 1890–1907* Cambridge, Mass.: Harvard University Press, 1971.

Chang Hsi-t'ang 張西堂. "Hsün-tzu 'Ch'üan-hsüeh p'ien' yüan-tz'u" 荀子勸學篇冤詞 (Remarks in defense of the [Authenticity] of the chapter "Exhortation to Learning" in *Hsun-tzu*). In Ku Chieh-kang 顧頡剛, ed., *Ku-shih pien* 古史辨 (Debates about ancient history), vol. 6. Reprinted—Shanghai: Ku-chi ch'u-pan she, 1982.

————. "Yen-Li chu-shu k'ao" 顏李著書考 (A study of the written works of Yen Yüan and Li Kung). In *YLHP*.

Chang Hsien-ch'ing 張顯清. "Ming Chia-ching ta-li i ti ch'i-yin, hsing-chih ho hou-kuo" 明嘉靖大禮議的起因, 性質和後果 (The background, nature, and consequences of the Great Rites Controversy of the Chia-ching reign). *Shih-hsüeh chi-k'an* 史學集刊 1988, no. 4: 7–15.

————. "Ming-tai kuan-shen yu-mien ho shu-min chung-hu ti yao-i fu-tan" 明代官紳優免和庶民中戶的徭役負擔 (The tax exemption of gentry-officials and the corvée burden on middle-ranking households in the Ming dynasty). *Li-shih yen-chiu* 歷史研究 1986, no. 2 (Apr.): 161–74.

————. "Ming-tai shen-chin ti-chu ch'ien-lun" 明代紳衿地主淺論 (A preliminary discussion of gentry landlords of the Ming dynasty). *Chung-kuo shih yen-chiu* 中國史研究 1984, no. 2 (May): 75–91.

284   Bibliography

Chang Hsiu-min 張秀民. *Chung-kuo yin-shua shih* 中國印刷史 (A history of Chinese printing). Shanghai: Jen-min ch'u-pan she, 1989.

Chang Hsüan 張萱. *Hsi-yüan chien-wen lu* 西園見聞錄 (Records of things seen and heard in the Western Garden). Taipei: Hua-wen shu-chü, 1969.

Chang Hsüeh-ch'eng 章學誠. *Chang-shih i-shu* 章氏遺書 (Works of the late Chang Hsüeh-ch'eng). 3 vols. Taipei: Han-sheng ch'u-pan she, 1973.

——. *Wen-shih t'ung-i* 文史通義 (General meaning of literature and history). Hong Kong: T'ai-p'ing shu-chü, 1973.

Chang Lieh 張烈. *Wang-hsüeh chih-i* 王學質疑 (Critique of Wang [Yang-ming]'s teachings). TSCCHP, vol. 23.

Chang Lü-hsiang 張履祥. *Yang-yüan hsien-sheng ch'üan-chi* 楊園先生全集 (Complete works of Chang Lü-hsiang). 1871.

Chang Mou 章懋. *Feng-shan Chang hsien-sheng chi* 楓山章先生集 (Collected writings of Mr. Chang of Feng-shan). TSCCHP, vol. 67.

Chang Mu 張穆. *T'ing-lin hsien-sheng nien-p'u* 亭林先生年譜 (Chronological biography of Ku Yen-wu). In Ts'un-ts'ui hsüeh-she 存粹學社, ed., *Ku T'ing-lin hsien-sheng nien-p'u hui-pien* 顧亭林先生年譜匯編 (Collected chronological biographies of Ku Yen-wu). Hong Kong: Ch'ung-wen shu-tien, 1975.

Chang Ping-lin 章炳麟. "Chien Lun" 檢論 (Collected discourses). In *Chang T'ai-yen ch'üan-shu* 章太炎全書 (Complete works of Chang T'ai-yen). Shanghai: Jen-min ch'u-pan she, 1984.

Chang Po-hsing 張伯行. *Cheng-i t'ang wen-chi* 正誼堂文集 (Collected writings from the Hall of Proper Duties). Ts'ung-shu chi-ch'eng chien-pien.

——. *Chin-ssu lu chi-chieh* 近思錄集解 (Collected annotations on *Record of Reflections at Hand*). Taipei: n.p., 1967.

——. *Hsiao-hsüeh chi-chieh* 小學集解 (Collected annotations on *Elementary Learning*). TSCCHP, vol. 33.

Chang Shun-hui 張舜徽. *Ch'ing jen wen-chi pieh-lu* 清人文集別錄 (Separate notes on the collected writings of Ch'ing scholars). Reprinted—Taipei: Ming-wen shu-chü, 1982.

——. *Ch'ing-tai Yang-chou hsüeh-chi* 清代揚州學記 (Account of scholarship in Yang-chou during the Ch'ing). Shanghai: Jen-min ch'u-pan she, 1962.

Chang Tsai 張載. *Chang Tsai chi* 張載集 (Collected works of Chang Tsai). Peking: Chung-hua shu-chü, 1978.

Chang Yen 張研. "Ch'ing-tai chiang-nan shou-tsu chi-kou ch'ien-lun" 清代江南收租機構淺論 (A preliminary study of rent-collecting institutions in Kiangnan). Paper presented at the Annual Conference on Studies in Ch'ing History, 1987.

——. "Ch'ing-tai tsu-t'ien ti hsing-chih chi tso-yung" 清代族田的性質及作用 (The nature and functions of lineage estates during the Ch'ing period). *Ch'ing-shih yen-chiu chi* 清史研究集, no. 6 (Aug. 1988): 195–227.

——. "Shih-lun Ch'ing-tai Chiang-su ti tsu-t'ien" 試論清代江蘇的族田 (Preliminary discussion on lineage estates in Kiangsu in the Ch'ing period). *Li-shih lun-ts'ung* 歷史論叢 (Shantung), vol. 5 (Jan. 1985): 305–41.

Chao I 趙翼. *Nien-erh shih cha-chi* 廿二史劄記 (Miscellaneous notes on the twenty-two dynastic histories). Taipei: Shih-chieh shu-chü, 1973.

Chao I-feng 趙軼峰. "Shih-lun Ming-mo ts'ai-cheng wei-chi ti li-shih ken-yüan chi ch'i shih-tai t'e-cheng" 試論明末財政危機的歷史根源及其時代特徵 (On the historical origins of the fiscal crisis of the late Ming and its characteristics). *Chung-kuo shih yen-chiu* 中國史研究 1986, no. 4 (Nov.): 55–68.

Chao Wei-pang 趙衛邦. "Yen Hsi-chai chu-shu pien-nien" 顏習齋著書編年 (Chronology of the writings of Yen Yüan). In *YLHP*.

Ch'en Ch'üeh 陳確. *Ch'en Ch'üeh chi* 陳確集 (Collected writings of Ch'en Ch'üeh). Peking: Chung-hua shu-chü, 1979.

Ch'en Fei-lung 陳飛龍. "Hsün Tzu li-hsüeh tui hou-shih chih ying-hsiang" 荀子禮學對後世之影響 (The influence of Hsün Tzu's ritual studies on later ages). *Cheng-chih ta-hsüeh hsüeh-pao* 政治大學學報, no. 44 (Dec. 1981): 1–36.

Ch'en K'o-yün 陳柯雲. "Lüeh lun Ming-Ch'ing Hui-chou ti hsiang-yüeh" 略論明清徽州的鄉約 (A brief discussion of village compacts in Hui-chou during the Ming and Ch'ing periods) *Chung-kuo shih yen-chiu* 中國史研究 1990, no. 4 (Nov.): 44–55.

Ch'en Li 陳澧. *Tung-shu tu-shu chi* 東塾讀書記 (Notes from the Studio of the East). Taipei: Shang-wu yin-shu-kuan, 1967.

Ch'en Min-yü 陳民裕. "Ku Ching-yang chi ch'i li-hsüeh" 顧涇陽及其禮學. Manuscript. Taipei, 1978.

Ch'en T'ieh-fan 陳鐵凡. "Wang Chung hsing-i k'ao-cheng" 汪中行誼考徵 (A evidential study of the moral conduct of Wang Chung). *Ta-lu tsa-chih* 大陸雜誌 35, no. 3 (Aug. 1967): 67–78.

Ch'en Yao-nan 陳耀南. *Wei Yüan yen-chiu* 魏源研究 (A study of Wei Yüan). Hong Kong: Chao-ming ch'u-pan she, 1979.

Cheng, Chung-ying. "Reason, Substance, and Human Desires in Seventeenth-Century Neo-Confucianism." In Wm. Theodore de Bary, ed., *The Unfolding of Neo-Confucianism*. New York: Columbia University Press, 1975.

Cheng Shih-hsing 鄭世興. "Yen Hsi-chai chiao-yü ssu-hsiang chih yen-chiu" 顏習齋教育思想之研究 (Study of the educational thought of Yen Yüan). In *YLHP*.

Ch'eng Chin-fang 程晉芳. *Mien-hsing t'ang chi* 勉行堂集 (Collected writings from the Hall of Making Strenuous Efforts). 1820.

Ch'eng I 程頤 and Ch'eng Hao 程顥. *Erh Ch'eng chi* 二程集 (Collected works of the two Ch'eng brothers). Peking: Chung-hua shu-chü, 1980.

Ch'eng T'ing-tso 程廷祚. *Ch'ing-hsi wen-chi* 青溪文集 (Collected writings of Green Brook). Taipei: Ta-t'ung shu-chü.

Ch'eng Yao-t'ien 程瑤田. *T'ung-i lu* 通藝錄 (Records of comprehensive learning). An-hui ts'ung-shu, ser. 2. Anhwei, 1933.

Ch'eng Yüan-min 程元敏. *Wang Po chih sheng-p'ing yü hsüeh-shu* 王柏之生平與學術 (The life and scholarship of Wang Po). Taipei: Hsüeh-hai ch'u-pan she, 1975.

Chi Yün 紀昀. *Chi Wen-ta kung i-chi* 紀文達公遺集 (Writings of the late Chi Yün). 1812.

Chiang Fan 江藩. *Kuo-ch'ao Han-hsüeh shih-ch'eng chi* 國朝漢學師承記 (Records of the lineage of Han learning of the present [Ch'ing] dynasty). Taipei: Chung-hua shu-chü, 1962.

———. *Kuo-ch'ao Sung-hsüeh yüan-yüan chi* 國朝宋學淵源記 (The lineage of Sung scholarship of the present [Ch'ing] dynasty). SPPY. Taipei: Chung-hua shu-chü, 1962.

Chiang Yung 江永. *Li-shu kang-mu* 禮書綱目 (Outline of books on rites). SKCS, vol. 127.

Chiao Hsün 焦循. "San-li pien-meng" 三禮便蒙 (Aid to beginners studying the three ritual Classics). Manuscript. East Asiatic Library, University of California, Berkeley.

———. *Tiao-ku chi* 雕菰集 (Collected writings from [the Studio of] Carved Bamboo). Ts'ung-shu chi-ch'eng chien-pien.

Ch'ien Ch'ien-i 錢謙益. *Mu-chai yu-hsüeh chi* 牧齋有學集 (Collected learning of Mu-chai). SPTK.

Ch'ien, Edward T. *Chiao Hung and the Restructuring of Neo-Confucianism in the Late Ming.* New York: Columbia University Press, 1986.

———. "Chiao Hung and the Revolt Against Ch'eng-Chu Orthodoxy." In Wm. Theodore de Bary, *The Unfolding of Neo-Confucianism.* New York: Columbia University Press, 1975.

Ch'ien I-chi 錢儀吉. *Pei-chuan chi* 碑傳集 (Collected biographies and tomb inscriptions). Preface dated 1826.

Ch'ien Mu 錢穆. *Chung-kuo chin san-pai-nien hsüeh-shu shih* 中國近三百年學術史 (History of Chinese scholarship during the last three centuries). Taipei: Shang-wu yin-shu-kuan, 1957.

———. *Chu-tzu hsin hsüeh-an* 朱子新學案 (A new study of Chu Hsi's learning). 5 vols. Taipei: San-min shu-chü, 1982.

———. *Liang Han ching-hsüeh chin-ku wen p'ing-i* 兩漢經學今古文平議 (An impartial assessment of the Old and New Text Classics in the Han dynasty). Hong Kong: Hsin-ya yen-chiu so, 1958.

Ch'ien Shih-fu 錢實甫. *Ch'ing-tai chih-kuan nien-piao* 清代職官年表 (Chronological tables of Ch'ing official appointments). 4 vols. Peking: Chung-hua shu-chü, 1980.

Ch'ien Ta-hsin 錢大昕. *Ch'ien-yen t'ang wen'chi* 潛研堂文集 (Collected essays from the Hall of Devotion to Studies). KHCPTS.

Ch'in Hui-t'ien 秦蕙田. *Wu-li t'ung-k'ao* 五禮通考 (Comprehensive study of the five categories of ritual). 1880.

Ch'in-ting Chou-kuan i'shu 欽定周官義疏 (Exegesis of the *Rites of Chou* compiled by imperial order). SKCS, vol. 98.

Ch'in-ting Li-chi i-shu 欽定禮記義疏 (Exegesis of the *Book of Rites* compiled by imperial order). SKCS, vol. 124.

Ch'in-ting Li-pu tse-li 欽定吏部則例 (Regulations and cases of the [Ch'ing] Board of Personnel compiled by imperial order). Taipei: Wen-ch'eng ch'u-pan she, 1966.

Ch'in-ting ta-Ch'ing hui-tien t'u shih-li 欽定大清會典圖事例 (Collected Ch'ing statutes, with illustrations, compiled by imperial order). Reprinted—Taipei, 1963.

Ching, Julia. "Chu Hsi on Personal Cultivation." In Wing-tsit Chan, ed., *Chu Hsi and Neo-Confucianism*. Honolulu: University of Hawaii Press, 1986.

Ch'ing-shih kao 清史稿 (Draft history of the Ch'ing dynasty). Hong Kong: Wen-hsüeh yen-chiu she, 1960.

Ch'ing-shih lieh-chuan 清史列傳 (Biographies for the history of the Ch'ing dynasty). Taipei: Chung-hua shu-chü, 1962.

Ch'iu Chün 邱濬. *Ch'iu Wen-chuang kung ch'üan-chi* 邱文莊公全集 (Complete writings of Ch'iu Chün). Taipei: T'ai-pei Ch'iu Wen-chuang kung ts'ung-shu chi yin wei-yüan hui, 1973.

Chou Ping-chun 周秉鈞. *Ku Han-yü kang-yao* 古漢語綱要 (An outline of Archaic Chinese). Changsha: Hu-nan chiao-yü ch'u-pan she, 1981.

Chow, Kai-wing [Chou Ch'i-jung 周啓榮]. "Ordering Ancestors and the State: Chang Hsüeh-ch'eng (1738–1801) and Lineage Discourse in Eighteenth-Century China." In *Family Process and Political Process in Modern Chinese History*. Taipei: Academia Sinica, Institute of Modern History, 1992.

————. "Discourse, Examinations, and Local Elites: The Invention of the T'ung-ch'eng School in Ch'ing China." In Benjamin A. Elman and Alexander Woodside, eds., *Society and Education in Late Imperial China*. Berkeley: University of California Press, forthcoming.

————. "Ritual, Cosmology, and Ontology: Chang Tsai's (1020–1077) Moral Philosophy and Neo-Confucian Ethics." *Philosophy East and West* 43, no. 2 (Apr. 1993): 201–28.

————. "Scholar and Society: The Textual Scholarship and Social Concerns of Wang Chung (1745–1794)." *Chinese Studies* 4, no. 1 (June 1986): 297–312.

————. "Ts'ung k'uang-yen tao wei-yen: Lun Kung Tzu-chen ti ching-shih ssu-hsiang yü ching chin-wen hsüeh" 從狂言到微言：論龔自珍的經世思想與經今文學 (From impetuous remarks to subtle expression: On Kung Tzu-chen's New Text scholarship and statecraft thought). In *Chin-shih Chung-kuo ching-shih ssu-hsiang yen-t'ao hui lun-wen chi* 近世中國經世思想研討會論文集 (Proceedings of the Conference on the Theory of Statecraft of Modern China). Taipei: Academia Sinica, Institute of Modern History, 1984.

Chow Kai-wing [Chou Ch'i-jung 周啓榮] and Liu Kuang-ching 劉廣京. "Hsüeh-shu ching-shih: Chang Hsüeh-ch'eng chih wen-shih lun yü ching-shih ssu-hsiang" 學術經世：章學誠之文史論與經世思想 (Scholarship and statecraft: Chang Hsüeh-ch'eng's theory of history and literature and his ideas on statecraft). In *Chin-shih Chung-kuo ching-shih ssu-hsiang yen-t'ao hui lun-wen chi* 近世中國經世思想研討會論文集 (Proceedings of the Conference on the Theory of Statecraft of Modern China). Taipei: Academia Sinica, Institute of Modern History, 1984.

Chow Tse-tsung. *The May Fourth Movement: Intellectual Revolution in Modern China*. Cambridge, Mass.: Harvard University Press, 1960.

Chu Hsi 朱熹. *Chu-tzu yü-lei* 朱子語類 (Classified remarks of Chu Hsi). Peking: Chung-hua shu-chü, 1986.

————. *Shih chi-chuan* 詩集傳 (Collected annotations on the *Book of Odes*). Taipei: Shih-chieh shu-chü, 1980.

Chu, Hung-lam. "The Debate over Recognition of Wang Yang-ming." *HJAS* 48, no. 1 (June 1988): 47–70.

Chu I-tsun 朱彝尊. *P'ao-shu t'ing chi* 曝書亭集 (Collected works from the Pavilion for Drying Books). KHCPTS.

Chu-ko Chih 諸葛治. "Ts'ung i-p'ien pei-wen t'an tao Ming-tai nung-min ti yao-i fu-tan" 從一篇碑文談到明代農民的徭役負擔 (The corvée burden of peasants druing the Ming period: observation from an inscription). In *Ming-Ch'ing shih kuo-chi hsüeh-shu t'ao-lun hui* 明清史國際學術討論會 (International Symposium on Ming-Ch'ing History). Tientsin: n.p., 1982.

Chu Kuo-chen 朱國楨. *Yung-ch'uang hsiao-p'in* 湧幢小品 (Flickering and bubbling notes). In *Pi-chi hsiao-shuo ta-kuan* 筆記小說大觀, ser. 22.

Ch'ü, T'ung-tsu. *Local Government in China Under the Ch'ing*. Stanford: Stanford University Press, 1969.

Ch'ü Wan-li 屈萬里. "Sung-jen i-ching ti feng-ch'i" 宋人疑經的風氣 (The skeptical current in Sung Classical scholarship). In *Ta-lu tsa-chih shih-hsüeh ts'ung-shu* 大陸雜誌史學叢書, 2nd ser., vol. 2.

Ch'üan Tsu-wang 全祖望. *Chieh-ch'i t'ing chi* 鮚埼亭集 (Writings from the Chieh-ch'i Pavilion). KHCPTS.

Cohen, Myron. "Lineage Organization in North China." *JAS* 49 (1990): 509–34.

Dardess, John W. "A Century of Social Change: T'ai-ho County, Kiangsi, 1400–1500." *Ming Studies*, no. 26 (Fall 1988): 56–60.

————. "The Cheng Communal Family: Social Organization and Neo-Confucianism in Yüan and Early Ming China." *HJAS* 34 (1974): 7–52.

————. *Confucianism and Autocracy: Professional Elites in the Founding of the Ming Dynasty*. Berkeley: University of California Press, 1983.

de Bary, Wm. Theodore. "Individualism and Humanitarianism." In idem, ed., *Self and Society in Ming Thought*. New York: Columbia University Press, 1970.

————. *The Message of the Mind in Neo-Confucianism*. New York: Columbia University Press, 1990.

————. "Neo-Confucian Cultivation and the Seventeenth-Century "Enlightenment." In idem, ed., *The Unfolding of Neo-Confucianism*. New York: Columbia University Press, 1975.

————. "Some Common Tendencies in Neo-Confucianism." In David S. Nivison and Arthur F. Wright, eds., *Confucianism in Action*. Stanford: Stanford University Press, 1959.

————, ed. *Sources of Chinese Tradition*. New York: Columbia University Press, 1960.

Dennerline, Jerry. *The Chia-ting Loyalists: Confucian Leadership and Social Change in Seventeenth-Century China*. New Haven: Yale University Press, 1981.

————. "Fiscal Reform and Local Control: The Gentry-Bureaucratic Alliance Survives the Conquest." In Frederic Wakeman, Jr., and Carolyn Grant, eds., *Conflict and Control in Late Imperial China*. Berkeley: University of California Press, 1975.

————. "Marriage, Adoption, and Charity in the Development of Lineages in Wu-hsi from Sung to Ch'ing." In Patricia B. Ebrey and James L. Watson, eds., *Kinship Organization in Late Imperial China, 1400–1900*. Berkeley: University of California Press, 1986.

Dimberg, Ronald G. *The Sage and Society: The Life and Thought of Ho Hsin-yin*. Honolulu: University of Hawaii Press, 1974.

Duara, Prasenjit. *Culture, Power, and the State: Rural North China, 1900–1942*. Stanford: Stanford University Press, 1988.

————. "Superscribing Symbols: The Myth of Guandi, Chinese God of War." *JAS* 47 (1988): 778–95.

Eberhard, Wolfram. *Social Mobility in Traditional China*. Leiden: E. J. Brill, 1962.

Ebrey, Patricia Buckley. *Confucianism and Family Rituals in Imperial China: A Social History of Writing About Rites*. Princeton: Princeton University Press, 1991.

————. "Conception of the Family in the Sung Dynasty." *JAS* 43 (1984): 219–45.

————. "Early Stages in the Development of Descent Group Organization." In idem and James L. Watson, eds., *Kinship Organization in Late Imperial China, 1400–1900*. Berkeley: University of California Press, 1986.

————. "Types of Lineages in Ch'ing China: A Re-examination of the Chang Lineage of T'ung-ch'eng." *Ch'ing-shih wen-t'i* 4, no. 9 (June 1983): 1–20.

————, trans. *Chu Hsi's Family Rituals: A Twelfth-Century Chinese Manual for the Performance of Cappings, Weddings, Funerals, and Ancestral Rites*. Princeton: Princeton University Press, 1991.

Ebrey, Patricia, and James L. Watson, eds. *Kinship Organization in Late Imperial China, 1400–1900*. Berkeley: University of California Press, 1986.

Elman, Benjamin A. *Classicism, Politics, and Kinship: The Ch'ang-chou School of New Text Confucianism in Late Imperial China*. Berkeley: University of California Press, 1990.

————. *From Philosophy to Philology: Intellectual and Social Aspects of Change in Late Imperial China*. Cambridge, Mass.: Harvard University Press, 1984.

————. "Philosophy (*i-li*) versus Philology (*k'ao-cheng*): The *Jen-hsin Tao-hsin* Debate." *T'oung Pao* 69, nos. 4–5 (1983): 175–222.

————. "Scholarship and Politics: Chuang Ts'un-yü and the Rise of the Ch'ang-chou New Text School in Late Imperial China." *Late Imperial China* 7, no. 1 (June 1986): 63–86.

Elvin, Mark. "Female Virtue and the State in China." *Past and Present*, no. 104 (Aug. 1984): 111–52.

Esherick, Joseph W., and Mary Backus Rankin, eds. *Chinese Local Elites and Patterns of Dominance*. Berkeley: University of California Press, 1990.

Fan Shu-chih 樊樹志. *Ming-Ch'ing Chiang-nan shih chen t'an-wei* 明清江南市鎮探微

(A study of the cities and towns of Kiangnan in the Ming and Ch'ing periods). Shanghai: Fu-tan ta-hsüeh ch'u-pan she, 1990.

Fang Hsiao-ju 方孝孺. *Hsün-chih chai chi* 遜志齋集 (Collected essays from the Studio of Humble Aspirations). SPPY.

Fang Pao 方苞. *Fang Pao chi* 方苞集 (Collected writings of Fang Pao). Shanghai: Ku-chi ch'u-pan she, 1983.

Fang Tung-shu 方東樹. *Han-hsüeh shang-tui* 漢學商兌 (A critical assessment of Han learning). KHCPTS.

Farmer, Edward. "Social Regulations of the First Ming Emperor: Orthodoxy as a Function of Authority." In K. C. Liu, ed., *Orthodoxy in Late Imperial China*. Berkeley: University of California Press, 1990, pp. 103–25.

Faure, David. *The Structure of Chinese Rural Society: Lineage and Village in the Eastern New Territories, Hong Kong*. Hong Kong: Oxford University Press, 1986.

————. "What Made Foshan a Town? The Evolution of Rural-Urban Identities in Ming-Ch'ing China." *Late Imperial China* 11, no. 2 (Dec. 1990): 1–31.

Feng Ch'en 馮辰. *Shu-ku hsien-sheng nien-p'u* 恕谷先生年譜 (Chronological biography of Li Kung). YLHP.

Feng Erh-k'ang 馮爾康. "Ch'ing-tai ti hun-yin chih-tu yü fu-nü ti she-hui ti-wei shu-lun" 清代的婚姻制度與婦女的社會地位述論 (On the institution of marriage and the social status of women in the Ch'ing period). *Ch'ing-shih yen-chiu chi* 清史研究集 1986, no. 5: 305–43.

Feng Kuei-fen 馮桂芬. *Chiao-pin lu k'ang-i* 校邠廬抗議 (Straightforward words from the Lodge of Early Chou Studies). Chin-tai Chung-kuo shih-liao ts'ung-k'an, ser. 62, vol. 612. Taipei: Wen-hai ch'u-pan she, 1966.

————. *Hsien-chih t'ang chi* 顯志堂集 (Collected writings from the Hall of Manifest Aspirations). Taipei: Hsüeh-hai ch'u-pan she, 1967.

Feng Ts'ung-wu 馮從吾. *Hsiao-hsü chi* 少墟集 (Collected writings of Feng Ts'ung-wu). SKCS, vol. 1293.

Feuerwerker, Albert. *Rebellion in Nineteenth-Century China*. Michigan Papers in Chinese Studies, no. 21. Ann Arbor: University of Michigan, Center for Chinese Studies, 1975.

Fisher, Carney T. "The Great Ritual Controversy in the Age of Ming Shih-tsung." *Society for the Study of Chinese Religion Bulletin*, no. 7 (Fall 1979): 71–87.

Fisher, Tom. "Loyalist Alternatives in the Early Ch'ing." *HJAS* 44 (1984): 83–122.

Freedman, Maurice. *Chinese Lineage and Society: Fukien and Kwangtung*. London: Athlone Press, 1966.

Fu I-ling 傅衣凌. *Ming-Ch'ing she-hui ching-chi shih lun-wen chi* 明清社會經濟史論文集 (Collected essays on the social and economic history of the Ming and Ch'ing periods). Peking: Jen-min ch'u-pan she, 1982.

————. *Ming-tai Chiang-nan shih-min ching-chi shih-t'an* 明代江南市民經濟試探 (A preliminary study of the urban economy of Kiangnan during the Ming period). Shanghai: Jen-min ch'u-pan she, 1975.

Furth, Charlotte. "Androgynous Males and Deficient Females: Biology and Gender Boundaries in Sixteenth and Seventeenth-Century China." *Late Imperial China*, 9, no. 2 (Dec. 1988): 1–31.

Gernet, Jacques. *China and the Christian Impact*. New York: Cambridge University Press, 1985.

Gilmore, Myron P. *The World of Humanism, 1453–1517*. New York: Harper, 1952.

Goodrich, Luther C., and Chaoying Fang, eds. *Dictionary of Ming Biography, 1368–1644*. 2 vols. New York: Columbia University Press, 1976.

Goody, Jack. *The Logic of Writing and the Organization of Society*. Cambridge, Mass.: Harvard University Press, 1986.

Greenblatt, Kristin Yü. "Chu-hung and Lay Buddhism in the Late Ming." In Wm. Theodore de Bary, ed., *The Unfolding of Neo-Confucianism*. New York: Columbia University Press, 1975.

Grieder, Jerome B. *Hu Shih and the Chinese Renaissance*. Cambridge, Mass.: Harvard University Press, 1970.

Guy, R. Kent. "Development of the Evidential Research Movement: Ku Yen-wu and the Ssu-k'u ch'üan-shu." *Ch'ing-hua hsüeh-pao* 16, nos. 1–2 (Dec. 1984): 97–116.

———. *The Emperor's Four Treasuries: Scholars and the State in the Late Ch'ien-lung Era*. Cambridge, Mass.: Harvard University Press, 1987.

Han Ta-ch'eng 韓大成. "Ming-tai kao-li-t'ai tzu-pen ti te-tien chi ch'i tso-yung" (The characteristics and functions of usurious capital in the Ming dynasty) 明代高利貸資本的特點及其作用. *Ming-shih yen-chiu lun-ts'ung* 明史研究論叢 (Kiangsu) 1991, no. 4: 348–67.

———. "Ming-tai shang-p'in ching-chi ti fa-chan yu tzu-pen" 明代商品經濟的發展與資本 (Capital and the growth of the commercial economy during the Ming). *Ming-Ch'ing she-hui ching-chi hsing-t'ai ti yen-chiu* 明清社會經濟形態的研究 (Studies of the social and economic conditions of the Ming and Ch'ing periods). Shanghai: Jen-min ch'u-pan she, 1957, pp. 1–100.

Hang Shih-chün 杭世駿. *Tao-ku t'ang chi* 道古堂集 (Collected writings from the Hall of Following the Ancients). 1888.

Hao Feng 薅峰. "Ming-tai ti i-nan mai-mai yü ku kung-jen" 明代的義男買賣與僱工人 (The "righteous male" trade and hired labor in the Ming period). *Shan-tung ta-hsüeh hsüeh-pao* 山東大學學報 1988, no. 4: 107–13. Reprinted—*Ming-Ch'ing shih* 1989, no. 4: 41–48.

Hazelton, Keith. "Patrilines and the Development of Localized Lineages: The Wu of Hsiu-ning City, Hui-chou, to 1528." In Patricia B. Ebrey and James L. Watson, eds., *Kinship Organization in Late Imperial China, 1400–1900*. Berkeley: University of California Press, 1986.

Hegel, Robert. "Distinguishing Levels of Audiences for Ming-Ch'ing Vernacular Literature." In David Johnson, Andrew J. Nathan, and Evelyn S.

Rawski, eds., *Popular Culture in Late Imperial China*. Berkeley: University of California Press, 1985.

―――. *The Novel in Seventeenth-Century China*. New York: Columbia University Press, 1981.

Henderson, John. *The Development and Decline of Chinese Cosmology*. New York: Columbia University Press, 1984.

Ho Ch'ang-ling 賀長齡 and Wei Yüan 魏源, eds. *Huang-ch'ao ching-shih wen-pien* 皇朝經世文編 (Collected Ch'ing dynasty writings on statecraft). Chin-tai Chung-kuo shih-liao ts'ung-k'an 近代中國史料叢刊 ser. 74. Taipei: Wen-hai ch'u-pan she, 1972.

Ho, Ping-ti. *The Ladder of Success in Imperial China*. New York: John Wiley & Sons, 1964.

Ho Yu-sen 何佑森. "Ku T'ing-lin ti ching-hsüeh" 顧林亭的經學 (The Classical scholarship of Ku Yen-wu). *Wen shih che* 文史哲 1967, no. 16 (Oct.): 183–205.

Hou Wai-lu 侯外廬. *Chin-tai Chung-kuo ssu-hsiang hsüeh-shuo shih* 近代中國思想學說史 (History of modern Chinese thought and theories). 2 vols. Shanghai: Sheng-huo shu-tien, 1947.

Hou Wai-lu et al. *Chung-kuo ssu-hsiang t'ung-shih* 中國思想通史 (A general history of Chinese thought). 5 vols. Peking: Jen-min ch'u-pan she, 1960.

Hsi, Angela Ning-Jy Sun. "Social and Economic Status of the Merchant Class of the Ming Dynasty, 1368–1644." Ph.D. Dissertation. University of Illinois, Urbana-Champaign, 1972.

Hsiao I-shan 蕭一山. *Ch'ing-tai t'ung-shih* 清代通史 (General history of the Ch'ing), vol. 5. Taipei: Shang-wu yin-shu-kuan, 1980.

Hsiao, Kung-chuan [Hsiao Kung-ch'üan] 蕭公權. *Chung-kuo cheng-chih ssu-hsiang shih* 中國政治思想史 (A history of Chinese political thought). Taipei: Chung-kuo wen-hua ta-hsüeh, 1980.

―――. *Rural China: Imperial Control in the Nineteenth Century*. Seattle: University of Washington Press, 1967.

Hsieh Kuo-chen 謝國楨. "Ming tai nu-pien k'ao" 明代奴變考 (A study of bond-servant rebellion in the late Ming). In idem, *Ming-Ch'ing chih chi t'ang-she yün-tung k'ao* 明清之際黨社運動考 (A study of the activities of factions and societies in the Ming-Ch'ing transition). Peking: Chung-hua shu-chü, 1982.

Hsiung Ping-chen 熊秉真. "Shih-ch'i shih-chi Chung-kuo cheng-chih ssu-hsiang chung fei ch'uan-t'ung ch'eng-fen ti fen-hsi" 十七世紀中國政治思想中非傳統成份的分析 (Analysis of non-traditional elements in the political thought of seventeenth-century China). *Chin-tai shih yen-chiu-so chi-k'an* 近代史研究所集刊 15, no. 1 (June 1986): 1–31.

Hsü Ch'ien-hsüeh 徐乾學. *Tu-li t'ung-k'ao* 讀禮通考 (A comprehensive study of rituals). 1881.

Hsü Fang 徐枋. *Chü-i t'ang chi* 居易堂集 (Hall of Dwelling in Flux). Taipei: Hsüeh-sheng shu-chü, 1973.

Hsü Fu-kuan 徐復觀. *Chung-kuo ssu-hsiang shih lun-chi hsü-pien* 中國思想史論集續編

(Collected essays on Chinese intellectual history, second series). Taipei: Shih-pao wen-hua ch'u-pan, 1982.

————. "Han-hsüeh lun-heng" 漢學論衡 (An assessment of Han learning). *Ta-lu tsa-chih* 大陸雜誌 54, no. 4 (Apr. 1977): 1–22.

————. *Liang Han ssu-hsiang shih* 兩漢思想史 (Intellectual history of the Former and Latter Han dynasties). Vols. 2–3. Taipei: Hsüeh-sheng shu-chü, 1976, 1979.

Hsü Heng 許衡. *Hsü Lu-chai chi* 許魯齋集 (Collected writings of Hsü Heng). Ts'ung-shu chi-ch'eng chien-pien.

Hsü Hung 徐泓. "Ming-tai she-hui feng-ch'i ti pien-ch'ien" 明代社會風氣的變遷 (Changes in social custom in Ming society). Paper presented at the Second International Conference on Sinology. Taipei: Academia Sinica, Dec. 1986.

Hsü I-k'uei 徐一夔. *Ta-Ming chi-li* 大明集禮 (Collected ceremonies of the Great Ming). SKCS, vol. 649.

Hsü K'o 徐柯. *Ch'ing pai lei-ch'ao* 清稗類鈔 (Classified notes for an unofficial history of the Ch'ing dynasty). Taipei: Shang-wu yin-shu-kuan, 1967.

Hsü Shih-ch'ang 徐世昌. *Ch'ing-ju hsüeh-an* 清儒學案 (Case studies of the scholarship of Ch'ing Confucians). Taipei: Shih-chieh shu-chü, 1962.

Hsü, Sung-peng. *A Buddhist Leader in Ming China: The Life and Thought of Han-shan Te-ch'ing.* State Park: Pennsylvania State University Press, 1979.

Hsü wen-hsien t'ung-k'ao 續文獻通考 (Comprehensive study of documents, supplement). In *Shih-t'ung* 十通 (Ten comprehensive studies). 24 vols. KHCPTS.

Hsüeh Yün-sheng 薛允升. *Tu-li ts'un-i* 讀例存疑 (Doubts about sub-statutes in the Ch'ing Code), vol. 2. Taipei: Ch'eng-wen ch'u-pan she, 1970.

Hu, Hsien-chin. *The Common Descent Group in China and Its Functions.* New York: Viking Funds Publications, 1948.

Hu, John. "Ming Dynasty Drama." In Colin Mackerras, ed., *Chinese Theater: From Its Origins to the Present Day.* Honolulu: University of Hawaii Press, 1983.

Hu Kuang 胡廣. *Hsing-li ta-ch'üan* 性理大全 (Complete repository of [teachings about] human nature and principle). SKCS, vol. 710.

Hu P'ei-hui 胡培翬. *Ti-hsia ta-wen* 禘祫答問 (Questions and answers about *ti* and *hsia*). TSCCHP, vol. 35.

Hu Shih 胡適. *Tai Tung-yüan ti che-hsüeh* 戴東原的哲學 (The philosophy of Tai Chen). Taipei: Shang-wu yin-shu kuan, 1971.

Hu Wei 胡渭. *I-t'u ming-pien* 易圖明辨 (A clarifying critique of the diagrams associated with the *Book of Changes*). TSCCHP, vol. 16.

Huang Huai 黃淮. *Huang Ming wen-heng* 皇明文衡.

Huang Pai-chia 黃百家 and Ch'üan Tsu-wang 全祖望. *Sung-yüan hsüeh-an* 宋元學案 (Case studies of Sung and Yüan scholarship). Taipei: Kuang-wen shu-chü, 1971.

Huang, Pei. *Autocracy at Work: A Study of the Yung-cheng Period, 1723–1735.* Bloomington: Indiana University Press, 1974.

Huang P'ei-chin 黃佩瑾. "Kuan-yü Ming-tai kuo-nei shih-ch'ang wen-t'i ti k'ao-ch'a" 關於明代國內市場問題的考察 (Observations on the domestic market of the Ming dynasty). In *Ming-Ch'ing she-hui ching-chi hsing-t'ai ti yen-chiu* 明清社會經濟形態的研究 (Studies of the social and economic conditions of the Ming and Ch'ing periods). Shanghai: Jen-min ch'u-pan she, 1957, pp. 198–262.

Huang, Ray. *1587—A Year of No Significance: The Ming Dynasty in Decline.* New Haven: Yale University Press, 1981.

————. *Taxation and Government Finance in Sixteenth-Century Ming China.* Cambridge, Eng.: Cambridge University Press, 1974.

Huang Tsung-hsi 黃宗羲. *Huang Tsung-hsi ch'üan-chi* 黃宗羲全集 (Complete works of Huang Tsung-hsi), vol. 1. Chekiang: Ku-chi ch'u-pan she, 1985.

————. *Li-chou i-chu hui-k'an* 梨洲遺箸彙刊 (Composite edition of the late Huang Tsung-hsi's writings). 1919.

————. *Ming-ju hsüeh-an* 明儒學案 (Case studies of the scholarship of Ming Confucians). Shanghai: Shang-wu yin-shu kuan, 1930.

————. *Nan-lei wen-ting* 南雷文定 (Writings from Mount Nan-lei). KHCPTS, 1936–37.

Huang Yung-wu 黃永武. *Hsü Shen chih ching-hsüeh* 許慎之經學 (The Classical learning of Hsü Shen). Taipei: Chung-hua shu-chü, 1972.

Hucker, Charles O. "The Tung-lin Movement of the Late Ming Period." In John K. Fairbank, *Chinese Thought and Institutions.* Chicago: University of Chicago Press, 1957.

Hui Chou-t'i 惠周惕. *Shih shuo* 詩說 (Exposition of the *Book of Odes*). Huang Ch'ing ching-chieh 皇清經解.

Hui Shih-ch'i 惠士奇. *Li-shuo* 禮說 (Explications of rituals). SKCS, vol. 101.

Hui Tung 惠棟. *Chiu-ching ku-i* 九經古義 (Ancient meanings of nine Classics). TSCCHP, vol. 10

————. *Ch'un-ch'iu Tso-chuan pu-chu* 春秋左傳補註 (Supplementary notes to the *Tso Commentary* on the *Spring and Autumn Annals*), Ed. Mo-hai chin-hu 墨海金壺 (Sea of Ink in a Gold Vase); comp. Chang Hai-p'ang. Taipei: n.p., 1969.

————. *Hui-shih tu Shuo-wen chi* 惠氏讀說文記 (Collected notes of Mr. Hui on the *Shuo-wen*). Ts'ung-shu chi-ch'eng chien-pien.

————. *Ming-t'ang ta-tao lu* 明堂大道錄 (The great way of the Hall of Illumination). TSCCHP, vol. 34.

Hummel, Arthur W., ed. *Eminent Chinese of the Ch'ing Period.* 2 vols. Washington, D.C.: U.S. Government Printing Office, 1943.

Hung Liang-chi 洪亮吉. *Chüan-shih ko wen chia chi* 卷施閣文甲集 (First collection of writings from the Chüan-shih Pavilion). In *Hung Pei-chiang shih-wen chi* 洪北江詩文集 (Collected essays and poems of Hung Liang-chi). KHCPTS.

Huters, Theodore. "From Writing to Literature: The Development of Late Qing Theories of Prose." *HJAS* 47, No. 1 (June 1987): 70–80.

Hymes, Robert. "Marriage, Descent Groups, and the Localist Strategy in Sung and Yüan Fu-chou." In Patricia B. Ebrey and James L. Watson, eds., *Kinship*

Organization in Late Imperial China, 1400–1900. Berkeley: University of California Press, 1986.

Inoue Susumu 井上進. "Han gaku no seiritsu" 漢学の成立 (The Rise of Ch'ing textual criticism). *Tōhō gakuhō* 東方学報 no. 61 (Mar. 1989): 223–319.

Inoue Tōru 井上徹. "Sōzoku no keisei to sono soshiki: Min Shin jidai no Shukō san deruta o taishō to shite" 宗族の形成とその組織——明清時代の珠江三デルタを對象として (The formation and structure of the *zongzu* system—especially in the Canton Delta during the Ming and the Ch'ing periods). *Shirin* 史林 72, no. 5 (Sept. 1989): 84–122.

Jen Ch'i-yün 任啓運. *Kung-shih k'ao* 宮室考 (Study of buildings and rooms). SKCS, vol. 109.

———. *T'ien-tzu ssu hsien lo k'uei-shih li* 天子肆獻祼饋食禮 (Various ceremonies). SKCS, vol. 109.

Johnson, David. "Communication, Class, and Consciousness in Late Imperial China." In idem, Andrew J. Nathan, and Evelyn S. Rawski, eds., *Popular Culture in Late Imperial China.* Berkeley: University of California Press, 1985.

Johnson, David, Andrew J. Nathan, and Evelyn S. Rawski, eds. *Popular Culture in Late Imperial China.* Berkeley: University of California Press, 1985.

Juan Yüan 阮元. *Yen-ching shih chi* 揅經室集 (Collected writings from the Studio for the Investigation of the Classics). I-chi, erh-chi, san-chi, and hsü-chi (Collections 1–4). SPTK.

———. *Yen-ching shih hsü-chi* 揅經室續集 (Collected writings from the Studio for the Investigation of the Classics, continued). Ts'ung-shu chi-ch'eng chien-pien.

———, ed. *Ku-ching ching-she wen-chi* 詁經精舍文集 (Collected writings from the Studio for the Philological Exposition of the Classics). Ts'ung-shu chi-ch'eng chien-pien.

———. *Shih-san ching chu-shu* 十三經注疏 (Commentaries and annotations on the Thirteen Classics). Peking: Chung-hua shu-chü, 1980.

Jung Chao-tsu 容肇祖. *Ming-tai ssu-hsiang shih* 明代思想史 (History of Ming thought). Shanghai: K'ai-ming shu-chü, 1941.

Kahn, Harold. *Monarchy in the Emperor's Eye: Image and Reality in the Ch'ien-lung Reign.* Cambridge, Mass.: Harvard University Press, 1971.

K'ang-hsi ti yü-chih wen-chi 康熙帝諭制文集 (Collected writings of the K'ang-hsi emperor) Chung-kuo shih-hsüeh ts'ung-shu 中國史學叢書. Taipei: Hsüeh-sheng shu-chü, 1966.

Kao P'an-lung 高攀龍. *Kao-tzu i-shu* 高子遺書 (Writings of the late Kao P'an-lung). 1876.

———. *Kao-tzu i-shu* SKCS, vol. 1292.

Kao T'ing-chen 高廷珍. *Tung-lin shu-yüan chih* 東林書院志 (An account of the Tung-lin Academy). Taipei: Kuang-wen shu-chü, 1968.

Kessler, Lawrence D. "Chinese Scholars and the Early Manchu State." *HJAS* 31 (1971): 179–200.

————. *K'ang-hsi and the Consolidation of Ch'ing Rule, 1661–1684*. Chicago: University of Chicago Press, 1976.

Ko, Dorothy. "Private Lives, Public Morality: Women and the State in the Ming-Qing Transition." In *Family Process and Political Process in Modern China*. Taipei: Academia Sinica, Institute of Modern History, 1992.

Kristeller, Paul Oskar. *Eight Philosophers of the Italian Renaissance*. Stanford: Stanford University Press, 1964.

————. *Renaissance Thought: The Classic, Scholastic, and Humanist Strains*. New York: Harper, 1961.

Ku Hsien-ch'eng 顧憲成. *Ching-kao ts'ang-kao* 涇皋藏稿 (Preserved manuscripts of the Riverbank Studio). 3 vols. SKCS chen-pen, ser. 8. Taipei: Shang-wu yin-shu kuan, n.d.

————. *Hsiao-hsin chai cha-chi* 小心齋劄記 (Notes from the Studio of Vigilance). Taipei: Kuang-wen shu-chü, 1975.

————. *Hsiao-hsin chai cha-chi* 小心齋劄記 (Notes from the Studio of Vigilance). SKCS.

————. *Ku Tuan-wen kung i-shu* 顧端文公遺書 (Writings of the late Ku Hsien-ch'eng). K'ang-hsi ed.

Ku Kung-hsieh 顧公燮. *Hsiao-hsia hsien-chi tsa-ch'ao* 消夏閑記雜抄 (Desultory scribblings that whiled away the summer). In *Han-fen lou mi-chi* 涵芬樓秘笈, vol. 9. Taipei: Shang-wu yin-shu kuan, 1967.

Ku Tung-kao 顧棟高. *Ch'un-ch'iu ta-shih piao* 春秋大事表 (Tables of momentous events during the Spring and Autumn period). 1888.

Ku Yen-wu 顧炎武. *Jih-chih lu chi-shih* 日知錄集釋 (Collected annotations on *Records of Daily Learning*), ed. Huang Ju-ch'eng 黃汝成. 4 vols. SPPY.

————. *Ku T'ing-lin shih wen chi* 顧亭林詩文集 (Collected prose and poetry of Ku Yen-wu). Peking: Chung-hua shu-chü, 1983.

————. *Wu-ching t'ung-i* 五經同異 (Concordances and differences in the Five Classics). In *T'ing-lin i-shu* 亭林遺書 (Writings of the late Ku Yen-wu). 1888.

Ku Yün-ch'eng 顧允成. *Hsiao-pien chai ou-ts'un* 小辨齋偶存 (Casually kept [writings] from the Hsiao-pien Studio). SKCS, vol. 1292.

Kuan Chih-tao 管志道. *T'i-jo chai chi* 惕若齋集 (Collected writings from the Studio of Worrying About Danger).

Kuhn, Philip A. "Local Self-Government Under the Republic: Problems of Control, Autonomy, and Mobilization." In Frederic Wakeman, Jr., and Carolyn Grant, eds., *Conflict and Control in Late Imperial China*. Berkeley: University of California Press, 1975.

————. *Rebellion and Its Enemies in Late Imperial China: Militarization and Social Structure, 1796–1864*. Cambridge, Mass.: Harvard University Press, 1970.

Kung Tzu-chen 龔自珍. *Kung Tzu-chen ch'üan chi* 龔自珍全集 (Complete writings of Kung Tzu-chen). Shanghai: Jen-min ch'u-pan she, 1975.

K'ung Ying-ta 孔穎達. *Li-chi cheng-i* 禮記正義 (Correct meanings of the *Book of Rites*). SSCCS.

Kuo Sung-t'ao 郭嵩燾. *Kuo Sung-t'ao shih-wen chi* 郭嵩燾詩文集 (Collected prose and poetry of Kuo Sung-t'ao). Changsha: Yüeh-lu shu-she, 1984.

Lai Fang-ling 賴芳玲. "*Yüeh-wei ts'ao t'ang pi-chi* yen-chiu" 閱微草堂筆記研究 (A study of *Notes from the Yüeh-wei Hut*). M.A. thesis, National Taiwan University, 1982.

Lamley, Harry J. "Hsieh-tou: The Pathology of Violence in Southern China." *Ch'ing-shih wen-t'i* 3, no. 7 (Nov. 1977): 1–39.

———. "Lineage and Surname Feuds in Southern Fukien and Eastern Kwangtung Under the Ch'ing." In Kwang-ching Liu, ed., *Orthodoxy in Late Imperial China*. Berkeley: University of California Press, 1990.

Lan Ting-yüan 藍鼎元. *Lu-chou kung-an* 鹿洲公案 (Legal cases [tried by] Lan Ting-yüan). Kweichow: Chün-chung ch'u-pan she, 1985.

Langlois, John D., Jr. "Chinese Culturalism and the Yüan Analogy: Seventeenth-Century Perspectives." *HJAS* 40, no. 1 (June 1980): 355–98.

Langlois, John D., Jr., and K'o-k'uan Sun. "Three Teachings Syncretism and the Thought of Ming T'ai-tsu." *HJAS* 43, no. 1 (June 1983): 97–139.

Leung, Angela [Liang Ch'i-tzu] 梁其姿. "Ming-mo Ch'ing-ch'u min-chien tz'u-shan huo-tung ti hsing-ch'i: i Chiang-che ti-ch'ü wei li" 明末清初民間慈善活動的興起：以江浙地區為例 (The rise of private philanthropy in the late Ming and early Ch'ing: Kiangsu and Chekiang). *Shih-huo* 食貨, n.s., 15, nos. 7–8 (Jan. 1986): 52–79.

———. "To Chasten the Society: The Development of Widow Homes in the Ch'ing, 1773–1911." In *Family Process and Political Process in Modern China*. Taipei: Academia Sinica, Institute of Modern History, 1992.

Levenson, Joseph R. *Confucian China and Its Modern Fate: A Trilogy*. Berkeley: University of California Press, 1965.

Lewis, Mark Edward. *Sanctioned Violence in Early China*. New York: State University of New York Press, 1990.

Li Chao-lo 李兆洛. *Yang-i chai wen-chi* 養一齋文集 (Collected writings from the Studio of Nurturing Oneness). 1874.

Li Chih 李贄. *Fen-shu* 焚書 (A book to be burned). Peking: Chung-hua shu-chü, 1975.

———. *Tsang-shu* 藏書 (Books to be hidden away). Peking: Chung-hua shu-chü, 1959.

Li Fu 李紱. *Mu-t'ang ch'u-kao* 穆堂初稿 (Manuscripts from the Solemn Hall). 1740.

———. *Mu-t'ang pieh-kao* 穆堂別稿 (Supplements to the Writings of Solemn Hall). 1747.

Li Hsin-ta 李新達. "Kuan-yü Man-chou ch'i-chih yü Han-chün ch'i-chih ti shih-chien wen-t'i" 關於滿洲旗制與漢軍旗制的始建問題 (On the initial date of the founding of the Manchu and Chinese Banner companies). *Ch'ing-shih lun-ts'ung* 清史論叢 1982, no. 4 (Dec.): 216–23.

Li Huan 李桓, ed. *Kuo-ch'ao ch'i-hsien lei-cheng* 國朝耆獻類徵 (Collected and classified biographies of elders from the present [Ch'ing] dynasty). 25 vols. Taipei: Wen-ch'eng ch'u-pan she, 1966.

Li Jo-yü 李若愚. "Ts'ung Ming-tai ti ch'i-yüeh k'an Ming-tai ti pi-chih" 從明代的契約看明代的幣制 (A discussion of currency in the Ming based on contracts). *Chung-kuo ching-chi shih yen-chiu* 中國經濟史研究 1988, no. 4: 39–43.

Li Kuang-ti 李光地. *Jung-ts'un chi* 榕村集 (Collected writings of Jung-ts'un). SKCS, vol. 1324.

————, comp. *Chu-tzu li-tsuan* 朱子禮纂 (Collected of Chu Hsi's [remarks on] ritual). SKCS, vol. 142.

Li Kung 李塨. *Chiao-she k'ao-pien* 郊社考辨 (A critical study of the *chiao-she* ceremonies. YLTS.

————. *Chou-i chuan-chu* 周易傳註 (Annoted commentary on the *Book of Changes*). YLTS.

————. *Hsüeh-li* 學禮 (Learning rituals). TSCCHP, vol. 34.

————. *Lun hsüeh* 論學 (On learning). YLTS.

————. *Lun-yü chuan-chu wen* 論語傳註問 (Questions about commentaries on the *Analects*). YLTS.

————. *Shu-ku hou-chi* 恕谷後集 (Recent collection of Li Kung's writings). TSCCCP.

————. *Ta-hsüeh pien-yeh* 大學辨業 (Exercises in defending the *Great Learning*). YLTS.

————. *Ti-hsia k'ao-pien* 禘祫考辨 (A critical study of the rites of *ti* and *hsia*). YLTS.

————. *Tsung-miao k'ao-pien* 宗廟考辨 (A critical study of temple systems). YLTS.

————. *Yen Hsi-chai nien-p'u* 顏習齋年譜 (Chronological biography of Yen Yüan). In *YLHP*.

Li Wen-chih 李文治. "Lun Ming-Ch'ing shih-tai ti tsung-tsu chih" 論明清時代的宗族制 (On the lineage institutions of Ming-Ch'ing times). *Ching-chi yen-chiu so chi-k'an* 經濟研究所集刊 1983, no. 4: 278–338.

Li Yüan-tu 李元度. *Kuo-ch'ao hsien-cheng shih-lüeh* 國朝先正事略 (Survey of earlier upright scholars of the present [Ch'ing] dynasty). SPPY.

Li Yün-kuang 李雲光. *San-li Cheng shih hsüeh fa-fan* 三禮鄭氏學發凡 (Study guide to Cheng Hsüan's learning of the three ritual Classics). Taipei: Chia-hsin shui-ni kung-ssu, 1966.

Liang Chang-chü 梁章鉅. *Kuei-t'ien so-chi* 歸田瑣記 (Miscellaneous notes on returning to the field). Peking: Chung-hua shu-chü, 1981.

Liang Ch'i-ch'ao 梁啓超. *Chung-kuo chin san pai nien hsüeh-shu shih* 中國近三百年學術史 (History of Chinese thought during the past three centuries). Shanghai: Chung-hua shu-chü, 1937.

Liang Fang-chung 梁方仲. "I-t'iao-pien-fa" 一條鞭法 (The single-whip method). *Chung-kuo chin-tai ching-chi-shih yen-chiu chi-k'an* 中國近代經濟史研究集刊 4, no. 1 (1936).

Liang Hsüeh-lang 梁雪郎. "Ch'ing Ch'u wen-tzu yü yü yü-lun" 清初文字獄與輿論 (Literary inquisitions and public opinion in the early Ch'ing). M.A. thesis, Cheng-chih ta-hsüeh, Taipei, 1960.

Liang Ju-yüan 梁汝元 [Ho Hsin-yin]. *Ho Hsin-yin chi* 何心隱集 (Collected works of Ho Hsin-yin). Ed. Jung Chao-tsu 容肇祖. Peking: Chung-hua shu-chü, 1960.

Lin Ch'ing-chang 林慶彰. *Ming-tai k'ao-chü hsüeh yen-chiu* 明代考據學研究 (A study of philological scholarship in the Ming). Taipei: Hsüeh-sheng shu-chü, 1983.

Lin Li-yüeh 林麗月. "Ming-mo Tung-lin yün-tung ch'u-t'an" 明末東林運動初探 (A preliminary examination of the Tung-lin movement of the Late Ming). Ph.D. dissertation, Taiwan Normal University, Institute for Historical Research, 1984.

—————. "Min-nan shih-shen yü Chia-ching nien-chien ti hai-shang tsou-ssu mao-i" 閩南士紳與嘉靖年間的海上走私貿易 (Southern Fukien gentry and the illegal coastal trade during the Chia-ching reign). *Ming shih yen-chiu lun-ts'ung* 明史研究論叢 (Taipei), ser. 2 (1984): 399–426.

Lin, Yü-sheng. *The Crisis of Chinese Consciousness: Radical Anti-Traditionalism in the May Fourth Era*. Madison: University of Wisconsin Press, 1979.

—————. "The Evolution of the Pre-Confucian Meaning of *Jen* and the Confucian Conception of Moral Autonomy." *Monumenta Serica* 31 (1974–75): 172–204.

Ling Hsi-ch'i 凌錫祺. *Lu-tzu nien-p'u* 陸子年譜 (Chronological biography of Lu Shih-i). In *Lu-tzu i-shu* 陸子遺書 (Writings of the late Lu Shih-i). 1899.

Ling T'ing-k'an 凌廷堪. *Chiao-li t'ang wen-chi* 校禮堂文集 (Collected writings from the Studio for Collating Rituals). In *Ling Chung-tzu i-shu* 凌仲子遺書.

—————. *Ling Chung-tzu i-shu* (Writings of the late Mr. Ling T'ing-k'an). An-hui ts'ung-shu, ser. 4. Anhwei, 1935

Liu Chih-ch'in 劉志琴. "Shih-lun Wan-li min-pien" 試論萬曆民變 (A preliminary study of popular riots in the Wan-li reign). In *Ming-Ch'ing shih kuo-chi hsüeh-shu t'ao lun hui* 明清史國際學術討論會 (International Symposium on Ming-Ch'ing History). Tientsin: n.p., 1982.

Liu Feng-lu 劉逢祿. *Liu Li-pu chi* 劉禮部集 (Collected writings of Liu Feng-lu). 1830.

Liu, Hui-chen Wang. *The Traditional Chinese Clan Rules*. Monographs of the Association for Asian Studies, no. 7. New York: Augustin, 1959.

Liu I-cheng 柳詒徵. *Chung-kuo wen-hua shih* 中國文化史 (A cultural history of China), vol. 2. Taipei: Cheng-chung shu-chü, 1958.

Liu, James T. C. *Ou-yang Hsiu: An Eleventh-Century Neo-Confucianist*. Stanford: Stanford University Press, 1967.

Liu, Kwang-ching [Liu Kuang-ching] 劉廣京. "The Ch'ing Restoration." In John King Fairbank and Kwang-ching Liu, eds., *The Cambridge History of China*, vol. 10, pt. 1. Cambridge, Eng.: Cambridge University Press, 1978.

—————. "Education for Its Own Sake: Notes on Tseng Kuo-fan's *Family Letters*." In Benjamin A. Elman and Alexander Woodside, eds., *Society and Education in Late Imperial China*. Berkeley: University of California Press, forthcoming.

—————. "The Military Challenge: The North-West and the Coast." In John King Fairbank and Kwang-ching Liu, eds., *The Cambridge History of China*, vol. 11, pt. 2. Cambridge, Eng.: Cambridge University Press, 1980.

————. "Socio-ethics as Orthodoxy: A Perspective." In idem, ed., *Orthodoxy in Late Imperial China*. Berkeley: University of California Press, 1990.

————. "Wei Yüan chih che-hsüeh yü ching-shih ssu-hsiang" 魏源之哲學與經世思想 (The philosophy and thinking on statecraft of Wei Yüan). In *Chin-shih Chung-kuo ching-shih ssu-hsiang yen-t'ao hui lun-wen chi* 近世中國經世思想研討會論文集 (Proceedings of the Conference on the Theory of Statecraft of Modern China). Taipei: Academia Sinica, Insitute of Modern History, 1984.

Liu Tsung-chou 劉宗周. *Liu Chi-shan chi* 劉蕺山集 (Collected writings of Liu Tsung-chou). SKCS, vol. 1294.

————. *Liu-tzu ch'üan-shu* 劉子全書 (Complete works of Liu Tsung-chou). Chung-hua wen-shih ts'ung-shu 中華文史叢書, ser. 7. Taipei: Hua-wen shu-chü, 1976.

Lo Lun 羅倫. *I-feng wen-chi* 一峰文集 (Collected writings of Lo Lun). SKCS chen-pen, ser. 4.

Lu Lung-ch'i 陸隴其. *Lu Chia-shu hsien-sheng wen-chi* 陸稼書先生文集 (Collected writings of Lu Lung-ch'i). Ts'ung-shu chi-ch'eng chien-pien.

————. *Tu-li chih-i* 讀禮質疑 (Doubts raised in studying rituals). TSCCHP, vol. 10.

Lu Pao-ch'ien 陸寶千. *Ch'ing-tai ssu-hsiang shih* 清代思想史 (Intellectual history of the Ch'ing period). Taipei: Kuang-wen shu-chü, 1978.

Lu Shih-i 陸世儀. *Ssu-pien lu chi-yao* 思辨錄輯要 (Selected records of reflections). TSCCHP, vol. 23.

Lu Wen-ch'ao 盧文弨. *Pao-ching t'ang wen-chi* 抱經堂文集 (Collected writings from the Studio of Embracing the Classics). TSCCCP.

Lü K'un 呂坤. *Ssu-li i* 四禮疑 (Doubts about four [orders] of rituals).

Lü Liu-liang 呂留良. *Lü Wan-ts'un hsien-sheng wen-chi* 呂晚村先生文集 (Collected writings of Lü Liu-liang). Taipei: Chung-ting wen-hua kung-ssu, 1967.

Lung Wen-pin 龍文彬. *Ming hui-yao* 明會要 (Collection of essential institutes of the Ming). Taipei: Shih-chieh shu-chü, 1963.

Ma T'ai-hsüan 馬太玄. "Wan Ssu-t'ung ti sheng-p'ing chi ch'i chu-shu" 萬斯同的生平及其著述 (The life and writings of Wan Ssu-t'ung). In *Chung-kuo chin san-pai-nien hsüeh-shu ssu-hsiang shih lun-chi* 中國近三百年學術思想史論集 (Historical essays on Chinese thought during the past three centuries), vol. 3. Hong Kong: Ts'un-ts'ui hsüeh-she, 1972.

Ma Tuan-lin 馬端臨. *Wen-hsien t'ung-k'ao* 文獻通考 (Comprehensive documents of statues). In *Shih-t'ung* 十通. 24 vols. KHCPTS.

Mackerras, Colin. "The Drama of the Qing Dynasty." In idem, ed., *Chinese Theater: From Its Origins to the Present Day*. Honolulu: University of Hawaii Press, 1983.

————. *The Rise of the Peking Opera*. London: Oxford University Press, 1972.

Mann, Nicholas. "Petrarch's Role as Moralist in Fifteenth-Century France." In A. H. T. Levi, ed. *Humanism in France at the End of the Middle Ages and in the Early Renaissance*. New York: Barnes & Noble, 1970.

Mann [Jones], Susan. "Classical Revival and the Gender Question: China's First

Quérelle des Femmes." In *Family Process and Political Process in Modern Chinese History*. Taipei: Academia Sinica, Modern Institute of History, 1992.

———. "Grooming a Daughter for Marriage: Brides and Wives in the Mid-Ch'ing Period." In Rubie S. Watson and Patricia Buckley Ebrey, eds., *Marriage and Inequality in Chinese Society*. Berkeley: University of California Press, 1991.

———. *Local Merchants and the Chinese Bureaucracy, 1750–1950*. Stanford: Stanford University Press, 1987.

———. "Scholasticism and Politics in Late Eighteenth Century China." *Ch'ing-shih wen-t'i* 3, no. 4 (Dec. 1975): 28–49.

———. "Widows in the Kinship, Class, and Community Structures of Qing Dynasty China," *JAS* 46 (1987): 37–56.

Mao Ch'i-ling 毛奇齡. *Chiao, she, ti, hsia wen* 郊社禘祫問 (Questions regarding *chiao, she, ti,* and *hsia*). TSCCHP, vol. 35.

———. *Hsi-ho wen-chi* 西河文集 (Collected writings of Mao Ch'i-ling). KHCPTS.

———. *Miao-chih che-chung* 廟制折衷 (Reconciled view of temple system). In *Hsi-ho ho-chi* 西河合集 (Composite works of Mao Ch'i-ling). 1770.

———. *Pien-ting chi-li t'ung-su p'u* 辨定祭禮通俗譜 (Manual for popular application of clarified ancestral rites). SKCS chen-pen, ser. 9.

———. *Ta-hsiao tsung t'ung-shih* 大小宗通釋 (Systematic explication of the great and lesser descent-lines). TSCCHP, vol. 35.

McDermott, Joseph P. "Bondservants in the T'ai-hu Basin During the Late Ming: A Case of Mistaken Identities." *JAS* 40 (1981): 675–701.

McMahon, Keith. *Causality and Containment in Seventeenth-Century Chinese Fiction*. Monographes du T'oung Pao, vol. 15. Leiden: E. J. Brill, 1988.

McMorran, Ian. "Wang Fu-chih and the Neo-Confucian Tradition." In Wm. Theodore de Bary, ed., *The Unfolding of Neo-Confucianism*. New York: Columbia University Press, 1975.

McMullen, David. *State and Scholars in T'ang China*. New York: Cambridge University Press, 1988.

Meijer, M. J. "The Price of *P'ai-lou*." *T'oung-pao* 67, nos. 3–5 (1981): 288–304.

Meng Sen 孟森. *Ming-tai shih* 明代史 (History of the Ming). Taipei: Chung-hua ts'ung-shu wei-yüan hui, 1957.

Meskill, Johanna M. "The Chinese Genealogy as a Research Guide." In Maurice Freedman, ed., *Family and Kinship in Chinese Society*. Stanford: Stanford University Press, 1970.

Ming shih-lu 明實錄 (Veritable records of the Ming emperors). 133 vols. Taipei: Academia Sinica, Institute of Philology and History, 1962–66.

Mori Masao. "The Gentry in the Ming: An Outline of the Relations Between the *Shih-ta-fu* and Local Gentry." *Acta Asiatica* 38 (Mar. 1980): 31–53.

Mote, Frederick. "The Growth of Chinese Despotism: A Critique of Wittfogel's Theory of Oriental Despotism as Applied to China." *Oriens Extremus* 8, no. 1 (1961): 1–41.

Naquin, Susan. *Millenarian Rebellion in China: The Eight Trigrams Uprising of 1813.* New Haven: Yale University Press, 1976.

————. *Shantung Rebellion: The Wang Lun Uprising of 1774.* New Haven: Yale University Press, 1981.

————. "Two Descent Groups in North China: The Wangs of Yung-p'ing Prefecture, 1500–1800." In Patricia B. Ebrey and James L. Watson, eds., *Kinship Organization in Late Imperial China, 1400–1900.* Berkeley: University of California, 1986.

Naquin, Susan, and Evelyn S. Rawski. *Chinese Society in the Eighteenth Century.* New Haven: Yale University Press, 1987.

Needham, Joseph, et al. *Science and Civilisation in China,* vol. 5, *Chemistry and Chemical Technology,* pt. 1, *Paper and Printing.* Cambridge, Eng.: Cambridge University Press, 1985.

Ng, On-cho. "Text in Context: *Chin-wen* Learning in Ch'ing Thought." Ph.D. dissertation, University of Hawaii, 1986.

Ng, Vivien W. "Ideology and Sexuality: Rape Laws in Qing China." *JAS* 46 (1987): 57–70.

Nivison, David S. *The Life and Thought of Chang Hsüeh-ch'eng.* Stanford: Stanford University Press, 1966.

Ocko, Jonathan K. "Hierarchy and Harmony: Family Conflict as Seen in Ch'ing Legal Cases." In Kwang-ching Liu, ed., *Orthodoxy in Late Imperial China.* Berkeley: University of California Press, 1990.

Ono Kazuko 小野和子. "Shinsho no kōkeikai ni tsuite" 清初の講経会について (Concerning the Society for the Discussion of the Classics in the early Ch'ing). *Tōhō gaku hō* 東方学報 36 (1964): 633–61.

Oyama Masaaki 小山正明. "Minmatsu Shinsho no daitochi shoyū: toku ni Kōnan deruta chitai o chūshin ni shite" 明末清初の大土地所有:とくに江南デルタ地帯を中心にして (Large landholdings in the late Ming and early Ch'ing: The Kiangnan Delta). *Shigaku zashi* 史學雜志 66 (1957): 1–30; 67, no. 1 (1957): 50–72.

Palmer, Richard E. *Hermeneutics.* Evanston, Ill.: Northwestern University Press, 1969.

Parsons, James Bunyan. *Peasant Rebellions of the Late Ming Dynasty.* Tucson: University of Arizona Press, 1970.

Peterson, Willard J. *Bitter Gourd: Fang I-chih and the Impetus for Intellectual Change.* New Haven: Yale University Press, 1979.

————. "From Interest to Indifference: Fang I-chih and Western Learning." *Ch'ing-shih wen-t'i* 3, no. 5 (Nov. 1976): 72–85.

————. "The Life of Ku Yen-wu (1613–1682)." *HJAS* 28 (1968): 114–56; 29 (1969): 201–47.

Pi Hsi-jui 皮錫瑞. *Ching-hsüeh li-shih* 經學歷史 (History of Classical learning). Hong Kong: Chung-hua shu-chü, 1961.

————. *Ching-hsüeh t'ung-lun* 經學通論 (General discussions on Classical learning). Hong Kong: Chung-hua shu-chü, 1961.

Plaks, Andrew. *The Four Masterworks of the Ming Novel*. Princeton: Princeton University Press, 1987.

Rankin, Mary Backus. *Elite Activism and Political Transformation in China, Zhejiang Province, 1865-1911*. Stanford: Stanford University Press, 1986.

―――. "The Emergence of Women at the End of the Ch'ing: The Case of Ch'iu Chin." In Margery Wolf and Roxane Witke, eds., *Women in Chinese Society*. Stanford: Stanford University Press, 1975.

Rawski, Evelyn S. "Economic and Social Foundations of Late Imperial Culture." In David Johnson, Andrew J. Nathan, and Evelyn S. Rawski, eds., *Popular Culture in Late Imperial China*. Berkeley: University of California Press, 1985.

―――. *Education and Popular Literacy in Ch'ing China*. Ann Arbor: University of Michigan Press, 1979.

―――. "A Historian's Approach to Chinese Death Ritual." In James L. Watson and Evelyn S. Rawski, eds., *Death Ritual in Late Imperial and Modern China*. Berkeley: University of California Press, 1988.

Robinson, James M. "Hermeneutics Since Barth." In James M. Robinson and John B. Cobb, eds., *The New Hermeneutics*. New Frontiers in Theology, vol. 1. New York: Harper & Row, 1964.

Ropp, Paul S. *Dissent in Early Modern China: "Ju-lin wai-shih" and Ch'ing Social Criticism*. Ann Arbor: University of Michigan Press, 1981.

Roth, Gertraude. "The Manchu-Chinese Relationship, 1618-1636." In Jonathan D. Spence and John E. Wills, Jr., eds., *From Ming to Ch'ing: Conquest, Region, and Continuity in Seventeenth-Century China*. New Haven: Yale University Press, 1979.

Rowe, William T. "Women and the Family in Mid-Ch'ing Social Thought: The Case of Ch'en Hung-mou." In *Family Process and Political Process in Modern Chinese History*. Taipei: Academia Sinica, Institute of Modern History, 1992.

Sakai Tadao. "Confucianism and Popular Educational Works." In Wm. Theodore de Bary, ed., *Self and Society in Ming Thought*. New York: Columbia University Press, 1970.

Sangren, P. Steven. "Traditional Chinese Corporations: Beyond Kinship." *JAS* 43 (1984): 391-415.

Sarton, George. "The Quest for Truth: Scientific Progress During the Renaissance." In Wallace K. Ferguson et al., *The Renaissance: Six Essays*. New York: Harper Torchbooks, 1962.

Schoppa, R. Keith. *Chinese Elites and Political Change: Zhejiang Province in the Early Twentieth Century*. Cambridge, Mass.: Harvard University Press, 1982.

Schwartz, Benjamin. "Foreword." In Liang Ch'i-ch'ao, *Intellectual Trends in the Ch'ing Period*. Tr. Immanuel C. Y. Hsü. Cambridge, Mass.: Harvard University Press, 1959.

―――. *The World of Thought in Ancient China*. Cambridge, Mass.: Harvard University Press, 1985.

Shek, Richard Hon-chun. "Religion and Society in Late Ming: Sectarianism and Popular Thought in Sixteenth–Seventeenth Century China." Ph.D. dissertation, University of California, Berkeley, 1980.

Shen Ch'ao-yang 沈朝陽. *Huang-Ming Chia–Lung liang-ch'ao wen-chien chi* 皇明嘉隆兩朝聞見記 (Collection of records of things seen and heard during the Chia-ching and Lung-ch'ing reigns). Taipei: Hsüeh-sheng shu-chü, 1969.

Shen T'ung 沈彤. *Chou-kuan lu-t'ien k'ao* 周官祿田考 (Study of remunerative estates in the *Rites of Chou*). SKCS, vol. 101.

————. *Kuo-t'ang chi* 果堂集 (Collected writings of Shen T'ung). SKCS chen-pen, ser. 4.

Sheng K'ang 盛康. *Huang-ch'ao ching-shih wen-pien hsü-pien* 皇朝經世文編續編 (Collected Ch'ing dynasty writings on statecraft, continued). Chin-tai Chung-kuo shih-liao ts'ung-k'an 近代中國史料叢刊, ser. 85. Taipei: Wen-hai ch'u-pan she, 1972.

Siu, Helen. "Where Were the Women? Rethinking Marriage Resistance and Regional Culture in South China." *Late Imperial China*, 11, no. 2 (Dec. 1990): 32–62.

Skinner, G. William. "Introduction: Urban Development in Imperial China." In idem, ed., *The City in Late Imperial China*. Stanford: Stanford University Press, 1977.

Smith, Joanna Handlin. *Action in Late Ming Thought: The Orientation of Lü K'un and Other Scholar-Officials*. Berkeley: University of California Press, 1983.

————. "Benevolent Societies: The Reshaping of Charity During the Late Ming and Early Ch'ing." *JAS* 46 (1987): 309–37.

————. "Lü K'un's New Audience: The Influence of Women's Literacy on Sixteenth-Century Thought." In Margery Wolf and Roxane Witke, eds., *Women in Chinese Society*. Stanford: Stanford University Press, 1975.

Smith, Richard J. "Ritual in Ch'ing Culture." In Kwang-ching Liu, ed. *Orthodoxy in Late Imperial China*. Berkeley: University of California Press, 1990.

Spence, Jonathan D. *The Death of Woman Wong*. New York: Penguin Books, 1980.

————. *Ts'ao Yin and the K'ang-hsi Emperor, Bondservant and Master*. New Haven: Yale University Press, 1966.

Spence, Jonathan D., and John E. Wills, eds. *From Ming to Ch'ing: Conquest, Region, and Continuity in Seventeenth-Century China*. New Haven: Yale University Press, 1979.

Ssu-k'u ch'üan-shu tsung-mu t'i-yao 四庫全書總目提要 (Concise annotated catalogue of the complete collection of the Four Treasuries). Chi Yün 紀昀 et al. KHCPTS.

Stockard, Janice E. *Daughters of the Canton Delta*. Stanford: Stanford University Press, 1989.

Strassberg, Richard E. *The World of K'ung Sheng-jen: A Man of Letters in Early Ch'ing China*. New York: Columbia University Press, 1983.

Struve, Lynn A. "Ambivalence and Action: Some Frustrated Scholars of the

K'ang-hsi Period." In Jonathan D. Spence and John E. Wills, Jr., eds., *From Ming to Ch'ing: Conquest, Region, and Continuity in Seventeenth-Century China*. New Haven: Yale University Press, 1979.

————. "The Early Ch'ing Legacy of Huang Tsung-hsi: A Reexamination." *Asia Major*, 3rd ser., 1, pt. 1 (1988): 83–122.

————. "Huang Zongxi in Context: A Reappraisal of His Major Writings." *JAS* 47 (1988): 474–502.

————. *The Southern Ming, 1644–1662*. New Haven: Yale University Press, 1984.

Su Po-heng 蘇伯衡. *Su P'ing-chung chi* 蘇平仲集 (Collected writings of Su Po-heng). TSCCHP, vol. 67.

Sun Ch'i-feng 孫奇逢. *Hsia-feng hsien-sheng chi* 夏峰先生集 (Collected writings of Mr. Sun Ch'i-feng). TSCCCP.

Sung shih 宋史 (History of the Sung dynasty). Peking: Chung-hua shu-chü, 1977.

Sweeten, Alan Richard. "Women and Law in Rural China: Vignettes from Sectarian Cases (*Chiao-an*) in Kiangsi, 1872–1878." *Ch'ing-shih wen-t'i* 3, no. 10 (Dec. 1978): 49–68.

Ta-Ch'ing li-ch'ao shih-lu 大清歷朝實錄 (Veritable records of successive reigns of the Ch'ing dynasty). 30 vols. Taipei: Hua-wen shu-chü, 1964.

Ta-Ming hui-tien 大明會典 (Collected statutes of the Ming empire). Comp. Shen Shih-hsing 申時行 and Li Tung-yang 李東陽. Taipei: Tung-nan shu-pao she, n.d. Reprint of 1587.

Taga Akigorō 多賀秋五郎. *Sōfu no kenkyū* 宗譜の研究 (A study of [Chinese] genealogies). Tokyo: Tōyō Bunko, 1960.

Tai Chen 戴震. *Meng-tzu tzu-i shu-cheng* 孟子字義疏證 (Verification of the literal meanings of the *Mencius*). In *Tai Chen chi* 戴震集 (Collected writings of Tai Chen). Shanghai: Ku-chi ch'u-pan she, 1980.

————. *Tai Chen chi* 戴震集 (Collected writings of Tai Chen). Shanghai: Ku-chi ch'u-pan she, 1980.

Tai Chün-jen 戴君仁. "Shu Chang Erh-ch'i *I-li Cheng-chu chü-tu* hou" 書張爾岐儀禮鄭注句讀後 (Comment on Chang Erh-ch'i's *I-li Cheng-chu chü-tu*). *Shu-mu chi-k'an* 書目季刊 1, no. 1 (Sept. 1955): 51–55.

T'an Ssu-t'ung 譚嗣同. *T'an Ssu-t'ung ch'üan-chi* 譚嗣同全集 (Complete writings of T'an Ssu-t'ung). Ed. Ts'ai Shang-ssu 蔡尚思 and Fang Hsing 方行. Peking: Chung-hua shu-chü, 1981.

T'an Ti-hua 譚棣華. "Kuan-yü Ch'ing chung-yeh i-hou Chu-chiang san-chiao chou hao-tsu ti fu-i cheng-shou wen-t'i" 關於清中葉以後珠江三角洲豪族的賦役徵收問題 (On issues regarding the collection of tax and corvée among powerful lineages in the Canton Delta after the mid-Ch'ing period). *Ch'ing-shih yen-ch'iu t'ung-hsin* 清史研究通信 1985, no. 2: 1–4.

————. "Lüeh-lun Ch'ing-tai tsung-tsu chih-tu" 略論清代宗族制度 (A brief study of Ch'ing lineage institutions). *Ch'ing-shih yen-chiu t'ung-hsin* 清史研究通信 1985, no. 3: 6–11.

T'an Ti-hua 譚棣華 and Yeh Hsien-en 葉顯恩. "Feng-chien tsung-fa shih-li tui Fo-shan ching-chi ti k'ung-chih chi ch'i ch'an-sheng ti ying-hsiang" 封建宗法 勢力對佛山經濟的控制及其產生的影響 (The feudal patrilineal establishment's control of the economy of Fo-shan and its consequences). In *Ming-Ch'ing Kuang-tung she-hui ching-chi hsing-t'ai yen-chiu* 明清廣東社會經濟形態 研究 (Studies in the social and economic patterns of Kwangtung during the Ming and Ch'ing periods). Kwangtung: Jen-min ch'u-pan she, 1985.

Tanaka Issei 田仲一成. "Shindai Setsutō sōzoku no soshiki keisei ni okeru sōshi engeki no kinō ni tsuite" 清代浙東宗族の組織形成における宗祠演劇の機能につ いて (A study of the function of ritual drama in the formation of lineage in eastern Chekiang during the Ch'ing period). *Tōyōshi Kenkyū* 東洋史研究 44 (1986): 32–67.

―――. "The Social and Historical Context of Ming-Ch'ing Local Drama." In David Johnson, Andrew J. Nathan, and Evelyn S. Rawski, eds., *Popular Culture in Late Imperial China*. Berkeley: University of California Press, 1985.

Tanaka Masatoshi. "Popular Uprisings, Rent Resistance, and Bondservant Rebellions in the Late Ming." In Linda Grove and Christian Daniels, eds., *State and Society in China: Japanese Perspectives on Ming-Qing Social and Economic History*. Tokyo: University of Tokyo Press, 1984.

T'ang Chien 唐鑑. *Ch'ing hsüeh-an hsiao shih* 清學案小識 (Brief notes on case studies of the Ch'ing period). Taipei: Shang-wu yin-shu kuan, 1975.

T'ang Chih-chün 湯志鈞. "Ch'ing-tai ching chin-wen hsüeh ti fu-hsing" 清代 經今文學的復興 (The Ch'ing revival of the New Text Classical tradition). *Chung-kuo shih yen-chiu* 中國史研究 1980, no. 2 (June): 145–56.

T'ang Chün-i 唐君毅. *Chung-kuo che-hsüeh yüan-lun: tao-lun pien* 中國哲學原論: 導論編 (Studies of the foundations of Chinese philosophy: introductory volume). Hong Kong: Hsin-ya shu-yüan yen-chiu so, 1974.

―――. "The Development of the Concept of Moral Mind from Wang Yang-ming to Wang Chi." In Wm. Theodore de Bary, ed., *Self and Society in Ming Thought*. New York: Columbia University Press, 1970.

―――. "Liu Tsung-chou's Doctrine of Moral Mind and Practice and His Critique of Wang Yang-ming." In Wm. Theodore de Bary, ed., *The Unfolding of Neo-Confucianism*. New York: Columbia University Press, 1975.

T'ang Pin 湯斌. *T'ang Ch'ien-an chi* 湯潛庵集 (Collected writings of T'ang Pin). TSCCCP.

T'ang Wen-chi 唐文基. *Ming-tai fu-i chih-tu shih* 明代賦役制度史 (A fiscal history of the Ming dynasty). N.p.: Chung-kuo she-hui k'o-hsüeh chu-pan she, 1991.

T'ang Yü-yüan 唐宇元. "Yüan-tai Liu Yin ti ssu-hsiang" 元代劉因的思想 (The thought of Liu Yin of the Yüan dynasty). *Chung-kuo shih yen-chiu* 中國史研究 1982, no. 3 (Sept.): 135–46.

Tatsuo Chikusa. "Succession to Ancestral Sacrifices and Adoption of Heirs." In

David C. Buxbaum, ed., *Chinese Family Law and Social Change in Historical Perspective*. Seattle: University of Washington Press, 1978.

Taylor, Romeyn. "Official and Popular Religion and the Political Organization of Chinese Society in the Ming." In Kwang-ching Liu, ed., *Orthodoxy in Late Imperial China*. Berkeley: University of California Press, 1990.

Telford, Ted A., et al. *Chinese Genealogies at the Genealogical Society of Utah: An Annotated Bibliography*. Taipei: Ch'eng-wen, 1983.

Teng Ch'iu 鄧球. *Huang-Ming yung-hua lei-pien* 皇明泳化類編 (Didactic and laudatory writings, by category). Taipei: Kuo-feng ch'u-pan she, 1965.

T'ien Ju-k'ang. *Male Anxiety and Female Chastity: A Comparative Study of Chinese Ethical Values in the Ming-Ch'ing Times*. Leiden: E. J. Brill, 1988.

Tillman, Hoyt. "A New Direction in Confucian Scholarship: Approaches to Examining the Differences Between Neo-Confucianism and *Tao-hsüeh*." *Philosophy East and West* (1992): 455–74.

Ting, Pang-hsin. "Chinese Phonology of the Wei-Chin Period: Reconstruction of the Finals as Reflected in Poetry." Ph.D. dissertation, University of Washington, 1972.

Tong, James. *Disorder Under Heaven: Collective Violence in the Ming Dynasty*. Stanford: Stanford University Press, 1992.

Topley, Majorie. "Marriage Resistance in Rural Kwangtung." In Arthur P. Wolf, ed., *Studies in Chinese Society*. Stanford: Stanford University Press, 1978.

Tseng Chao 曾釗. *Mien-ch'eng lou tsa ch'ao* 面城樓雜鈔 (Miscellaneous writings from the Tower Facing the Walled City). Hsüeh-hai t'ang ts'ung-k'o 學海堂叢刻, ser. 2.

Tso Yün-p'eng 左雲鵬. "Tz'u-t'ang tsu-chang tsu-ch'üan ti hsing-ch'eng chi ch'i tso-yung shuo" 祠堂族長族權的形成及其作用說 (On the development of ancestral halls, lineage heads, and lineage power). *Li-shih yen-chiu* 歷史研究 1964, nos. 5–6 (Dec.): 97–116.

Ts'ui Shu 崔述. *Ts'ui Tung-pi i-shu* 崔東壁遺書 (Writings of the late Ts'ui Shu). Shanghai: Ku-chi ch'u-pan she, 1983.

Ts'ung Hsiao-p'ing 叢小平. "Li Yung ti hui-kuo tzu-hsin shuo" 李顒的悔過自新說 (Li Yung's teaching: "Confess and Renew"). In Chung-kuo che-hsüeh shih-hsüeh hui 中國哲學史學會 and Che-chiang sheng she-hui k'o-hsüeh yen-chiu so 浙江省社會科學研究所, eds. *Lun Chung-kuo che-hsüeh shih* 論中國哲學史 (On the history of Chinese philosophy). Chekiang: Jen-min ch'u-pan she, 1983.

Tu Wan-yen 杜婉言 and Wang Ch'un-yü 王春喻. *Ming-tai huan-kuan yü ching-chi shih-liao ch'u-t'an* 明代宦官與經濟史料初探 (A preliminary study of the historical sources on the relationship of eunuchs to the Ming economy). Peking: Chung-kuo she-hui k'o-hsüeh ch'u-pan she, 1986)

———. "Ming-tai huan-kuan yü Ming-tai ching-chi" 明代宦官與明代經濟 (Eunuchs and economy in the Ming dynasty). *Chung-kuo shih yen-chiu* 中國史研究 1982, no. 2 (June): 50–65.

Tu Wei-ming. *Neo-Confucian Thought in Action: Wang Yang-ming's Youth (1472-1509)*. Berkeley: University of California Press, 1976.

———. "Yen Yüan: From Inner Experience to Lived Concreteness." In Wm. Theodore de Bary, ed., *The Unfolding of Neo-Confucianism*. New York: Columbia Press, 1975.

Tu Wei-yün 杜維運. *Ch'ing-tai shih-hsüeh yü shih-chia* 清代史學與史家 (Historical studies and historians of the Ch'ing dynasty). Taipei: Tung-ta t'u-shu, 1984.

Tuan Yü-ts'ai 段玉裁. *Ching-yün lou chi* 經韻樓集 (Collected writings from the Chamber of the Rhymes of the Classics). In *Tuan Yü-ts'ai i-shu* 段玉裁遺書 (Writings of the late Tuan Yü-ts'ai). 2 vols. Taipei: Ta-hua shu-chü, 1977.

Turner, Victor. *The Forest of Symbols: Aspects of Ndembu Ritual*. Ithaca, N.Y.: Cornell University Press, 1967.

Twitchett, Dennis. "The Fan Clan's Charitable Estate, 1050–1760." In David S. Nivison and Arthur F. Wright, eds., *Confucianism in Action*. Stanford: Stanford University Press, 1959.

Von Glahn, Richard. "Municipal Reform and Urban Social Conflict in Late Ming Jiangnan." *JAS* 50 (1991): 280–307.

Wakeman, Frederic, Jr. "China and the Seventeenth Century Crisis." *Late Imperial China* 7, no. 1 (June 1986): 1–26.

———. *The Great Enterprise: The Manchu Reconstruction of Imperial Order in Seventeenth-Century China*. 2 vols. Berkeley: University of California Press, 1985.

———. "Localism and Loyalism During the Ch'ing Conquest of Kiangnan: The Tragedy of Chiang-yin." In idem and Carolyn Grant, eds., *Conflict and Control in Late Imperial China*. Berkeley: University of California Press, 1975.

———. "The Shun Interregnum of 1644." In Jonathan D. Spence and John E. Wills, Jr., eds., *From Ming to Ch'ing: Conquest, Region, and Continuity in Seventeenth-Century China*. New Haven: Yale University Press, 1979.

———. *Strangers at the Gate: Social Disorder in South China, 1839–1861*. Berkeley: University of California Press, 1966.

Waltner, Ann. "Widows and Remarriage in Ming and Early Qing China." *Historical Reflection* 8, no. 3 (Fall 1981): 129–46.

Wan Ssu-ta 萬斯大. *Ching-hsüeh wu-shu* 經學五書 (Five studies on the Classics). Preface dated 1796.

———. *Chou-kuan pien-fei* 周官辨非 (Clarifying errors in the *Rites of Chou*). *CHWS*.

———. *Hsüeh-li chih-i* 學禮質疑 (Doubts regarding the study of rituals). *CHWS*.

———. *Hsüeh-li chih-i* 學禮質疑 (Doubts regarding the study of rituals). SKCS, vol. 129.

———. *I-li shang* 儀禮商 (Discussion of the *Book of Etiquette and Decorum*). *CHWS*.

———. *Li-chi ou-chien* 禮記偶箋 (Casual notations on the *Book of Rites*). TSCCHP, vol. 34. Also in *CHWS*.

Wan Ssu-t'ung 萬斯同. *Ch'ün-shu i-pien* 群書疑辨 (Doubts about and criticism of various books). 1816.

Wang Ch'ang 王昶. *Ch'un-jung t'ang chi* 春融堂集 (Collected writings from the Studio of Harmonious Spring). 1892.

Wang Chi 王畿. *Wang Lung-hsi ch'üan-chi* 王龍溪全集 (Complete work of Wang Chi). Taipei: Hua-wen shu-chü, 1970.

Wang Chien 汪鑑, ed. *Chu-tzu chia-li* 朱子家禮 (The Family Rituals by Master Chu). Preface dated 1701.

Wang Chung 汪中. *Jung-fu hsien-sheng i-shu* 容甫先生遺書 (Writings of the late Wang Chung). In *Chiang-tu Wang-shih ts'ung-shu* 江都汪氏叢書 (Collected works of the Wangs of Chiang-tu). 1925.

Wang Fu 汪紱. *Ts'an Tu-li chih-i* 參讀禮質疑 (Collection of [Lu Lung-chi's] *Doubts Raised in Studying Rituals*). SKCS, vol. 129.

Wang Fu-chih 王夫之. *Li-chi chang-chü* 禮記章句 (The *Book of Rites* in chapters and verses). In *Ch'uan-shan i-shu ch'üan-chi* 船山遺書全集 (Complete collected works of the late Wang Fu-chih), vol. 5. Taipei: Chung-kuo Ch'uan-shan hsüeh-hui and Tzu-yu ch'u-pan she, 1972.

——. *Ssu chieh* 俟解 (Awaiting explanations). In *Ssu-wen lu* 思問錄 (Records of reflections and inquiries). Peking: Chung-hua shu-chü, 1956.

——. *Ssu-wen lu* 思問錄 (Records of reflections and inquiries). Peking: Chung-hua shu-chü, 1956.

Wang Hsi-sun 汪喜孫. *Wang Jung-fu nien-p'u* 汪容甫年譜 (Chronological biography of Wang Chung). In *Chiang-tu Wang-shih ts'ung-shu* 江都汪氏叢書. 1925.

Wang Hsien-ch'ien 王先謙. *Hsün-tzu chi-chieh* 荀子集解 (Collected annotations on *Hsün-tzu*). Taipei: Hsin-hsing shu-chü, 1956.

Wang Hsing-ya 王興亞. "Ming-tai chung hou ch'i Ho-nan she-hui feng-shang ti pien-hua" 明代中後期河南社會風尚的變化 (Change in social customs and mores in Honan during the middle and late Ming period). *Chung-chou hsüeh-k'an* 中州學刊 1989, no. 4: 107–10.

Wang Ken 王艮. *Wang Hsin-chai ch'üan-chi* 王心齋全集 (Complete works of Wang Ken). Taipei: Kuang-wen shu-chü, 1987.

Wang Kuei-min 王貴民. *Shang-Chou chih-tu k'ao-hsin* 商周制度考信 (A study of institutions of the Shang and Chou dynasties). Taipei: Ming-wen shu-chü, 1989.

Wang Li-ch'i 王利器. *Cheng K'ang-ch'eng nien-p'u* 鄭康成年譜 (Chronological biography of Cheng Hsüan). Shantung: Ch'i-Lu shu-she, 1983.

——. *Yüan Ming Ch'ing san-tai chin-hui hsiao-shuo hsi-ch'ü shih-liao* 元明清三代禁毀小說戲曲史料 (Historical sources on the censorship of fiction and drama in the Yüan, Ming, and Ch'ing dynasties). Shanghai: Ku-chi ch'u-pan she, 1981.

Wang Mou-hung 王懋竑. *Pai-t'ien tsao-t'ang ts'un-kao* 白田草堂存稿 (Preserved manuscripts from the Hut in White Field). Taipei: Han-hua wen-hua shih-yeh, 1972.

Wang Pi 王襞. *Tung-yai hsien-sheng i-chi* 東崖先生遺集 (Writings of the late Wang Pi). Preface dated 1610.

Wang Shou-jen 王守仁 (Yang-ming 陽明). *Ch'uan-hsi lu* 傳習錄 (Instructions for practical living). In idem, *Wang Yang-ming ch'üan-chi*. Hong Kong: Kuang-chih shu-chü, 1959.

——. *Instructions for Practical Living and Other Writings by Wang Yang-ming.* Trans. Wing-tsit Chan. New York: Columbia University Press, 1963.

——. *Wang Yang-ming ch'üan-chi* 王陽明全集 (Complete works of Wang Yang-ming). Hong Kong: Kuang-chih shu-chü, 1959.

Wang Ssu-chih 王思治. "Tsung-tsu chih-tu ch'ien lun" 宗族制度淺論 (A brief discussion of lineage institutions). *Ch'ing-shih lun-ts'ung* 清史論叢 1982, no. 4 (Dec.): 152–78.

Wang Tao-k'un 汪道昆. *T'ai-han chi* 太函集 (Collected writings of Wang Tao-k'un). Preface dated 1591.

Wang Wan 汪琬. *Yao-feng wen-chi* 堯峰文集 (Collected writings of Wang Wan). SPTK, vol. 169.

Wang Yin-lan 王蔭蘭. "Ming-tai ti hsiang-yüeh yü min-chung chiao-yü 明代的鄉約與民衆教育 (The community compact and popular education in the Ming period). *Ming-shih yen-chiu lun-ts'ung* 明史研究論叢 (Taipei), ser. 2 (1984): 275–99.

Wang Yü-ch'üan 王毓銓. "Ming-tai yao-i shen-pien yü t'u-ti" 明代徭役審編與土地 (Registration of corvée and landholding in the Ming period). *Li-shih yen-chiu* 歷史研究 1988, no. 1 (Feb.): 162–80.

Wang Yüan 王源. *Chü-yeh t'ang wen-chi* 居業堂文集 (Collected writings of the Chü-yeh Hall). TSCCCP.

Watson, James L. "Standardizing the Gods: The Promotion of Tien-hou ('Empress of Heaven') Along the South China Coast, 960–1960." In David Johnson, Andrew J. Nathan, and Evelyn S. Rawski, eds., *Popular Culture in Late Imperial China.* Berkeley: University of California Press, 1985.

——. "The Structure of Chinese Funeral Rites: Elementary Forms, Ritual Sequence, and the Primacy of Performance." In idem and Evelyn S. Rawski, eds., *Death Ritual in Late Imperial and Modern China.* Berkeley: University of California Press, 1988.

Watson, James L., and Patricia B. Ebrey. "Introduction." In idem, eds., *Kinship Organization in Late Imperial China, 1400–1900.* Berkeley: University of California Press, 1986.

Watson, Rubie. "The Creation of a Chinese Lineage: The Teng of Ha Tsuen, 1669–1751." *Modern Asian Studies* 16, no. 1 (Feb. 1982): 69–99.

——. *Inequality Among Brothers: Class and Kinship in South China.* Cambridge, Eng.: Cambridge University Press, 1985.

Weber, Max. *The Religion of China.* Trans. and ed. Hans H. Gerth. New York: Free Press, 1951.

——. *The Theory of Social and Economic Organization.* Ed. Talcott Parsons. New York: Free Press, 1964.

Wechsler, Howard. *Offerings and Jade: Ritual and Symbol in the Legitimation of the T'ang Dynasty.* New Haven: Yale University Press, 1985.

Wei Hsiang-shu 魏象樞. *Han-sung t'ang chi* 寒松堂集 (Collected writings from the Hall of Cold Pine Trees). TSCCCP.

Wei Hsiu-mei 魏秀梅. "Ho Ch'ang-ling chih ching-shih ssu-hsiang" 賀長齡之經世思想 (Ho Ch'ang-ling's thinking on statecraft). In *Chin-shih Chung-kuo ching-shih ssu-hsiang yen-t'ao hui lun-wen chi* 近世中國經世思想研討會論文集 (Proceedings of the Conference on the Theory of Statecraft of Modern China). Taipei: Academia Sinica, Institute of Modern History, 1984.

———. *T'ao Chu tsai Chiang-nan* 陶澍在江南 (Tao Chu in Kiangnan). Taipei: Academia Sinica, 1985.

Wei Yüan 魏源. *Wei Yüan chi* 魏源集 (Collected writings of Wei Yüan). Peking: Chung-hua shu-chü, 1976.

Weng Fang-kang 翁方綱. *Fu-ch'u chai wen-chi* 復初齋文集 (Collected essays from the Studio of Return to Beginnings). Chin-tai Chung-kuo shih-liao ts'ung-k'an 近代中國史料叢刊, ser. 43. Taipei: Wen-hai ch'u-pan she.

Widmer, Ellen. "The Epistolary World of Female Talent in Seventeenth-Century China." *Late Imperial China* 10, no. 2 (Dec. 1989): 1–43.

———. "Xiaoqing's Literary Legacy and the Place of the Woman Writer in Late Imperial China." *Late Imperial China* 13, no. 1 (June 1992): 111–55.

Wiens, Mi Chu. "Lord and Peasants: The Sixteenth to the Eighteenth Century." *Modern China* 6, no. 1 (Jan. 1980): 3–39.

———. "Social Change and Fiscal Reform in the Fifteenth Century." *Ming Studies*, no. 26 (Fall 1988): 18–36.

Woon, Yuen-fong. *Social Organization in South China, 1911–1949: The Case of the Kuan Lineage in K'ai-p'ing County.* Michigan Monographs in Chinese Studies. Ann Arbor: University of Michigan, 1984.

Wu Ch'eng-ming 吳承明. *Chung-kuo tzu-pen chu-i yü kuo-nei shih-ch'ang* 中國資本主義與國內市場 (The domestic market and Chinese capitalism). Peking: Chung-kuo she-hui k'o-hsüeh ch'u-pan she, 1985.

Wu Chin-ch'eng 吳金成. "Ming-tai Chiang-hsi nung-ts'un ti she-hui pien-hua yü shen-shih" 明代江西農村的社會變化與紳士 (Gentry and social change in rural areas of Kiangsi in the Ming dynasty). Paper presented at the Second International Conference on Sinology, Academia Sinica, Dec. 1986.

Wu Han 吳晗. "Ming-tai ti hsin shih-huan chieh-chi, she-hui ti cheng-chih ti wen-hua ti kuan-hsi chi ch'i sheng-huo" 明代的新仕宦階級、社會的政治的文化的關系及其生活 (The social, political, and cultural relationships and life of the new gentry-officials of the Ming). *Ming-shih yen-chiu lun-ts'ung* 明史研究論叢 1991, no. 5: 1–68.

Wu Jen-an 吳任安. "Ming-tai Chiang-nan she-hui feng-shang ch'u-t'an" 明代江南社會風尚初探 (A preliminary study of social customs and mores of Kiangnan in the Ming period). *She-hui k'o-hsüeh chia* 社會科學家 1987, no. 2: 39–46.

Wu, Kwang-tsing. "Ming Printing and Printers." *HJAS* 7, no. 3 (1943): 203–60.

Wu, Nelson Ikon. "Tung Ch'i-ch'ang (1555–1636): Apathy in Government and Fervor in Art." In Arthur F. Wright and Dennis Twitchett, eds., *Confucian Personalities.* Stanford: Stanford University Press, 1962.

————. "T'ung Ch'i-ch'ang: The Man, His Time and His Landscape Painting." Ph.D. dissertation, Yale University, 1957.

Wu, Pei-i. "Self-Examination and Confession of Sins in Traditional China." *HJAS* 39, no. 1 (June 1979): 5–38.

Wu, Silas. *Communication and Imperial Control in China: Evolution of the Palace Memorial System, 1693–1735*. Cambridge, Mass.: Harvard University Press, 1970.

Wu Tan-ko 伍丹戈. "Ming-tai shen-chin ti-chu ti fa-chan" 明代紳衿地主的發展 (The development of gentry landlords in the Ming dynasty). *Ming-shih yen-chiu lun-ts'ung* 明史研究論叢 1983, no. 2: 10–14.

Wu T'ing-hua 吳廷華. *I-li chang-chü* 儀禮章句 (*Book of Etiquette and Decorum* in chapters and verses). SKCS, vol. 109.

Yagisawa Hajime 八木澤元. *Ming-tai chü-tso-chia yen-chiu* 明代劇作家研究 (A study of Ming playwrights). Trans. Lo Chin-t'ang 羅錦堂. Taipei: Chung-hsin shu-chü, 1977.

Yang Ch'un 楊椿. *Meng-lin t'ang chi* 孟鄰堂集 (Collected writings from the Meng-lin Hall). 1942.

Yang Hsiang-k'uei 楊向奎. "Ch'ing-tai ti chin-wen ching-hsüeh" 清代的今文經學 (The New Text Classical scholarship of the Ch'ing period). In idem, *I-shih chai hsüeh-shu lun-wen chi* 繹史齋學術論文集 (Collected scholarly essays from the Studio for Unraveling History). Shanghai: Jen-min ch'u-pan she, 1983.

Yang T'ien-shih 楊天石. "Kung Tzu-chen chieh shih yü hsüeh Fo" 龔自珍戒詩與學佛 (Kung Tzu-chen's vow not to write poems and his pursuit of Buddhism). *Fu-tan hsüeh-pao* 复旦學報 1980, no. 3 (May): 99–102.

————. *T'ai-chou hsüeh-p'ai* 泰州學派 (The T'ai-chou school). Peking: Chung-hua shu-chü, 1980.

Yao Ch'un 姚椿, comp. *Ch'ing-ch'ao wen-lu* 清朝文錄 (An anthology of Ch'ing dynasty writings). 6 vols. Taipei: Ta-hsin shu-tien, 1965.

Yao Nai 姚鼐. *Hsi-pao hsüan ch'üan-chi* 惜抱軒全集 (Complete works from the Studio of Embraced Regrets). Hong Kong: Kuang-chi shu-chü, n.d.

Yeh Hsien-en 叶顯恩. *Ming-Ch'ing Hui-chou nung-ts'un she-hui yü tien-p'u chih* 明清徽州農村社會與佃僕制 (Rural society and the tenant-servant system in Hui-chou during the Ming and Ch'ing). Anhwei: Jen-min ch'u-pan she, 1983.

Yeh Hsien-en 叶顯恩 and T'an Ti-hua 譚棣華. "Lun Chu-chiang san-chiao chou ti tsu-t'ien" 論珠江三角洲的族田 (On the corporate estates of lineages in the Canton Delta). *Ming-Ch'ing Kuang-tung she-hui ching-chi hsing-t'ai yen-chiu* 明清廣東社會經濟形態研究 (Studies on the social and economic patterns of Kwantung during the Ming and Ch'ing periods). Kwangtung: Jen-min ch'u-pan she, 1985.

Yeh Kuo-liang 葉國良. *Sung-jen i-ching kai-ching k'ao* 宋人疑經改經考 (Study of the Sung Confucians' skepticism regarding the Classics and the changes they made in the Classics). Taipei: National Taiwan University, 1980.

Yen Jo-chü 閻若璩. *Ch'ien-ch'iu cha-chi* 潛邱劄記 (Reading notes of Ch'ien-ch'iu). SKCS chen-pen, ser. 4.

————. *Shang-shu ku-wen shu-cheng* 尙書古文疏證 (Evidential study of the *Book of Documents*). SKCS, vol. 66.

Yen Yüan 顏元. *Chu-tzu yü-lei p'ing* 朱子語類評 (Evaluation of *Chu-tzu yü-lei*). YLTS, vol. 1.

————. *Hsi-chai chi-yü* 習齋記餘 (More notes from the Studio of Practice). TSCCHP, vol. 76.

————. *Ssu-shu cheng-wu* 四書正誤 (Corrections of errors in the Four Books). YLTS, vol. 1.

————. *Ssu-ts'un p'ien* 四存篇 (Four treatises on preservation [of nature, learning, government, and humanity]). Taipei: Ho-Lo t'u-shu ch'u-pan she, 1975.

Yin Hui-i 尹會一. *Chien-yü hsien-sheng wen-chi* 健餘先生文集 (Collected writings of Yin Hui-i). Ts'ung-shu chi-ch'eng chien-pien.

Yü Cheng-hsieh 俞正燮. *Kuei-ssu ts'un-kao* 癸巳存稿 (Preserved notes of the Kuei-ssu year [1833]). Taipei: Shang-wu yin-shu kuan, 1971.

Yü Chih 余治. *Te-i lu* 得一錄 (Records of getting hold of goodness). Chung-hua wen-shih ts'ung-shu 中華文史叢書, ser. 10. Taipei: Hua-wen shu-chü, 1968–69.

Yü, Chün-fang. *The Renewal of Buddhism in China: Chu-hung and the Late Ming Synthesis.* New York: Columbia University Press, 1980.

Yü Lung-kuang 余龍光. *Shuang-ch'ih hsien-sheng nien-p'u* 雙池先生年譜 (Chronological biography of Wang Fu). 1894.

Yü Shen-hsing 于慎行. *Ku-shan pi-ch'en* 穀山筆塵 (Dust from Mount Grain). Peking: Chung-hua shu-chü, 1984.

Yü Ying-shih 余英時. "Ch'ing-tai hsüeh-shu ssu-hsiang chung-yao kuan-nien t'ung-shih 清代學術思想重要觀念通釋 (General exposition of some major concepts in Ch'ing scholarship and thought). *Shih-hsüeh p'ing-lun* 史學評論 1983, no. 5 (Jan.): 19–98.

————. *Li-shih yü ssu-hsiang* 歷史與思想 (History and thought). Taipei: Lien-ching ch'u-pan, 1977.

————. *Lun Tai Chen yü Chang Hsüeh-ch'eng: Ch'ing-tai chung-ch'i hsüeh-shu ssu-hsiang shih yen-chiu* 論戴震與章學誠:清代中期學術思想史研究 (On Tai Chen and Chang Hsüeh-ch'eng: a study of scholarship and thought in the mid-Ch'ing period). Taipei: Hua-shih ch'u-pan she, 1977.

————. "Some Preliminary Observations on the Rise of Ch'ing Intellectualism." *Ch'ing-hua hsüeh-pao* 11, nos. 1–2 (1975): 105–29.

————. "Ts'ung Sung-Ming ju-hsüeh ti fa-chan lun Ch'ing-tai ssu-hsiang shih" 從宋明儒學的發展論清代思想史 (Discussion of Ch'ing intellectual history from the perspective of the development of Sung-Ming Confucianism). In idem, *Li-shih yü ssu-hsiang* 歷史與思想 (History and thought). Taipei: Lien-ching ch'u-pan, 1977.

Yüan Mei 袁枚. *Sui-yüan ch'üan-chi* 隨園全集 (Complete works of Yüan Mei). Hong Kong: Kuang-chih shu-chü, n.d.

Yuan, Tsing. "Urban Riots and Disturbances." In Jonathan D. Spence and John E. Wills, Jr., eds., *From Ming to Ch'ing: Conquest, Region, and Continuity in Seventeenth-Century China.* New Haven: Yale University Press, 1979.

Zurndorfer, Harriet T. *Change and Continuity in Chinese Local History: The Development of Hui-chou Prefecture, 800–1800.* Leiden: E. J. Brill, 1989.

———. "The 'Constant World' of Wang Chao-yüan: Women, Education, and Orthodoxy in 18th Century China." *Family Process and Political Process in Modern Chinese History.* Taipei: Academia Sinica, Institute of Modern History, 1992.

———. "*Han-hsüeh*, 'Evidential Research,' and Female Chastity: A Re-examination of Intellectual Attitudes and Social Ideals in 18th Century China." In W. L. Idema and E. Zürcher, eds., *Thought and Law in Qin and Han China: Studies Presented to Anthony Hulsewé on the Occasion of His Eightieth Birthday.* Leiden: E. J. Brill, 1990.

———. "Local Lineages and Local Development: A Case Study of the Fan Lineage, Hsiu-ning Hsien, Hui-chou, 800–1500," *T'oung-pao* 70, nos. 1–3 (1984): 18–59.

Character List

an-i 安逸
An Hsi-fan 安希范
Ao Chi-kung 敖繼公

Ch'ai Shao-ping 柴紹炳
Chan Jo-shui 湛若水
Ch'an 禪
Chang Chia-ling 張嘉玲
Chang Chü-cheng 張居正
Chang Erh-ch'i 張爾歧
Chang Hai-shan 張海珊
Chang Hsüeh-ch'eng 章學誠
Chang Lieh 張烈
Chang Lü-hsiang 張履祥
Chang Po-hsing 張伯行
Chang P'u 張溥
Chang Shun-hui 張舜徽
Chang T'ing-yü 張廷玉
Chang Tsai 張載
Chang Ts'ai 張采
Chang Ts'ung 張璁
Ch'ang-chou 常州
Chao I 趙翼
Chao K'uang 趙匡
chao-mu 昭穆
Chao Nan-hsing 趙南星
Chao Ta-chou 趙大洲
Ch'en Ch'üeh 陳確
Ch'en Hao 陳澔
Ch'en Hsiang-tao 陳詳道

Ch'en Huan 陳奐
Ch'en Hung-mou 陳宏謀
Ch'en Li (1252–1333) 陳櫟
Ch'en Li (1809–69) 陳立
Ch'en Li (1810–82) 陳澧
Ch'en Liang 陳亮
Ch'en Lung-cheng 陳龍正
Ch'en Shou-ch'i 陳壽祺
Ch'en Tuan 陳摶
Ch'en Tzu-chih 陳紫芝
cheng-hsin 正心
Cheng Hsüan 鄭玄
Cheng-hsüeh chai 鄭學齋
Cheng Hu-wen 鄭虎文
cheng-i 正義
cheng-jen 證人
cheng-meng 正蒙
cheng-ming 正名
Cheng Tso 鄭佐
cheng-t'ung 正統
Cheng Yung 鄭泳
Ch'eng Chin-fang 程晉芳
Ch'eng Hao 程顥
Ch'eng I 程頤
ch'eng-i 誠意
Ch'eng T'ing-tso 程廷祚
Ch'eng Yao-t'ien 程瑤田
chi 祭
Chi-fa 祭法
chi kung-fu chi pen-t'i 即工夫即本體

chi-ti 吉禘

Chi Yün 紀昀

ch'i 氣

Ch'i Chao-nan 齊召南

chia-chieh 假借

chia-chieh i 假借義

chia-hsün 家訓

Chia I 賈誼

Chia K'uei 賈逵

Chia Kung-yen 賈公彥

Chia-li cho 家禮酌

chia-miao 家廟

"Chia-miao chi-hsiang li lüeh" 家廟祭
享禮畧

chia-t'ang 家堂

chia-tz'u 家祠

chiang 講

Chiang Chao-hsi 姜兆錫

Chiang Fan 江藩

Chiang Hsiang-nan 蔣湘南

chiang-hsüeh 講學

chiang li 講理

Chiang Yung 江永

ch'iang-tsung 強宗

chiao (canonical teaching,
    teaching) 教

chiao (worship in the suburb) 郊

Chiao Hsün 焦循

Chiao Hung 焦竑

Chiao-pin lu k'ang-i 校邠廬抗議

chiao-she 郊社

Chiao-she k'ao-pien 郊社考辨

Chiao, she, ti, hsia wen 郊社禘祫問

chieh-hsing 節性

Chieh-hsing chai 節性齋

Chieh-hsing chai lao-jen 節性齋老人

Ch'ien Ch'eng-chih 錢澄之

Ch'ien Ch'ien-i 錢謙益

Ch'ien I-pen 錢一本

Ch'ien Shih-sheng 錢士升

Ch'ien Ta-hsin 錢大昕

chih 知

chih-chih 知止

chih-chung 至中

chih-hsing ho-i 知行合一

chih li ch'eng hsing 知禮成性

chih-pen 知本

chih-p'ing 治平

chih-shu 制數

chih-tu 制度

chih-tzu 支子

chih-tzu pu chi 支子不祭

Chin Lü-hsiang 金履祥

chin-shih 進士

Chin-ssu lu 近思錄

Ch'in Hui-t'ien 秦蕙田

ch'in-ying 親迎

ching 敬

ching-hsüeh chi li-hsüeh 經學即理學

ching i chih nei 敬以直內

ching-shih 經世

ching-tsung shou-tsu 敬宗收族

ch'ing (deputy) 卿

ch'ing (feelings) 情

ch'ing ta-fu 卿大夫

Chiu-chieh 九解

Chiu-ti 九諦

ch'iu 求

Ch'iu Chün 邱濬

Chou Ho 周何

Chou Ju-teng 周汝登

"*Chou-kuan* cheng-wen" 周官徵文

Chou-kuan chi-chu 周官集注

Chou-kuan i-shu 周官義疏

Chou-kuan pien-fei 周官辨非

"*Chou-kuan* pien-wei" 周官辨偽

Chou K'ung-chiao 周孔教

Chou-li 周禮

Chou-li Han tu k'ao 周禮漢讀考

Chou Tun-i 周敦頤

Chu Hsi 朱熹

Chu-hung 株宏

Chu I-tsun 朱彝尊
Chu Shih 朱軾
Chu-tzu ch'üan-shu 朱子全書
Chu-tzu chia-li 朱子家禮
Chu-tzu yü-lei 朱子語類
Chu Yüan-chang 朱元璋
Chu Yün 朱筠
ch'u-pi 除蔽
Ch'u Yin-liang 褚寅亮
chü (conformity) 拘
chü (gather together) 聚
ch'ü-ssu 去私
chuan-chu 轉注
ch'uan-hsin 傳心
chüan 卷
ch'üan-miao 全廟
Ch'üan Tsu-wang 全祖望
Chuang Ts'un-yü 莊存與
chüeh ch'u sheng-min chih tsu 厥初
    生民之祖
chüeh-tsu 絕族
Ch'un-ch'iu 春秋
Ch'un-ch'iu chi-chieh 春秋集解
Chün-hsien lun 郡縣論
ch'ün-miao 群廟
Ch'ün-shu i-pien 群書疑辨
chung 忠
chung-ti 終禘
Chung-yung 中庸

Erh-ya 爾雅

fan-lun i-li chih shuo 泛論義理之說
Fang Hsiao-ju 方孝孺
Fang I-chih 方以智
Fang Kuan-ch'eng 方觀承
Fang Pao 方苞
Fang Ta-chen 方大鎮
fang-tse 方澤
Fang Tung-shu 方東樹
fei-li 非禮

fen 分
fen-chü 分居
fen-li 分理
Fen-shu 焚書
feng-chien 封建
Feng-chien lun 封建論
Feng Kuei-fen 馮桂芬
feng-su jen-hsin 風俗人心
Feng Tao 馮道
Feng Ts'ung-wu 馮從吾
fu 復
fu-chu 祔主
fu-hsing 復性
fu-hsing ku-hsüeh 復興古學
fu-ku 復古
Fu-li lun 復禮論
Fu Shan 傅山
Fu she 復社

Han Chen 韓貞
Han-hsüeh 漢學
Han-shan Te-ch'ing 憨山德清
Hang Shih-chün 杭世駿
Hao Ching 郝敬
Hao I-hsing 郝懿行
hao-shen 豪紳
hao-wu 好惡
ho 和
Ho Ch'o 何焯
Ho Hsin-yin 何心隱
Ho Hsiu 何休
Ho-t'u Lo-shu 河圖洛書
Hou-chi 后稷
Hou K'ang 侯康
hsi 習
hsi-chai 習齋
hsi-i 蜥易
"Hsi-tz'u" 繫辭
hsia 祫
Hsia Yen 夏言
hsiang 象

hsiang san-wu 鄉三物

hsiang-yüan 鄉愿

hsiang-yüeh 鄉約

hsiao 孝

Hsiao-hsüeh (Elementary learning) 小學

hsiao-hsüeh (philology) 小學

Hsiao-shan 蕭山

hsiao-tsung 小宗

hsiao-tsung tz'u 小宗祠

Hsieh Chao-che 謝肇淛

hsin 信

hsin-chih 心知

hsin-shuo ch'ü-i 新說曲議

hsing (conduct, practice) 行

hsing (form) 形

hsing (nature) 性

Hsing-li ching-i 性禮精義

Hsing-li ta-ch'üan 性理大全

hsing-ling 性靈

hsing-ming 性命

hsing-o 性惡

hsing-shan 性善

hsiu-ch'i 修齊

hsiu-shen 修身

hsiu tao chih wei chiao 修道之謂教

hsiu-te 修德

Hsiung Tz'u-lü 熊賜履

Hsü Chieh 徐階

Hsü Ch'ien-hsüeh 徐乾學

Hsü Chou-t'ang 徐畫堂

Hsü Fang 徐枋

Hsü Fu-yüan 許孚遠

Hsü Heng 許衡

hsü-i 虛義

Hsü I-k'uei 徐一夔

Hsü San-li 許三禮

Hsü Shen 許慎

Hsü Tung 徐棟

Hsü Yüan-meng 徐元夢

Hsü Yüan-wen 徐元文

Hsüeh-cheng ch'üan-shu 學政全書

hsüeh-ch'i 血氣

Hsüeh Ch'un-ch'iu sui-pi 學春秋隨筆

Hsüeh Fu-chiao 薛敷教

Hsüeh-hai t'ang 學海堂

"Hsüeh-le ko" 學樂歌

Hsüeh-li 學禮

Hsüeh-li chih-i 學禮質疑

Hsüeh-shu pien 學術辨

hsün-fen shou-chieh 循份守節

hsün-li 循吏

Hsün-tzu 荀子

Hu An-kuo 胡安國

Hu Ch'eng-kung 胡承珙

Hu Chih-wei 胡稚威

Hu Hung 胡宏

hu-hsün 互訓

Hu Kuang 胡廣

Hu Shih 胡適

Hu Wei 胡渭

Hu Ying-lin 胡應麟

Hu Yüan 胡瑗

Hua Hsüeh-ch'üan 華學泉

Huang-ch'ao ching-shih wen-pien 皇朝
經世文編

Huang-Ch'ing wen-ying kuan 皇清
文穎館

Huang Kan 黃幹

Huang Tsung-hsi 黃宗羲

Huang Tsung-yen 黃宗炎

hui 會

Hui-chou 徽州

hui-kuo tzu-hsin 悔過自新

Hui Shih-ch'i 惠士奇

Hui Tung 惠棟

Hun-li pien-cheng 婚禮辨正

Hung Liang-chi 洪亮吉

Hung Sheng 洪昇

i 義

I Cheng t'ang 儀鄭堂

i-hsing (change name) 易姓
i-hsing (different clan) 異姓
I-hsüeh hsiang-shu lun 易學象數論
i i fang-wai 義以方外
i-li 義理
I-li 儀禮
I-li chang chü 儀禮章句
I-li Cheng-chu chü-tu 儀禮鄭註句讀
I-li chieh-yao 儀禮節要
i-li chih-hsing 義理之性
I-li ching-chuan t'ung-chieh 儀禮經傳
    通解
I-li hsi-i 儀禮析疑
I-li i-shu 儀禮義疏
i-li po-wen, hsüeh-li yeh 以禮博文,
    學禮也
I-li shang 儀禮商
I-li shih-i 儀禮釋疑
I-li shih-kung 儀禮釋官
I-li t'u 儀禮圖
i-li wei chiao 以禮為教
i-nan 義男
I-t'u ming-pien 易圖明辨
i-tuan 異端
I-tuan pien 異端辨
i-tzu shu-yin 一字數音
i-yin shu-tzu 一音數字

jen (humaneness, humanity) 仁
jen (trust) 任
Jen Ch'i-yün 任啓運
jen chih shih shih 仁之實事
Jen-ho 仁和
jen-hsin 人心
jen-i 仁義
jen-kuei 人鬼
jen-lun 人倫
Jen-p'u 人譜
Jen Ta-ch'un 任大椿
jen-yü 人欲
Jih-chih lu 日知錄

ju 儒
ju-che 儒者
Juan Yüan 阮元

kan 干
kan-hsia 干袷
Kan Ju-lai 甘汝來
kan-sheng shang-ti 感生上帝
kan-sheng ti 感生帝
kang-ch'ang 綱常
K'ang Yu-wei 康有為
Kao P'an-lung 高攀龍
k'ao-cheng 考證
k'ao-cheng hsüeh 考證學
k'ao-ku i chun-chin 考古以準今
Kao Yü 高愈
Keng Chü 耿橘
ko-chih 格致
ko-wu 格物
k'o-chi fu-li 克己復禮
Ku-chin t'u-shu chi-ch'eng 古今圖書集成
Ku Hsien-ch'eng 顧憲成
ku-hsün 古訓
Ku-liang 穀梁
Ku Tsu-yü 顧祖輿
Ku Tung-kao 顧棟高
Ku-wen Shang-shu 古文尚書
Ku Yen-wu 顧炎武
Ku Yün-ch'eng 顧允成
kuan 冠
Kuan Chih-tao 管志道
kuan-shih 官師
K'uang-Ch'an 狂禪
kuei 貴
Kuei Yu-kuang 歸有光
K'un-ch'ü 崑曲
kung-fu 功夫
kung-kung chih li 公共之理
kung-kuo ko 功過格
Kung-shih k'ao 宮室考
kung-tzu 公子

Kung Tzu-chen 龔自珍
kung-tz'u 公祠
Kung-yang 公羊
k'ung 空
K'ung Kuang-sen 孔廣森
K'ung Shang-jen 孔尚任
K'ung Ying-ta 孔穎達
kuo (country) 國
kuo (fault) 過
Kuo-ch'ao Han-hsüeh shih-ch'eng chi 國朝漢學師承記
Kuo Hsiang 郭象
Kuo-yü 國語
k'uo-ch'ung 擴充

Lei Hung 雷鋐
li (precedents) 例
li (principle) 理
li (ritual, ritual propriety, ritual institution) 禮
Li Ao 李翱
Li Chao-lo 李兆洛
Li-chi 禮記
Li-chi chang-chü 禮記章句
Li-chi chang-i 禮記章義
Li-chi chi-shuo 禮說集說
Li-chi hsi-i 禮記析疑
Li-chi hui-pien 禮記彙編
Li-chi i-chang 禮記義章
Li-chi i-shu 禮記義疏
Li-chi ou-chien 禮記偶箋
Li-chi shih-i 禮記釋疑
"*Li-chi* t'u-shuo" 禮記圖說
li-chia 里甲
li-chia cheng-i 里甲正役
li-chiao 禮教
li che t'ien-li chih chieh-wen 禮者天理之節文
li-chieh 禮節
Li Chih 李贄
li-chih (establish one's will) 立志
li-chih (ritual institutions) 禮制

Li-ching kang-mu 禮經綱目
Li Fu 李紱
li-hsüeh (study of principle) 理學
li-hsüeh (study of ritual) 禮學
Li-hsüeh hui-pien 禮學彙編
li-i (principle propriety) 理義
li-i (ritual propriety) 禮義
Li Ju-kuei 李如圭
Li Kuang-ti 李光地
Li Kung 李塨
Li-shu kang-mu 禮書綱目
Li Tun 李惇
Li Wei 李緯
Li-wei 禮緯
Li-wen shou-ch'ao 禮文手鈔
Li Yin-tu 李因篤
Li Yüan-tu 李元度
li-yüeh 禮樂
Li Yung 李顒
Liang Ch'i-ch'ao 梁啓超
liang-chih 良知
Liao P'ing 廖平
Lin Chao-en 林兆恩
Ling Shu 凌曙
Ling T'ing-k'an 凌廷堪
Liu Chi 劉基
Liu En 劉恩
Liu Feng-lu 劉逢祿
liu-fu san-shih 六府三事
Liu Hsiang 劉向
Liu Hsien-t'ing 劉獻廷
Liu Hsin 劉歆
liu-i 六藝
Liu Jung 劉蓉
liu-li 六禮
liu-shu 六書
liu-te, liu-hsing 六德六行
liu-tsei 六賊
Liu Tsung-chou 劉宗周
Liu Tsung-yüan 柳宗元
Liu Yin 劉因
Lo Ch'in-shun 羅欽順

Lo Ju-fang 羅汝芳
Lu-chiang 廬江
Lu Chiu-yüan 陸九淵
Lu Lung-ch'i 陸隴其
Lu Shih-i 陸世儀
Lu Wen-ch'ao 盧文弨
Lu Yao 陸燿
Lu Yüan-fu 陸元輔
Lü K'un 呂坤
Lü Liu-liang 呂留良
Lü Nan 呂楠
Lung-ch'ang 龍場

Ma Jung 馬融
Ma Tuan-lin 馬端臨
Mao Ch'i-ling 毛奇齡
Meng-tzu tzu-i shu-cheng 孟子字義疏證
mei-shih 媒氏
miao 廟
miao-chih 廟制
min-shu 民庶
ming (destiny) 命
ming (status, name) 名
ming-chiao 名教
ming-fen 名分
Ming-i tai-fang lu 明夷待訪錄
Ming-ju hsüeh-an 明儒學案
ming-li 明理
Ming-t'ang 明堂
"Ming-t'ang wei" 明堂位
Ming-teng tao-ku lu 明燈道古錄
ming-wu 名物
mu 睦
Mu-ling chi-yao 牧令輯要

nan-chiao 南郊
Nieh Ch'ung-i 聶崇義
nu-p'u 奴僕
nung-tsung 農宗

O-er-t'ai 鄂爾泰
Ou-yang Hsiu 歐陽修

Pai-hu t'ung 白虎通
p'ai-lou 牌樓
P'an P'ing-ko 潘平格
pao-chia 保甲
Pao Ching-yen 鮑敬言
P'ei-ts'un 裴村
pen (origin) 本
pen (run away) 奔
pen-i 本義
pen-t'i 本體
pi 蔽
Pi Yüan 畢沅
pieh-tzu 別子
pieh-tzu wei tsu 別子為祖
pien-cheng 辨正
pien-hua ch'i-chih 變化氣質
Pien-ting chi-li t'ung-su p'u 辨定祭
    禮通俗譜
p'ien 偏
po-hsüeh 博學
po-hsüeh hung-ju 博學鴻儒
po-hsüeh hung-tz'u 博學宏詞
po-hsüeh yü wen, hsing chi yu ch'ih
    博學於文, 行己有恥
po-hsüeh yü wen, yüeh chih i li 博學
    於文, 約之以禮
po-wen 博文
po-wen i chi-i 博文以集義
po-wen yüeh-li 博文約禮
po-yüeh 博約
pu-cheng-shih ssu 布政使司
pu-i 不易
pu tai wang-cheng chih shih 不待王政之施
P'u Sung-ling 蒲松齡
p'u-t'ien 蒲田

san-chiao ho-i 三教合一
San-chiao k'ai-mi kuei-cheng yen-i 三教
    開迷歸正演義
san-i chiao 三一教
san-kang 三綱
san-kang chin 三綱巾

san-kang wu-ch'ang i 三綱五常衣

San-li hsü-lu 三禮紋錄

San-li kuan 三禮館

San-li t'u chi chu 三禮圖集注

San-nien fu-chih k'ao 三年服制考

san-nien wu kai fu chih chih 三年無改父之志

"Sang-fu chuan" 喪服傳

"Sang-fu hsiao-chi" 喪服小記

Sang-fu i-chu 喪服翼注

"Sang-li i" 喪禮議

Sang-li tsa-shuo 喪禮雜說

Sang-li wu-shuo 喪禮吾說

"Seng-fo tzu-shuo" 僧佛字說

shan 善

Shang-shu ku-wen shu-cheng 尙書古文疏證

Shao Yung 邵雍

she (archery) 射

she (literary associations) 社

shen 紳

shen-chin 紳矜

Shen Ch'in-han 沈欽韓

shen-shih 紳士

"Shen i" 深衣

Shen T'ing-fang 沈廷芳

shen-tu 慎獨

shen-tu kung-fu 慎獨工夫

Shen T'ung 沈彤

Shen Yün 沈昀

sheng (life) 生

sheng (sage) 聖

shih (actual experience) 事

shih (scholar-gentry, officer) 士

shih-chi (first to lay the foundation) 始基

shih-chi (seasonal worship) 時祭

Shih-chi 史記

Shih-ch'i shih shang-ch'üeh 十七史商榷

Shih Chieh 石介

Shih Meng-lin 史孟麟

shih-ming 實名

"Shih sang-li" 士喪禮

shih-shih 實事

shih-shih ch'iu shih 實事求是

shih-ti 時禘

shih-tsu (aristocratic clans) 士族

shih-tsu (first ancestor) 始祖

shih-tsu miao 始祖廟

shih-wu 事物

shou-hsing chih tsu 受姓之祖

shou-pei 守備

shou-tsu 收族

shu (mathematics) 數

shu (sympathy) 恕

shu (writing) 書

shu-tzu 庶子

shu-yüan 書院

Shuo-wen chieh-tzu 說文解字

so tzu ch'u 所自出

ssu 私

ssu-ch'in 四親

ssu-hsin 私心

Ssu-li yüeh-yen 四禮約言

Ssu-ma Ch'ien 司馬遷

Ssu-ma Kuang 司馬光

Ssu-pien lu chi-yao 思辨錄輯要

ssu-yü 私欲

Su Ch'e 蘇轍

Sun Ch'i-ao 孫淇奧

Sun Ch'i-feng 孫奇逢

Sun Hsing-yen 孫星衍

Sung Lao 宋犖

Ta-Ch'ing hui-tien 大清會典

Ta-Ch'ing i-t'ung chih 大清一統志

Ta-Ch'ing lü-li 大清律例

"Ta-chuan" 大傳

ta-fu 大夫

ta-fu shih 大夫士

ta-hsia 大祫

Ta hsiao tsung t'ung-shih 大小宗通釋

ta-hsien 大賢

Ta-hsüeh pien 大學辨

Ta-hsüeh pien-yeh 大學辨業

Ta-li i 大禮議

Ta-Ming chi-li 大明集禮

Ta-Ming hui-tien 大明會典

ta-shih 大事

Ta-Tai li 大戴禮

ta-ti 大禘

ta-tsung 大宗

ta-tsung-fa 大宗法

ta-tsung-tz'u 大宗祠

Tai Chen 戴震

Tai Ming-shih 戴名世

"T'ai-chi t'u" 太極圖

T'ai-chou 泰州

t'ai-tsu 太祖

Tan Chu 啖助

T'an Ssu-t'ung 譚嗣同

tang 蕩

tang-hsia 當下

T'ang Chen 唐甄

T'ang Pin 湯斌

T'ang Shun-chih 唐順之

tao 道

tao-hsin 道心

Tao-hsüeh 道學

tao-i 道義

tao wen-hsüeh 道問學

T'ao Chu 陶澍

te 德

te-hsing 德性

te-hsing tzu yü hsüeh-wen 德性資於學問

T'eng Yüan-hsi 鄧元錫

ti 禘

ti-hsia 禘祫

Ti-hsia k'ao-pien 禘祫考辨

ti-sun 嫡孫

t'i-yung 體用

Tiao Pao 刁包

t'iao-chu 祧主

t'iao-li 條理

tien-chang chih-tu 典章制度

T'ien-ch'üan cheng-tao 天泉證道

t'ien-hsia 天下

t'ien-li 天理

t'ien-li chih chieh-wen 天理之節文

t'ien-ming chih hsing 天命之性

t'ien-shen 天神

t'ien ti chün ch'in shih 天地君親師

T'ien-tzu ssu hsien lo k'uei-shih li
        天子肆獻祼饋食禮

T'ien Wen-ching 田文鏡

t'ou-hsien 投獻

Toyotomi Hideyoshi 豐臣秀吉

tsa-pan 雜辦

tsa-yao 雜徭

ts'ai 才

ts'an-chiang 參將

Tsang shuo 葬說

Ts'ang-shu 藏書

Ts'ao Tuan 曹端

tse 則

Tseng Kuo-fan 曾國藩

Tso-chuan pu-chu 左傳補注

Tsou Yüan-piao 鄒元標

tsu 族

tsu-chang 族長

tsu-cheng 族正

Ts'ui Shu 崔述

ts'un-hsin 存心

ts'un-i (preserve differences) 存異

ts'un-i (preserve doubts) 存疑

tsun te-hsing 尊德性

tsung 宗

tsung-chang 宗長

Tsung-chi li 宗祭禮

tsung-chiao 宗教

tsung-fa 宗法

tsung-fa pu i shih-chüeh 宗法不以世爵

tsung-lun 總論

tsung-miao 宗廟

Tsung-miao k'ao-pien 宗廟考辨

tsung-tsu 宗族

tsung-tzu 宗子

tsung-tz'u 宗祠

Tsung-tz'u ssu-tien 宗祠祀典

tsung-yüeh 宗約

"Tu Chou-kuan" 讀周官

Tu-li chih-i 讀禮志疑

Tu-li ou-chien 讀禮偶箋

Tu-li t'ung-k'ao 讀禮通考

Tu Yü 杜預

t'u 圖

tuan 端

tuan i li 斷以理

Tuan Yü-ts'ai 段玉裁

Tung Ch'i-ch'ang 董其昌

Tung Chung-shu 董仲舒

Tung-lin 東林

T'ung-hsiang 桐鄉

t'ung-hsin 童心

t'ung-lun 通論

tzu ch'eng ming wei chih hsing 自誠
   明謂之性

tzu-jan 自然

tzu-jan chih hsing 自然之性

tzu-jan liang-chih 自然良知

Tzu-po Ta-kuan 紫柏大觀

tz'u-t'ang 祠堂

Wan Ssu-ta 萬斯大

Wan Ssu-t'ung 萬斯同

Wang An-shih 王安石

Wang Ch'ang 王昶

Wang Chien 汪鑑

wang-che ti ch'i tsu chih so-tzu ch'u
   王者禘其祖之所自出

Wang Chi 王畿

"Wang chih" 王制

Wang Chung 汪中

Wang Fu 汪紱

Wang Fu-chih 王夫之

Wang Fu-li 王復禮

Wang Hsi-sun 汪喜孫

Wang Hsin-ching 王心敬

Wang-hsüeh chih-i 王學質疑

Wang Hung-chuan 王宏撰

Wang Ken 王艮

Wang K'un-sheng 王崑繩

Wang Mang 王莽

Wang Ming-sheng 王鳴盛

Wang Mou-hung 王懋竑

Wang Nien-sun 王念孫

Wang Pi (226–49) 王弼

Wang Pi (1511–87) 王襞

Wang Po 王柏

Wang Shih-chen 王世貞

Wang Shih-p'eng 王十朋

Wang Su 王肅

Wang Tao-k'un 汪道昆

Wang Wan 汪琬

Wang Yang-ming 王陽明

Wang Yin-chih 王引之

Wang Yüan 王源

wei (attain) 為

wei (false) 偽

Wei Chi 魏驥

Wei Chih 衛湜

Wei Chin-hsi

Wei Hsiang-shu 魏象樞

Wei Hsüan-ch'eng 韋玄成

wei jen yu chi 為仁由己

wei-shu 緯書

Wei T'ing-chen 魏廷珍

wei-yen ta-i 微言大義

Wei Yüan 魏源

Wei Yüan-ch'eng 韋元成

wen-chien chih chih 聞見之知

wen-hsüeh 問學

"Wen-yen" 文言

Weng Fang-kang 翁方綱

wu-ch'ang 五常

Wu-ch'ang lü 五常履

Wu Ch'eng 吳澄
Wu Ch'ien-mu 吳謙木
Wu-ching i-i 五經異義
Wu-ching t'ung-i 五經同異
Wu Chung-mu 吳仲木
Wu Fan-ch'ang 吳蕃昌
wu-fu 五服
wu-hsing 五行
Wu I 武億
Wu-li t'ung-k'ao 五禮通考
wu-lu pu-chi 無祿不祭
wu-lun 五倫
wu-nien tsai yin chi 五年再殷祭
Wu T'ing-hua 吳廷華
Wu Yü 吳棫

yang-ch'i 陽氣
Yang Ch'i-yüan 楊起元
Yang Ch'un 楊椿
Yang Fu 楊復
Yang Ming-shih 楊名時
Yang Shen 楊慎
Yang T'ing-yün 楊廷筠
Yang Tung-ming 楊東明
Yang Yin 楊峴
Yao Chi-heng 姚際恆
Yao Nai 姚鼐
Yen Chün 嚴均

Yen Jo-chü 閻若璩
Yen K'o-chün 嚴可均
Yen Sung 嚴嵩
Yen Yüan 顏元
yin (affinity) 姻
yin (sound) 音
Yin Hui-i 尹會一
yin-pi hsi-jan 引蔽習染
yin-yang 陰陽
Ying Hui-ch'ien 應撝謙
yu 友
yu-hsia 游俠
yü (chariot driving) 御
yü (desires) 欲
Yü-ch'eng 虞城
yü-fu ÿu-fu 愚夫愚婦
Yü K'ung-chien 于孔兼
yü-lun 餘論
"*Yü-tsao*" 玉藻
Yüan Huang 袁黃
Yüan Mei 袁枚
Yüan Tsung-tao 袁宗道
yüeh 樂
"*Yüeh-chi*" 樂記
yüeh-li 約禮
yüeh-li, hsing-li yeh 約禮, 行禮也
Yung-le ta-tien 永樂大典

Index

In this index an "f" after a number indicates a separate reference on the next page, and an "ff" indicates separate references on the next two pages. A continuous discussion over two or more pages is indicated by a span of page numbers, e.g., "57–59." *Passim* is used for a cluster of references in close but not consecutive sequence. Entries are alphabetized letter by letter, ignoring word breaks, hyphens, and accents.

Absentee landlordism, 15
Academies, 224; Chi-shan, 49, 216; Cheng-jen, 56; Ku-ching ching-she, 201. *See also* Tung-lin Academy
Adoption, 131
Agnates, 83, 89f, 94, 96, 100ff, 103f, 109, 125
Analects, 68f, 139ff, 142, 146, 180, 194, 200, 204
Ancestral cult, 87, 204, 224
Ancestral hall, 4, 66, 75, 77f, 83, 87f, 100, 104, 138, 143, 217f, 220; free-standing, 76, 214, 228; crucial to kinship unity, 92; lesser descent-line, 93, 117; building and wealth, 93, 122; for quaternary ancestry, 94; structure and types, 96, 105–9, 117, 125, 127, 132; in the Chou dynasty, 114–17; admission to, 218
Ancestral rites, 7f, 78, 90ff, 94, 122–25, 132, 166, 214f; popular practice of, 22, 116; and lineage, 76, 84–86, 99f, 129; and descent-line system, 84–86; theory, 89, 99; quaternary ancestry (*ssu-chin*), 90, 94–95, 96, 100–102, 105, 107, 115–17, 120f, 125ff; tablets, 93, 103, 217; *fu-chu*

(appended ancestors), 93; displaced (*t'iao-chu*), 93, 113, 143, 263n58; identical with mourning grades, 95, 100–101; worship three generations, 98f, 115, 120; controversy over, 109–24; *shih-chi* (regular rites), 138f. *See also* Ancestral hall; Descent-line System; First ancestor; Lineage; *Ta-tsung-tz'u*
Ancestral temple, *see* Ancestral hall
Anhwei, 179; Hui-chou, 75, 77, 93, 108, 207, 219, 252n20; T'ung-ch'eng county, 77, 256n98; Hsi county, 216
Anhwei school, 163
Anti-Buddhism, *see* Buddhism
Anti-Manchu feelings, 98, 117–18, 164, 166
Antiquity, 89, 99, 229
Ao Chi-kung, 151, 154, 160
Apical ancestor, *see* First ancestor
Apical lineage hall, *see* Ta-tsung-tz'u
Apocryphal texts, 58, 140f, 147, 157, 167. *See also* Spurious texts
Appetites, 188f
Archaic Chinese, 158f, 162, 176–79, 185, 229. *See also* Language
Aristocracy, 88, 102, 111, 117f, 125
Astronomy, 187

Authoritarianism, 193, 228

Barbarians, 44, 91, 109
Berling, Judith, 27
Betrothed girl, 205ff, 208. *See also*
　Fiancée chastity
Bible, 162, 229
Bloch, Maurice, 11, 13
Board of Personnel, 32, 81, 106
Board of Punishment, 235*n*12
Board of Rites, 150, 235*n*12
Boccaccio, Giovanni, 229
Bondservants, 18f, 23, 77, 87, 252*n*17,
　253*n*29
Book of Changes, 57f, 68, 167, 180, 194,
　248*n*66
Book of Etiquette and Decorum, 41, 46, 49,
　51ff, 67, 79, 130, 134, 139, 143, 147,
　151–56 *passim*, 169, 192, 196f
Book of History, 147, 167f, 181, 199
Book of Odes, 68, 139ff, 142, 147, 179, 181
Book of Rites, 65, 104, 112, 114, 119f, 125,
　132, 139, 142–47 *passim*, 152ff, 155f,
　159, 169, 208
Book of Rites by Senior Tai, 59, 194, 200
Buddhism/Buddhist, 14, 21, 28f, 33, 36,
　44, 50, 93; scripture, 5, 68; rites, 11,
　22, 36–37, 130f, 185; releasing ani-
　mals, 11, 36, 75; and syncretism, 22,
　25; spiritual cultivation, 27; Ch'an,
　34, 47, 55, 62, 191f, 248*n*60; origin
　of *pen-ti*, 47; language, 54, 188; and
　Wang Yang-ming's teachings, 61f;
　anti-Buddhism, 61, 185–86; and
　human relationships, 61; societies,
　74; as members of lineage, 78;
　corruption of, 184–85; perverted
　Confucianism, 184–85, 188; mode
　of thinking, 188; purge of, 192;
　influence on Confucianism, 197,
　201; aversion toward, 197; chari-
　table organization, 252*n*15; Manchu
　emperors' interest in, 271*n*139
Bureaucracy, 23, 71, 73, 82, 108f, 118,
　127f, 225
Burial rite, 22, 130f
Busch, Heinrich, 35

Calvin, John, 229

Canton Delta, 208
Ch'ai Shao-ping, 92
Chan, Wing-tsit, 7
Ch'an Buddhism, *see* Buddhism
Chang Chia-ling, 96
Chang Erh-ch'i, 45, 49ff, 83, 132ff, 135f,
　154, 182–83
Chang Hai-shan, 221
Chang Hsüeh-ch'eng, 172–73, 207,
　217, 220
Chang Lieh, 61
Chang Lü-hsiang, 55, 249*n*80; on
　moral nature, 49; and lineage, 76;
　ritual reform, 92–96 *passim*; and
　the Manchu regime, 122, attack on
　Buddhist rites, 130f; and genealogy,
　215
Chang Po-hsing, 52, 157
Chang P'u, 42
Chang T'ing-yü, 150
Chang Tsai, 30, 42f, 47, 53, 61, 64,
　100, 139, 223; and *ch'i* ontology,
　39; on moral cultivation, 39, 50;
　ritualist ethics, 48–49, 250*n*115; on
　descent-line system, 102, 110, 113
Chang Ts'ung, 184
Ch'ang-chou school, 210
Chao I, 184
Chao K'uang, 134, 140f, 146f, 155
Chao-mu (generational order), 93, 116,
　147
Chao Nan-hsing, 32
Charitable estates, 75f, 78. *See also*
　Lineage
Charitable funds, *see* Charity
Charitable schools, 77
Charity, 72f, 74–75, 252*n*15
Chekiang, 49, 95, 156, 164, 217, 220;
　Jen-ho county, 92; Hai-ning
　county, 94; Hsiao-shan county,
　106; Chin-hua county, 107, 258*n*30;
　Shao-hsing prefecture, 216
Ch'en Ch'üeh, 76, 120, 163, 191; on
　Buddhism, 47, 54, 130f; habits, 48;
　and purism, 54–55, 166; on neo-
　Confucianism, 54–56, 111, 163;
　iconoclasm, 55; on the *Great Learn-
　ing*, 55, 59; and ancestral rites, 92,
　111; and lineage reform, 94–95; and

ritual reform, 96; and *Family Ritual*, 111f, 135
Ch'en Hao, 152, 160
Ch'en Huan, 182, 185, 273*n*53
Ch'en Hung-mou, 220
Ch'en Li (1252–1333), 120
Ch'en Li (1810–82), 182
Ch'en Lung-cheng, 74, 235*n*16
Ch'en Shou-i, 221
Ch'en T'uan, 58
Ch'en Tzu-chih, 259*n*59
Cheng-hsin (rectification of the mind), 195
Cheng Hsüan, 104, 111, 118ff, 125, 151–60 *passim*, 177, 194, 198; on descent-line system, 112; and ritual Classics, 113, 182–84; in early Ch'ing scholarship, 133–34; on *hsia*, 138; on *ti*, 138–39, 140; criticized by Sung neo-Confucians, 139–40; criticized in the early Ch'ing, 140ff, 143f; and exegetical scholarship in ascendancy, 182–84; on ancestral rite, 256*n*4; schedule of *ti* and *hsia*, 263*n*59
Cheng Hu-wen, 207
Cheng Liang, 56
Cheng-ming (rectification of names), 10
Cheng Tso, 252*n*17
Cheng Yung, 258*n*30
Ch'eng Chin-fang, 180, 209
Ch'eng-Chu neo-Confucianism, 5, 58–63 *passim*, 69, 104, 108, 122ff, 134, 151, 153, 184, 223f; revival, 7, 40, 56, 129, 225, 234*n*1; as state orthodoxy, 6, 165–66; criticized by Li Chih, 29–30; ritualism and new interpretations of, 39, 50–51; and Wang Yang-ming school, 41, 49, 54; Classical tradition, revival of, 53, 168; and textual criticism, 56; under attack, 60, 161; dualism challenged, 68, 271–72*n*4; and ancestral rites, 98–103; and ritual scholarship, 135–36; and the Manchu regime, 165; perverted teaching of, 166; and *ko-wu*, 195; and female chastity, 207. *See also* Ch'eng I; Chu Hsi
Ch'eng Hao, 30, 48, 120

Ch'eng Hsiang-tao, 257*n*28
Ch'eng I, 30, 89, 98, 117, 120, 134, 139f, 146, 148, 167, 175, 188, 213; exegetical legacy, 7; on ancestral rite, 7, 125f; and Ch'an Buddhism, 55; on rituals, 60, 65; on human nature, 63; on four immediate ancestors, 95, 100–102, 115; and two approaches to kinship organization, 99–103; on worship of first ancestor (*shih-tsu*), 102–8 *passim*, 114; on descent-line system, 110, 113–14; on mourning rite, 125f; on remarriage of widows, 210
Ch'eng-i (sincerity in intention), 195
Ch'eng T'ing-tso, 117
Ch'eng Yao-t'ien, 190
Chi kung-fu chi pen-t'i (moral effort is the substance of the mind), 46
Chi-ti (auspicious rite), 143. *See also* Ti
Chi Yün, 5, 210, 215
Ch'i Shao-nan, 145
Chia-chieh (borrowing character), 158, 177. *See also* Archaic Chinese; Language; Philology
Chia-ching emperor, 107
Chia K'uei, 138, 158, 176
Chia Kung-yen, 134, 156f, 176
Chia-li cho, 135
Chia-miao (official family shrine), 92–93, 106, 108–9
Chiang Chao-hsi, 134
Chiang Fan, 172, 175, 185, 210, 216
Chiang Hsiang-nan, 181
Chiang-hsüeh (public lecturing), 16, 21, 23f, 27–28, 31, 42, 73, 87, 226f
Chiang-li (discussion of principles), 226
Chiang Yung, 51, 136, 196
Chiao (sacrifice in suburb), 145
Chiao Hsün, 6, 226
Chiao Hung, 29, 34
Chiao-she ti-hsia wen, 144
Chieh-hsing (restraining human nature), *see* Human nature
Ch'ien Ch'eng-chih, 181
Ch'ien Ch'ien-i, 215
Ch'ien I-pen, 40, 74
Ch'ien-lung emperor, 149f, 155, 158, 220

Ch'ien Mu, 55, 56, 168
Ch'ien Ta-hsin, 136; on novels, 6; and
    k'ao-cheng, 157, 202; on Classics,
    171, 174; on Buddhism, 185; on ko-
    wu, 195; on Han exegeses, 177; and
    lineage, 215–16
Chih (wisdom), 38
Chih li ch'eng-hsing (learning ritual to
    establish one's nature), 39, 49, 53
Chih-tzu (secondary son), 95, 215
Chin Lü-hsiang, 153
Chin-ssu lu, 104, 106
Ch'in Hui-t'ien, 51, 117, 136, 224
Chinese culture, 45, 91, 110, 118
Chinese identity, 44–46, 49, 110
Ching (reverence), 50
Ching-shih (ordering the world), 24.
    See also Statecraft
Ch'ing law, 122, 212–13
Ch'ing ta-fu (great officials), 100
Ch'iu Chün, 92, 106f, 109, 114, 135,
    235n12
Ch'iu Fang, 206
Chou dynasty, 88, 99f, 111, 115, 117,
    140, 145f, 153, 157, 179; feudal struc-
    ture, 110; descent-line system, 113,
    255n70; kings, 139, 146, 147. See also
    Descent-line system; Feng-chien
Chou Ju-teng, 29, 34, 40, 62
Chou-kuan i-shu, 150
Chou K'ung-chiao, 254n50
Chou-li Han-tu k'ao, 179
Chou Tun-i, 30, 55, 57, 237n41
Christianity, 229
Chu Hsi, 30, 66, 68, 79, 93; opposed
    popular literature, 5; Classical
    scholarship, 7, 53, 60, 129, 170f; on
    ancestral worship, 7, 99; on the
    Doctrine of the Mean, 50; I-li ching-
    chuan t'ung-chieh, 51, 135f, 151; ritual
    scholarship, 52–53, 60f, 69, 98, 130,
    134ff, 160, 223; and Book of Etiquette
    and Decorum, 53; and Buddhism,
    55, 188; and heterodoxy, 56; dual-
    ism, 57; on Book of Changes, 57f;
    on human nature, 63; Hsiao-hsüeh,
    78; on worship of first ancestor,
    103–5, 106, 114f; on ti, 139, 146f,

259n52; on so tzu ch'u, 146; on Spring
    and Autumn Annals, 148; and ritual
    Classics, 152–57 passim; honored in
    Confucian temple, 165; distrusted
    Old Text Book of History, 167; and
    cult of women's purity, 207, 213
Chu I-tsun, 136, 184
Chu Shih, 61, 135, 149f, 153, 159
Chu-tzu ch'üan-shu, 165
Chu-tzu yü-lei, 165
Chu Yin-liang, 182
Chu Yün, 185, 204
Chu Yüan-chang, see Ming T'ai-tsu
Chuan-chu (explain in different terms),
    177–78
Ch'üan-miao (all enshrined ancestors),
    146
Ch'üan Tsu-wan, 47
Chuang Ts'un-yü, 210
Chuang-tzu, 158, 197
Ch'un-ch'iu chi-chieh, 174. See also Spring
    and Autumn Annals
Chung-ti (concluding ceremony), 138.
    See also Ti
Chung-yung (the mean), 51. See also
    Doctrine of the Mean
Classical studies, 1f, 5, 46, 66, 131, 156,
    159, 167, 217, 227; and ritual, 1, 41–
    43, 52, 64–65, 97, 119, 121, 124–26,
    128, 138, 180–83; and purism, 1,
    53–60, 67; empiricism in, 2, 6; im-
    portant in cultural reform, 3; and
    social conservatism, 6–8; and lin-
    eage building, 7, 78–79, 98–99, 128;
    revival, 57; and ancestral rites, 115–
    17, 138; and ritual debate, 124–28;
    historical approach, 129, 137, 175;
    eclectic approach to, 133–34, 148–
    49, 152–53, 160; in Han dynasty,
    141, 182; linguistic, evidence, 175,
    197; polarization of, 209, 224
Classicism, 2, 6, 41, 52, 104, 122; rise
    of, 1, 43, 110; Yüan, 54; Sung, 54,
    164; and Renaissance humanism,
    228–30; New Text, 228
Classic of Filial Piety, 59, 122, 180, 200
Classics, 30, 64, 110f, 117, 119, 141; Five
    Classics, 22, 131; as history of the

Three Dynasties, 45, 172–73; and ritual, 52–53; corruption of, 57, 171; textual integrity, 59, 67, 149; spurious parts, 60, 67, 154; and lineage, 76, 78–79; New Text, 151; Old Text, 151; authenticity, 152, 163, 167, 177; meaning misconstrued, 162, 166; textual order rearranged, 167, 170; growing faith in, 168–69; and moral truth, 170–71; direct reading of, 171, 175; hidden meaning of, 174–75; and Archaic Chinese, 177. *See also* Book of Changes; Book of History; Book of Odes; Book of Rites; Spring and Autumn Annals

Clerks and runners, 80f, 218, 221

Coastal evacuation, 220

Cohen, Myron, 76

Commemorative arch, *see* P'ai-lou

Commentaries, *see* Exegeses

Commercialization, 1, 76

Community compact, *see* Hsiang-yüeh

Concubines, 119, 212

Confucian elite, 98

Confucianism, 66, 130; and ritualism, 2, 172, 223; moral orthodoxy, 5, 24, 33; popular, 26–28; confused with heterodoxy, 37; Classical, 55, 188; purification of, 62; subverted by heterodoxy, 69; skewed by commentaries, 137; New Text school, 176, 228; as learning of ritual, 181, 194, 223–24; perverted by Buddhism, 184–85, 188; redefined, 223–24; Han dynasty, 234n4. *See also* Ritualism

Confucian syncretism, *see* Syncretism

Confucian values, 3, 5, 167, 200; transformed, 36–37; instilled through lineages, 86–88; and the common people, 226

Confucius, 30, 53, 55, 61, 63, 66f, 132, 156, 159, 167, 170ff, 173f, 194, 200; on *jen* and *li*, 9–10

Corporate estates, 75, 215, 218f. *See also* Lineage

Cosmology, 13, 40, 54, 56f, 166f, 173, 200

Cremation, 130

Critical scholarship, 58, 65ff; danger of, 55. *See also* Classical studies; Textual skepticism

Cult of women's purity, 1, 3, 201, 204, 207–9, 211–14, 227. *See also* Fiancée chastity; Widow; Women

Cultural identity, 44–45, 69

Cultural nexus, 72

Cultural purity, 7

Cultural reformism, 2. *See also* Gentry

Cultural symbolism, *see* Ritual

Culturalism, 44–46, 61, 69

Degree-holders, in lineage leadership, 218f

de Bary, William Theodore, 7

Dennerline, Jerry, 19

Descent (*tsung*), 75f, 90, 95; group, 76, 78, 84f, 95, 101, 104, 107, 109, 114, 118, 121, 124, 127, 139, 215, 217, 220; falsified, 77, 253n29

Descent-line heir (*tsung-tzu*), 84f, 89, 95, 100f, 109, 112, 126, 221; and government office, 91; authority of, 101–2; qualifications, 122–24; expansion of meaning of, 255n72

Descent-line system, 99, 131f, 166, 214, 218, 221; principle, 79, 87ff, 98, 124, 143f; definition, 84; types of, 84–85; and lineage, 88–97, 100–105; obstacle to revival, 109, 127–28; at odds with meritocracy, 109; as heavenly principle, 110; and aristocracy, 110–12; debate over revival, 110–28, 130; and kinship cohesion, 112; as symbol of Chinese culture, 118; critics of, 121–24; and property, 121–22; and gentry status, 122–24; practiced in the Ch'ing, 123; and centralization of ritual authority, 124; as part of feudal polity, 126; and meaning of *ti*, 142–44. *See also* Hsü San-li; Li Kuang-ti; Li Kung; Mao Ch'i-ling, Wan Ssu-ta; Wan Ssu-t'ung

Desire, 28, 39, 57, 188–89, 193, 198–99, 201

Dictatores, 229
Didacticism, 13, 21, 26, 31, 46, 72, 87, 225
Dikes, 73f
Doctrine of the Mean, 41, 50–51, 68f, 132, 146, 153, 195, 199
Drama, 4f, 23, 227, 235*nn*12, 15, 20
Dream of the Red Chamber, 236*n*35
Duara, Prasenjit, 72
Duke of Chou, 45, 61, 146, 156, 169f, 196, 199f
Duke of Lu, 144

Ebrey, Patricia, 76, 84, 100
Economy, 15–16
Education, 1, 42, 48, 219
Elman, Benjamin A., 2, 57, 228
Emotions, 50. *See also* Feelings; Moral cultivation
Erasmus, Desiderius, 228
Erh-ya, 178f
Ethics, erosion of Confucian, 19–21; and hierarchy, 27, 30, 227; intuitive approach, 28, 35, 49; reorientation of neo-Confucian, 31; Confucian, 44, 187, 197, 204, 229; ritualist, 48–50, 64, 71, 94, 186, 187, 201, 207; and metaphysics, 54; metaethics, 69; philologized, 187. *See also* Juan Yüan; Li Kung; Ling T'ing-k'an; Ritualism; Tai Chen; Yen Yüan
Etymology, 178. *See also* Archaic Chinese; Classical studies; Language; Philology
Eunuch, 3, 15, 32, 80, 82, 224
Evil, 63, 189
Examinations, 22, 73, 106, 108, 209, 224, 229; degrees, 4, 118, 121, 127; *po-hsüeh hung-tz'u*, 118, 164, 260*n*112; "Eight-legged" essays, 230
Exegeses, 68, 99f, 105. *See also* Classical studies; Han exegeses; Sung exegeses; Yüan exegeses
Extortion, 218, 221. *See also* Clerks and runners

Factional struggle, 15
Family instructions, 75, 78

Family Rituals by Master Chu (*Chu-tzu chia-li*), 61, 63f, 66, 79, 116, 169, 215, 254*n*50, 259*n*59; and ancestral rites, 90–97; and lineage, 91–97, 104–11, 122–28; and ritual reform, 95–97; and first ancestor, 104–8; and ancestral hall of Ming official, 106–7; and descent-line system, 109, 120–24; and Ming dynasty, 110; and Chinese culture, 110, 135; criticism of, 110–11, 131; defense of, 111–15; and cultural symbolism, 135; and ritual studies in the early Ch'ing, 135–36; and Ch'ing official rituals, 165–66. *See also* Ancestral rites; Chu Hsi; Ritual; Ritual studies
Famine, 74f
Fang Hsiao-ju, 92, 107
Fang I-chih, 254*n*50
Fang Kuan-ch'eng, 136
Fang Pao, 66, 133f, 136, 149, 156, 158, 169f, 177–78, 205, 218; *I-li shih-i*, 143; "Sang-li i," 150; and the San-li kuan, 150–53; eclecticism, 152
Fang Ta-chen, 254*n*50
Fang-tse (altar of the earth), 138
Fang Tung-shu, 193, 201
Feelings, 68, 188f, 193, 198, 201, 230
Female sexuality, 3
Fen (station), 10
Feng-chien (feudal system), 9, 64, 80ff, 83, 88, 119, 127. *See also* Chou dynasty; Ku Yen-wu
Feng Tao, 29
Feng Ts'ung-wu, 34, 37, 39, 43
Feudal system, *see Feng-chien*
Fiancée chastity, 209ff. *See also* Widow
Filial piety, 3, 24f, 36–37, 45, 74, 180, 193
First ancestor (*shih-tsu*) worship, 90, 92ff, 109, 111, 139f, 144, 146, 217; of *t'ai-tsu*, 100, 105, 114, 142; and kinship organization, 102–3; definition of, 103, 257*n*13; migrant ancestor, 103–5, 107, 121, 127, 216; in lineage hall, 105, 107f; worshipped in family shrine, 106–8; official recognition of, 107–8; and great

descent-line, 113; and aristocracy, 114–15. *See also* Ancestral rites; Apical lineage hall

Five Pecks of Grain, 31. *See also* Peasant rebellion

Forgery, 58f, 154, 160, 169, 177

Four Books, 22, 50–51, 195. See also *Analects*; *Doctrine of the Mean*, *Great Learning*; *Mencius*

Freeman, Maurice, 75f

Fu-hsing ku-hsüeh (reviving ancient learning), 42

Fu-she (Restoration society), 42, 72

Fukien, 27, 75f, 93, 208, 220

Fundamentalism, 236–37*n*40

Funeral rite, 22, 74, 92, 102, 130ff

Genealogy, 6, 75ff, 78, 94, 103–4, 105, 124, 212–19 *passim*; and falsified descent, 77, 253*n*29; tax for compiling, 219, 277*n*91; chronological distribution of, 276*n*55

Gentry: culture reformed, 1, 2–6, 227; and local society, 2–3, 19, 71–75, 224, 277; and common people, 2–3, 87, 225–26; privileges, 3, 8; and the imperial state, 3, 73, 224–25; as bearers of Confucian values, 8; and purism, 8–9; and ritualism, 8–9, 227–28; engaged in commerce, 16; exploitation by, 16–18; and taxes, 17, 82, 239*n*17; effects of commercialization on, 19; and syncretism, 22; and Tung-lin Academy, 31; and cultural identity, 69; urban, 72; activism in the late Ming, 72, 73–75; culture, 73, 204; and lineage, 75–79, 110, 214–19, 220, 224; status, and descent-line system, 122–24; and *Family Rituals*, 135; and cult of women's purity, 208; women, 209; and genealogy, 219; as ritual experts, 224; and vernacular literature, 227; and drama, 227, 235*n*16

Golden Lotus, 236*n*5

Grammar, 229. *See also* Archaic Chinese; Language

Granaries, 73

Grand Canal, 164

Grave site, 130

Great Learning, 67, 69, 132, 153, 167, 195, 199; and Buddhism, 55; neo-Confucian exposition, 59. See also *Four Books*

Great descent-line system, *see Ta-tsung-fa*

Great Rite Controversy, 107, 133

Greek classics, 229

Greek philosophy, 230

Guy, R. Kent, 81

Habit and moral cultivation, 37, 39, 48, 63, 193

Hairstyle, 33, 44, 46

Han Chen, 77

Han (Chinese) culture, 44–45, 207

Han dynasty, 67, 85, 138, 140; scholars, 104, 155f, 158f, 168

Han exegeses, 69, 105, 129, 133f, 138–39, 141, 148f, 157ff, 160, 163, 199, 223; revival of, 6, 169; growing respect for, 134, 166; criticism of, 139–44; and ancient phonology, 176–79; and Archaic Chinese, 176–79; preferred over T'ang and Sung, 179

Han learning (*Han-hsüeh*) scholars, 68f, 141, 178, 180, 201, 226, 229; rejected Ch'eng-Chu learning, 7; and the cult of female chastity, 209–11; and compiling genealogies, 215–16; and lineage building, 215–16

Han learning movement, 2, 8, 54, 60, 70, 129, 148, 155, 158, 161ff, 223ff, 226f; methodological principles, 68, 170–79; and purism, 188, 191–202; rise of, 204; and Sung learning, 213

Han-lin Academy, 82, 158, 260*n*112

Han-shan Te-ch'ing, 25

Hang Shih-chün, 159, 196

Hao I-hsing, 174

Heaven, 138, 142, 189

Heavenly principle (*t'ien-li*), 49, 51, 53, 57, 95, 110

Hermeneutics, 8, 133, 167, 227. *See under* Purism
Heroism, 27ff
Heterodoxy, 8, 54–63 *passim*, 171, 185ff, 188, 191, 196, 202, 226; and late Ming literati, 22; and Confucianism, 37, 171; and syncretism, 54; purge of, 57, 59, 62, 68, 137, 184–86; opposition to, 161, 192, 230. *See also* Purism
Hierarchy, imperial, 79
Historical empiricism, 137–47, 174. *See also* Classical studies
Ho Ch'o, 157
Ho Hsin-yin, 28ff, 77–78, 79, 95
Ho Hsiu, 174
Ho-t'u Lo-shu, 57
Homonyms, 178. *See also* Archaic Chinese; Language; Philology
Hou-chi (Chou ruler), 143, 145
Hou K'ang, 182
Hsi (practice), 50, 61
Hsi-chai (Studio of practice), 61
Hsia (collective worship), 66, 125, 130f, 137–40, 155, 166
Hsia I, 249*n*102
Hsia Yen, 93, 107f
Hsiang san-wu, 66f, 250*n*143
Hsiang-yüeh (community compact), 20f, 72, 75
Hsiao-hsüeh (philology), 179. *See under* Classical studies; Language; Philology
Hsiao-hsüeh (elementary learning), 191
Hsiao-hsüeh (Elementary learning), 78, 104, 106, 191
Hsiao Kung-chuan, 217, 219
Hsiao tsung-fa (lesser descent-line system), 84–85, 96, 100–102, 110ff, 113, 117, 124, 127, 221
Hsieh Chao-che, 31
Hsin-chih (mind-intellect), 188–89, 198. *See also* Mind
Hsing (conduct/practice), 200. *See also* Moral cultivation
Hsing-li ching-i, 165
Hsing-li ta-ch'üan, 106
Hsiu-shen (moral cultivation), 40–41, 46

Hsiu-te (cultivation of virtues), 46
Hsiung Tz'u-li, 165
Hsü Chieh, 16
Hsü Ch'ien-hsüeh, 51, 133, 135ff, 164f, 224
Hsü Chou-t'ang, 150
Hsü Fang, 215
Hsü Fu-yüan, 29, 40, 75
Hsü Heng, 103–5, 107, 114, 257*n*29
Hsü I-k'uei, 106
Hsü San-li, 91, 122f, 218
Hsü Shen, 133, 138, 154, 158, 176, 178, 198; on *ti*, 140; and Archaic Chinese, 177, 179
Hsü Yüan-meng, 150
Hsü Yüan-wen, 82
Hsüan Hsi, 206
Hsüeh-ch'i (physical force), 188. *See also* Human nature; Ontology
Hsüeh-hai t'ang (Hall of the Sea of Learning), 201
Hsün-tzu, 158, 202, 228, 272–73*n*53; and Han Classical learning, 10; and ritualist ethics, 190f, 194–95, 223; on human nature, 194–95
Hu An-kuo, 155
Hu Ch'eng-kung, 179, 210
Hu-hsün (method of mutual explanation), 178. *See also* Archaic Chinese; Language; Philology
Hu Huan, 250*n*115
Hu Shih, 191
Hu Wei, 57f, 164
Hu Ying-lin, 5
Huai-nan-tzu, 158
Huang-Ch'ing wen-ying kuan, 150
Huang Kan, 136
Huang Tsung-hsi, 46–48, 51–57 *passim*, 80f, 110f, 117, 136, 164, 215
Hucker, Charles, O., 35
Hui (bring together), 177
Hui Shih-ch'i, 158–59, 168, 173, 176, 181, 183, 266*n*171
Hui Tung, 157, 162f, 181, 266*n*171; and philology, 158–59; against skepticism, 168f; on moral truth, 172; preferred Han exegeses, 176; and *Shuo-wen chieh-tzu*, 179

Human nature, 38, 46f, 54, 64, 67, 86, 173, 192, 194–95, 202; physical, 39, 49, 63, 68, 188; and cosmology, 40; and heavenly nature, 50; monistic view of, 63, 187ff, 197, 201; dualist notion of, 63, 68, 188, 199, 271–72*n*4; and moral principle, 188; evil, 195; *chieh-hsing*, 196, 198–99, 200
Humanists, Renaissance, 228–30
Hun-li pien-cheng, 261*n*13
Hunan, 128
Hundred philosophers, 151
Hung Liang-chi, 185, 220
Hung Sheng, 235*n*14

I (duty), 38. *See also I-li*
I-hsing (different aristocratic clans), 104
I-hsing (one imperial family), 45
I-hsüeh hsiang-shu lun, 57. *See also Book of Changes*; Hu Wei; Huang Tsung-hsi
I-li (moral principle, principle of duty), 63, 110, 115, 117, 142, 157, 172ff, 189, 192. *See also* Principle
I-li Cheng-chu chü-tu, 45
I-li chieh-yao, 135
I-li i-shu, 150
I-li shih kung, 151
I-li t'u, 151
I-nan (righteous son), 18, 77. *See also* Bondservants
I-tzu shu-yin (polyphonemy), 177
I-yin shu-tzu (homonymy), 177
Iconoclasm, 35, 173, 228
Idealism, 71
Individuality, 230
Inheritable magistracy, 81–82, 86
Innate knowledge of the good, see *Liang-chih*
Intellect, 188
Intellectualism, 7, 53, 201, 203
Introspection, 46, 193
Irrigation, 73, 251*n*7
Italian humanism, 229

Japan, 16
Japanese pirates, 75, 252*n*17
Jen, 9–10, 38, 40, 195, 199–200
Jen Ch'i-yün, 134f, 149, 153f, 156

Jen-hsin (human mind), 41, 57. *See also* Mind; Ontology; *Pen-t'i*; *Tao-hsin*
Jen-lun (human ethical relations), 24, 196
Jen Ta-ch'un, 169f
Jesuits, 229
Johnson, David, 23
Journey to the West, 236*nn*23, 35
Juan Yüan, 8, 170, 181, 184–85, 187, 199–201, 216

Kan Ju-lai, 155
Kan-sheng shang-ti (deity in heaven), 146
K'ang-hsi emperor, 164, 166, 224
K'ang Yu-wei, 228
Kao P'an-lung, 32ff, 74, 223, 246*n*158; purist approach to ritual, 37; criticized syncretism, 37, 62; on Chang Tsai, 39; Classical learning, 42; on moral cultivation, 64; compiled a genealogy, 78
Kao-tzu, 198
K'ao-cheng (evidential) scholarship, 2, 6, 60, 161, 188, 201; scholars, 5–6, 53, 181, 204; and social conservatism, 6–8; movement, 162; futility of, 228. *See also* Han learning; Philology; Textual criticism
Keng Chü, 40
Kiangnan, 77, 118. *See also* Lower Yangtze area
Kiangsi, 107, 208, 220
Kiangsu, 16, 49, 121, 156, 164; Wu-hsi, 32; Soochow, 163, 253*n*29; Yang-hu county, 207f; Wu-chin county, 207; Ch'ang-chou prefecture, 207
King Kao, 143, 145f
King Wen, 146
Kinship, 1, 15, 76ff, 83, 88, 91, 98, 102, 127, 214. *See also* Descent-line system; Lineage
Ko-chih (extension of knowledge), 43
Ko-li (investigation of ritual propriety), 195
Ko-wu (investigation of things), 67, 195, 245–46*n*158
K'o-chi fu-li (suppressing the ego to return to ritual), 50, 68, 199

Kristeller, Paul, 229f
Ku-ching ching-she (Academy of ex-
    plaining the Classics), 201. *See also*
    Academies
Ku Hsien-ch'eng, 32–37 *passim*, 42f, 48,
    60, 62, 78, 223
Ku-liang Commentary, 173ff, 181f. *See
    also Spring and Autumn Annals*
Ku Tsu-yü, 164
Ku Tung-kao, 67, 124, 126, 145ff, 148,
    175, 218
Ku Yen-wu, 16f, 215; and ritual, 45, 49–
    50, 83; and Hsü Ch'ien-hsüeh, 51,
    136; and Classical studies, 52, 131,
    170; and Chu Hsi, 53; and purism,
    55, 191; on political decentraliza-
    tion, 80; *Jih-chih lu*, 80, 131; localist
    approach to social order, 80–84, 86;
    "Chün-hsien lun," 81; on feudal-
    ism, 81–83; on *she*, 82–83; in North
    China, 83; on lineage, 83–88, 110,
    220; on descent-line system, 84f,
    127f; on hereditary governor, 89;
    Wu-ching t'ung-i, 117, 131; on Bud-
    dhism, 131; and Cheng Hsüan, 134,
    140f, 149; and Han exegeses, 141–
    42; as Ming loyalist, 164; and Han
    learning, 183
Ku Yün-ch'eng, 34, 41f
Kuan Chih-tao, 31, 34
Kuan-tzu, 158
Kuei Yu-kuang, 211
Kuhn, Philip, 81, 222
K'un-chü, 4. *See also* Drama
Kung-shih k'ao, 153
Kung-tzu (ducal son), 104
Kung-tz'u (lineage hall), 121. *See also*
    Ancestral hall; *Ta-tsung-tz'u*
Kung Tzu-chen, 221
Kung-yang Commentary, 41, 144, 173ff,
    181f, 210, 256n4
Kung-yang School, 221, 228
K'ung An-kuo, 159
K'ung Kuang-sen, 184
K'ung Shang-jen, 235n14
K'ung Ying-ta, 104, 113, 115, 119, 134,
    155ff, 182, 256n4
Kuo (dynasty), 45
Kuo-ch'ao Han-hsüeh ssu-ch'eng chi, 172

Kuo Hsiang, 180
Kuo-yü, 146f
K'uo-ch'ung (full extension), 47

Laborers, 18
Land, false registration of, 17
Landlords, 15, 71
Language, 1, 8, 78, 159, 162, 178, 228f;
    lexical meaning, 67, 155f, 178f; and
    meaning of Classics, 174; corrupted
    by Buddhism, 185
Lao-tzu, 30
Lay Buddhism, 25, 34, 44. *See also*
    Buddhism
Lei Hung, 265n119
Lesser descent-line system, *see Hsiao
    tsung-fa*
Lexicography, 178f
Li (ritual propriety and institutions),
    see Ritual
Li Ao, 198
Li Chao-lo, 210
Li-chi i-chang, 134
Li-chi i-shu, 150
Li-chia system, 17
Li-chiao (doctrine of propriety and
    ritual), 10, 47, 228. *See also* Purism;
    Ritualism
Li-chieh (ritualized acts), 12
Li Chih, 18, 28–35 *passim*, 62
Li Fu, 5, 124, 126ff, 155–57, 158, 168
Li-hsüeh hui-pien, 131
Li-i (principle of duty), 148
Li-i (ritual-propriety), 12
Li Ju-kuei, 151
Li Jung, 132
Li Kuang-ti, 5, 91, 93, 123, 159, 165, 218
Li Kung: and purism, 7, 56, 170; on
    "Diagram of the Great Ultimate,"
    57; on *Old Text Book of History*, 59,
    168; on Ch'eng-Chu scholarship,
    60; and Yen Yüan, 60, 121, 131; and
    Classical studies, 64–69; *Ta-hsüeh
    pien-yeh*, 67; on public lecturing,
    87, 226; and Ch'eng T'ing-tso,
    117; on descent-line system and
    lineage hall, 121, 127; *Hsüeh-li*,
    132; and ritual studies, 133, 143;
    Ti-hsia k'ao-pien, 144; on Cheng

Hsüan, 144; and Han and Sung exegeticial traditions, 149, 166; on neo-Confucianism, 163, 187f, 191; and chastity, 209

Li-shu kang-mu, 51, 136. *See also* Chiang Yung

Li Tun, 185

Li-wei, 140, 263*n*59. *See also* Spurious texts

Li Yin-tu, 50

Li Yüan-tu, 128

Li-yüeh (rites and music), 9

Li Yung, 48–49, 55

Liang Ch'i-ch'ao, 59f, 186

Liang-chih (innate knowledge of the good), 23–24, 27–28, 34–35, 38, 87, 198

Lin Chao-en, 26, 31

Lineage, 2, 7, 22, 73, 92, 131, 226; and cultural reform, 3; rules, 6, 78, 211–12, 218; and local government, 72, 75, 79, 83–91 *passim*; development, variations in, 75, 224; in late Ming, 75–79; and gentry, 75–79, 110, 214–19, 220, 224; in Kwangtung, 75f, 212, 220f, 252*n*20, 256*n*98; school, 76, 216; scope of, 76, 89; types, 76, 224, 252–53*n*21; building, 76–79, 91–97, 144, 214–19, 220; control of property, 77, egalitarianism in, 77, 79; and tax collection, 77, 221; and social order, 77, 219–22; *tsung-yüeh* (compact), 78; and the state, 79–85, 220–21, 225; and litigation, 84; internal differentiation, 84; and social stability, 85; charitable estates, 85, 94, 96, 212, 221; promotion of Confucian values, 86–88, 221; in Kiangsi, 219f, 256*n*98; ancestral rites, 95–97, 114, 142, 161; corporate estates, 96, 211; as basis of local power, 98; two approaches to organizing, 99–103; and descent-line system, 100–105, 118, 121–22, 127; orientation, of kin group, 104; proliferation of, 128, 213f, 224; and patriarchy, 211; promoted widow chastity, 211f; managers, 218; and degree-holders, 218f; *tsu-chang*

(elders), 219–20; Manchu attitude toward, 220; in Kiangsu, 221; in Chekiang, 221; in Hunan, 222; and militarization, 222, 225; sponsor dramas, 235*n*4; in Anhwei, 252*n*20, 256*n*98

Lineage hall (*tsung-tz'u*), 93ff, 124f, 139, 145, 166, 216, 225; *See also* Ancestral hall; Ancestral rites; Descent-line system; *Ta-tsung-tz'u*

Ling Shu, 181

Ling T'ing-k'an, 8, 60, 64, 170, 187, 191–202 *passim*, 216, 223

Linguistic purism, *see* Purism

Literacy, 15

Literary associations, 82

Literati, 22f, 98, 165. *See also* Gentry

Litigation, 84, 226

Liturgical governance, 71–72

Liturgy, in ancestral hall, *see* Ancestral rites

Liu En, 172

Liu Hsiang, 144

Liu Hsien-t'ing, 164

Liu Hsin, 138, 153, 169f, 177

Liu Jung, 219

Liu-tsei (six destructive elements), 63

Liu Tsung-chou, 34, 39ff, 46ff, 49, 52, 78, 92, 131

Liu Tsung-yüan, 126

Lo Ju-fang, 29, 31, 34, 75, 77

Local defense, 72

Local elite, 72f. *See also* Gentry

Local gazetteers, 209

Local government, 71–73, 80ff, 86f. *See also* Local society

Localism, 72, 75, 79, 80–83. *See also* Gentry; Ku Yen-wu; Lineage; Lu Shih-i

Local society, 1ff, 19, 85, 88. *See also* Local government

Lower Yangtze area, 65, 72, 76f, 82, 87, 118, 156, 164

Loyalty, 24f, 36, 45, 61, 92, 180, 193, 206

Lu (state of), 138, 145–46

Lu Chiu-yüan, 56, 61, 68, 124, 157

Lu Lung-ch'i, 52f, 61f, 134, 149, 165, 180, 184, 248*n*80; opposed popu-

lar literature, 5; criticized Cheng
Hsüan, 142
Lu Shih-i, 49, 51, 74, 93, 110, 122, 127f,
130f, 143, 220; monism, 63; on
descent-line system, 88–91
Lu Wen-ch'ao, 171, 174, 207, 210, 215,
273n53
Lu Yüan-fu, 136
Lü K'un, 18, 20, 26, 75, 258n41
Lü Liu-liang, 61f, 80, 215, 249n58
Lü Nan, 135

Ma Jung, 176
Ma Tuan-lin, 141
Magistrates, 88–89
Manchus, 49, 82, 117; and Ch'eng-Chu
learning, 6; threat to the Ming,
43; conquest and consolidation
of rule, 43f, 61, 78f, 91, 109, 164;
and culturalism, 44–46, and Chinese scholars, 122; and gentry, 164;
adopted Chinese rituals, 165–66
Mao Ch'i-ling, 261n13; on Sung neo-
Confucianism, 57; on Old Text Book
of History, 59; and Li Kung, 65f; and
Classical studies, 67, 148f; on the
descent-line system, 118–21, 124ff,
127f, 215, 218; on Family Rituals,
120, 122, 131; on Cheng Hsüan,
134, 140; on ti and hsia, 143–44; and
Sung exegeses, 166, 168; doubts
about Classics, 169f; and Spring and
Autumn Annals, 181; and purism,
191; on chastity, 209
Mao Kung (Master Mao), 179
Market, 15f
Marriage, 65, 102, 177–78, 206, 208f
Mathematics, 64, 187
May Fourth movement, 213
Melanchthon, Philip, 229
Mencius/Mencius, 63, 68, 156, 188–89,
194f, 199f, 202
Merchants, 72, 219, 235n17
Metaphysics, 41, 54, 60, 129, 167, 173,
234n4, 248n66
Miao (temple), see Ancestral hall
Miao-chih (temple system), 114, 131. See
also Ancestral hall; Ancestral rites

Military uprising, 74. See also Peasant
rebellion; Popular uprising
Militia, 225
Mind, 29, 40, 50, 198; Learning of the
Mind and syncretism, 25; beyond
good and evil, 33f; pen-t'i, 29, 38,
43, 47, 54; and moral cultivation,
46–47, 51, 188–89, 198
Ming (destiny), 47, 67
Ming-chiao (doctrine of names), 10
Ming History project, 118, 133, 164–65
Ming-li (understanding principle), 61
Ming loyalists, 79, 164
Ming scholarship, 133
Ming T'ai-tsu, 22, 28, 92, 106
Ming-t'ang (Hall of illumination), 169
Ming-wu (names and articles), 157, 180
Mo-tzu, 36, 158
Moral cultivation, 1, 35–49 passim, 63ff,
68f, 172, 186–93 passim, 196ff, 199
Moral effort, see Moral cultivation
Morality books, 18, 73, 255n78
Moral knowledge, see Moral truth
Moral ledgers (kung-kuo ko), 26, 87,
255n78
Moral orthodoxy, 33. See also Confu-
cianism; Ethics, San-kang
Moral truth, 172–77, 180, 183
Mourning rites, 61ff, 64f, 92, 102, 117,
120, 122, 125, 130–36 passim; and
ancestral rite, 95, 100–101; circle,
101f, 111; length, 143, 150, 165, 205

Nan-chiao (southern suburb), 146
Nanking, 29, 216
Natural disasters, 73
Neo-Confucianism, 39, 57, 62, 132f,
234n4; and Classicism, 53–54;
ontology, 54, 188, 192; and Tao-
ism, 56; distortion of Classics, 68;
and linguistic principles, 177; and
Buddhism, 188, 191–92. See also
Ch'eng-Chu neo-Confucianism
Nieh Ch'ung-i, 151
Non-Han ethnic communities, 208
Novel, 2–6, 20, 23, 227, 230, 235–36n23

Objective moralism, 40

Objectivity, 173f. *See also* Historical empiricism
Oboi Regency, 164
Offering at the grave, 75, 95, 102, 104
Official corruption, 18
Old Text Book of History, 57ff, 66, 167f. *See also* Li Kung; Mao Ch'i-ling; Wan Ssu-t'ung; Yen Jo-chü
Ontology, 36–37, 40, 44, 54; *ch'i* (physical/material), 38–39, 188, 193, 198, 234*n*1; dualistic, 57f, 63, 188; Monism, 63; Buddhist, 68, 191; neo-Confucian, 68, 192, 166f. *See also* Human nature; Mind
Opium War, 222
Ou-yang Hsiu, 152, 157–58, 167

Pai-hu t'ung, 158
P'ai-lou (commemorative arch), 208, 212
Paleography, 176
P'an P'ing-ko, 55–56, 163, 191
Pao-chia (mutual surveillance system), 20, 75, 221
Parallel prose, 230
Paternal authority, 204, 206
Paternalism, 15, 19, 35, 73
Patriline, 215, 218. *See also* Descent; Descent-line heir; Descent-line system
Patronage of scholars, 164–65, 224
Peasant rebellion: and popular lectures, 31, 79, 83, 87f, 226, 228. *See also* Bondservants; Riots
P'ei-ts'un, 83
Pen-t'i (substance of the Mind), *see* Mind
Personal network, 72
Peterson, Willard, 23
Petrarch, Francesco, 229
Philology, 2, 5, 161f, 227; and anti-heterodoxy/purism, 69, 184–86; ancient, 155, 158; criticism, 163; notation, 179; and Han classical scholarship, 182; and Buddhist scriptures, 191; and social criticism, 204–7. *See also* Archaic Chinese; Language; Phonology

Phonology, 155, 158f, 162, 176, 177–79, 227, 229. *See also* Archaic Chinese; Language; Philology
Pi Yün, 204
Pieh-tzu (differentiated son), 103f, 111ff, 119–20. *See also* Descent-line system
Pieh-tzu wei tsu (differentiated son as the ancestor), 119
Pien-hua ch'i-chih (transformation of physical nature), 39
P'ien (excessive), 39
Plaks, Andrew, 20
Plays, *see* Drama
Po-hsüeh yü-wen, yüeh chih i li (learning extensively and disciplining oneself in accordance with ritual), 43
Po-wen (learning extensively), 43, 64
Po-wen i chi-i (learning extensively in order to accumulate knowledge of propriety), 39
Po-wen yüeh-li (learning extensively and disciplining oneself in accordance with ritual), 53, 66
Political order: and moral order, 86
Political power, 79ff, 82f
Popular culture, 4–5, 31, 227
Popular mobilization, 226
Popular morality, 40. *See also* Populism
Popular uprising, 20, 80, 83, 87. *See also* Peasant rebellion; Riots
Population, 16, 19, 26, 71f, 228
Populism, 23f, 27, 31, 42, 78
Primogenitor, *see* First ancestor
Principle (*li*), 47, 68, 87, 171, 192–93, 226, 248*n*60. *See also* Heavenly principle; *I-li*
Printing, 22–23
Property, 77, 88, 121–22
P'u Sung-ling, 215
Public lectures, *see* Chiang-hsüeh
Public works, 72
Purism, 8, 33, 140, 228; rise of, 1, 110; anti-heterodoxy, 8, 36, 160; quest for Confucian doctrine, 41, 69, 149, 191, 197; and culturalism, 44; and Manchu conquest, 44; textual, 53, 58–60, 66–67; and philology, 54,

184–86; linguistic, 54–55, 161f, 167, 172, 187, 194, 197, 223; and ritualism, 57, 69, 70, 170, 187, 202, 213f; ambivalence of, 58–60; and neo-Confucianism, 60–70; quest for authentic Confucian rites, 64, 69f, 98, 137, 166, 197; hermeneutics, 69, 160f, 167, 175, 201; and charity, 75, 252n15; and anti-Manchu sentiment, 98; and Yen Yüan, 121; and Li Kung, 121; and historical empiricism, 137; logic, 165; and Han Learning, 188, 191–203; discredited popular values, 227. See also Classical studies; Li Kung; Ritualism; Yen Yüan

Quaternary ancestry, see Ancestral rites
Queue, 44. See also Hairstyle
Quiet-sitting, 63, 193

Remarriage, see Widow
Renaissance Classicists, 228
Republican period, 222
Retribution, 36
Rhetoric, 229
Riots, 20, 73, 87, 226, 252n17
Rites of Chou, 41, 64, 66f, 130, 151–57 passim, 168, 170, 180; doubts about, 59, 169, 177
Ritual, 13, 38, 40, 61, 78, 172, 196, 224; and ethics, 1, 48–50; cultural symbolism of, 7, 44–45, 91, 95, 109, 163, 165f; and social station, 9–11, 226; and transmission of values, 11, 12–14, 87; symbolic domain, 11–12, 36, 196, 224; performative domain, 11–12, 166, 196; and intellect, 13, 188; and Classical studies, 41–42, 180–82; and self-cultivation, 47; and proper conduct, 53; purge of non-canonical, 57; Classical, 60, 79, 83, 95, 98, 113, 121, 137, 166, 197; neo-Confucian, 63; ancient, 65ff, 111; authority, 84; rectification of, 92–93, 96, 124; as heavenly principle, 95; unity of, 96; Sung dynasty, 98;

adjustment, 123, 128; resurrecting Confucian, 130; cultural symbolism of, 163–66
Ritual Classics, 52f, 67, 130, 132, 137, 160, 180f, 224. See also Book of Etiquette and Decorum; Book of Rites; Rites of Chou
Ritualism, 44, 69f, 133, 161, 223, 225, 227f; rise of, 1f, 14, 43, 48–49, 223f; purged heterodoxy, 8; neo-Confucian, 60. See also Ethics
Ritual purism, see Purism
Ritual studies, 52, 130–37, 152, 155–60, 227; and lineage building, 7, 78–79, 99; and history of Classical antiquity, 124–27, 137
River conservancy, 164, 251n7
Robinson, James H., 162
Romance of the Three Kingdom, 236n35

Sacrifice at the grave, see Offering at the grave
Sacrifice to earth, 66
Sacrifice to heaven, 66, 138–39, 140, 143f
Sacrificial fields, 77f. See also Lineage
San-kang (three bonds), 10–11, 35, 38, 47, 206. See also Filial piety; Loyalty
San-li hsü-li, 153
San-li kuan (Bureau for the Compilation of the Three Ritual Classics), 130, 149–55, 224
San-li t'u-chi, 151
San-nien fu chih k'ao, 261n13
Scholasticism, 228
Schwartz, Benjamin, 9
Secret societies, 220
Self, 27, 38. See also K'o-chi fu-li
Self-cultivation, 193, 195, 199–200
Selfishness, 28, 30, 68, 190, 199
Sex segregation, 3
Shansi, 83
Shao Yung, 57
She (association), 82–83, 145
Shen (official-gentry), 8. See Gentry
Shen-chin (official-gentry), 8. See Gentry

Shen Ch'in-han, 174, 181
Shen-shih (scholar-official), 8. See
    Gentry
Shen-tu (vigilance in solitude), 46
Shen T'ing-fang, 265n119
Shen T'ung, 157–58, 168
Shen Yün, 131
Shih (officer), 100
Shih Meng-lin, 32, 35, 38
Shih-shih (concrete action/things), 172,
    180–81, 200
Shih-shih ch'iu-shih (seeking truth in
    concrete matters), 172, 180–81
Shih-ti (seasonal oblation), 143. See also
    Ti
Shih-tsu miao (temple of the first ances-
    tor), 94. See Ancestral rites; First
    ancestor; Ta-tsung-tz'u
Shou-tsu (unifying agnates), 121
Shu-tzu (son of concubine), 119
Shuo-wen chieh-tzu, 133, 138, 158, 178f,
    198
Silver, 15–16, 238–39n2, 239n19
Six Arts, 64f
Skinner, G. William, 71
Smith, Joanna Handlin, 74
So tzu ch'u, 139, 142ff, 145f. See also First
    ancestor
Social conservatism, 1, 4, 6
Social ethics, 24, 71, 162. See also Ethics
Social hierarchy, 27, 44, 87, 193, 224f
Social mobility, 20, 209
Social order: ritualist approach to, 1f;
    localist approach, 72, 75, 80, 83, 88;
    and lineage, 77. See also Gentry;
    Lineage; Localism; Ritualism
Society for Sharing Goodness, 74
Society of Joint Benefit, 74
Soup kitchen, 74
Speech, 162, 229. See also Language
Spring and Autumn Annals, 67f, 111, 124,
    141–48 passim, 173–75, 181–82, 200,
    263n59
Spurious texts, 60, 67, 154. See also
    Apocryphal texts; Classics
Ssu-k'u ch'üan-shu, 153, 174, 179, 183,
    186, 215, 234n1, 266n171

Ssu-li yüeh-yen, 135
Ssu-ma Ch'ien, 147
Ssu-ma Kuang, 99, 167, 237n41,
    257n12, 258n41
Ssu-pien lu chi-yao, 131
Statecraft, 42, 64f, 131
Su Chieh, 237n41
Su Shih, 257n11
Subjectivism, 40, 171
Suicide, 205, 207, 211ff
Sun Ch'i-feng, 48, 62
Sun Hsing-yen, 216
Sung dynasty, 141, 179; Northern, 102;
    Southern, 103f
Sung exegeses, 68, 129, 141, 149, 159f,
    164, 173, 223; and eclecticism,
    133–34; prominence of, 151–55;
    methodology, 167
Sung learning, 129f, 161
Sung Lo, 135
Sung neo-Confucianism, 39, 47, 62,
    69, 128, 144, 234n4, 248n66; and
    Three Bonds, 10–11; metaphysics,
    41; textual criticism, 53, 129; on-
    tology and cosmology, 54, 166f;
    and Buddhism, 56, 61–62; excelled
    in moral truths, 192; and female
    chastity, 209, 213
Sung neo-Confucians: and the Clas-
    sics, 67, 162; and descent-line sys-
    tem, 100, 113–14; concocted rites,
    110; on Cheng Hsüan, 139; and exe-
    gesis, 148; non-canonical texts, 168;
    Chiang Fan on, 172
Syncretism, 31, 41, 56, 61f, 227; rejec-
    tion of, 8, 54; Confucian, 20, 27;
    Three Teachings, 22, 25, 36, 37;
    and Buddhism, 22, 25; varieties of,
    25–26; Three-in-One Religion, 27

Ta-Ch'ing hui-tien, 110, 165, 236n27
Ta-Ch'ing i-t'ung chih, 164
Ta-Ch'ing lü-li, 236n27
Ta-fu (great official), 113ff, 120
Ta-hsien (great worthy), 110
Ta-Ming chi-li, 106ff
Ta-Ming hui-tien, 92

Ta-tsung-fa (great descent-line system), 84–85, 102f, 112–21 *passim*, 124, 127, 144, 215. *See also* Ancestral rites; First ancestor

Ta-tsung-tz'u (great descent-line hall), 96, 105ff, 108f, 124, 128. *See also* Ancestral hall; First ancestor; *Ta-tsung-fa*

T'ai-chou school, 25, 27–28, 32–33, 38, 42, 49, 77ff

T'ai-tsu (first ancestor), *see* First Ancestor

Tablets of ancestors, *see* Ancestral rites

Tadao Sakai, 26

Tai Chen, 8, 60, 64, 67, 136, 157, 162f, 166, 180, 191–202 *passim*, 217, 226; defended the Classics, 169–70, 173; on Classics, 171, 176–78; on ethics, 171, 187, 188–91; *Meng-tzu tzu-i shu-cheng*, 190, 215; attitude toward female chastity, 209–10

Tai Ming-shih, 152

Taiping rebellion, 222

Tan Chu, 134

T'an Ssu-t'ung, 228

T'ang dynasty, 83, 100, 140f, 179

T'ang exegetes, 104, 134, 155

T'ang Pin, 5

T'ang Shun-chih, 17

Tao-hsin (moral mind), 41, 57

Tao-hsüeh (Learning of the Way), 234n4, 237n41. *See also* Sung neo-Confucianism

T'ao Chu, 207

Taoism, 29, 31, 37, 62, 184; priests, 14, 22; and syncretism, 25; spiritual cultivation, 27; Taoists as members of lineage, 78; deities, 93; aversion toward, 197; influence on Confucianism, 197, 201

Taxes, 3, 17, 71, 77, 85, 238–39n2; delinquency case of 1661, 164, 260n112

Te-hsing (moral nature), 40. *See also* Human nature

Textual criticism, 55–59, 66–67, 69, 227. *See also* Classical studies; Purism

Textualism, 161, 201

Textual skepticism, 57, 67, 149, 152, 157f, 160, 166, 171; in the K'ang-hsi period, 58, 129–30; in Classical studies, 137–38; decline of, 167; fight against, 168–70. *See also* Classical studies; Purism; Textual criticism

Textual Studies, *see* Textual criticism

Theatrical performances, 4f

Theology, 229

Three Dynasties, 45, 64, 85, 143, 172, 176, 179, 190, 196

Ti, 66, 103, 130f, 137, 166, 263n59; meaning in Han exegeses, 138–39, 140f; neo-Confucian legacy in debate, 139–40; and descent-line system, 142–44; and lineage building, 144–45. See also *Hsia*, Ku Tung-kao; Mao Ch'i-ling; Wan Ssu-ta; Wan Ssu-t'ung; Yang Ch'un

T'i-yung (substance-function), 191–92

T'ien-hsia (the realm under heaven), 45

T'ien Ju-k'ang, 207

T'ien-li chih chieh-wen (manifested rules of heavenly principle), 49, 51

T'ien-ming chih hsing (heavenly-endowed nature), 50. *See also* Human nature; Ontology

T'ien-shen (heavenly deities), 138

T'ien-tzu ssu hsien lo k'uei-shih li, 153

T'ien Wen-ching, 5

T'ou-hsien (commendation of land), 17

Trade, overseas, 16

Translation, 162

Tsa-pan (miscellaneous surcharges), 17. *See also* Taxes

Tseng Chao, 260n84

Tseng Kuo-fan, 222, 224

Tseng-tzu, 197, 200, 202

Tso Commentary, 173–74, 175, 181f, 263n59

Tsou Yüan-piao, 244n123

Tsu (ancestor), 113, 119. *See also* Ancestral Hall; Ancestral rites; Descent-line system; First ancestor; *Ta-tsung-tz'u*

Tsu (kin group), 102. *See also* Descent

Tsu-chang (lineage elders), 121

Ts'ui Shu, 173
Ts'un-hsin (preserve the moral mind),
    40
Tsung (descent-line), see Descent;
    Descent-line heir; Descent-line
    system
Tsung-chi li, 130
Tsung-fa, see Descent-line system
Tsung-miao (lineage hall), see Ancestral
    hall; Lineage hall
Tsung-tzu, see Descent-line heir
Tsung-tz'u ssu-tien, 78
Tu-li chih-i, 52–53
Tu-li t'ung-k'ao, 135ff
Tu Yü, 155, 174
Tuan Yü-ts'ai, 171, 178–79
Tung Ch'i-ch'ang, 18
Tung Chung-shu, 198
Tung-lin Academy, 48, 223f, 244n123;
    and public lectures, 31; on syn-
    cretism, 32, 33–34, 56–57, 62; con-
    servatism of, 32, 35; on Buddhism,
    32–38 passim; and the T'ai-chou
    school, 32–35, 42; purism, 33; on
    Union of the Three Teachings, 36;
    deemphasis of ontology, 37–38;
    on moral cultivation, 38–39; em-
    phasized Classical studies, 41–42;
    elite mobilization, 72; and chari-
    table activities, 74–75; and lineage
    building, 78–79
T'ung-hsin (child mind), 30
Tzu-jan (natural), 27
Tzu-po Ta-kuan, 18
Tzu-ssu, 200
Tz'u-t'ang, see Ancestral hall; Chia-
    miao; Lineage hall

Unorthodox ideas, 55, 69, 140, 151, 158.
    See also Heterodoxy
Urban culture, 4, 15
Urbanization, 1, 15, 19, 76

Valla, Lorenzo, 228
Virtues, see Confucian values
Voluntary associations, 82f

Wakeman, Frederic, 3

Wan Ssu-ta, 111, 132, 134, 215; and
    ritual studies, 52, 131f; on Rites of
    Chou, 66, 152, 154; on descent-line
    system, 113–15, 118–20, 124, 126–27;
    on quaternary system of ancestral
    rites, 115–17; Classical scholarship,
    117, 137; on ti, 139f, 147; on Cheng
    Hsüan, 140; on hsia, 144; and Sung
    Classical scholarship, 168
Wan Ssu-t'ung, 56, 65f, 118, 133; Tu-li
    t'ung-k'ao, 51, 133, 136; on Old Text
    Book of History, 59, 67; and Ming
    History Project, 132–33; on ti, 140–
    41, 144; on Cheng Hsüan, 147;
    and Spring and Autumn Annals, 148;
    and Han exegeses, 149; and Sung
    exegeses, 152
Wang An-shih, 40, 152, 237n41
Wang Ch'ang, 136, 183
Wang Chi, 24f, 33–34
Wang Chung, 170, 185, 204–7, 210
Wang Fu, 126
Wang Fu-chih, 45, 50, 80, 132, 262n19
Wang Fu-li, 57
Wang Hsi-sun, 185
Wang Hsin-ching, 132
Wang-hsüeh chih-i, 61
Wang Hung-chuan, 49f, 87
Wang Ken, 24, 26–27, 28, 31, 33f, 77
Wang K'un-ch'eng, 64
Wang Mang, 169
Wang Ming-sheng, 136, 157, 175, 216
Wang Mou-hung, 58
Wang Nien-sun, 179
Wang Pi (226–49), 180
Wang Pi (1511–87), 77
Wang Po, 167
Wang Shih-chen, 5, 31, 235n12
Wang Shih-p'eng, 141–42
Wang Su, 141, 144, 151, 153, 256n3
Wang Tao-k'un, 108, 235n12
Wang Wan, 45, 121f, 131, 136, 142, 154,
    172, 254n65
Wang Yang-ming, 5, 33ff, 40f, 48f, 54f,
    57, 61, 68, 110, 124, 157, 165; rejected
    as heterodox, 7, 61; and syncretism,
    23, 24–25; populism, 24, 27; ethics,
    24, 64; on the Mind, 29; intuition-

ism, 53; and Buddhism, 62, 241n58; and community compact, 75
Wang Yang-ming school, 41, 46, 60, 195
Wang Yin-chih, 179, 185
Wang Yüan, 215
Water Margin, 235n23, 236n35
Way (*tao*), 41, 51, 64, 190, 196
Weber, Max, 72
Wedding ceremony, 74, 131
Wei Chi, 106
Wei Chih, 159
Wei-Chin period, 185
Wei Hsiang-shu, 165, 259n59
Wei-shu (spurious text), 134, 140f. See also Apocryphal texts
Wei Yüan, 221
Wei Yüan-ch'eng, 146
Well-field system, 64, 88
Weng Fang-kang, 180, 209, 215
Widow, 206f, 234n6; chaste, 3, 228; widowhood, 205, 210; remarriage of, 208ff, 234n6, 236n6; property of, 211f; greater protection of, in Ch'ing law, 212–13
Widow chastity, 3, 8, 74, 207–11, 228
Wife, 3, 84, 119, 206, 209
Women, 1, 204f, 207ff
Wu Ch'eng, 57, 153, 155, 160
Wu Ch'ien-mu, 96
Wu-ching i-i, 138
Wu-ching t'ung-i, 117, 131
Wu Fan-ch'ang, 135
Wu-fu (five mourning grades), 100, 102. See also Mourning rites
Wu-hsing (five elements), 193
Wu-li t'ung-k'ao, 51, 117, 133, 136f. See also Ch'in Hui-t'ien
Wu-lun (five relationships), 10
Wu San-kuei, 164
Wu T'ing-chen, 150
Wu T'ing-hua, 149, 153–54, 156
Wu Yü, 57, 167

Yang Ch'i-yüan, 29

Yang-chou, 216, 235n17
Yang Chu, 185
Yang Ch'un, 124–26, 145–46
Yang Fu, 136, 151
Yang Ming-shih, 150
Yang Shen, 5, 235n12
Yang T'ing-yün, 254n50
Yang Tung-ming, 73
Yao Chi-heng, 59
Yao Nai, 184, 215f
Yellow Turbans, 31. See also Peasant rebellion
Yen Chün, 28
Yen Hui, 53, 198, 202
Yen Jo-chü, 57ff, 66f, 132f, 136, 164, 172
Yen K'o-chün, 273n53
Yen-Li school, 60
Yen Sung, 28
Yen Yüan, 117, 131, 226, 237n40; and purism, 7, 56, 121, 166, 168; criticized neo-Confucianism, 54, 60–64, 163, 187f, 191; and pragmatism, 64; and *hsiang san-wu*, 66f; on *k'o-chi fu-li*, 68; and chastity, 209
Yen Yüan (Confucius' disciple), see Yen Hui
Yin Hui-i, 126, 218
Yin-yang, 198
Ying Hui-ch'ien, 131, 134, 136
Yu-hsia (knight-errant), 28
Yu Ying-shih, 2, 41
Yü Chün-fang, 25
Yü-fu yü-fu (common people), 24
Yüan dynasty, 172
Yüan exegeses, 120, 129, 133f, 151f, 155, 223
Yüan Huang, 25f, 40
Yüan Mei, 207
Yüan neo-Confucians, 171
Yüan Tsung-tao, 34
Yüeh-li (self-discipline through ritual), 43
Yün-ch'i Chu-hung, 25f, 29, 36
Yung-cheng emperor, 150, 155, 184
Yung-lo ta-tien, 156

Library of Congress Cataloging-in-Publication Data

Chow, Kai-wing, 1951–
    The rise of Confucian ritualism in late imperial China :
ethics, classics, and lineage discourse / Kai-wing Chow.
        p.   cm.
    Includes bibliographical references and index.
    ISBN 0-8047-2173-4 (cl.) : ISBN 0-8047-2791-0 (pbk.)
    1. Confucianism—Rituals.   2. Confucian ethics—History.
3. China—Intellectual life—1644–1912.   1. Title.
BL1833.R57C48   1994
299'.51238—dc20

93-16633
CIP
Rev.

⊗ This book is printed on acid-free, recycled paper.

Original Printing 1994
Last figure below indicates year of this printing:
05   04   03   02   01   00   99   98   97   96